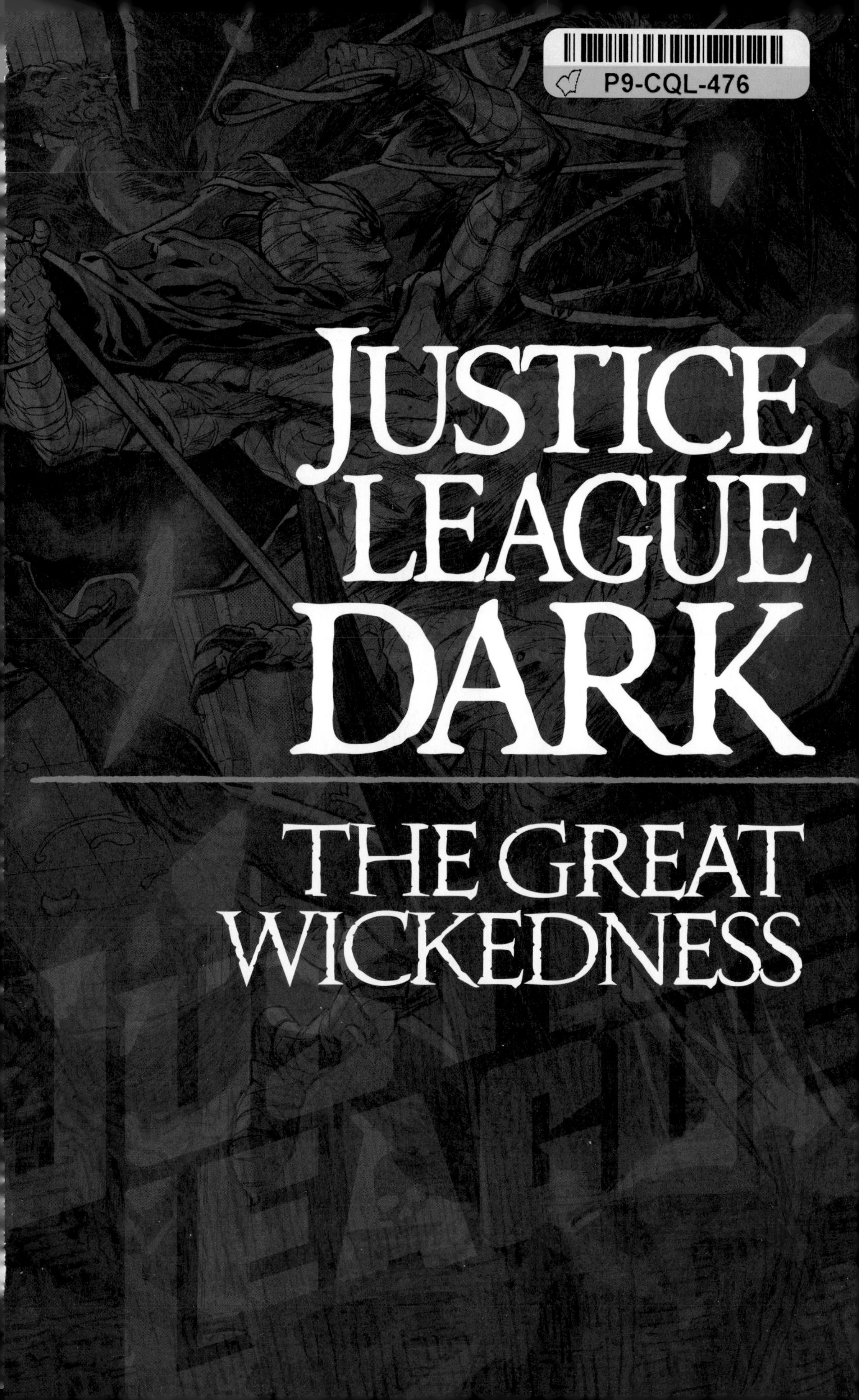

JUSTICE LEAGUE DARK

THE GREAT WICKEDNESS

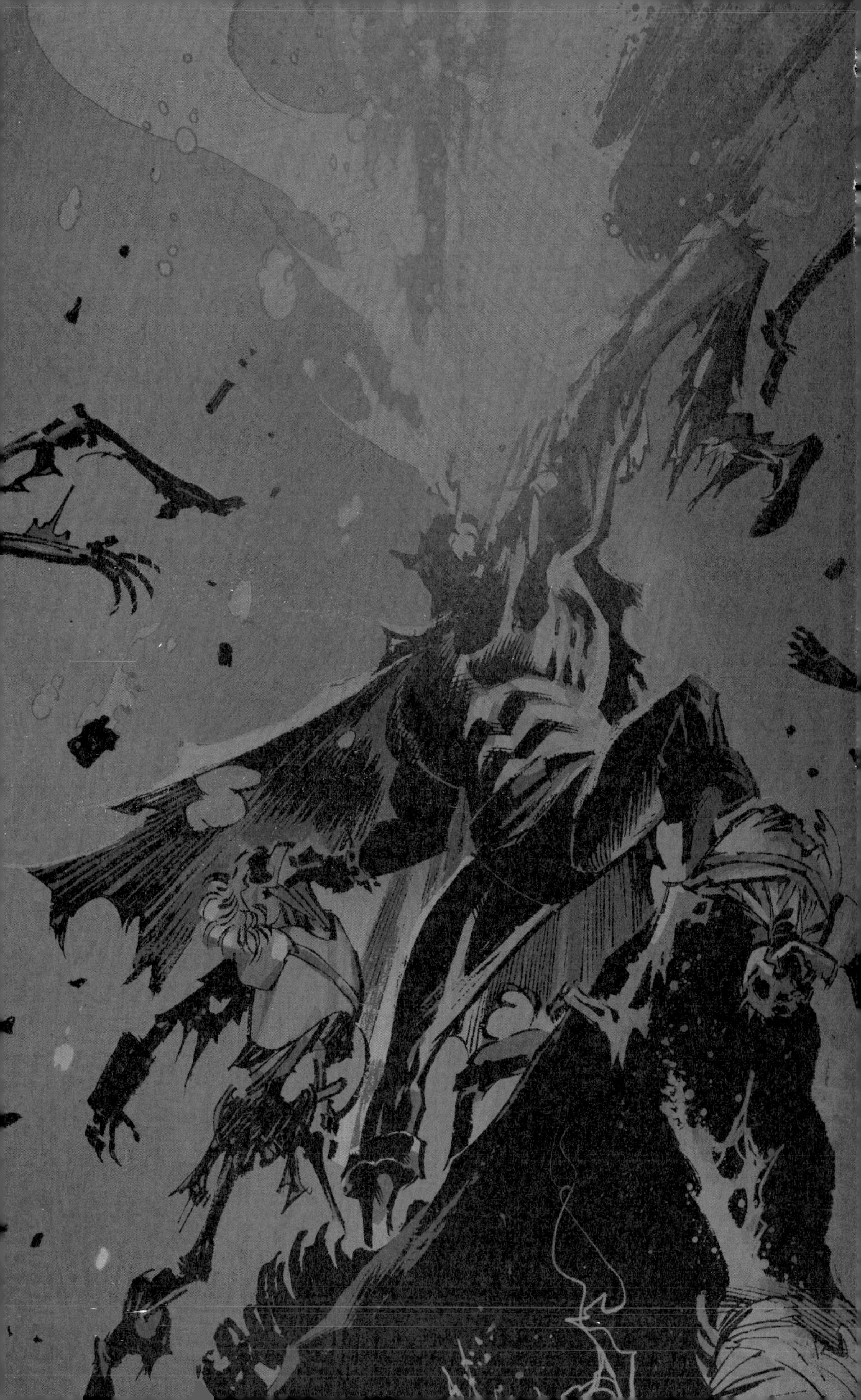

JUSTICE LEAGUE DARK

THE GREAT WICKEDNESS

Ram V   Dan Watters   WRITERS

Sumit Kumar   Xermánico   Christopher Mitten   PENCILLERS

Sumit Kumar   Xermánico   Christopher Mitten   Jose Marzan Jr.   INKERS

Romulo Fajardo Jr.   Nick Filardi   COLORISTS

Rob Leigh   LETTERER

Paul Renaud   COLLECTION COVER ARTIST

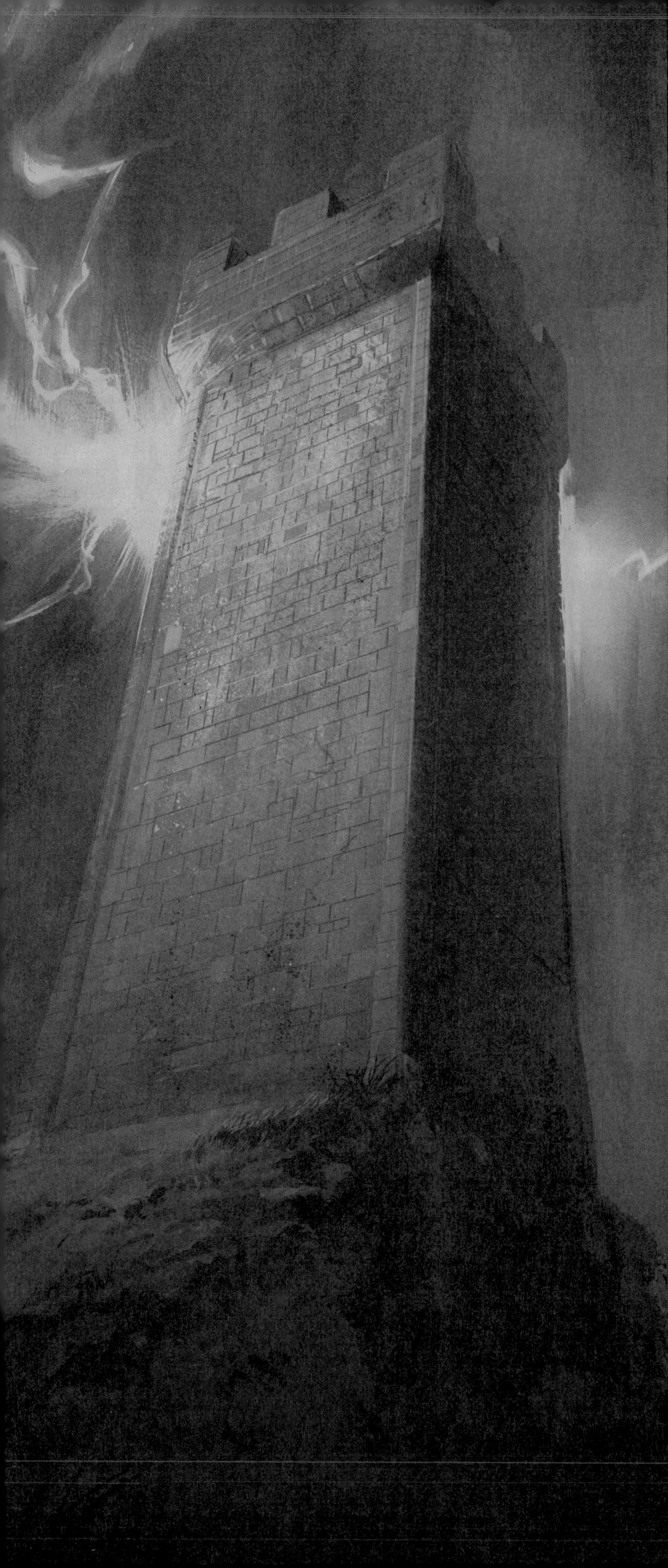

Brittany Holzherr
Editor – Original Series & Collected Edition
Alex R. Carr
Editor – Original Series
Andrea Shea
Associate Editor – Original Series
Jillian Grant
Assistant Editor – Original Series
Steve Cook
Design Director – Books
Curtis King Jr.
Publication Design
Erin Vanover
Publication Production

Marie Javins
Editor-in-Chief, DC Comics

Anne DePies
Senior VP – General Manager
Jim Lee
Publisher & Chief Creative Officer
Don Falletti
VP – Manufacturing Operations & Workflow Management
Lawrence Ganem
VP – Talent Services
Alison Gill
Senior VP – Manufacturing & Operations
Jeffrey Kaufman
VP – Editorial Strategy & Programming
Nick J. Napolitano
VP – Manufacturing Administration & Design
Nancy Spears
VP – Revenue

JUSTICE LEAGUE DARK:
THE GREAT WICKEDNESS

DC Comics,
2900 West Alameda Ave., Burbank, CA 91505

Printed by Solisco Printers,
Scott, QC, Canada. 5/13/22. First Printing.

ISBN: 978-1-77951-551-3

Library of Congress
Cataloging-in-Publication Data is available.

PEFC Certified
This product is from sustainably managed forests and controlled sources
PEFC/26-31-02
www.pefc.org

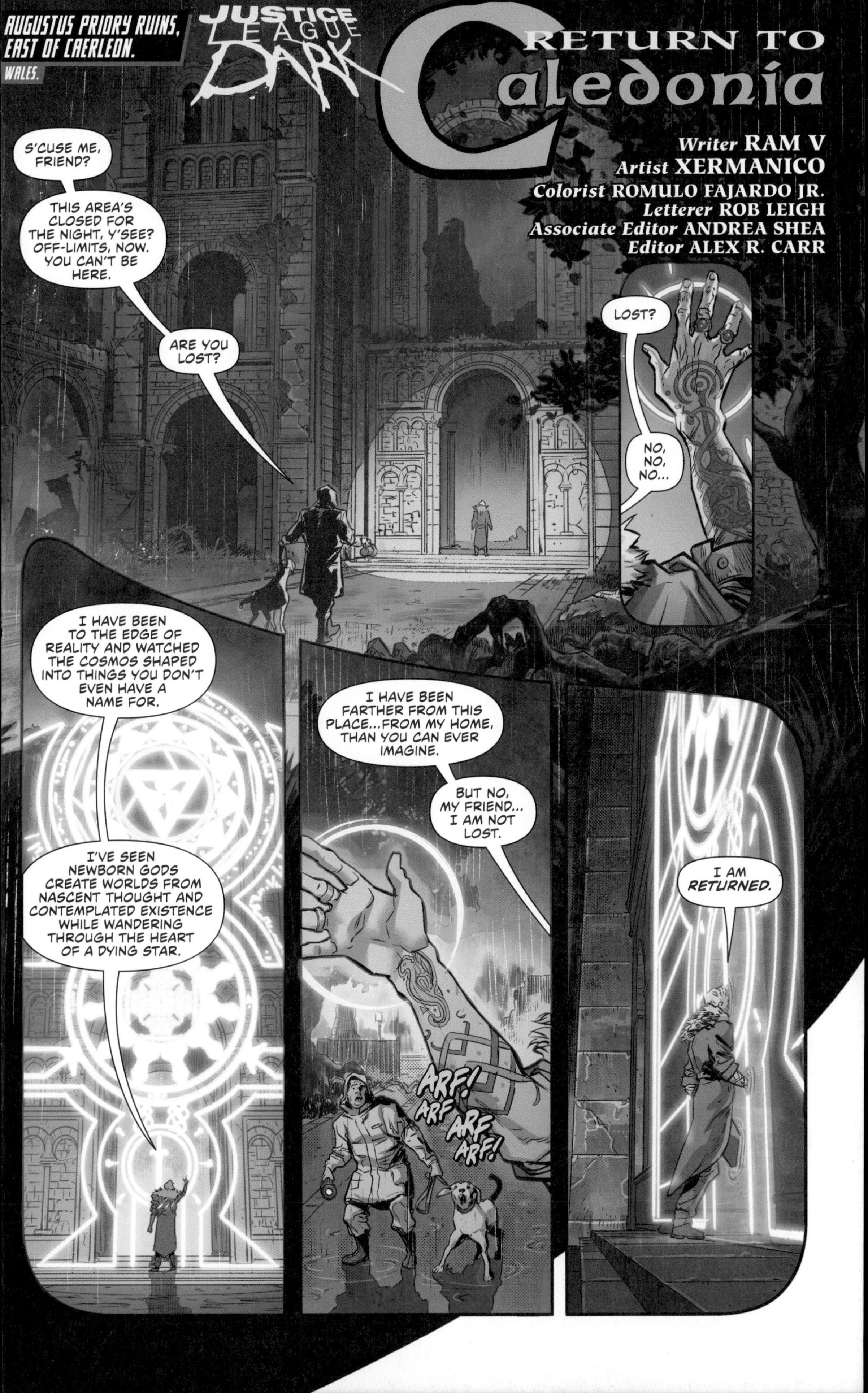
AUGUSTUS PRIORY RUINS, EAST OF CAERLEON.
WALES.
JUSTICE LEAGUE DARK
RETURN TO Caledonia
Writer RAM V
Artist XERMANICO
Colorist ROMULO FAJARDO JR.
Letterer ROB LEIGH
Associate Editor ANDREA SHEA
Editor ALEX R. CARR
S'CUSE ME, FRIEND?
THIS AREA'S CLOSED FOR THE NIGHT, Y'SEE? OFF-LIMITS, NOW. YOU CAN'T BE HERE.
ARE YOU LOST?
LOST?
NO, NO, NO...
I HAVE BEEN TO THE EDGE OF REALITY AND WATCHED THE COSMOS SHAPED INTO THINGS YOU DON'T EVEN HAVE A NAME FOR.
I'VE SEEN NEWBORN GODS CREATE WORLDS FROM NASCENT THOUGHT AND CONTEMPLATED EXISTENCE WHILE WANDERING THROUGH THE HEART OF A DYING STAR.
I HAVE BEEN FARTHER FROM THIS PLACE...FROM MY HOME, THAN YOU CAN EVER IMAGINE.
BUT NO, MY FRIEND... I AM NOT LOST.
ARF! ARF ARF ARF!
I AM RETURNED.

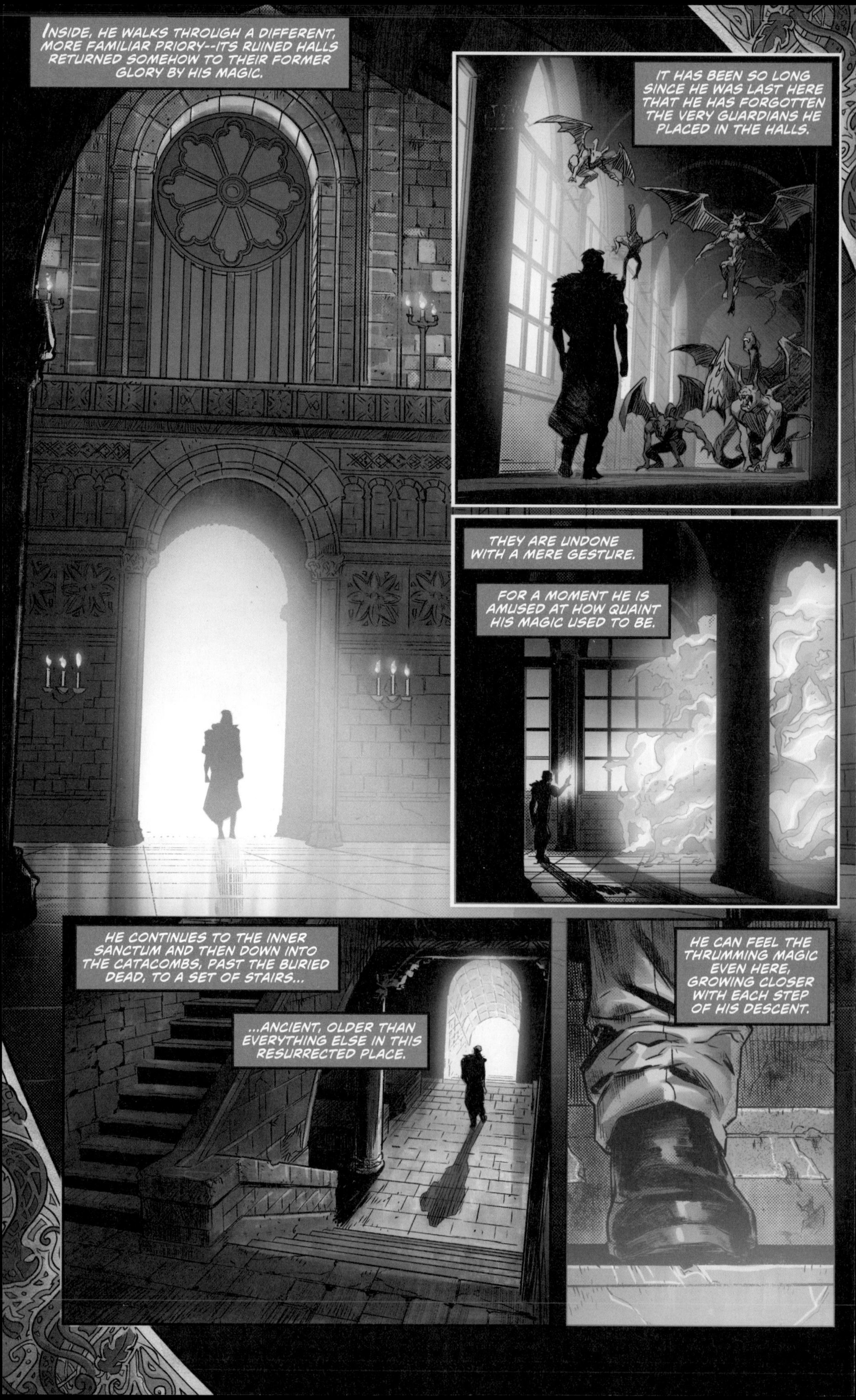
INSIDE, HE WALKS THROUGH A DIFFERENT, MORE FAMILIAR PRIORY--ITS RUINED HALLS RETURNED SOMEHOW TO THEIR FORMER GLORY BY HIS MAGIC.
IT HAS BEEN SO LONG SINCE HE WAS LAST HERE THAT HE HAS FORGOTTEN THE VERY GUARDIANS HE PLACED IN THE HALLS.
THEY ARE UNDONE WITH A MERE GESTURE.
FOR A MOMENT HE IS AMUSED AT HOW QUAINT HIS MAGIC USED TO BE.
HE CONTINUES TO THE INNER SANCTUM AND THEN DOWN INTO THE CATACOMBS, PAST THE BURIED DEAD, TO A SET OF STAIRS...
...ANCIENT, OLDER THAN EVERYTHING ELSE IN THIS RESURRECTED PLACE.
HE CAN FEEL THE THRUMMING MAGIC EVEN HERE, GROWING CLOSER WITH EACH STEP OF HIS DESCENT.

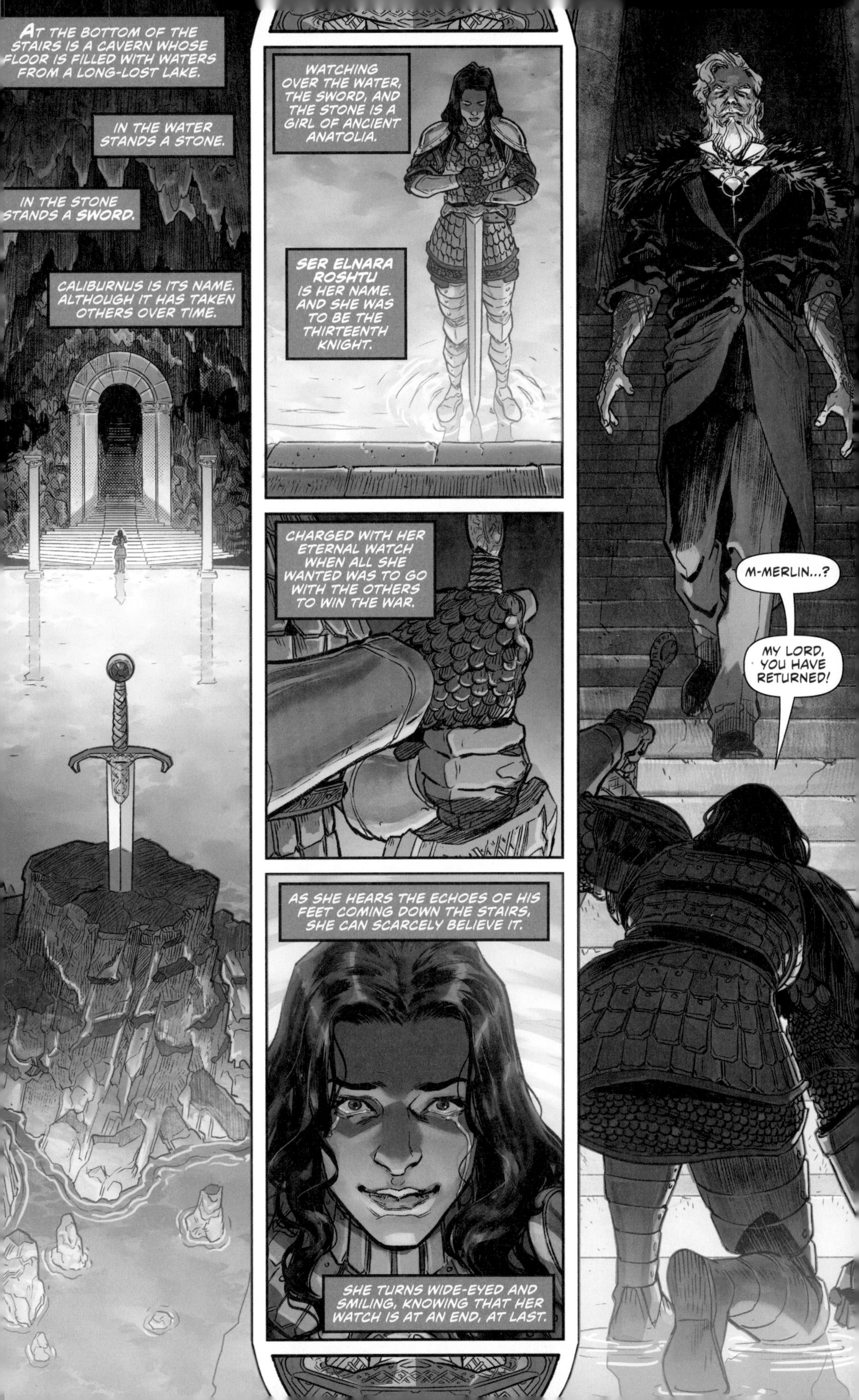
AT THE BOTTOM OF THE STAIRS IS A CAVERN WHOSE FLOOR IS FILLED WITH WATERS FROM A LONG-LOST LAKE.
IN THE WATER STANDS A STONE.
IN THE STONE STANDS A SWORD.
CALIBURNUS IS ITS NAME. ALTHOUGH IT HAS TAKEN OTHERS OVER TIME.
WATCHING OVER THE WATER, THE SWORD, AND THE STONE IS A GIRL OF ANCIENT ANATOLIA.
SER ELNARA ROSHTU IS HER NAME. AND SHE WAS TO BE THE THIRTEENTH KNIGHT.
CHARGED WITH HER ETERNAL WATCH WHEN ALL SHE WANTED WAS TO GO WITH THE OTHERS TO WIN THE WAR.
AS SHE HEARS THE ECHOES OF HIS FEET COMING DOWN THE STAIRS, SHE CAN SCARCELY BELIEVE IT.
SHE TURNS WIDE-EYED AND SMILING, KNOWING THAT HER WATCH IS AT AN END, AT LAST.
M-MERLIN...?
MY LORD, YOU HAVE RETURNED!

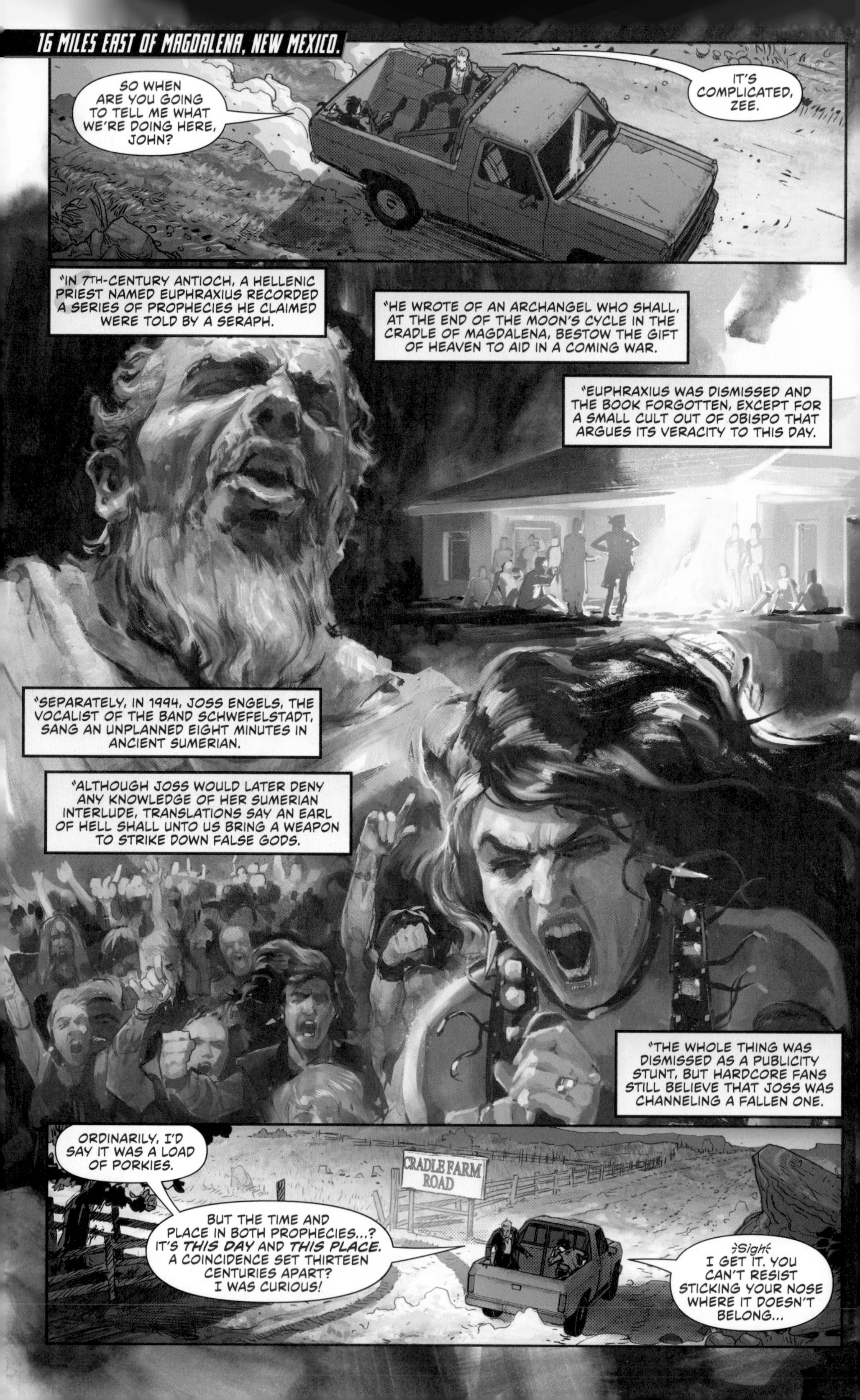
16 MILES EAST OF MAGDALENA, NEW MEXICO.
SO WHEN ARE YOU GOING TO TELL ME WHAT WE'RE DOING HERE, JOHN?
IT'S COMPLICATED, ZEE.
"IN 7TH-CENTURY ANTIOCH, A HELLENIC PRIEST NAMED EUPHRAXIUS RECORDED A SERIES OF PROPHECIES HE CLAIMED WERE TOLD BY A SERAPH.
"HE WROTE OF AN ARCHANGEL WHO SHALL, AT THE END OF THE MOON'S CYCLE IN THE CRADLE OF MAGDALENA, BESTOW THE GIFT OF HEAVEN TO AID IN A COMING WAR.
"EUPHRAXIUS WAS DISMISSED AND THE BOOK FORGOTTEN, EXCEPT FOR A SMALL CULT OUT OF OBISPO THAT ARGUES ITS VERACITY TO THIS DAY.
"SEPARATELY, IN 1994, JOSS ENGELS, THE VOCALIST OF THE BAND SCHWEFELSTADT, SANG AN UNPLANNED EIGHT MINUTES IN ANCIENT SUMERIAN.
"ALTHOUGH JOSS WOULD LATER DENY ANY KNOWLEDGE OF HER SUMERIAN INTERLUDE, TRANSLATIONS SAY AN EARL OF HELL SHALL UNTO US BRING A WEAPON TO STRIKE DOWN FALSE GODS.
"THE WHOLE THING WAS DISMISSED AS A PUBLICITY STUNT, BUT HARDCORE FANS STILL BELIEVE THAT JOSS WAS CHANNELING A FALLEN ONE.
ORDINARILY, I'D SAY IT WAS A LOAD OF PORKIES.
CRADLE FARM ROAD
BUT THE TIME AND PLACE IN BOTH PROPHECIES...? IT'S *THIS DAY* AND *THIS PLACE.* A COINCIDENCE SET THIRTEEN CENTURIES APART? I WAS CURIOUS!
Sigh I GET IT. YOU CAN'T RESIST STICKING YOUR NOSE WHERE IT DOESN'T BELONG...

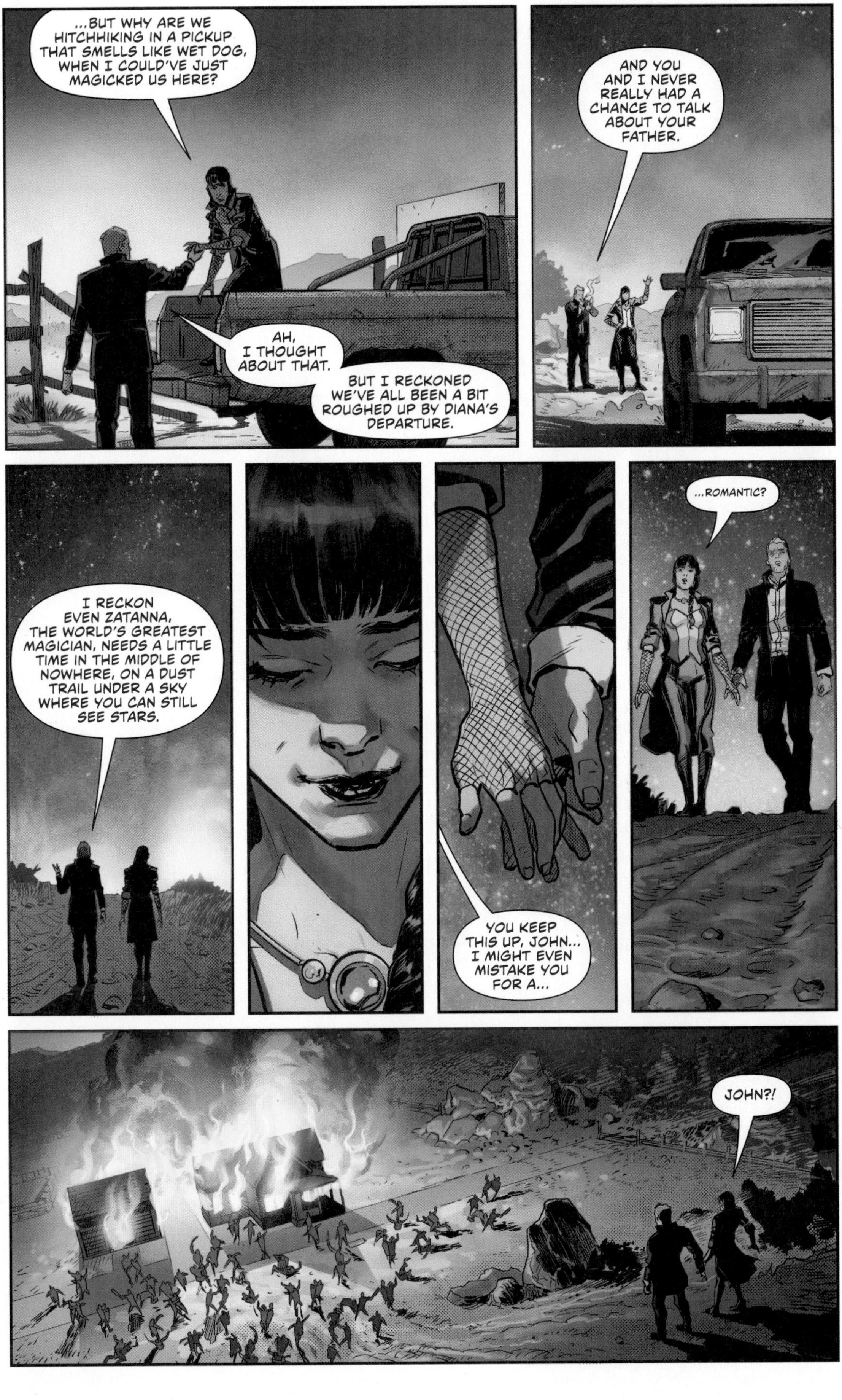
...BUT WHY ARE WE HITCHHIKING IN A PICKUP THAT SMELLS LIKE WET DOG, WHEN I COULD'VE JUST MAGICKED US HERE?
AH, I THOUGHT ABOUT THAT.
BUT I RECKONED WE'VE ALL BEEN A BIT ROUGHED UP BY DIANA'S DEPARTURE.
AND YOU AND I NEVER REALLY HAD A CHANCE TO TALK ABOUT YOUR FATHER.
I RECKON EVEN ZATANNA, THE WORLD'S GREATEST MAGICIAN, NEEDS A LITTLE TIME IN THE MIDDLE OF NOWHERE, ON A DUST TRAIL UNDER A SKY WHERE YOU CAN STILL SEE STARS.
YOU KEEP THIS UP, JOHN... I MIGHT EVEN MISTAKE YOU FOR A...
...ROMANTIC?
JOHN?!

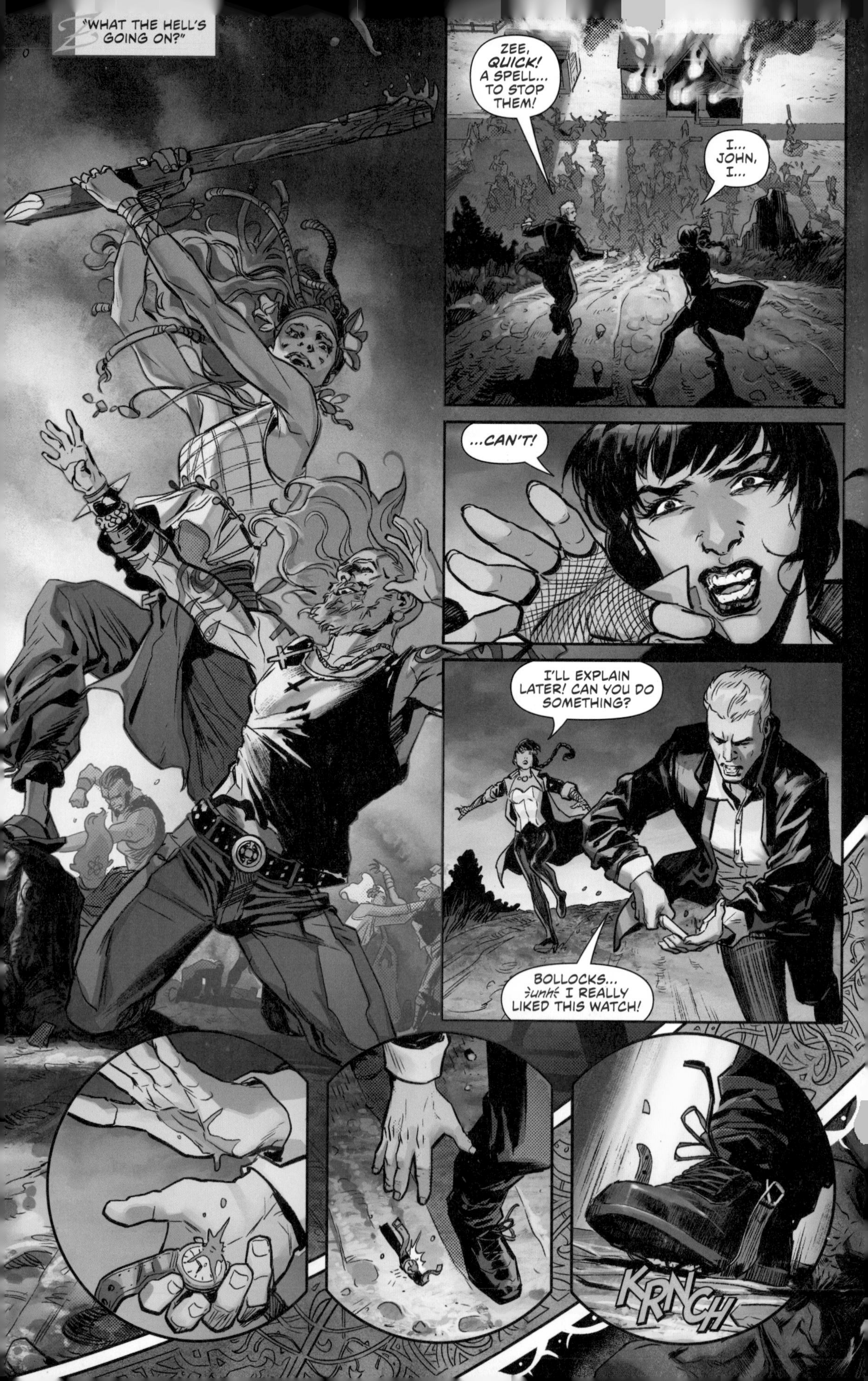

"WHAT THE HELL'S GOING ON?"
ZEE, QUICK! A SPELL... TO STOP THEM!
I... JOHN, I...
...CAN'T!
I'LL EXPLAIN LATER! CAN YOU DO SOMETHING?
BOLLOCKS... unh! I REALLY LIKED THIS WATCH!
KRNCH

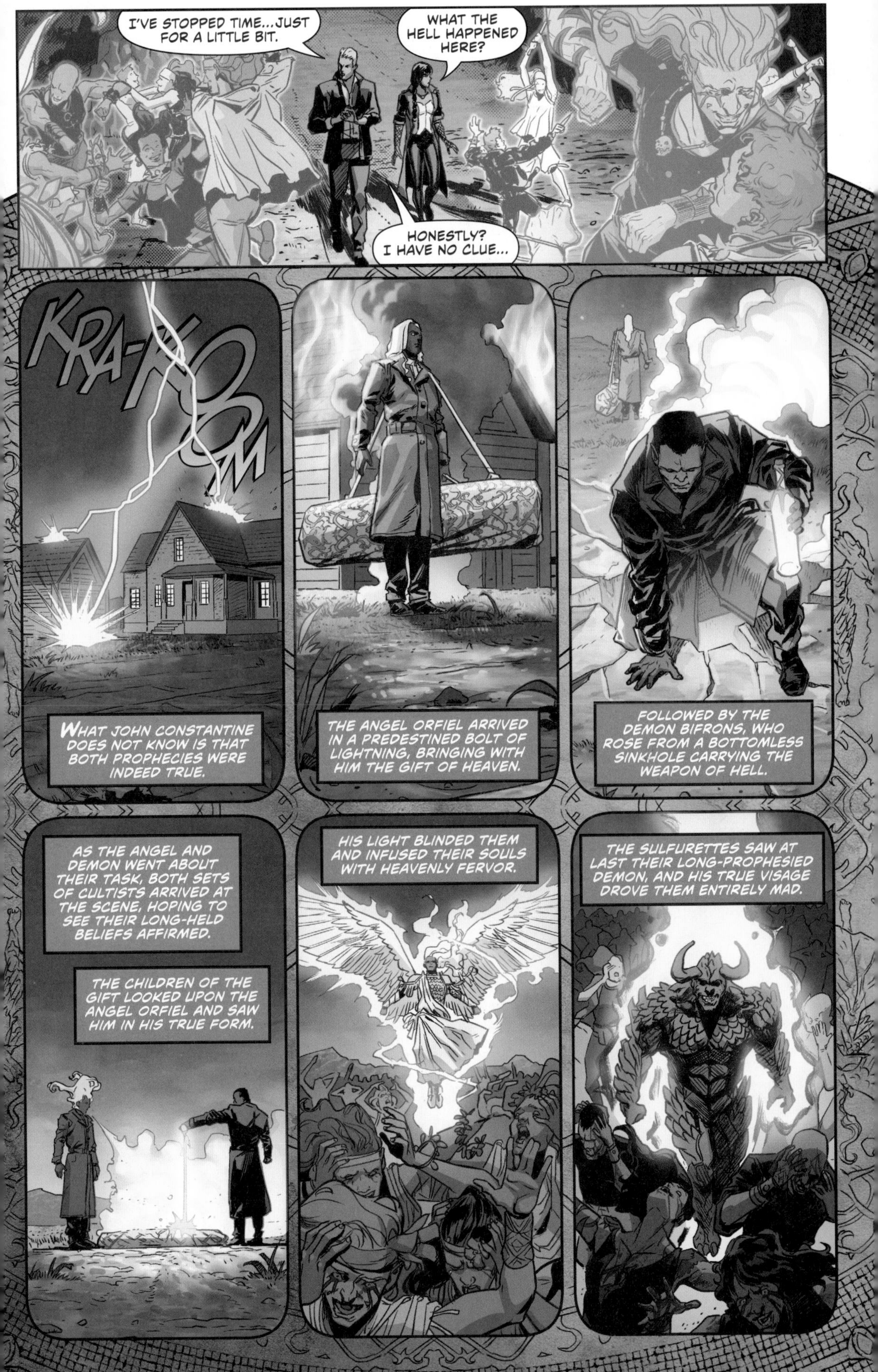
I'VE STOPPED TIME...JUST FOR A LITTLE BIT.
WHAT THE HELL HAPPENED HERE?
HONESTLY? I HAVE NO CLUE...
KRA-KOOOM
WHAT JOHN CONSTANTINE DOES NOT KNOW IS THAT BOTH PROPHECIES WERE INDEED TRUE.
THE ANGEL ORFIEL ARRIVED IN A PREDESTINED BOLT OF LIGHTNING, BRINGING WITH HIM THE GIFT OF HEAVEN.
FOLLOWED BY THE DEMON BIFRONS, WHO ROSE FROM A BOTTOMLESS SINKHOLE CARRYING THE WEAPON OF HELL.
AS THE ANGEL AND DEMON WENT ABOUT THEIR TASK, BOTH SETS OF CULTISTS ARRIVED AT THE SCENE, HOPING TO SEE THEIR LONG-HELD BELIEFS AFFIRMED.
THE CHILDREN OF THE GIFT LOOKED UPON THE ANGEL ORFIEL AND SAW HIM IN HIS TRUE FORM.
HIS LIGHT BLINDED THEM AND INFUSED THEIR SOULS WITH HEAVENLY FERVOR.
THE SULFURETTES SAW AT LAST THEIR LONG-PROPHESIED DEMON, AND HIS TRUE VISAGE DROVE THEM ENTIRELY MAD.

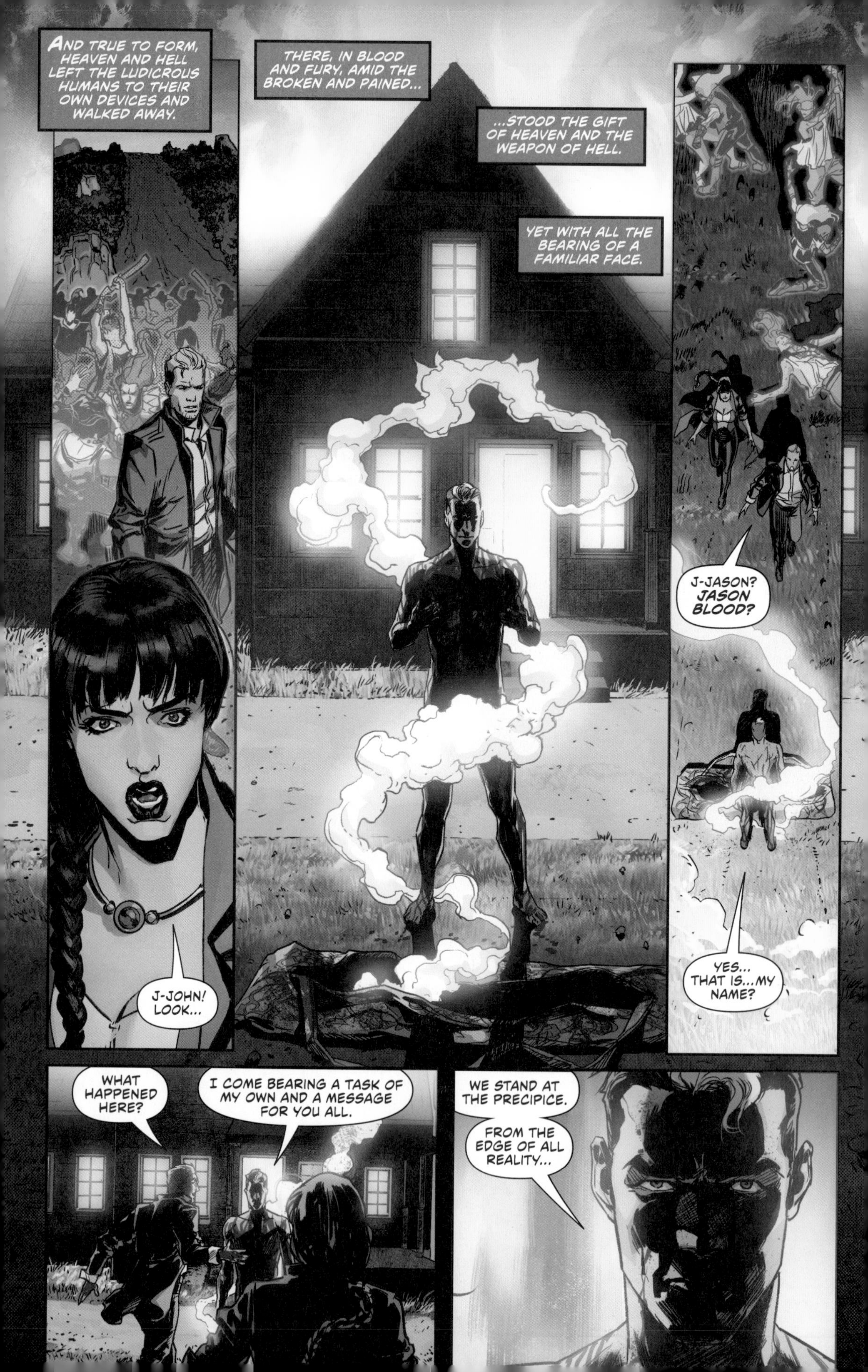
AND TRUE TO FORM, HEAVEN AND HELL LEFT THE LUDICROUS HUMANS TO THEIR OWN DEVICES AND WALKED AWAY.
THERE, IN BLOOD AND FURY, AMID THE BROKEN AND PAINED...
...STOOD THE GIFT OF HEAVEN AND THE WEAPON OF HELL.
YET WITH ALL THE BEARING OF A FAMILIAR FACE.
J-JOHN! LOOK...
J-JASON? JASON BLOOD?
YES... THAT IS...MY NAME?
WHAT HAPPENED HERE?
I COME BEARING A TASK OF MY OWN AND A MESSAGE FOR YOU ALL.
WE STAND AT THE PRECIPICE.
FROM THE EDGE OF ALL REALITY...

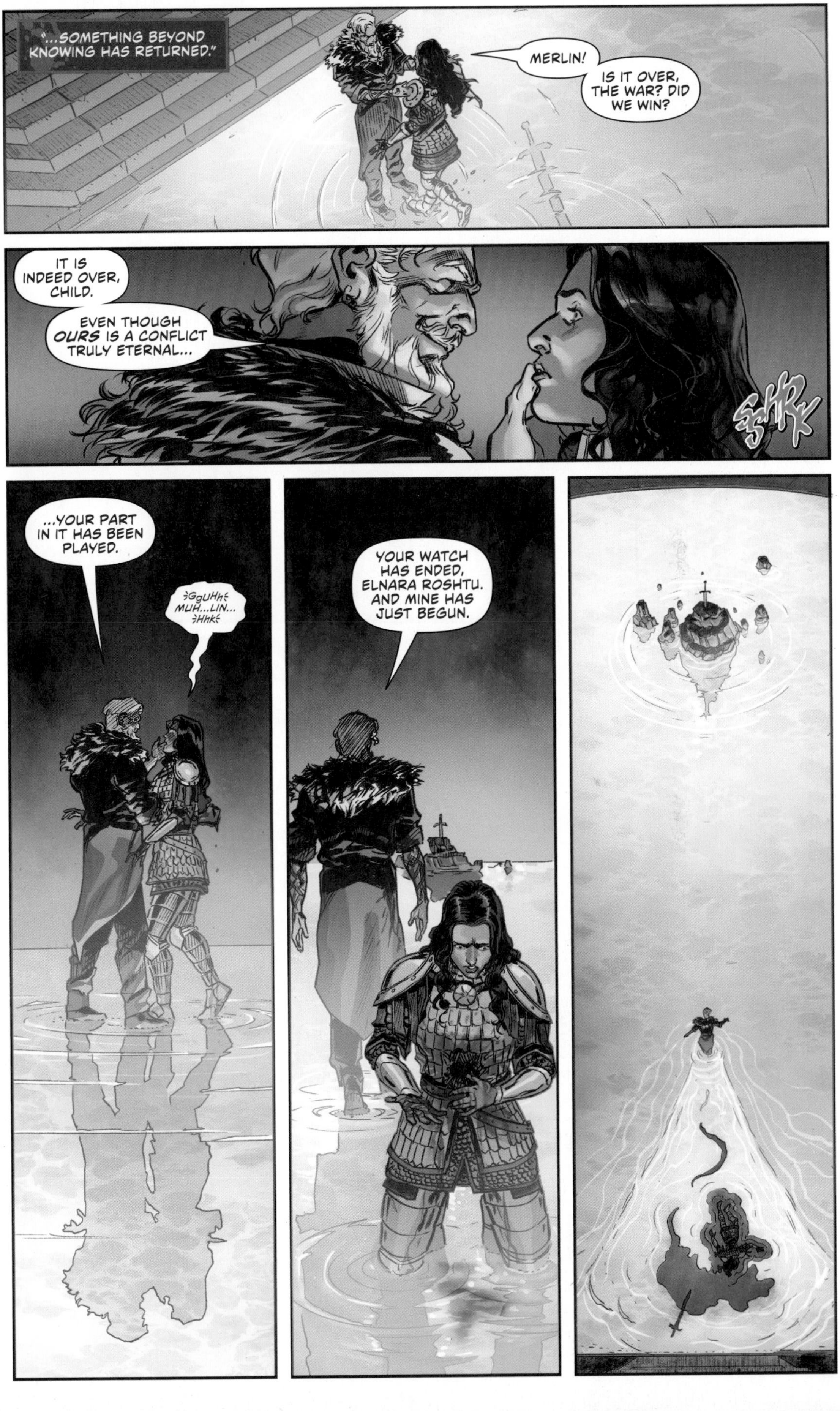
"...SOMETHING BEYOND KNOWING HAS RETURNED."
MERLIN!
IS IT OVER, THE WAR? DID WE WIN?
IT IS INDEED OVER, CHILD.
EVEN THOUGH *OURS* IS A CONFLICT TRULY ETERNAL...
SSHRK
...YOUR PART IN IT HAS BEEN PLAYED.
GGUHH MUH...LIN... HHK
YOUR WATCH HAS ENDED, ELNARA ROSHTU. AND MINE HAS JUST BEGUN.

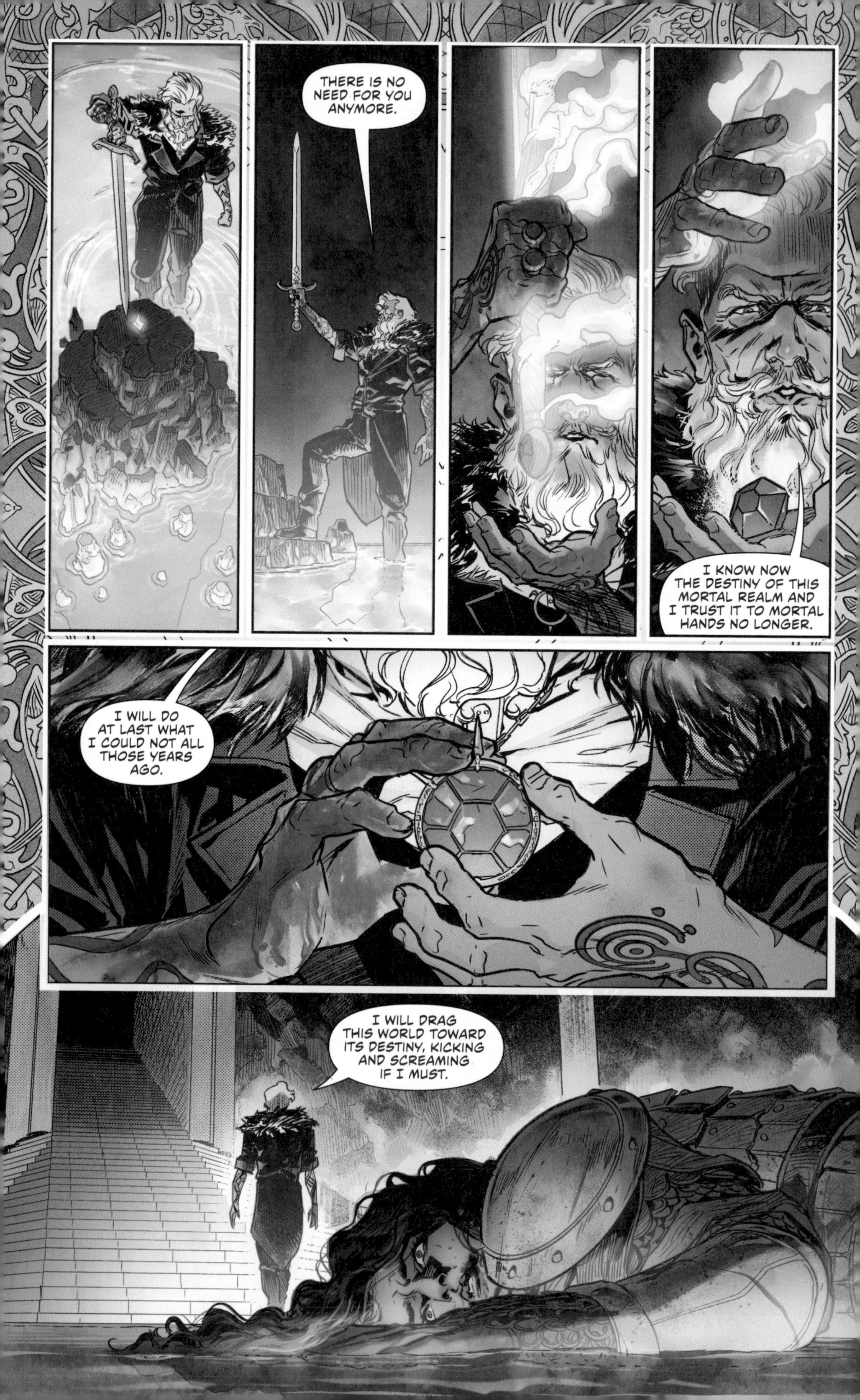
THERE IS NO NEED FOR YOU ANYMORE.
I KNOW NOW THE DESTINY OF THIS MORTAL REALM AND I TRUST IT TO MORTAL HANDS NO LONGER.
I WILL DO AT LAST WHAT I COULD NOT ALL THOSE YEARS AGO.
I WILL DRAG THIS WORLD TOWARD ITS DESTINY, KICKING AND SCREAMING IF I MUST.

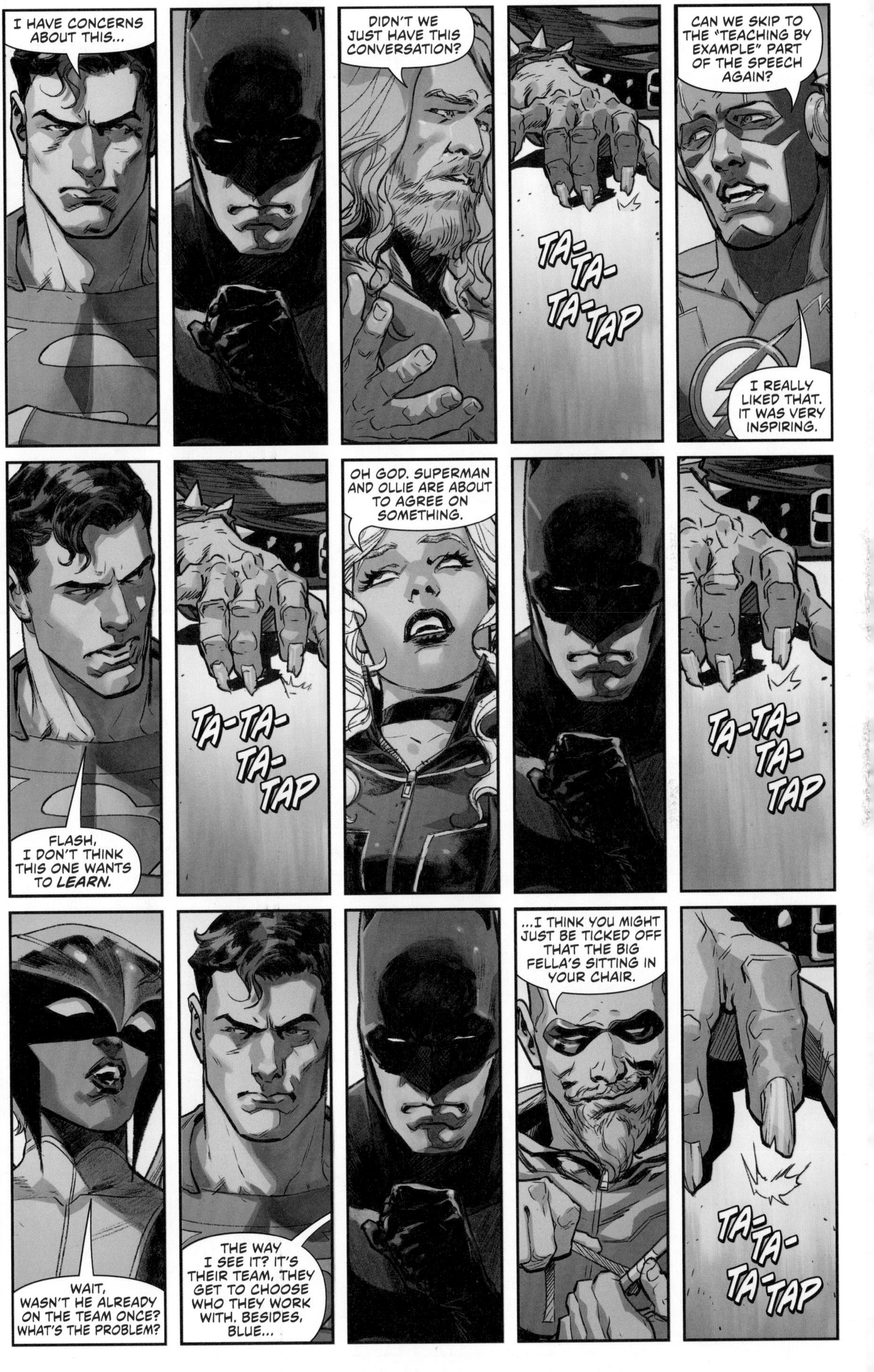
I HAVE CONCERNS ABOUT THIS...
DIDN'T WE JUST HAVE THIS CONVERSATION?
TA-TA-TA-TAP
CAN WE SKIP TO THE "TEACHING BY EXAMPLE" PART OF THE SPEECH AGAIN?
I REALLY LIKED THAT. IT WAS VERY INSPIRING.
FLASH, I DON'T THINK THIS ONE WANTS TO LEARN.
TA-TA-TA-TAP
OH GOD. SUPERMAN AND OLLIE ARE ABOUT TO AGREE ON SOMETHING.
TA-TA-TA-TAP
WAIT, WASN'T HE ALREADY ON THE TEAM ONCE? WHAT'S THE PROBLEM?
THE WAY I SEE IT? IT'S THEIR TEAM, THEY GET TO CHOOSE WHO THEY WORK WITH. BESIDES, BLUE...
...I THINK YOU MIGHT JUST BE TICKED OFF THAT THE BIG FELLA'S SITTING IN YOUR CHAIR.
TA-TA-TA-TAP

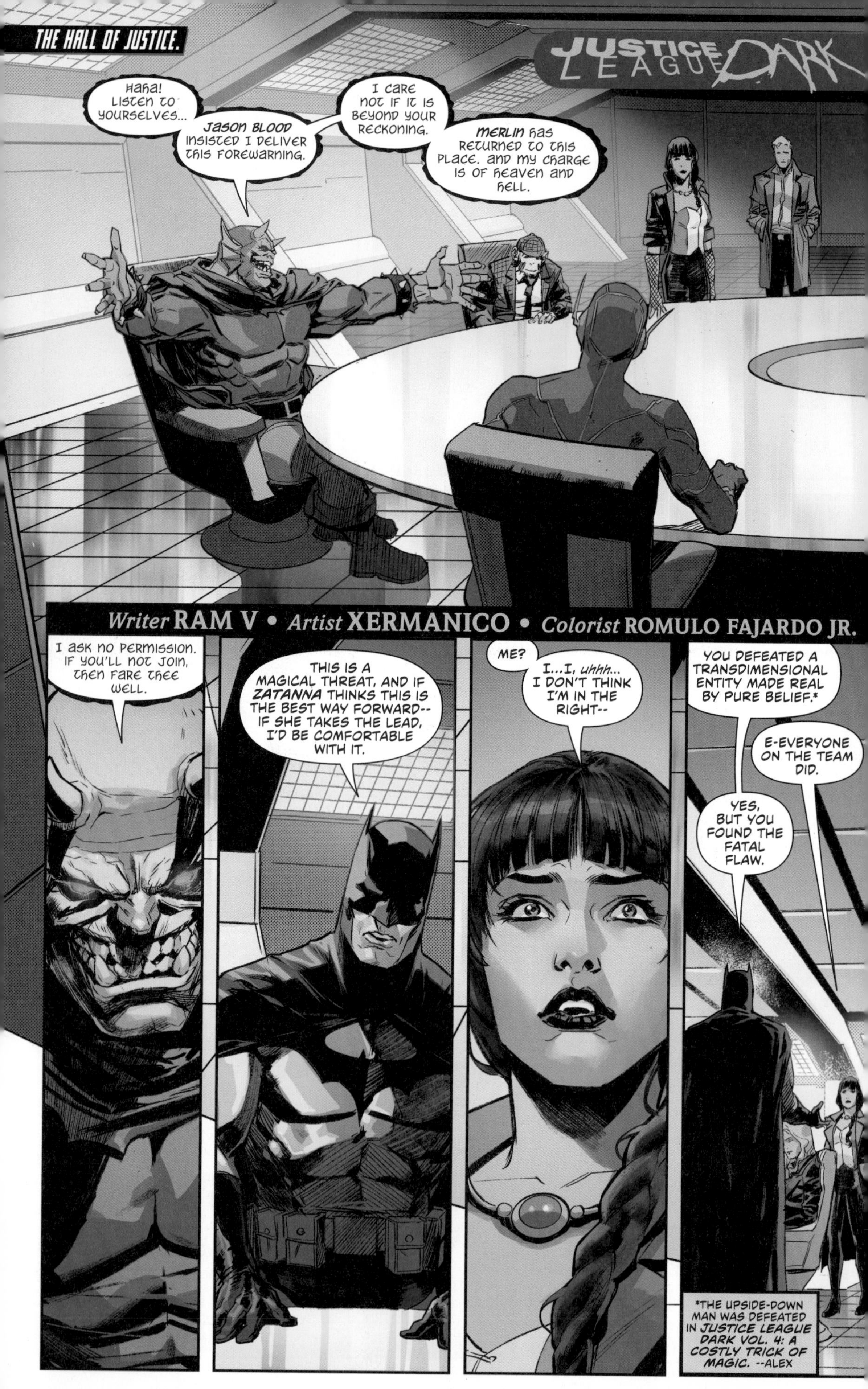
THE HALL OF JUSTICE.
JUSTICE LEAGUE DARK
HAHA! LISTEN TO YOURSELVES...
JASON BLOOD INSISTED I DELIVER THIS FOREWARNING.
I CARE NOT IF IT IS BEYOND YOUR RECKONING.
MERLIN HAS RETURNED TO THIS PLACE. AND MY CHARGE IS OF HEAVEN AND HELL.
Writer RAM V • Artist XERMANICO • Colorist ROMULO FAJARDO JR.
I ASK NO PERMISSION. IF YOU'LL NOT JOIN, THEN FARE THEE WELL.
THIS IS A MAGICAL THREAT, AND IF ZATANNA THINKS THIS IS THE BEST WAY FORWARD-- IF SHE TAKES THE LEAD, I'D BE COMFORTABLE WITH IT.
ME?
I...I, uhhh... I DON'T THINK I'M IN THE RIGHT--
YOU DEFEATED A TRANSDIMENSIONAL ENTITY MADE REAL BY PURE BELIEF.*
E-EVERYONE ON THE TEAM DID.
YES, BUT YOU FOUND THE FATAL FLAW.
*THE UPSIDE-DOWN MAN WAS DEFEATED IN JUSTICE LEAGUE DARK VOL. 4: A COSTLY TRICK OF MAGIC. --ALEX

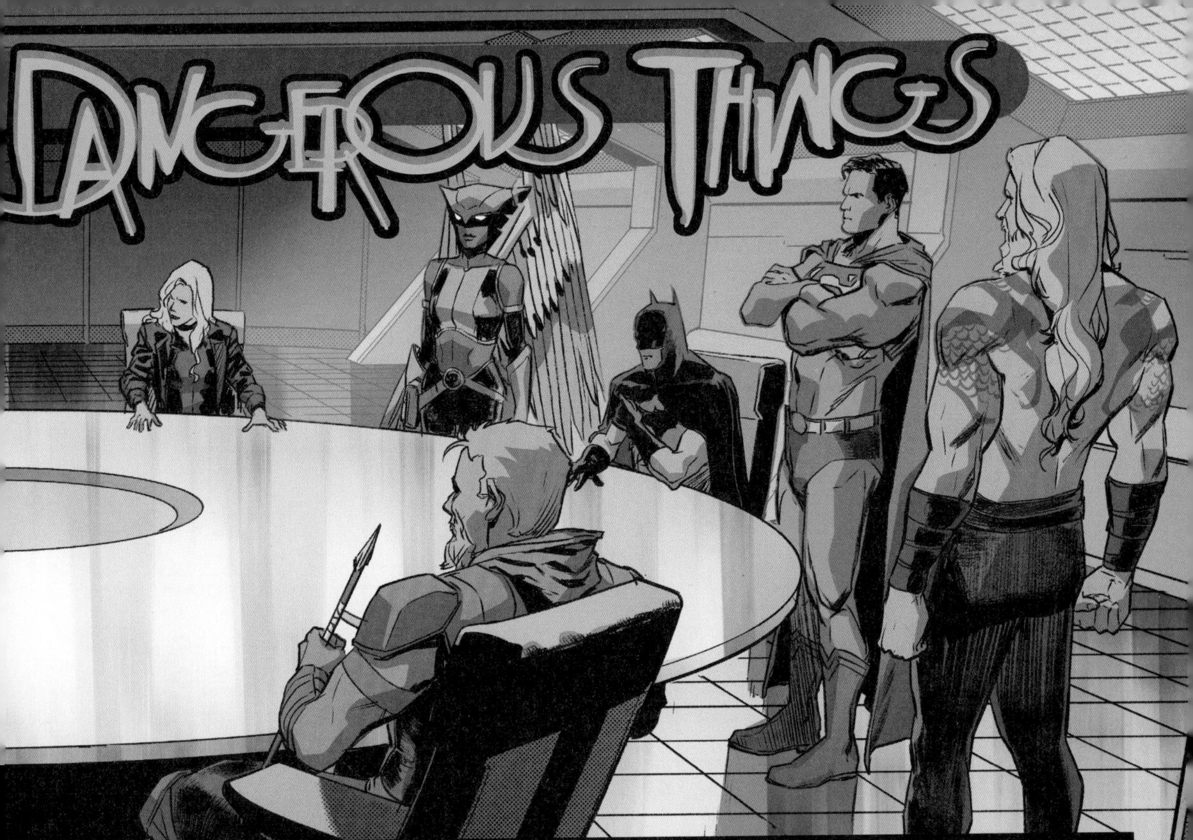
DANGEROUS THINGS

Letterer **ROB LEIGH** • *Associate Editor* **ANDREA SHEA** • *Editor* **ALEX R. CARR**

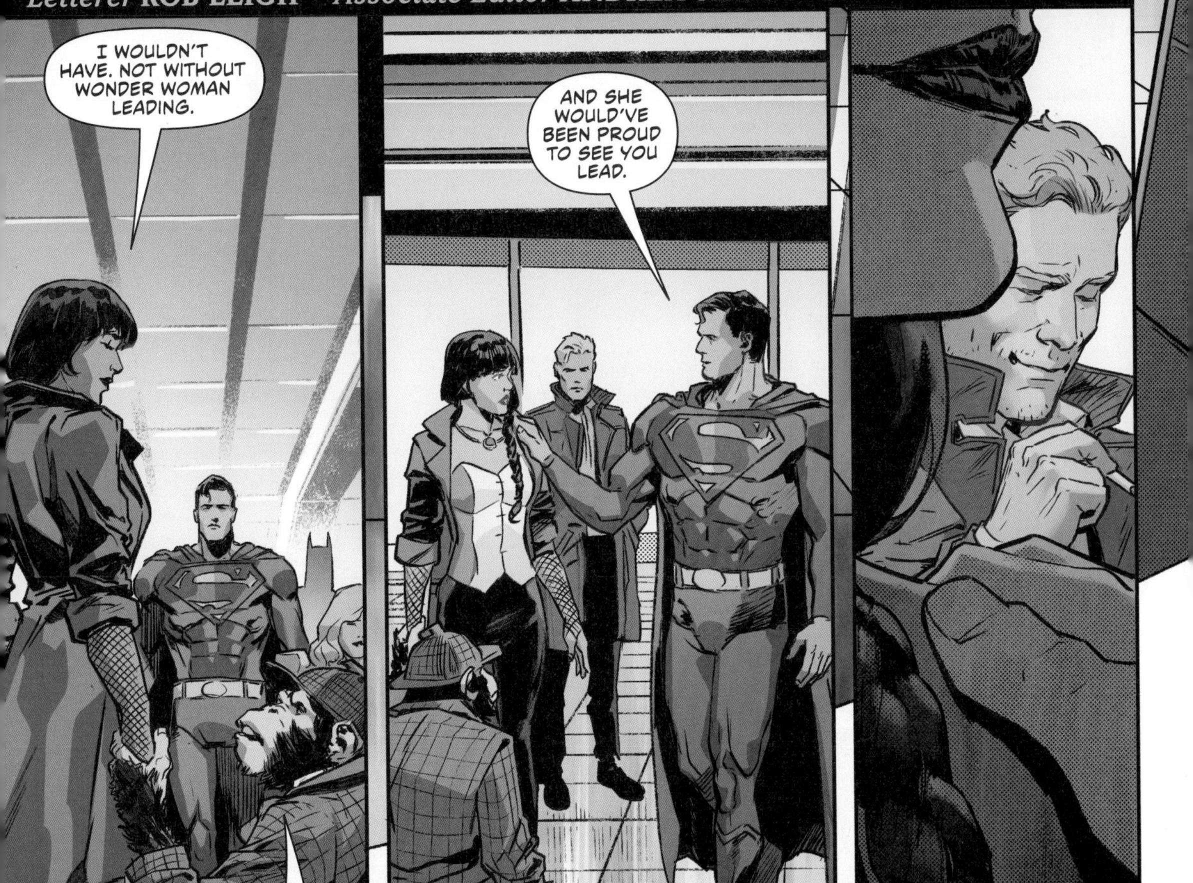
I WOULDN'T HAVE. NOT WITHOUT WONDER WOMAN LEADING.
DIANA IS GONE, ZEE.
AND SHE WOULD'VE BEEN PROUD TO SEE YOU LEAD.

SUPERMAN created by Jerry Siegel and Joe Shuster. By special arrangement with the Jerry Siegel family.

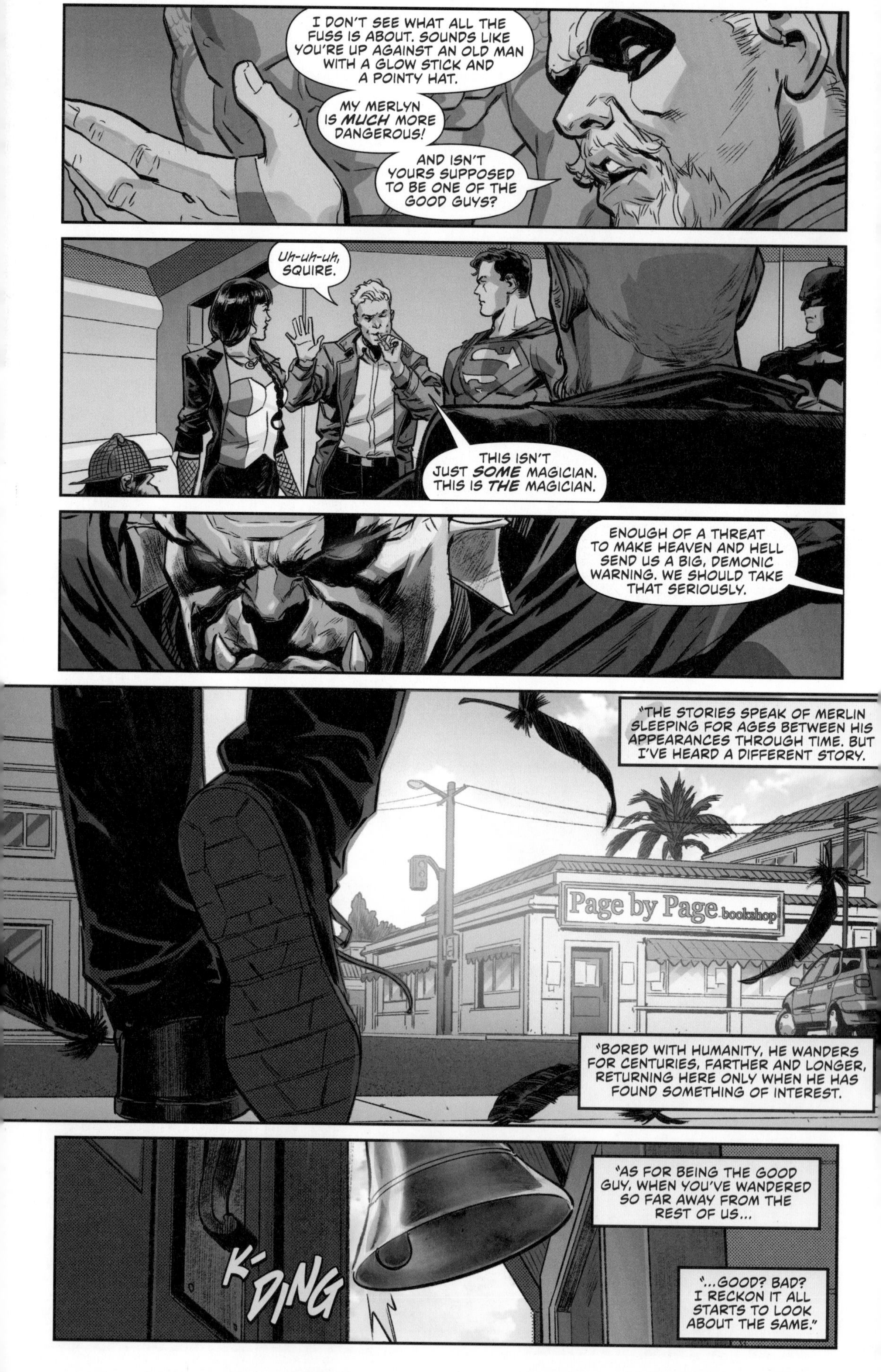
I DON'T SEE WHAT ALL THE FUSS IS ABOUT. SOUNDS LIKE YOU'RE UP AGAINST AN OLD MAN WITH A GLOW STICK AND A POINTY HAT.
MY MERLYN IS MUCH MORE DANGEROUS!
AND ISN'T YOURS SUPPOSED TO BE ONE OF THE GOOD GUYS?
Uh-uh-uh, SQUIRE.
THIS ISN'T JUST SOME MAGICIAN. THIS IS THE MAGICIAN.
ENOUGH OF A THREAT TO MAKE HEAVEN AND HELL SEND US A BIG, DEMONIC WARNING. WE SHOULD TAKE THAT SERIOUSLY.
"THE STORIES SPEAK OF MERLIN SLEEPING FOR AGES BETWEEN HIS APPEARANCES THROUGH TIME. BUT I'VE HEARD A DIFFERENT STORY.
Page by Page bookshop
"BORED WITH HUMANITY, HE WANDERS FOR CENTURIES, FARTHER AND LONGER, RETURNING HERE ONLY WHEN HE HAS FOUND SOMETHING OF INTEREST.
"AS FOR BEING THE GOOD GUY, WHEN YOU'VE WANDERED SO FAR AWAY FROM THE REST OF US...
K-DING
"...GOOD? BAD? I RECKON IT ALL STARTS TO LOOK ABOUT THE SAME."

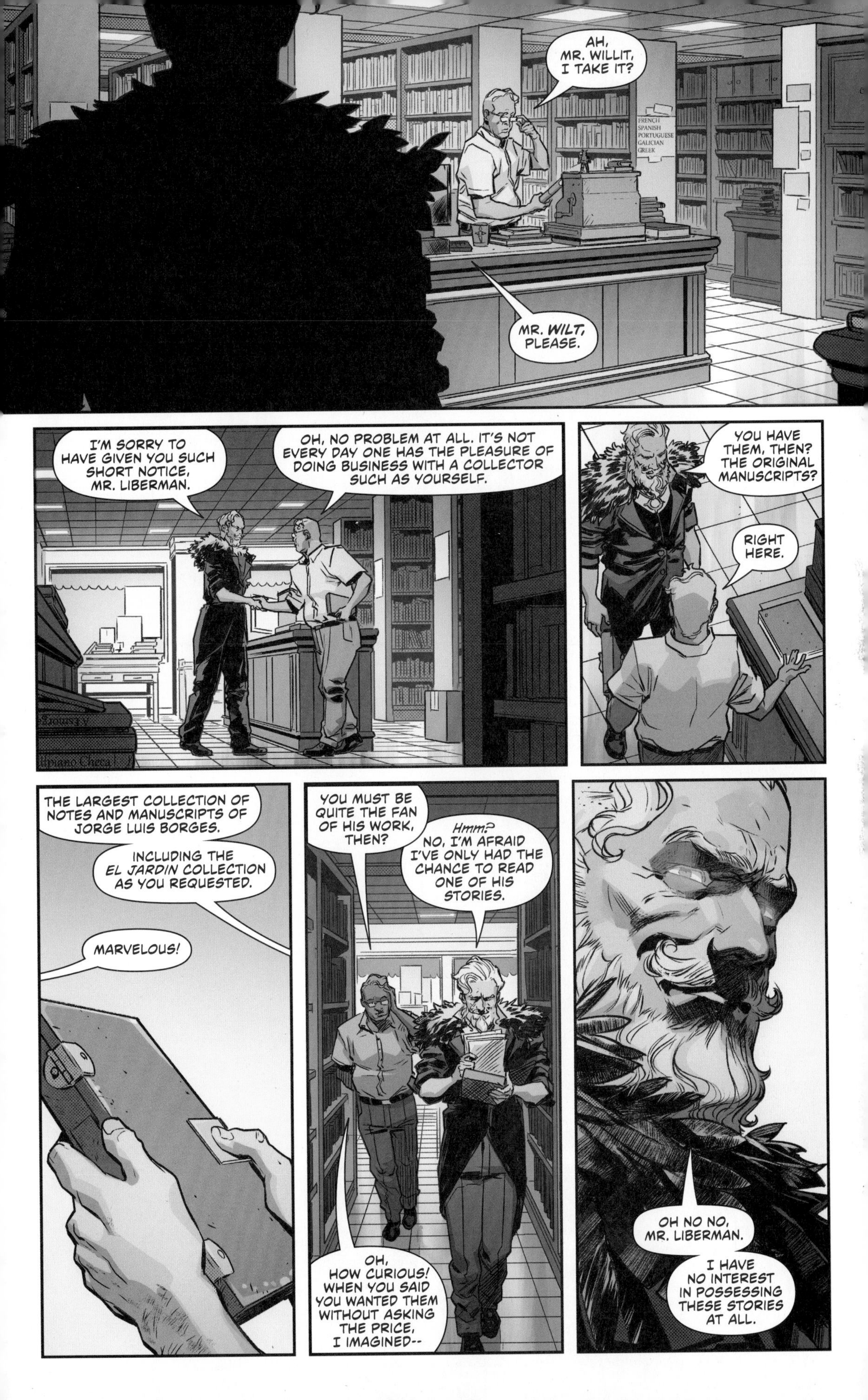
AH, MR. WILLIT, I TAKE IT?
FRENCH
SPANISH
PORTUGUESE
GALICIAN
GREEK
MR. *WILT,* PLEASE.
I'M SORRY TO HAVE GIVEN YOU SUCH SHORT NOTICE, MR. LIBERMAN.
OH, NO PROBLEM AT ALL. IT'S NOT EVERY DAY ONE HAS THE PLEASURE OF DOING BUSINESS WITH A COLLECTOR SUCH AS YOURSELF.
YOU HAVE THEM, THEN? THE ORIGINAL MANUSCRIPTS?
RIGHT HERE.
THE LARGEST COLLECTION OF NOTES AND MANUSCRIPTS OF JORGE LUIS BORGES.
INCLUDING THE *EL JARDIN* COLLECTION AS YOU REQUESTED.
MARVELOUS!
YOU MUST BE QUITE THE FAN OF HIS WORK, THEN?
Hmm? NO, I'M AFRAID I'VE ONLY HAD THE CHANCE TO READ ONE OF HIS STORIES.
OH, HOW CURIOUS! WHEN YOU SAID YOU WANTED THEM WITHOUT ASKING THE PRICE, I IMAGINED--
OH NO NO, MR. LIBERMAN.
I HAVE NO INTEREST IN POSSESSING THESE STORIES AT ALL.

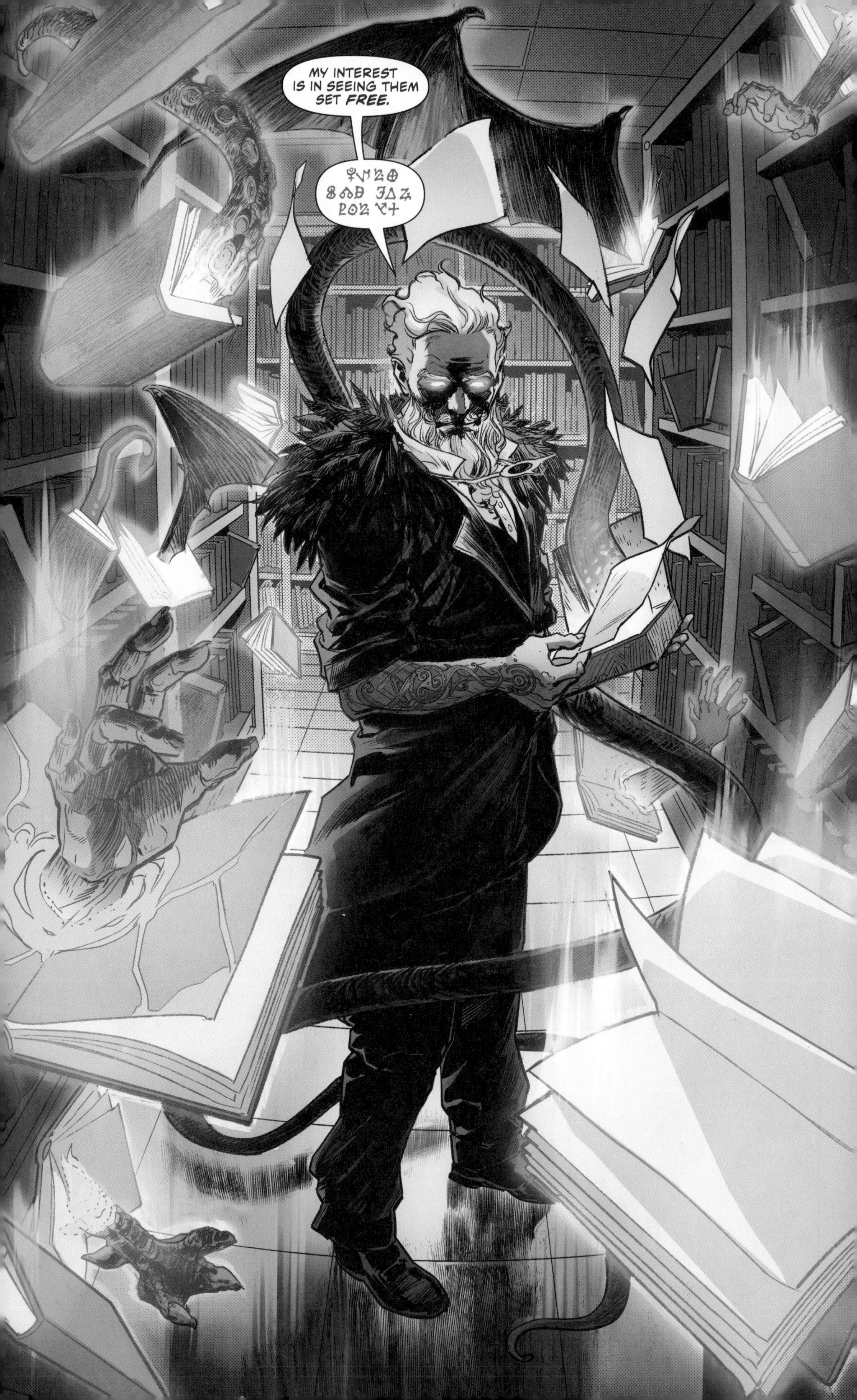
MY INTEREST IS IN SEEING THEM SET FREE.

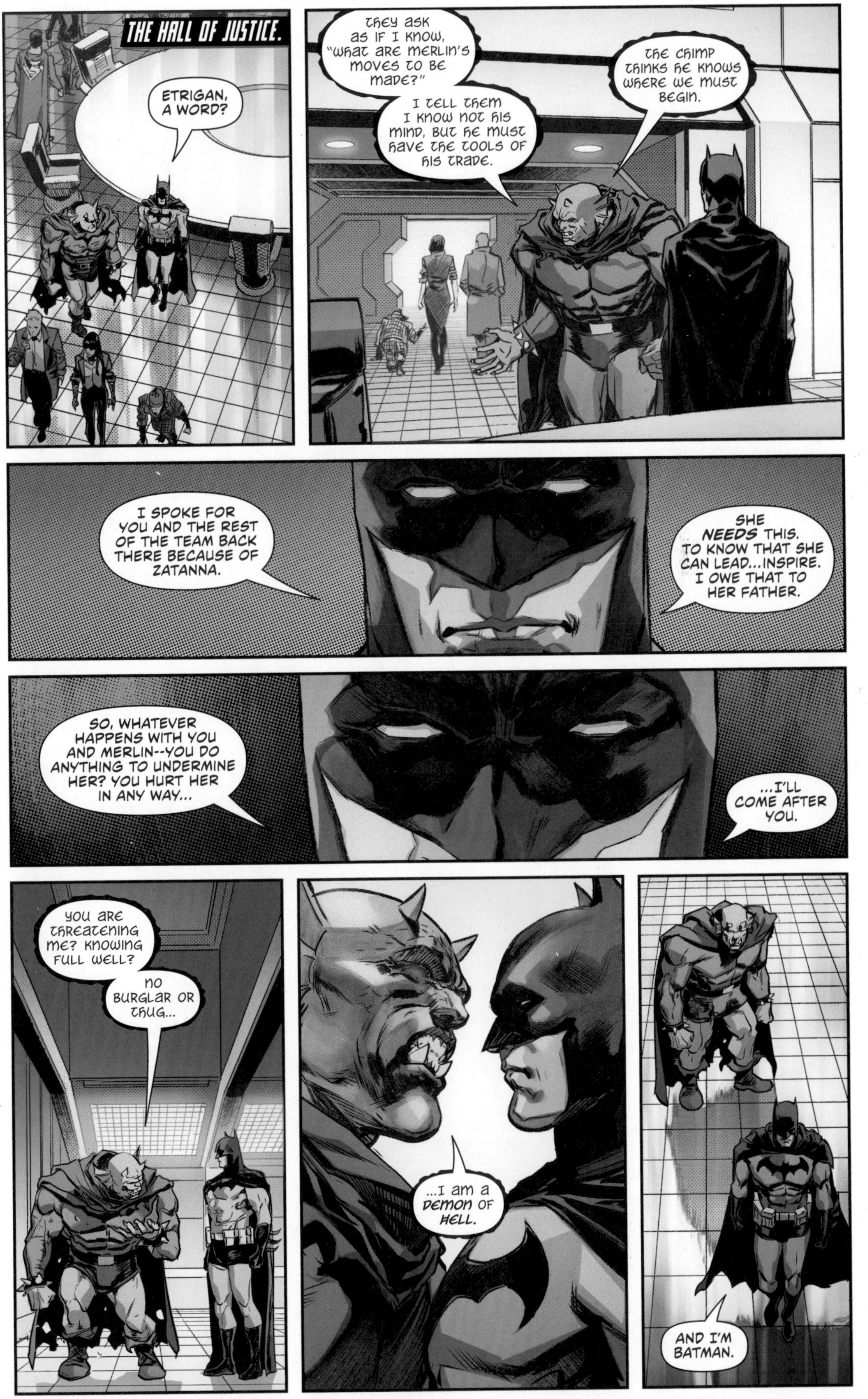
THE HALL OF JUSTICE.
ETRIGAN, A WORD?
THEY ASK AS IF I KNOW, "WHAT ARE MERLIN'S MOVES TO BE MADE?"
I TELL THEM I KNOW NOT HIS MIND, BUT HE MUST HAVE THE TOOLS OF HIS TRADE.
THE CHIMP THINKS HE KNOWS WHERE WE MUST BEGIN.
I SPOKE FOR YOU AND THE REST OF THE TEAM BACK THERE BECAUSE OF ZATANNA.
SHE NEEDS THIS. TO KNOW THAT SHE CAN LEAD...INSPIRE. I OWE THAT TO HER FATHER.
SO, WHATEVER HAPPENS WITH YOU AND MERLIN--YOU DO ANYTHING TO UNDERMINE HER? YOU HURT HER IN ANY WAY...
...I'LL COME AFTER YOU.
YOU ARE THREATENING ME? KNOWING FULL WELL?
NO BURGLAR OR THUG...
...I AM A DEMON OF HELL.
AND I'M BATMAN.

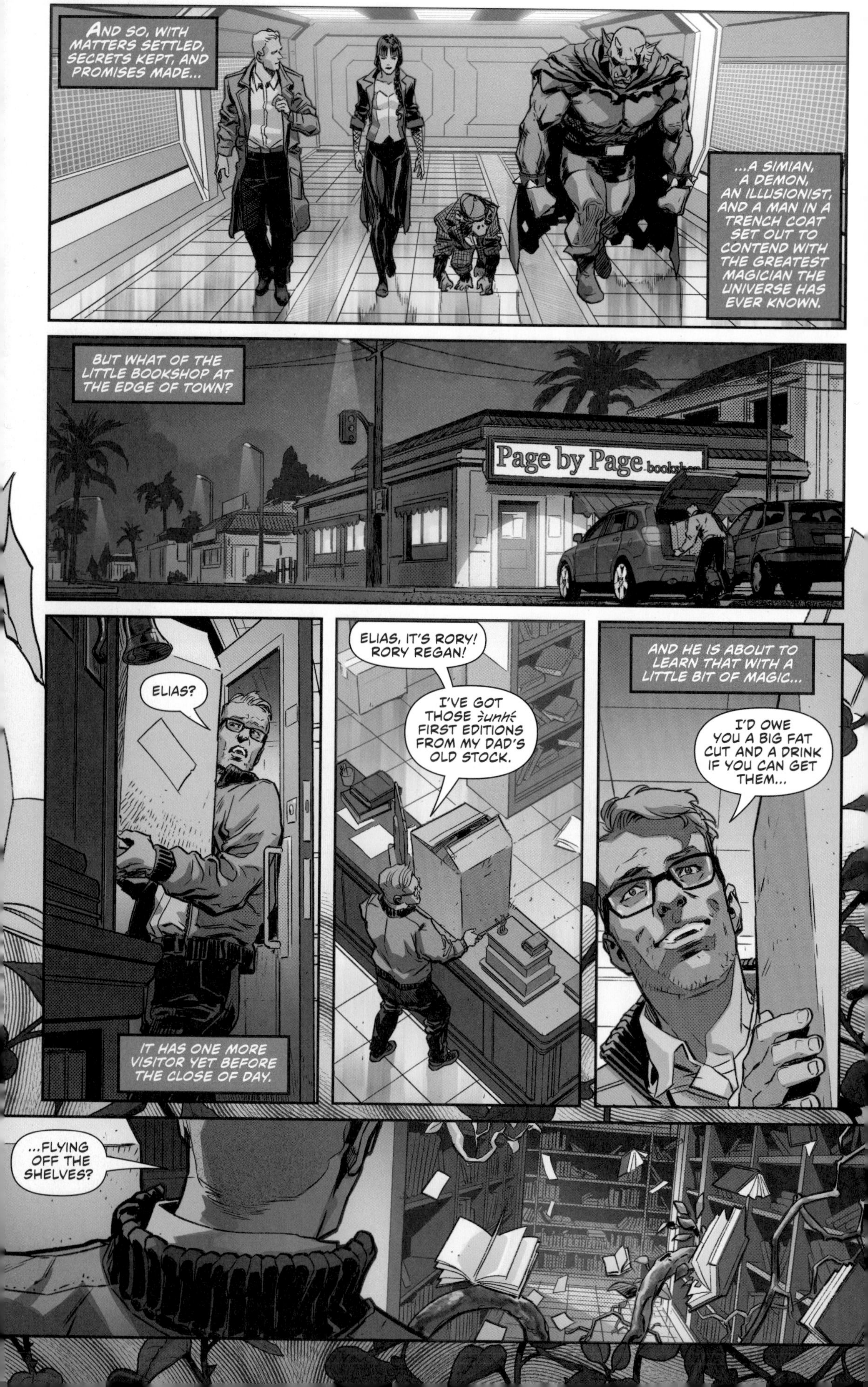
AND SO, WITH MATTERS SETTLED, SECRETS KEPT, AND PROMISES MADE...
...A SIMIAN, A DEMON, AN ILLUSIONIST, AND A MAN IN A TRENCH COAT SET OUT TO CONTEND WITH THE GREATEST MAGICIAN THE UNIVERSE HAS EVER KNOWN.
BUT WHAT OF THE LITTLE BOOKSHOP AT THE EDGE OF TOWN?
Page by Page
ELIAS?
IT HAS ONE MORE VISITOR YET BEFORE THE CLOSE OF DAY.
ELIAS, IT'S RORY! RORY REGAN!
I'VE GOT THOSE ≈unh≈ FIRST EDITIONS FROM MY DAD'S OLD STOCK.
AND HE IS ABOUT TO LEARN THAT WITH A LITTLE BIT OF MAGIC...
I'D OWE YOU A BIG FAT CUT AND A DRINK IF YOU CAN GET THEM...
...FLYING OFF THE SHELVES?

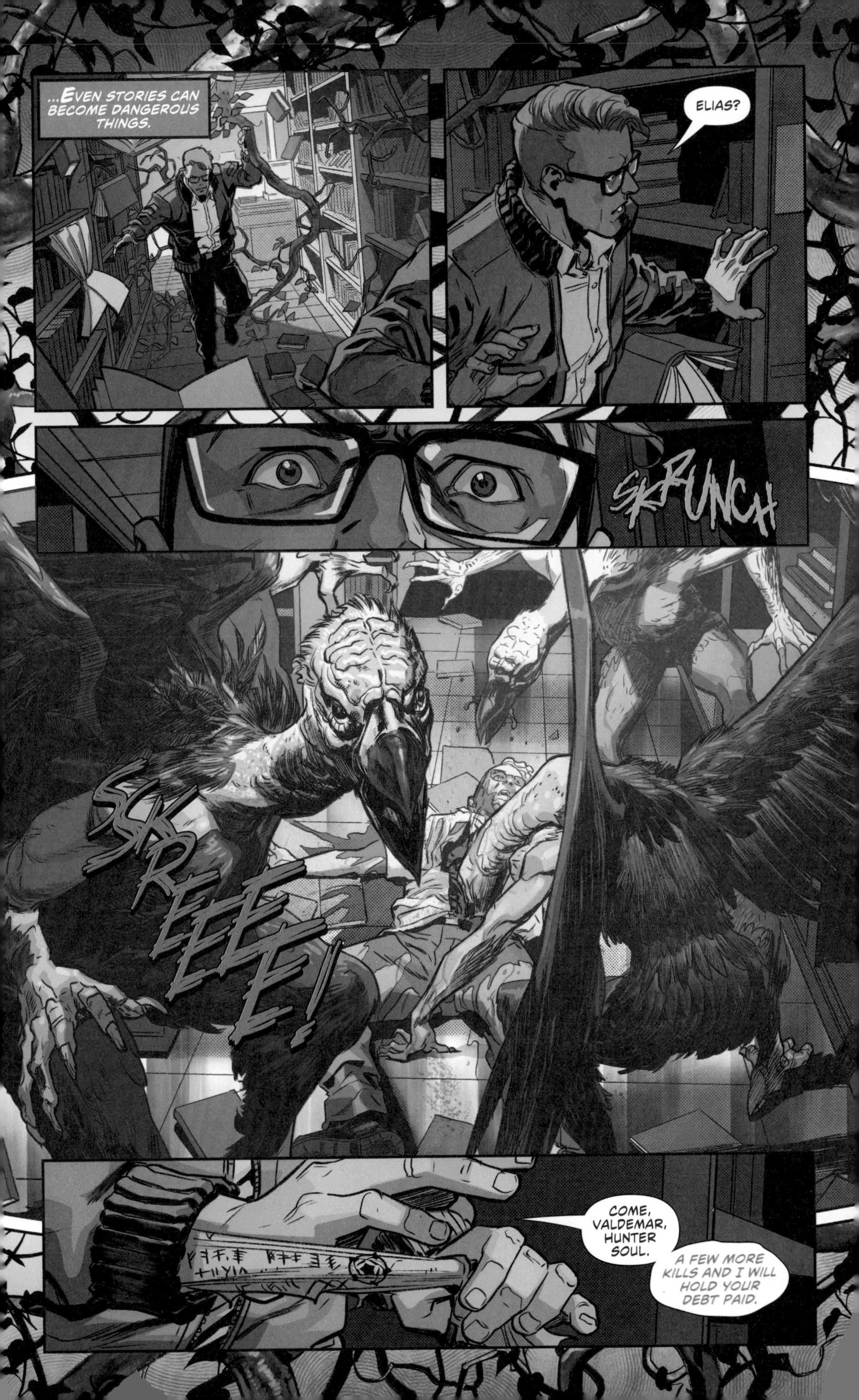

...EVEN STORIES CAN BECOME DANGEROUS THINGS.
ELIAS?
SKRUNCH
SSKREEEEE!
COME, VALDEMAR, HUNTER SOUL.
A FEW MORE KILLS AND I WILL HOLD YOUR DEBT PAID.

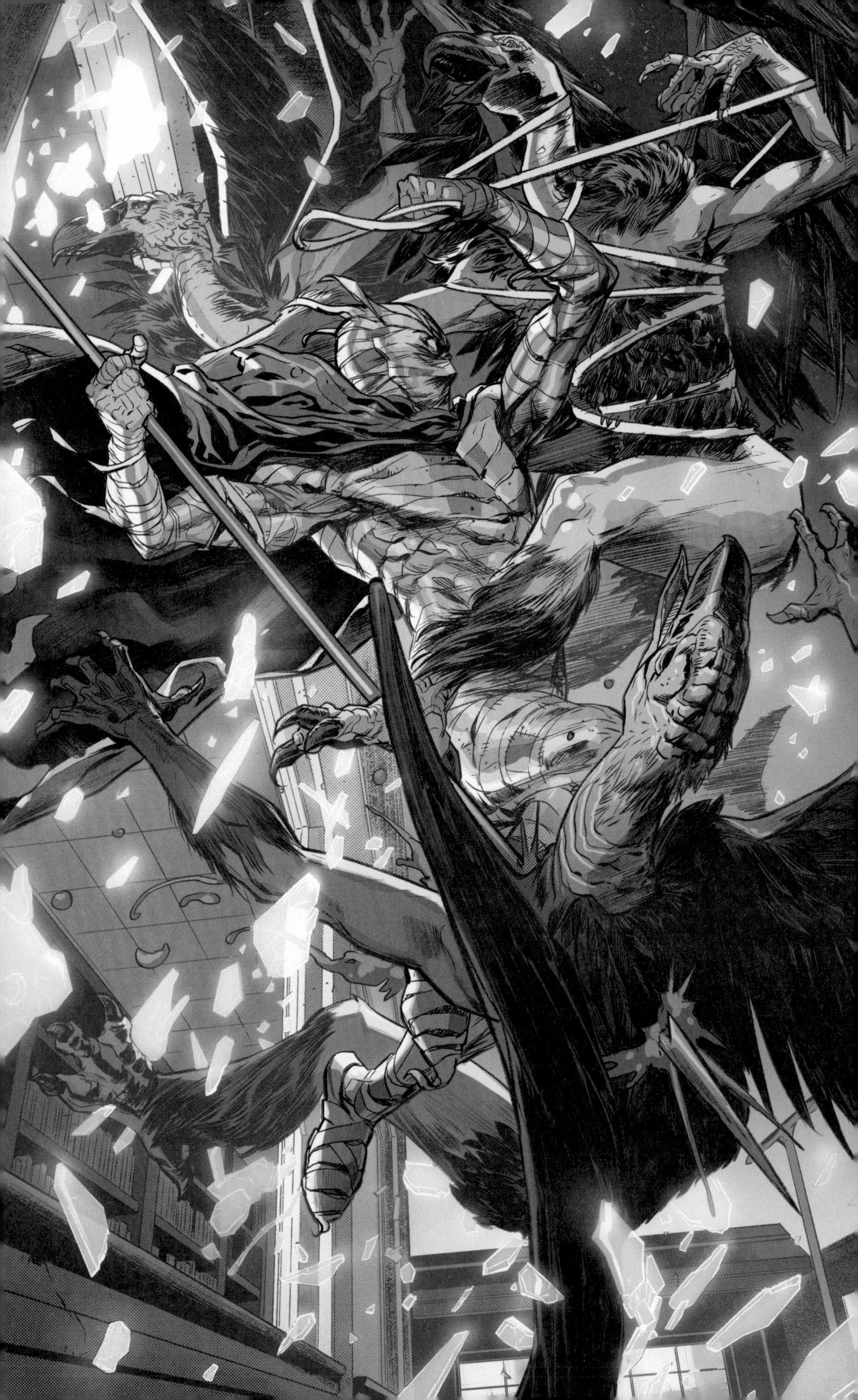

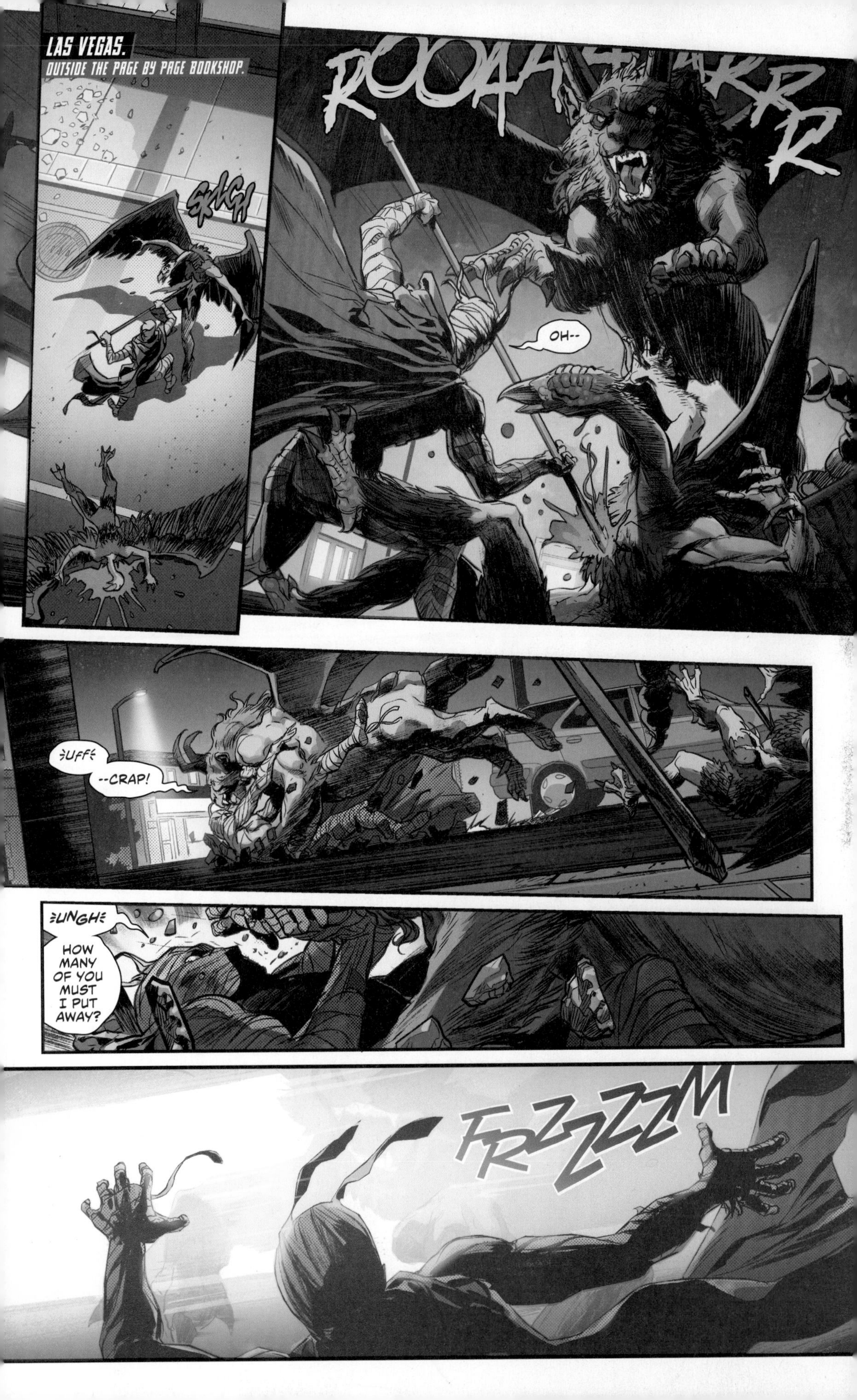
LAS VEGAS.
OUTSIDE THE PAGE BY PAGE BOOKSHOP.
OH--
UFF
--CRAP!
UNGH
HOW MANY OF YOU MUST I PUT AWAY?
FRZZZZM

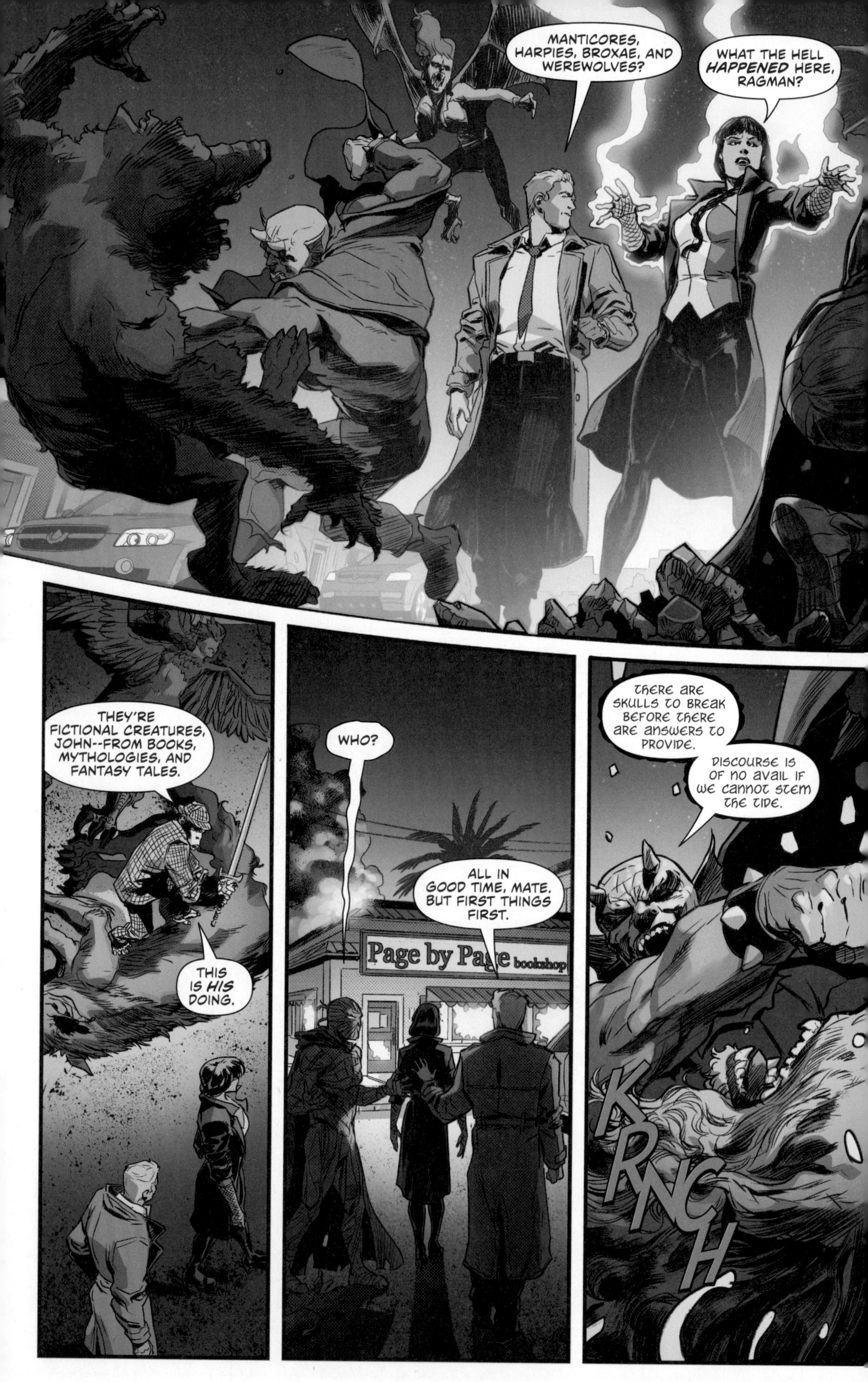
MANTICORES, HARPIES, BROXAE, AND WEREWOLVES?
WHAT THE HELL HAPPENED HERE, RAGMAN?
THEY'RE FICTIONAL CREATURES, JOHN--FROM BOOKS, MYTHOLOGIES, AND FANTASY TALES.
THIS IS HIS DOING.
WHO?
Page by Page bookshop
ALL IN GOOD TIME, MATE. BUT FIRST THINGS FIRST.
THERE ARE SKULLS TO BREAK BEFORE THERE ARE ANSWERS TO PROVIDE.
DISCOURSE IS OF NO AVAIL IF WE CANNOT STEM THE TIDE.
KRNCH

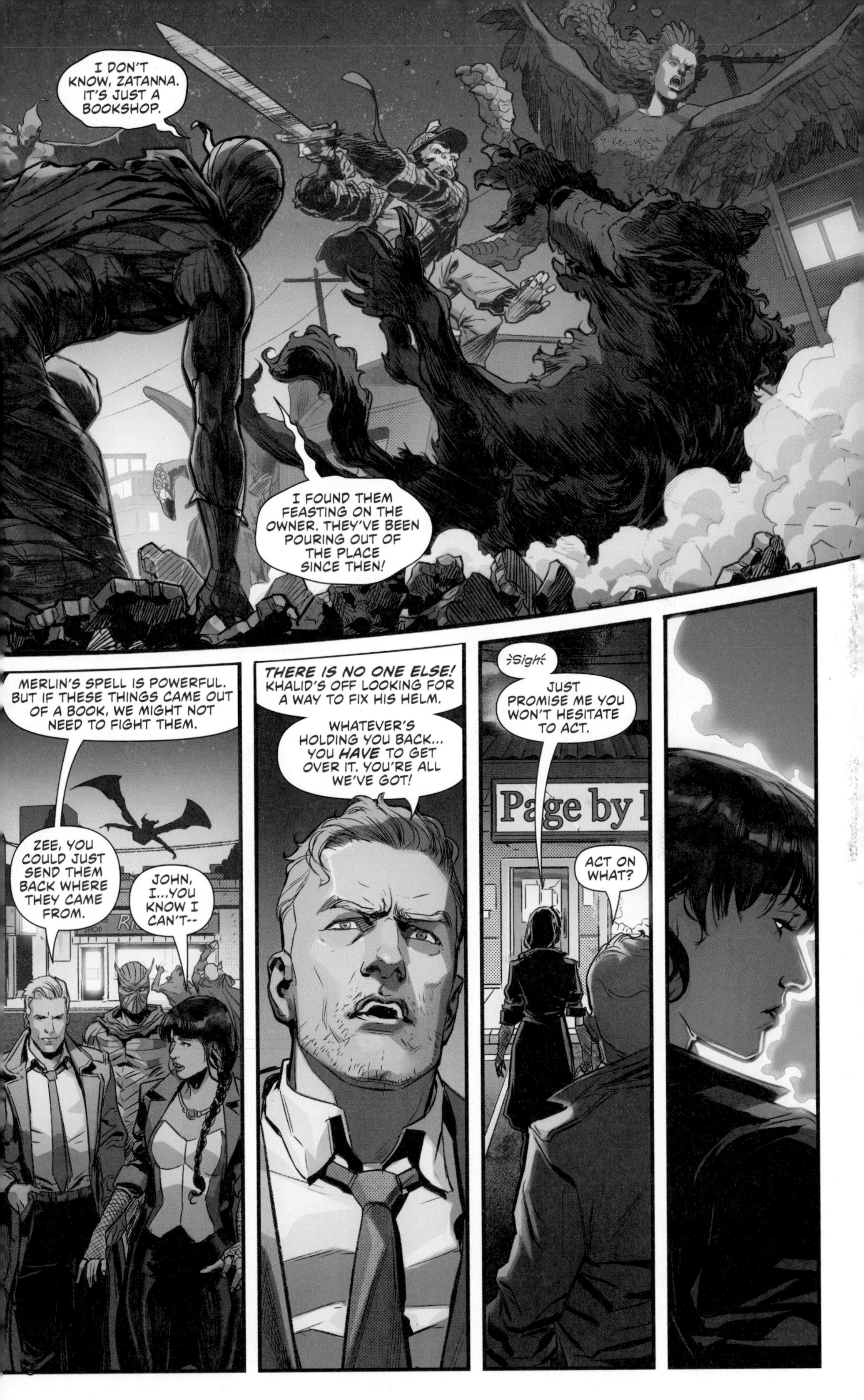

I DON'T KNOW, ZATANNA. IT'S JUST A BOOKSHOP.
I FOUND THEM FEASTING ON THE OWNER. THEY'VE BEEN POURING OUT OF THE PLACE SINCE THEN!
MERLIN'S SPELL IS POWERFUL. BUT IF THESE THINGS CAME OUT OF A BOOK, WE MIGHT NOT NEED TO FIGHT THEM.
ZEE, YOU COULD JUST SEND THEM BACK WHERE THEY CAME FROM.
JOHN, I...YOU KNOW I CAN'T--
THERE IS NO ONE ELSE! KHALID'S OFF LOOKING FOR A WAY TO FIX HIS HELM.
WHATEVER'S HOLDING YOU BACK... YOU *HAVE* TO GET OVER IT. YOU'RE ALL WE'VE GOT!
Sigh
JUST PROMISE ME YOU WON'T HESITATE TO ACT.
Page by
ACT ON WHAT?

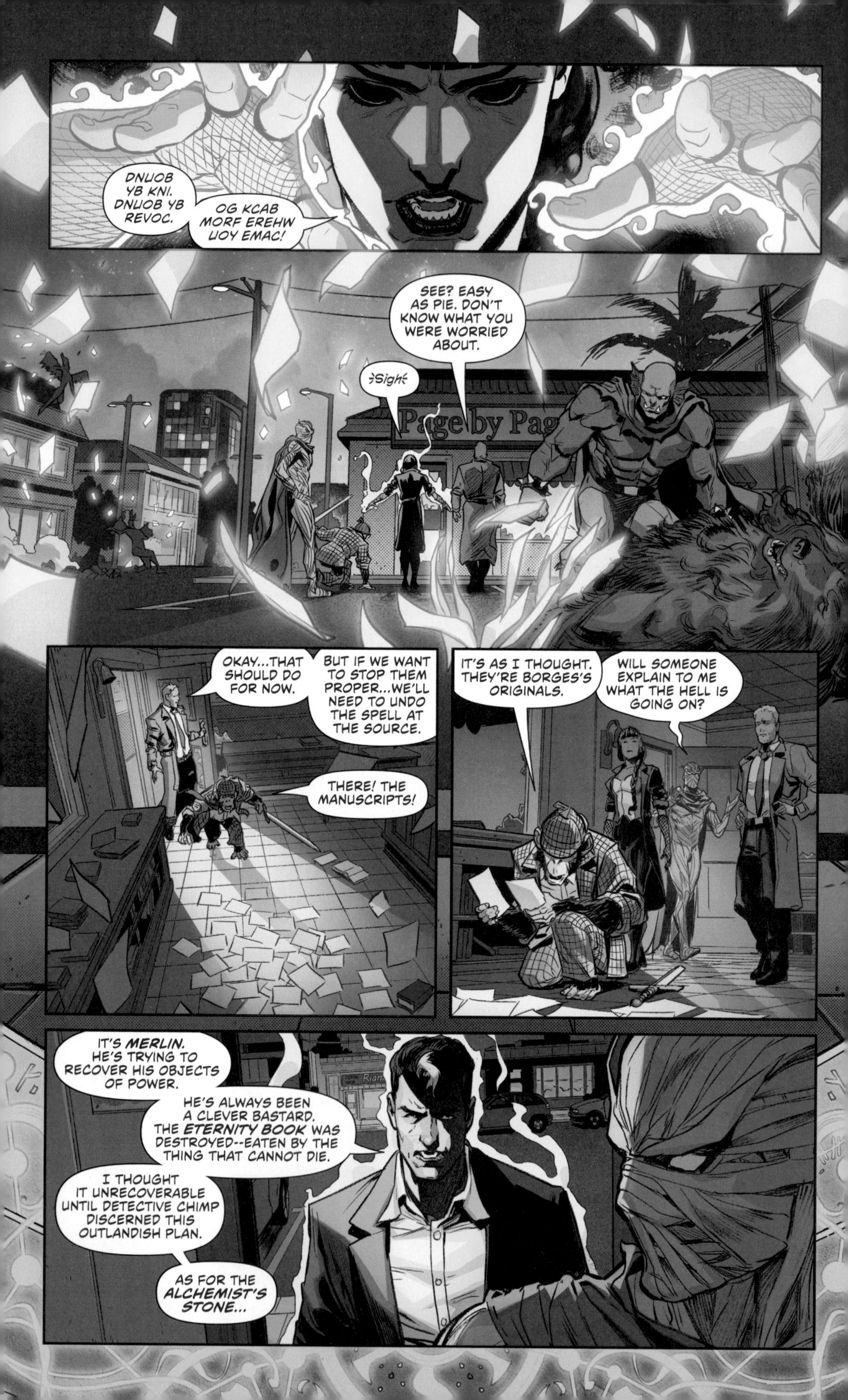
DNUOB YB KNI. DNUOB YB REVOC.
OG KCAB MORF EREHW UOY EMAC!
SEE? EASY AS PIE. DON'T KNOW WHAT YOU WERE WORRIED ABOUT.
Sigh
Page by Pag
OKAY...THAT SHOULD DO FOR NOW.
BUT IF WE WANT TO STOP THEM PROPER...WE'LL NEED TO UNDO THE SPELL AT THE SOURCE.
THERE! THE MANUSCRIPTS!
IT'S AS I THOUGHT. THEY'RE BORGES'S ORIGINALS.
WILL SOMEONE EXPLAIN TO ME WHAT THE HELL IS GOING ON?
IT'S MERLIN. HE'S TRYING TO RECOVER HIS OBJECTS OF POWER.
HE'S ALWAYS BEEN A CLEVER BASTARD. THE ETERNITY BOOK WAS DESTROYED--EATEN BY THE THING THAT CANNOT DIE.
I THOUGHT IT UNRECOVERABLE UNTIL DETECTIVE CHIMP DISCERNED THIS OUTLANDISH PLAN.
AS FOR THE ALCHEMIST'S STONE...

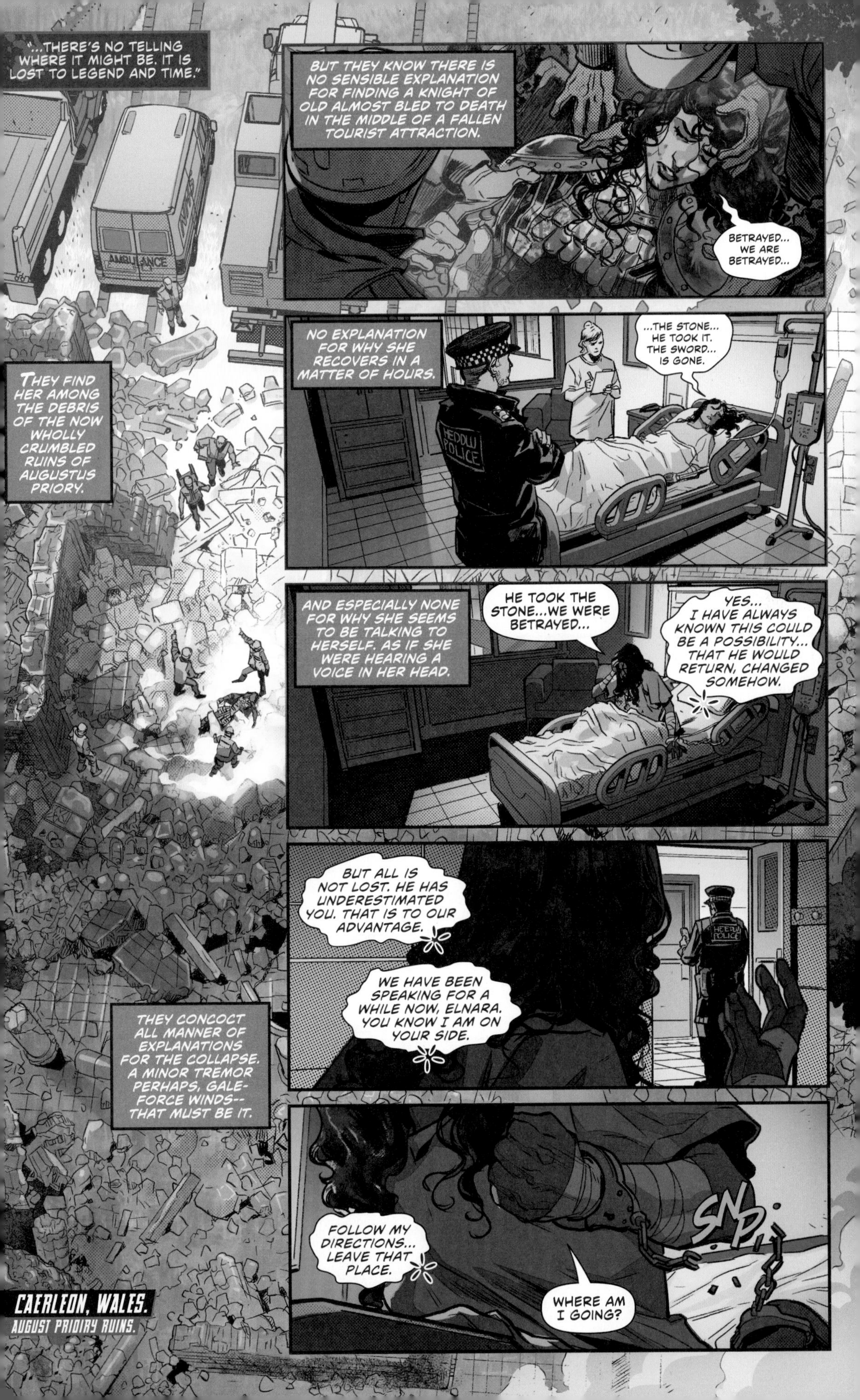
"...THERE'S NO TELLING WHERE IT MIGHT BE. IT IS LOST TO LEGEND AND TIME."
BUT THEY KNOW THERE IS NO SENSIBLE EXPLANATION FOR FINDING A KNIGHT OF OLD ALMOST BLED TO DEATH IN THE MIDDLE OF A FALLEN TOURIST ATTRACTION.
BETRAYED... WE ARE BETRAYED...
AMBULANCE
THEY FIND HER AMONG THE DEBRIS OF THE NOW WHOLLY CRUMBLED RUINS OF AUGUSTUS PRIORY.
NO EXPLANATION FOR WHY SHE RECOVERS IN A MATTER OF HOURS.
...THE STONE... HE TOOK IT. THE SWORD... IS GONE.
HEDDLU POLICE
AND ESPECIALLY NONE FOR WHY SHE SEEMS TO BE TALKING TO HERSELF. AS IF SHE WERE HEARING A VOICE IN HER HEAD.
HE TOOK THE STONE...WE WERE BETRAYED...
YES... I HAVE ALWAYS KNOWN THIS COULD BE A POSSIBILITY... THAT HE WOULD RETURN, CHANGED SOMEHOW.
BUT ALL IS NOT LOST. HE HAS UNDERESTIMATED YOU. THAT IS TO OUR ADVANTAGE.
WE HAVE BEEN SPEAKING FOR A WHILE NOW, ELNARA. YOU KNOW I AM ON YOUR SIDE.
THEY CONCOCT ALL MANNER OF EXPLANATIONS FOR THE COLLAPSE. A MINOR TREMOR PERHAPS, GALE-FORCE WINDS-- THAT MUST BE IT.
FOLLOW MY DIRECTIONS... LEAVE THAT PLACE.
SNP
WHERE AM I GOING?
CAERLEON, WALES.
AUGUST PRIOIRY RUINS.

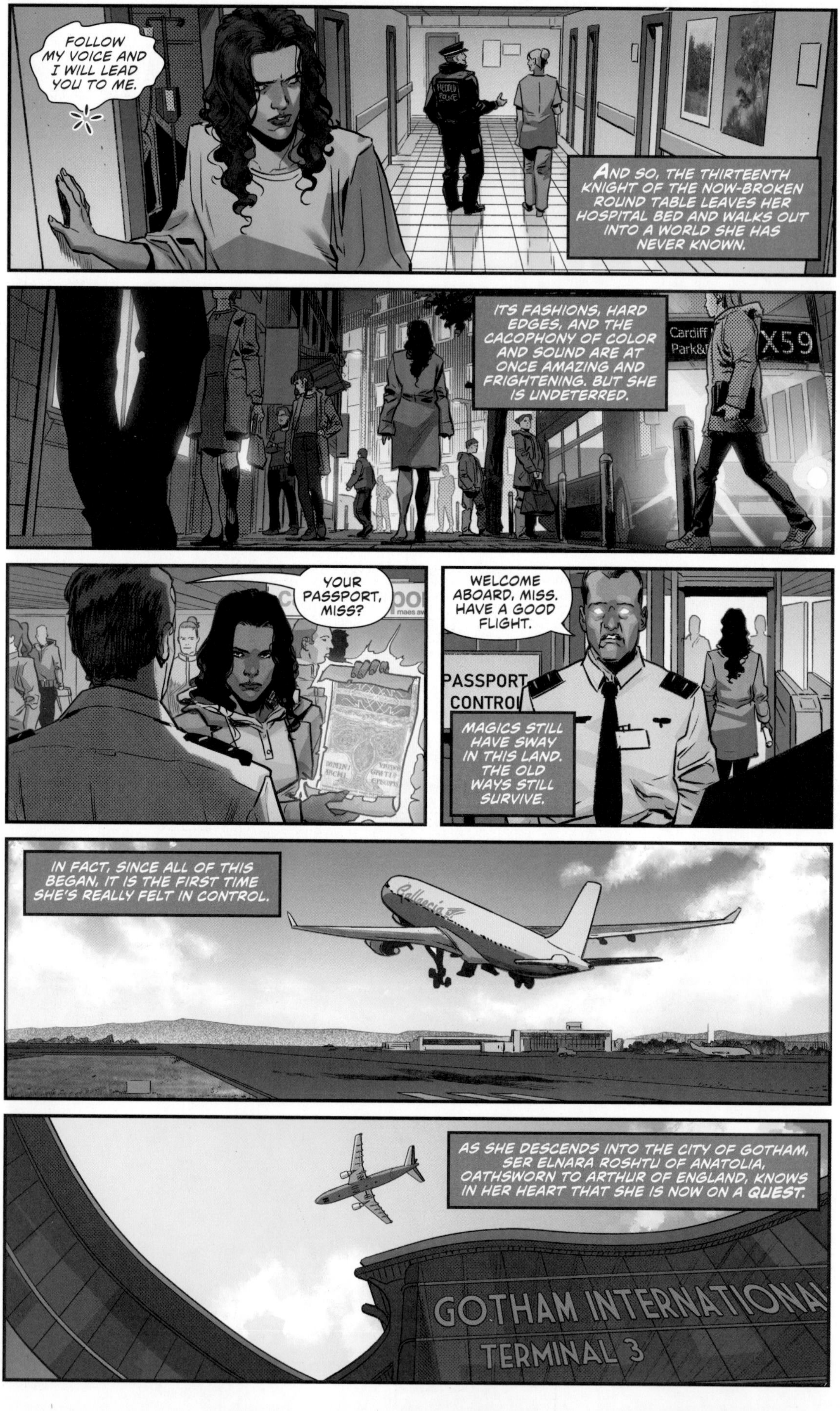
FOLLOW MY VOICE AND I WILL LEAD YOU TO ME.
AND SO, THE THIRTEENTH KNIGHT OF THE NOW-BROKEN ROUND TABLE LEAVES HER HOSPITAL BED AND WALKS OUT INTO A WORLD SHE HAS NEVER KNOWN.
ITS FASHIONS, HARD EDGES, AND THE CACOPHONY OF COLOR AND SOUND ARE AT ONCE AMAZING AND FRIGHTENING. BUT SHE IS UNDETERRED.
X59
YOUR PASSPORT, MISS?
WELCOME ABOARD, MISS. HAVE A GOOD FLIGHT.
PASSPORT CONTROL
MAGICS STILL HAVE SWAY IN THIS LAND. THE OLD WAYS STILL SURVIVE.
IN FACT, SINCE ALL OF THIS BEGAN, IT IS THE FIRST TIME SHE'S REALLY FELT IN CONTROL.
AS SHE DESCENDS INTO THE CITY OF GOTHAM, SER ELNARA ROSHTU OF ANATOLIA, OATHSWORN TO ARTHUR OF ENGLAND, KNOWS IN HER HEART THAT SHE IS NOW ON A QUEST.
GOTHAM INTERNATIONA
TERMINAL 3

IT WAS JUST A BIT OF MAGICAL THINKING. IF I WERE A MAGICIAN AND I WANTED TO FIND A BOOK THAT WAS DEFINITELY DESTROYED, WHERE WOULD I GO?

THERE'S ONLY ONE PLACE YOU COULD STILL FIND THE BOOK. IN 1941 BORGES WROTE A STORY ABOUT A LIBRARY.

"AN INFINITE LIBRARY-- A PLACE WHERE EVERY BOOK THAT EVER WAS OR WILL BE WRITTEN IS KEPT."

HE WAS A FRIEND OF MY DAD'S.

HE THOUGHT HE WAS SELLING THE MANUSCRIPT. HE WAS SO HAPPY TO HAVE FOUND A BUYER.

I'M SORRY, RORY.

BY DEFINITION, THE LIBRARY IS A PLACE THAT WOULD SURELY CONTAIN THE ETERNITY BOOK, IF ONLY IT WAS REAL.

HOW HARD COULD IT BE FOR SOMEONE LIKE MERLIN TO TURN FICTION INTO REALITY?

ARE YOU SAYING MERLIN'S IN THOSE PAGES?

CAN WE FOLLOW HIM, JOHN?

WELL... IF IT'S A PLACE THAT IS NOW MANIFEST, HOUDINI'S KEY SHOULD GET US THERE.

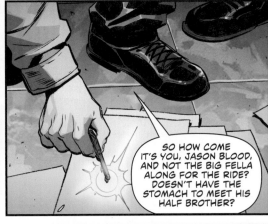

SO HOW COME IT'S YOU, JASON BLOOD, AND NOT THE BIG FELLA ALONG FOR THE RIDE? DOESN'T HAVE THE STOMACH TO MEET HIS HALF BROTHER?

ETRIGAN'S GOT THE STOMACH FOR A LOT OF THINGS, CONSTANTINE.

BUT BOOKSHOPS OR LIBRARIES, I'M AFRAID, AREN'T ONE OF THEM.

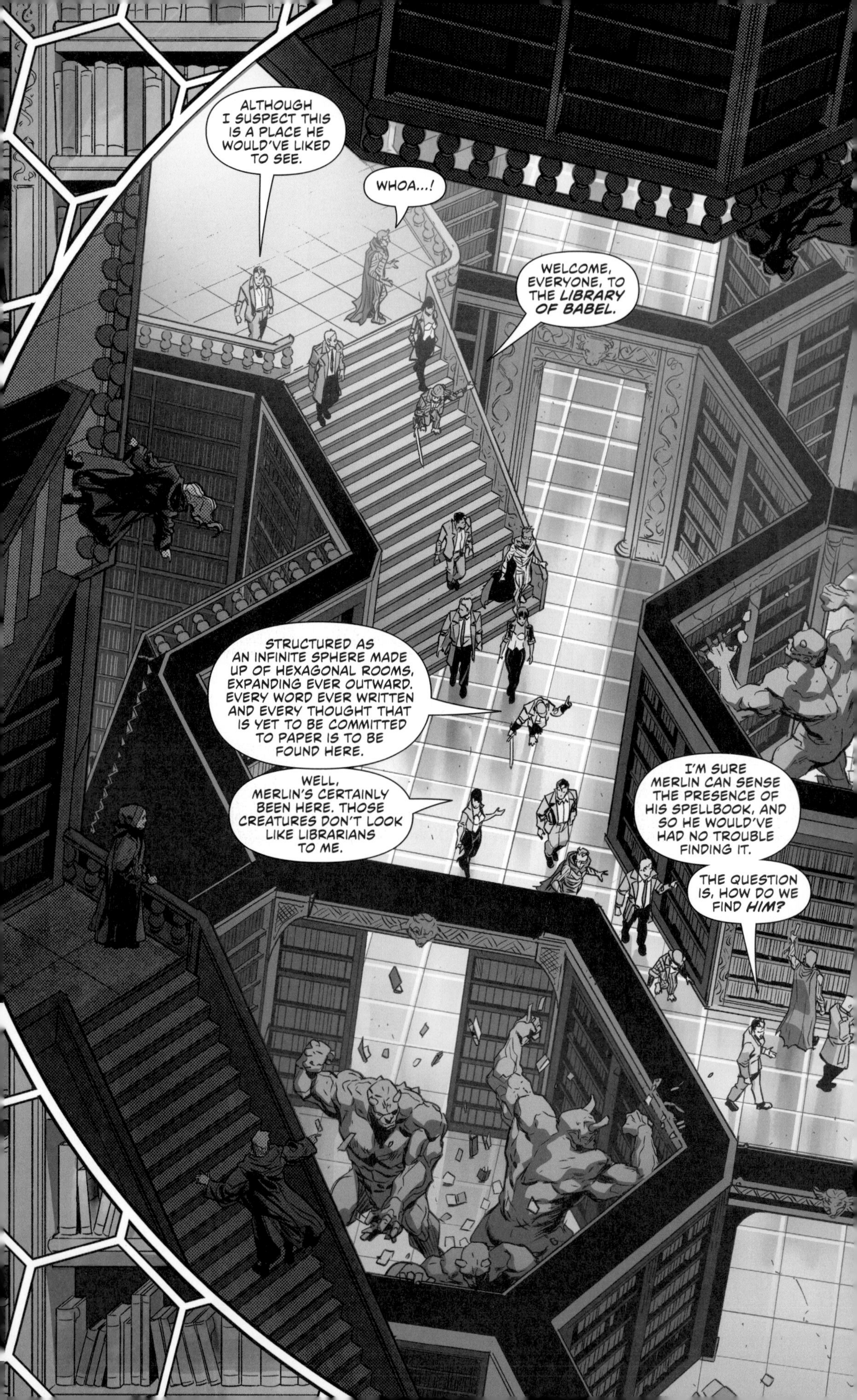
ALTHOUGH I SUSPECT THIS IS A PLACE HE WOULD'VE LIKED TO SEE.
WHOA...!
WELCOME, EVERYONE, TO THE *LIBRARY OF BABEL.*
STRUCTURED AS AN INFINITE SPHERE MADE UP OF HEXAGONAL ROOMS, EXPANDING EVER OUTWARD. EVERY WORD EVER WRITTEN AND EVERY THOUGHT THAT IS YET TO BE COMMITTED TO PAPER IS TO BE FOUND HERE.
WELL, MERLIN'S CERTAINLY BEEN HERE. THOSE CREATURES DON'T LOOK LIKE LIBRARIANS TO ME.
I'M SURE MERLIN CAN SENSE THE PRESENCE OF HIS SPELLBOOK, AND SO HE WOULD'VE HAD NO TROUBLE FINDING IT.
THE QUESTION IS, HOW DO WE FIND *HIM?*

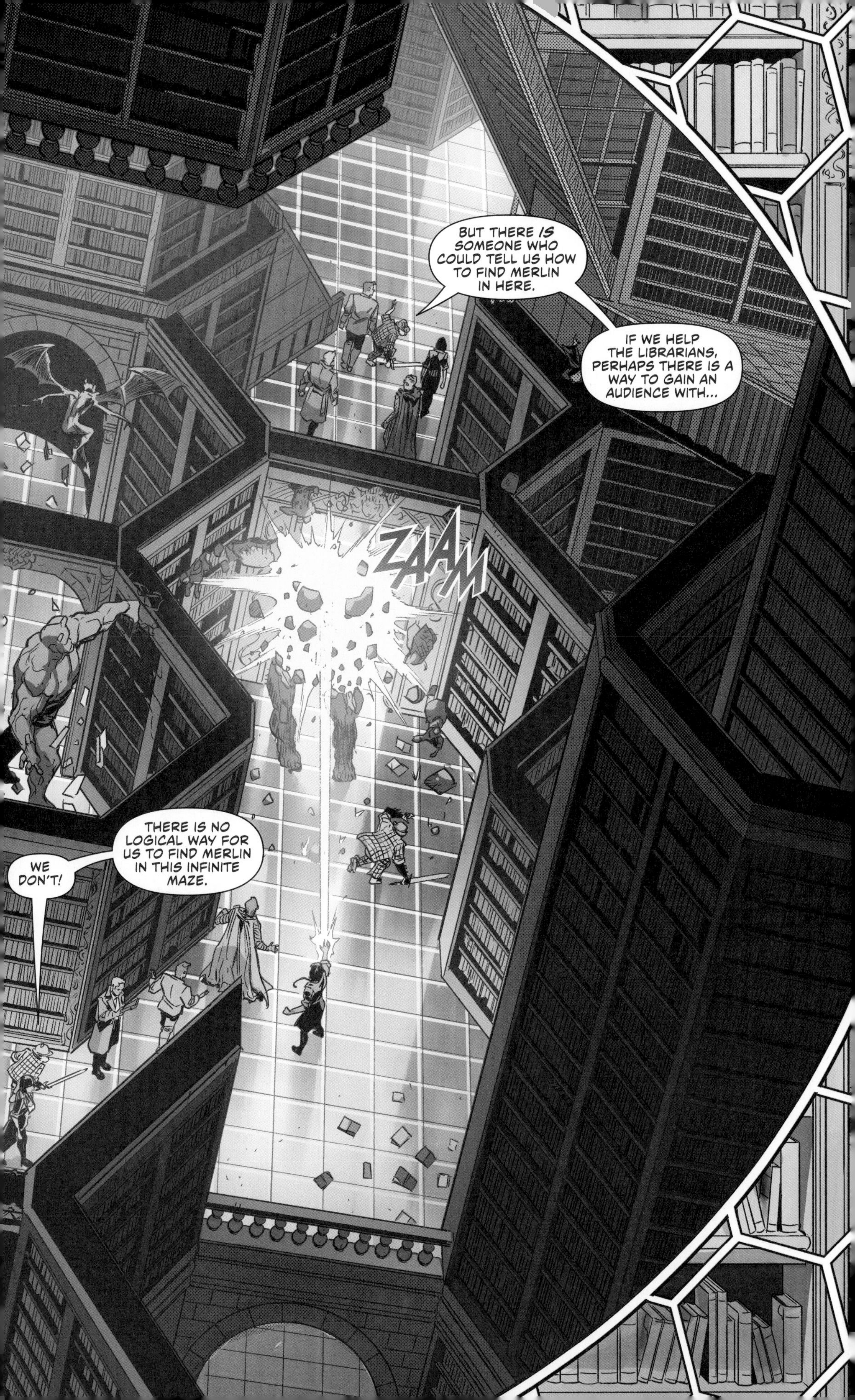
THERE IS NO LOGICAL WAY FOR US TO FIND MERLIN IN THIS INFINITE MAZE.
WE DON'T!
ZAAM
BUT THERE *IS* SOMEONE WHO COULD TELL US HOW TO FIND MERLIN IN HERE.
IF WE HELP THE LIBRARIANS, PERHAPS THERE IS A WAY TO GAIN AN AUDIENCE WITH...

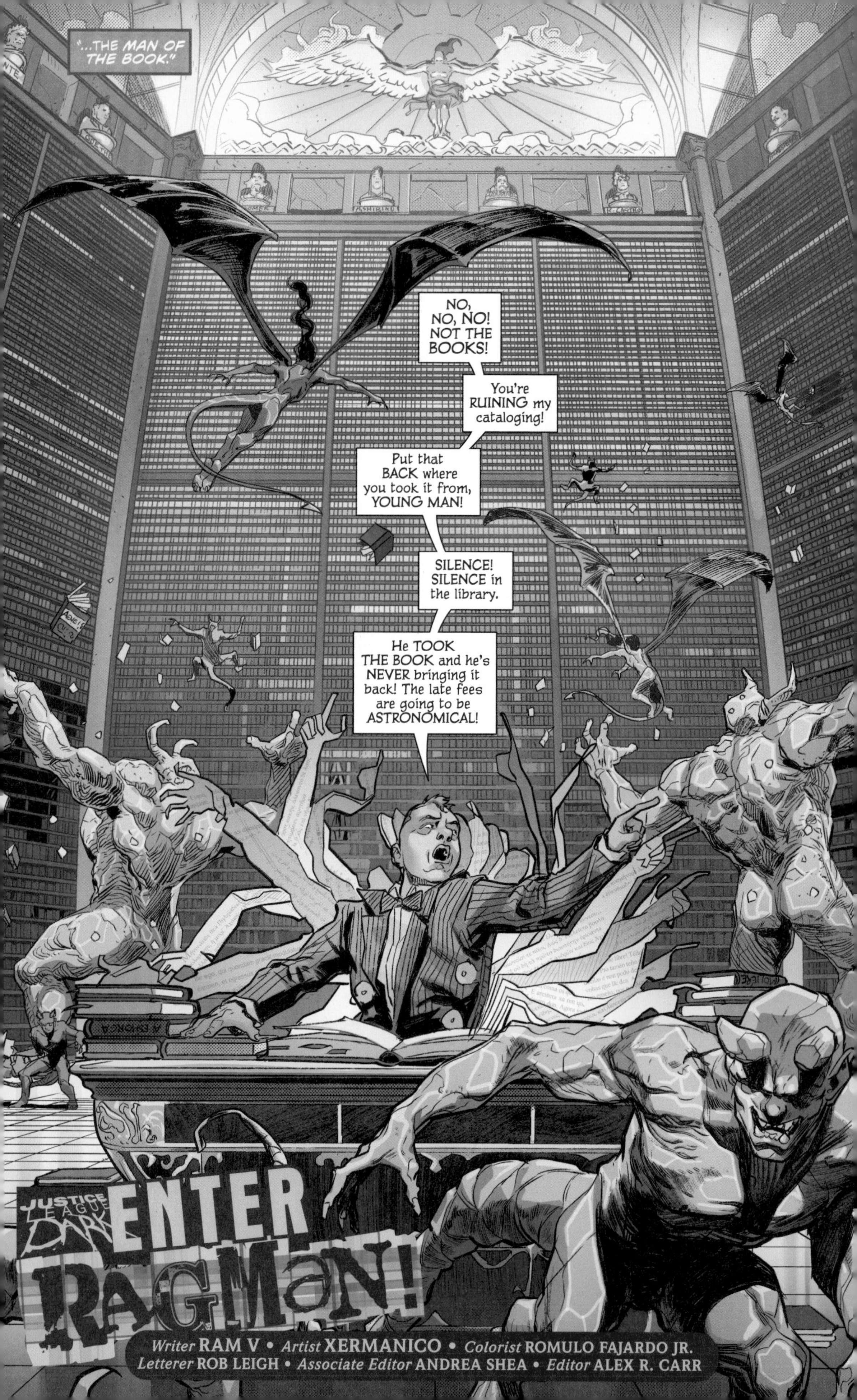
"...THE MAN OF THE BOOK."
NO, NO, NO! NOT THE BOOKS!
You're RUINING my cataloging!
Put that BACK where you took it from, YOUNG MAN!
SILENCE! SILENCE in the library.
He TOOK THE BOOK and he's NEVER bringing it back! The late fees are going to be ASTRONOMICAL!
JUSTICE LEAGUE DARK
ENTER RAGMAN!
Writer RAM V • Artist XERMANICO • Colorist ROMULO FAJARDO JR.
Letterer ROB LEIGH • Associate Editor ANDREA SHEA • Editor ALEX R. CARR

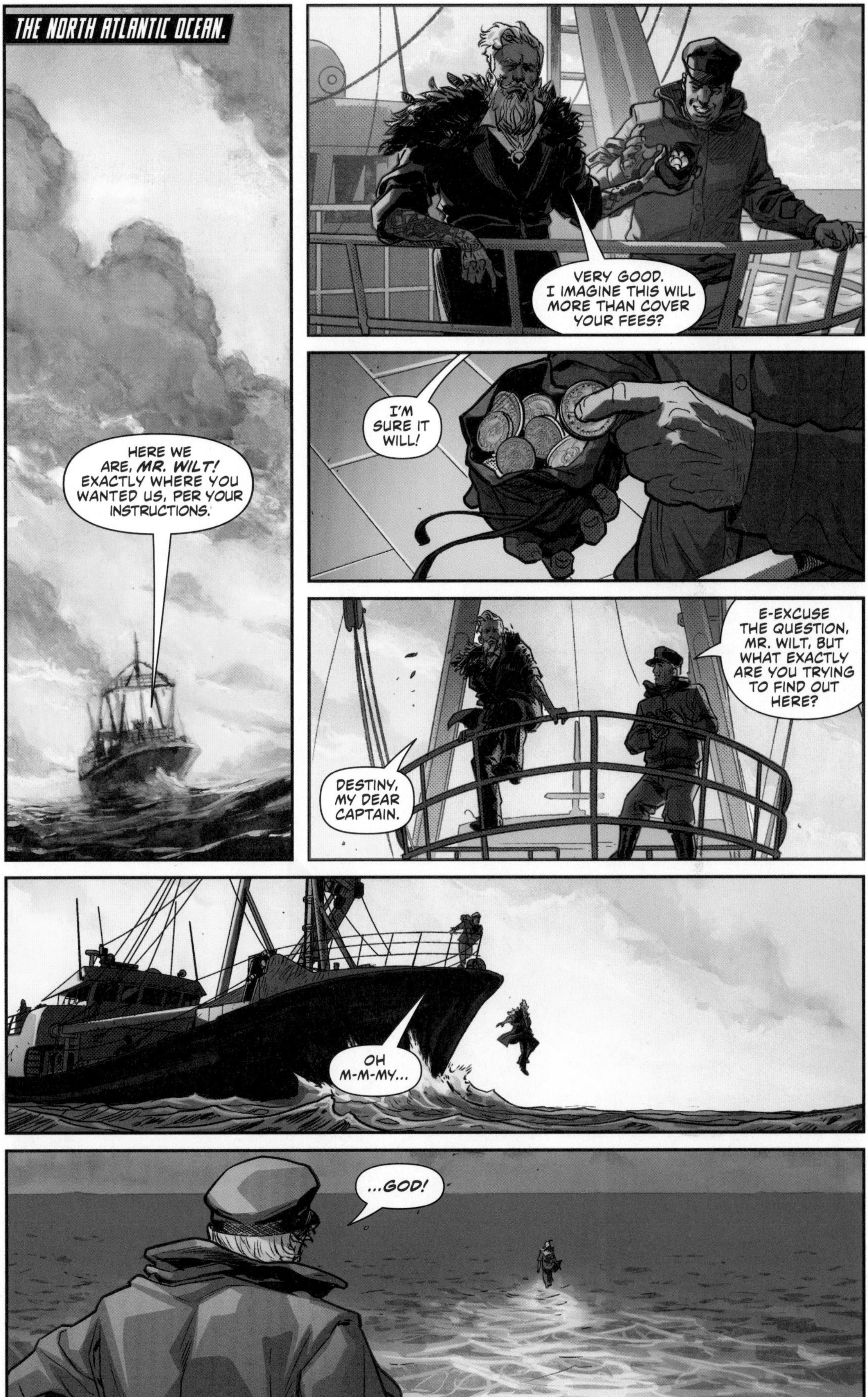
THE NORTH ATLANTIC OCEAN.
HERE WE ARE, MR. WILT! EXACTLY WHERE YOU WANTED US, PER YOUR INSTRUCTIONS.
VERY GOOD. I IMAGINE THIS WILL MORE THAN COVER YOUR FEES?
I'M SURE IT WILL!
E-EXCUSE THE QUESTION, MR. WILT, BUT WHAT EXACTLY ARE YOU TRYING TO FIND OUT HERE?
DESTINY, MY DEAR CAPTAIN.
OH M-M-MY...
...GOD!

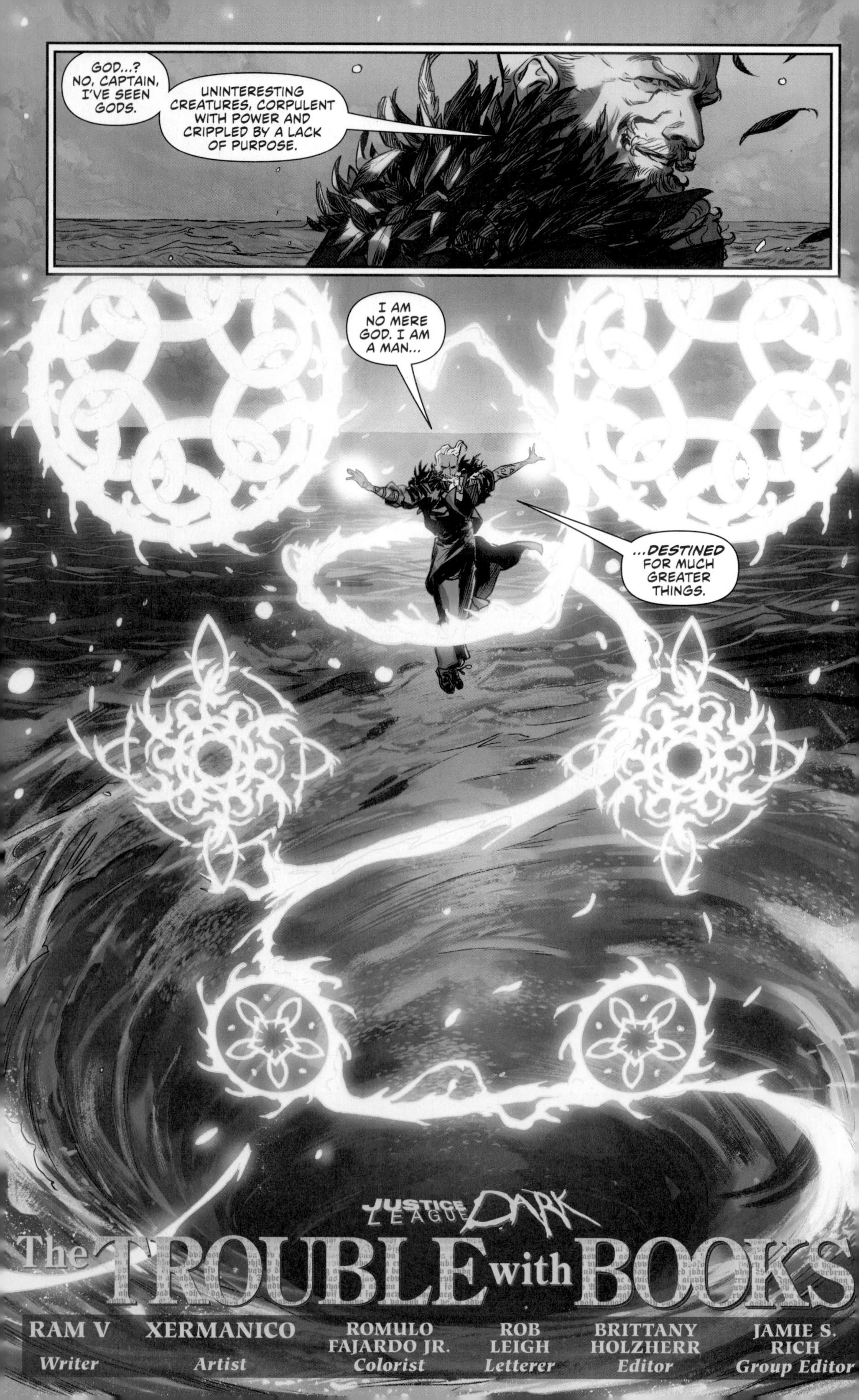
GOD...? NO, CAPTAIN, I'VE SEEN GODS.
UNINTERESTING CREATURES, CORPULENT WITH POWER AND CRIPPLED BY A LACK OF PURPOSE.
I AM NO MERE GOD. I AM A MAN...
...DESTINED FOR MUCH GREATER THINGS.
JUSTICE LEAGUE DARK
The TROUBLE with BOOKS
RAM V Writer
XERMANICO Artist
ROMULO FAJARDO JR. Colorist
ROB LEIGH Letterer
BRITTANY HOLZHERR Editor
JAMIE S. RICH Group Editor

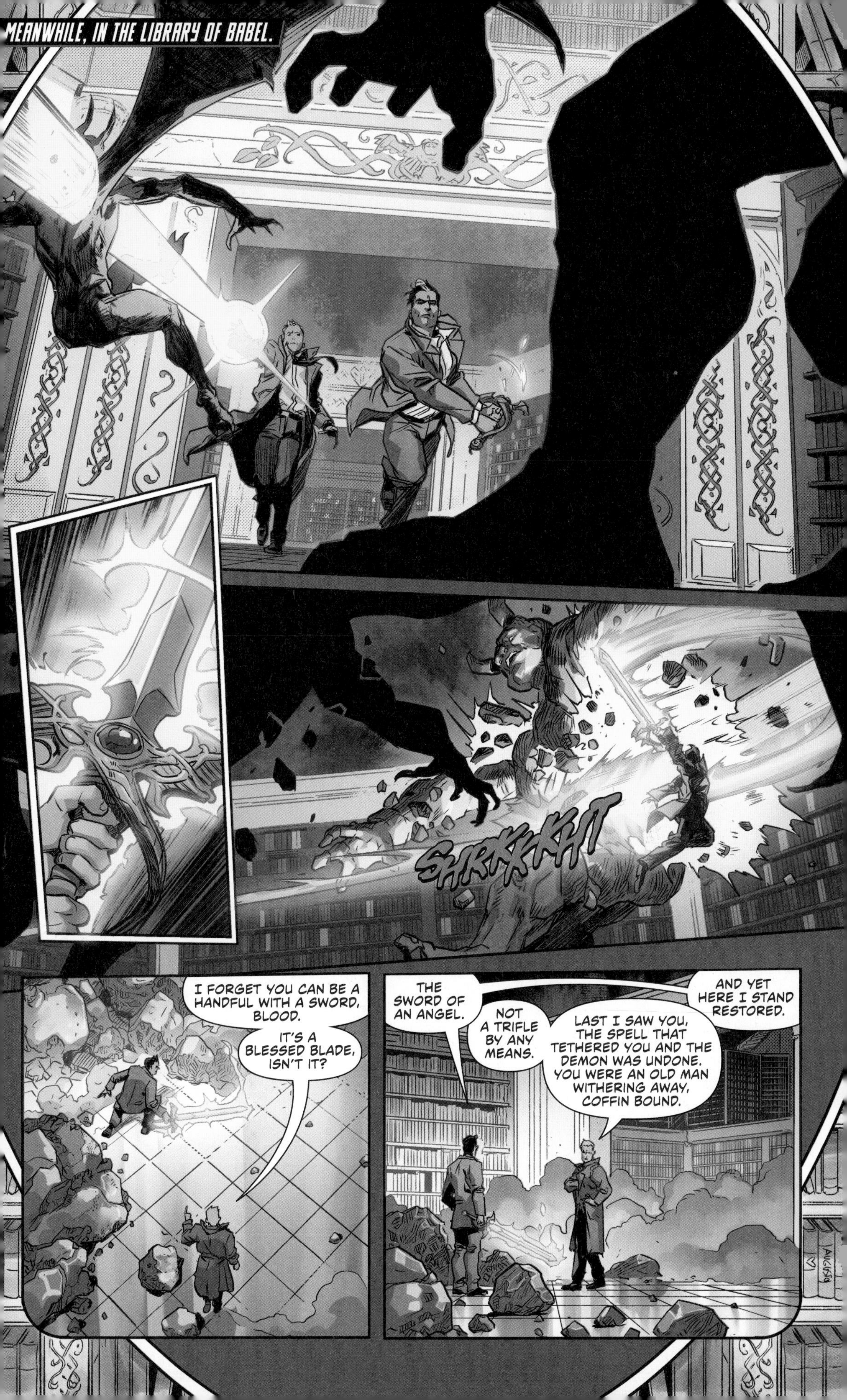
MEANWHILE, IN THE LIBRARY OF BABEL.
SHRKKKHT
I FORGET YOU CAN BE A HANDFUL WITH A SWORD, BLOOD.
IT'S A BLESSED BLADE, ISN'T IT?
THE SWORD OF AN ANGEL.
NOT A TRIFLE BY ANY MEANS.
LAST I SAW YOU, THE SPELL THAT TETHERED YOU AND THE DEMON WAS UNDONE. YOU WERE AN OLD MAN WITHERING AWAY, COFFIN BOUND.
AND YET HERE I STAND RESTORED.

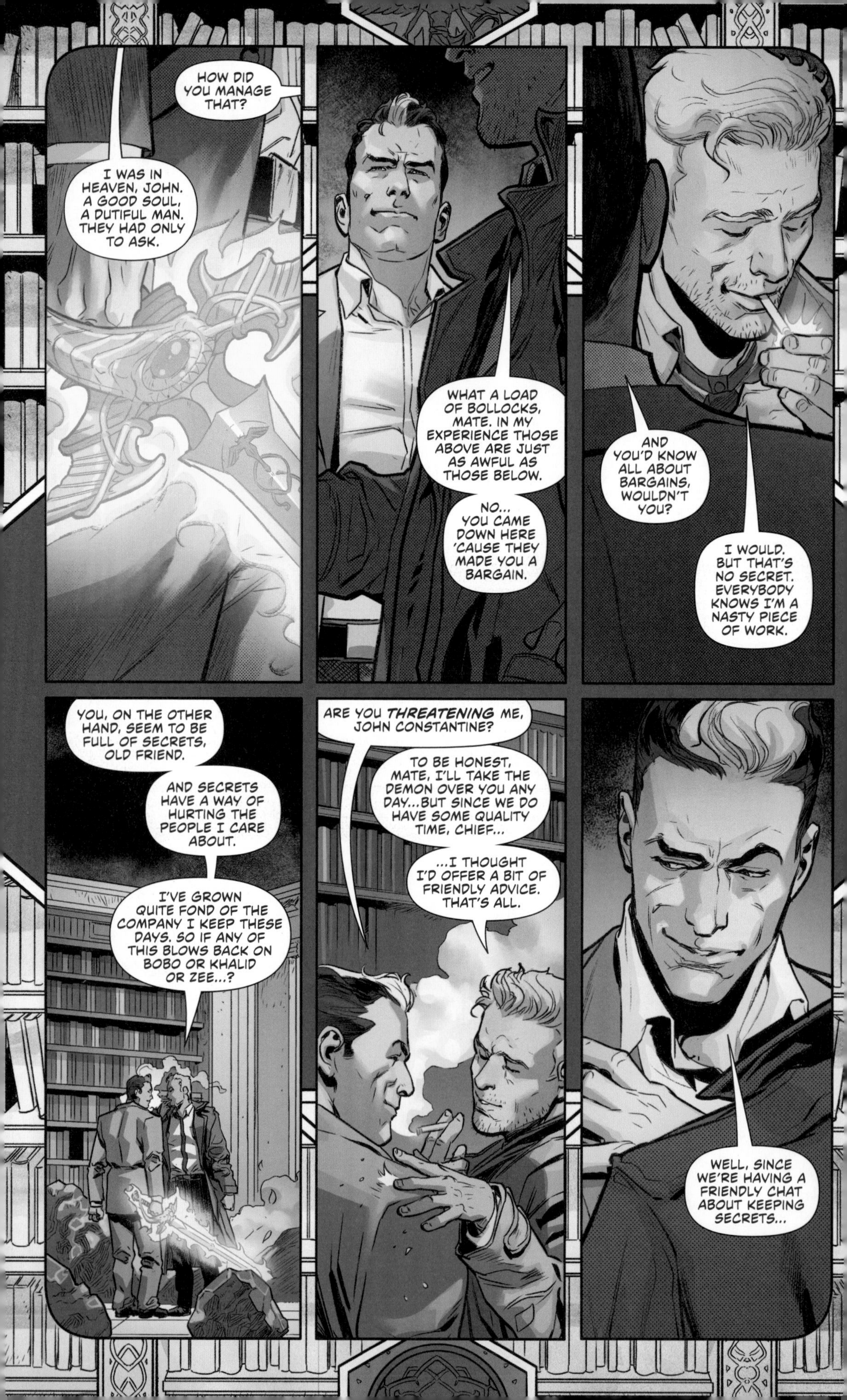
HOW DID YOU MANAGE THAT?
I WAS IN HEAVEN, JOHN. A GOOD SOUL, A DUTIFUL MAN. THEY HAD ONLY TO ASK.
WHAT A LOAD OF BOLLOCKS, MATE. IN MY EXPERIENCE THOSE ABOVE ARE JUST AS AWFUL AS THOSE BELOW.
NO... YOU CAME DOWN HERE 'CAUSE THEY MADE YOU A BARGAIN.
AND YOU'D KNOW ALL ABOUT BARGAINS, WOULDN'T YOU?
I WOULD. BUT THAT'S NO SECRET. EVERYBODY KNOWS I'M A NASTY PIECE OF WORK.
YOU, ON THE OTHER HAND, SEEM TO BE FULL OF SECRETS, OLD FRIEND.
AND SECRETS HAVE A WAY OF HURTING THE PEOPLE I CARE ABOUT.
I'VE GROWN QUITE FOND OF THE COMPANY I KEEP THESE DAYS. SO IF ANY OF THIS BLOWS BACK ON BOBO OR KHALID OR ZEE...?
ARE YOU *THREATENING* ME, JOHN CONSTANTINE?
TO BE HONEST, MATE, I'LL TAKE THE DEMON OVER YOU ANY DAY...BUT SINCE WE DO HAVE SOME QUALITY TIME, CHIEF...
...I THOUGHT I'D OFFER A BIT OF FRIENDLY ADVICE. THAT'S ALL.
WELL, SINCE WE'RE HAVING A FRIENDLY CHAT ABOUT KEEPING SECRETS...

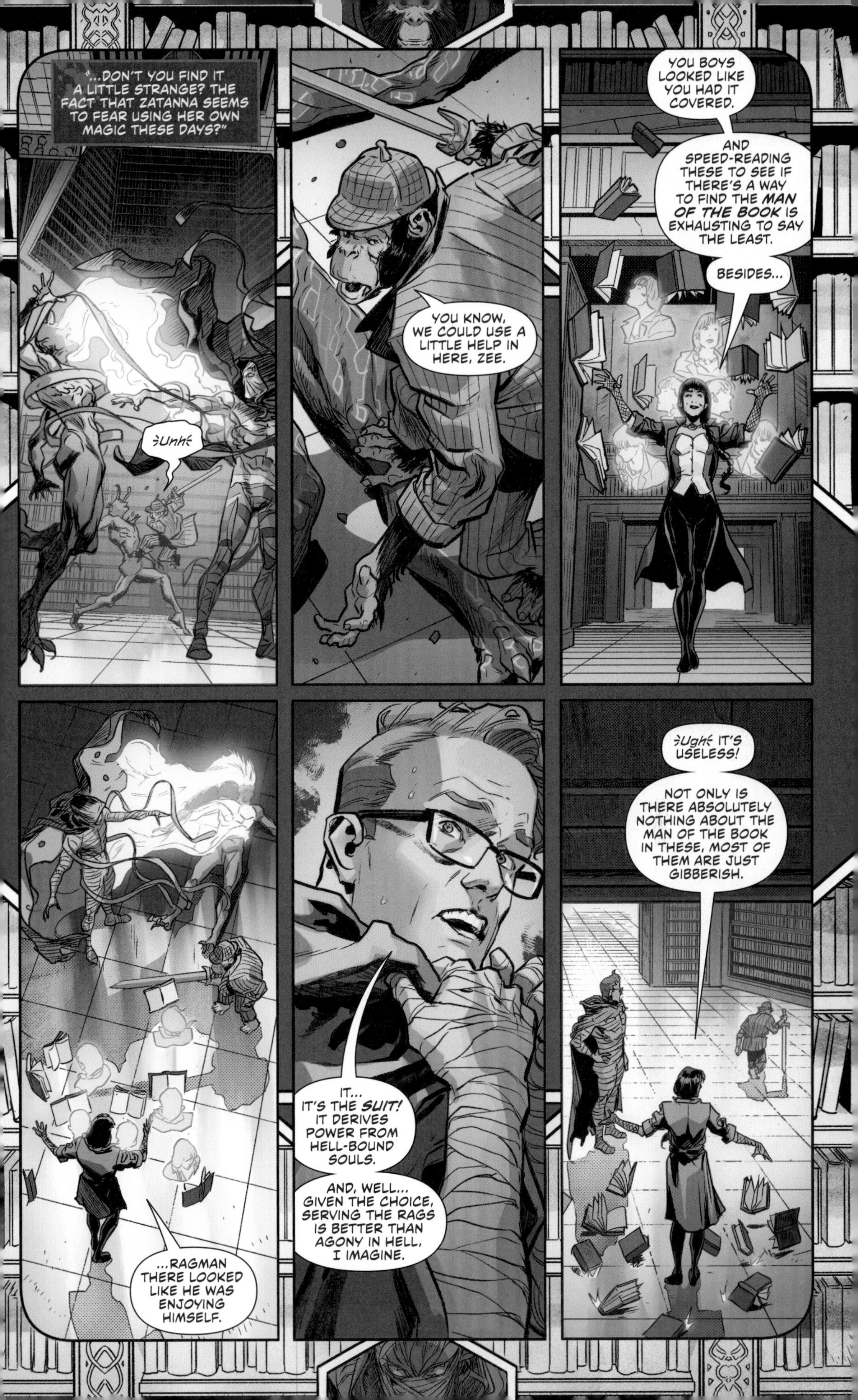
"...DON'T YOU FIND IT A LITTLE STRANGE? THE FACT THAT ZATANNA SEEMS TO FEAR USING HER OWN MAGIC THESE DAYS?"
UNH
YOU KNOW, WE COULD USE A LITTLE HELP IN HERE, ZEE.
YOU BOYS LOOKED LIKE YOU HAD IT COVERED.
AND SPEED-READING THESE TO SEE IF THERE'S A WAY TO FIND THE MAN OF THE BOOK IS EXHAUSTING TO SAY THE LEAST.
BESIDES...
...RAGMAN THERE LOOKED LIKE HE WAS ENJOYING HIMSELF.
IT... IT'S THE SUIT! IT DERIVES POWER FROM HELL-BOUND SOULS.
AND, WELL... GIVEN THE CHOICE, SERVING THE RAGS IS BETTER THAN AGONY IN HELL, I IMAGINE.
UGH IT'S USELESS!
NOT ONLY IS THERE ABSOLUTELY NOTHING ABOUT THE MAN OF THE BOOK IN THESE, MOST OF THEM ARE JUST GIBBERISH.

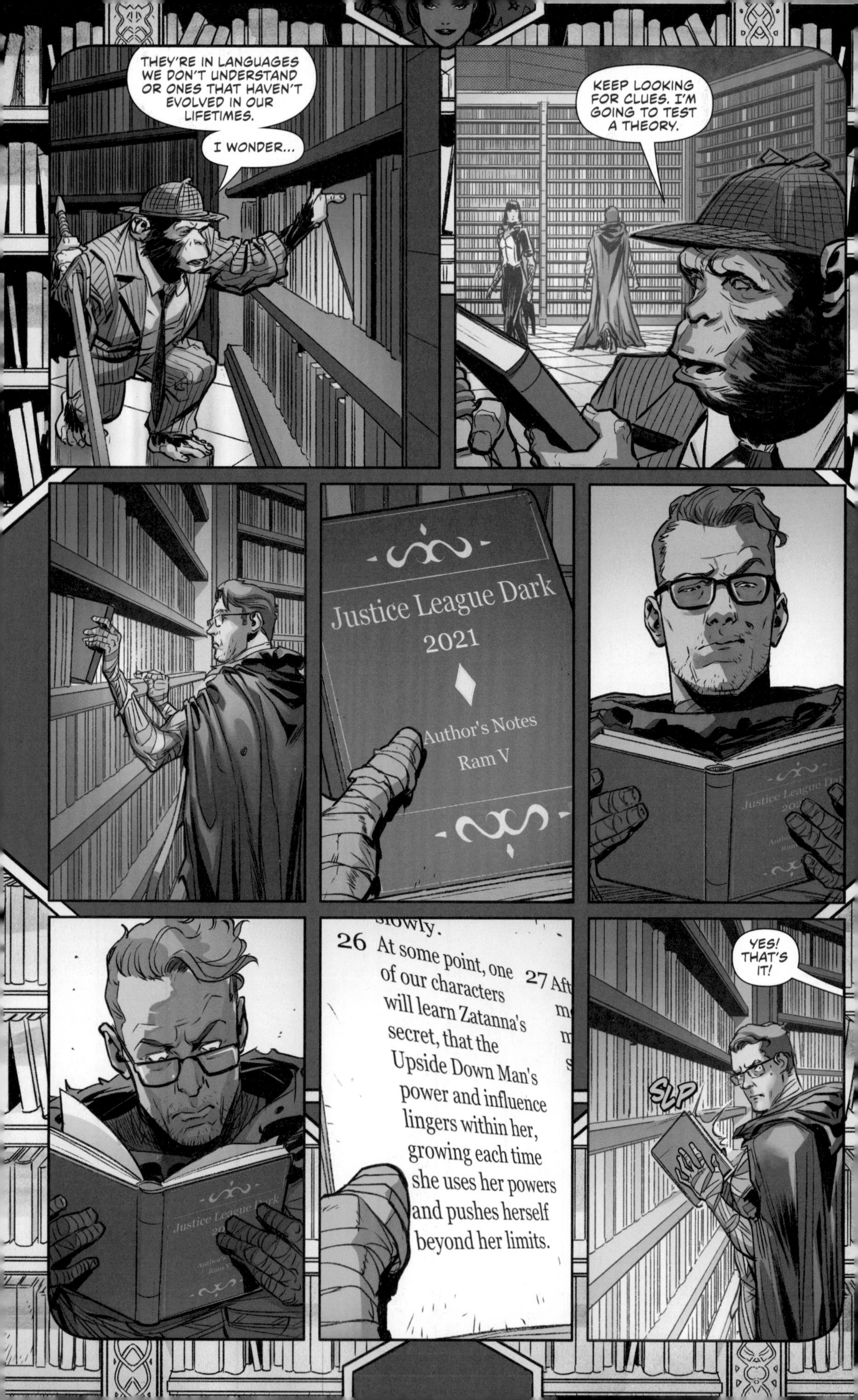
THEY'RE IN LANGUAGES WE DON'T UNDERSTAND OR ONES THAT HAVEN'T EVOLVED IN OUR LIFETIMES.
I WONDER...
KEEP LOOKING FOR CLUES. I'M GOING TO TEST A THEORY.
Justice League Dark
2021
Author's Notes
Ram V
26 At some point, one of our characters will learn Zatanna's secret, that the Upside Down Man's power and influence lingers within her, growing each time she uses her powers and pushes herself beyond her limits.
SLP
YES! THAT'S IT!

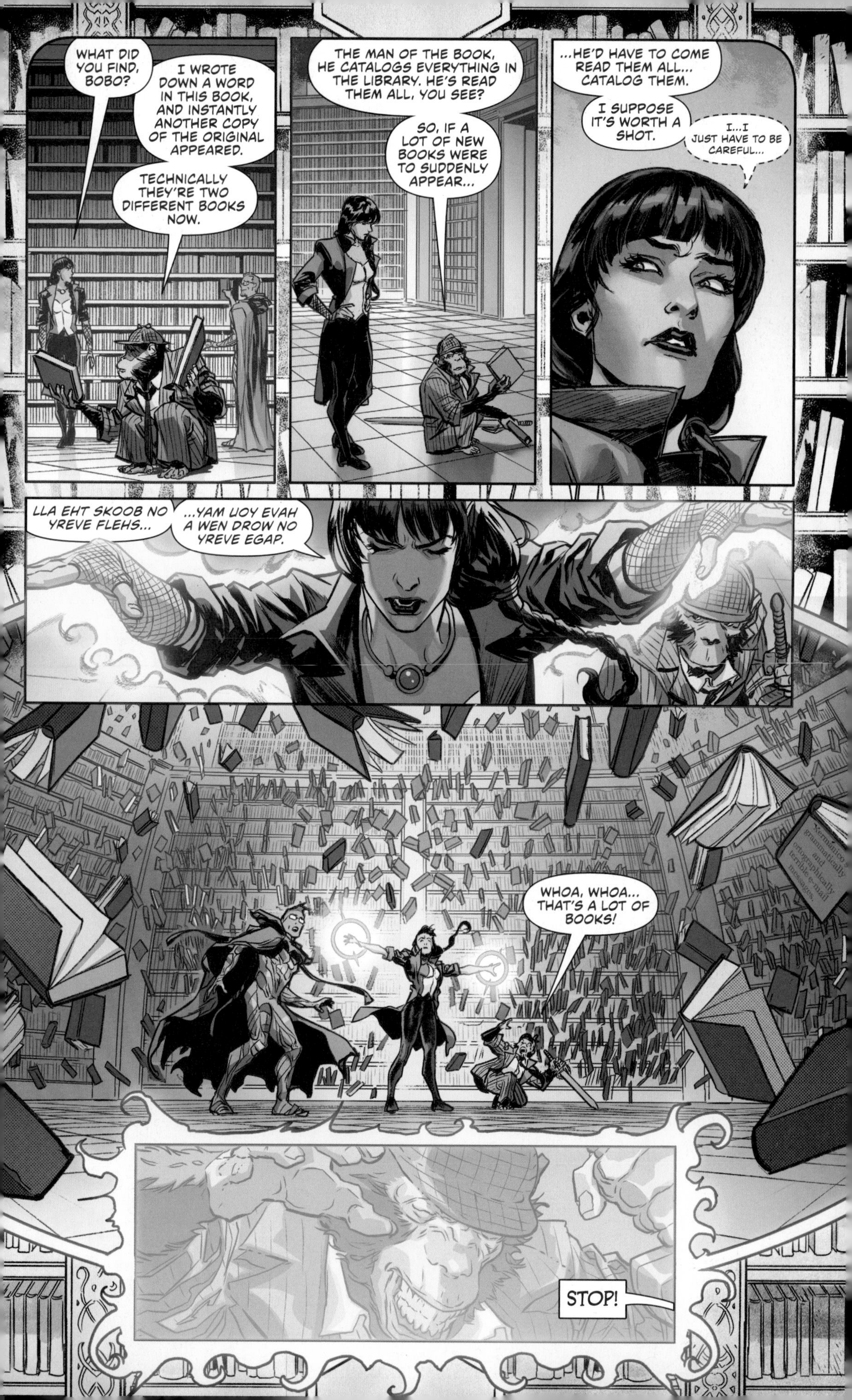
WHAT DID YOU FIND, BOBO?
I WROTE DOWN A WORD IN THIS BOOK, AND INSTANTLY ANOTHER COPY OF THE ORIGINAL APPEARED.
TECHNICALLY THEY'RE TWO DIFFERENT BOOKS NOW.
THE MAN OF THE BOOK, HE CATALOGS EVERYTHING IN THE LIBRARY. HE'S READ THEM ALL, YOU SEE?
SO, IF A LOT OF NEW BOOKS WERE TO SUDDENLY APPEAR...
...HE'D HAVE TO COME READ THEM ALL... CATALOG THEM.
I SUPPOSE IT'S WORTH A SHOT.
I...I JUST HAVE TO BE CAREFUL...
LLA EHT SKOOB NO YREVE FLEHS...
...YAM UOY EVAH A WEN DROW NO YREVE EGAP.
grammatically
and
ortographically
terrible e-mail
messages.
WHOA, WHOA... THAT'S A LOT OF BOOKS!
STOP!

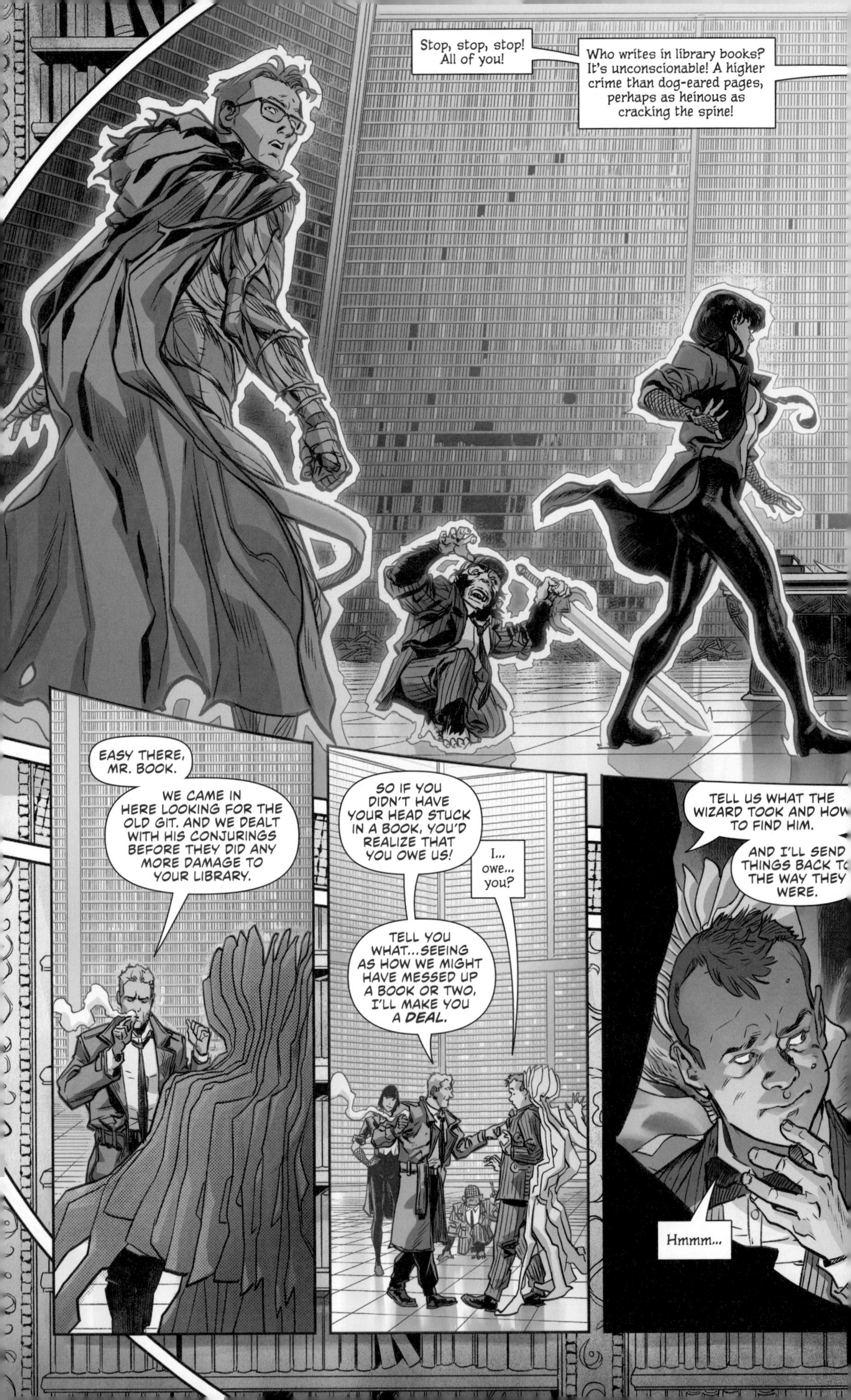
Stop, stop, stop! All of you!
Who writes in library books? It's unconscionable! A higher crime than dog-eared pages, perhaps as heinous as cracking the spine!
EASY THERE, MR. BOOK.
WE CAME IN HERE LOOKING FOR THE OLD GIT. AND WE DEALT WITH HIS CONJURINGS BEFORE THEY DID ANY MORE DAMAGE TO YOUR LIBRARY.
SO IF YOU DIDN'T HAVE YOUR HEAD STUCK IN A BOOK, YOU'D REALIZE THAT YOU OWE US!
I... owe... you?
TELL YOU WHAT...SEEING AS HOW WE MIGHT HAVE MESSED UP A BOOK OR TWO, I'LL MAKE YOU A DEAL.
TELL US WHAT THE WIZARD TOOK AND HOW TO FIND HIM.
AND I'LL SEND THINGS BACK TO THE WAY THEY WERE.
Hmmm...

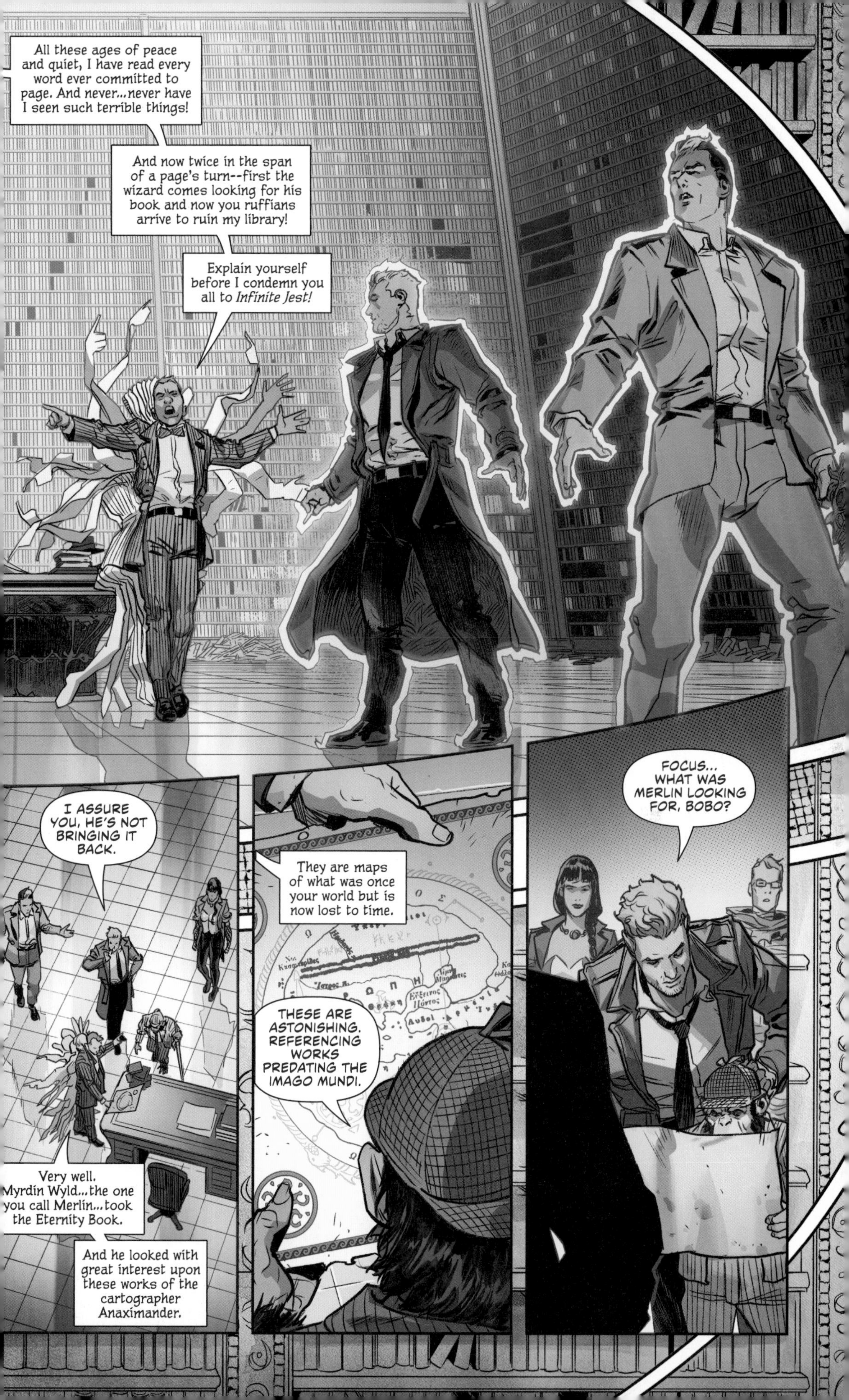
All these ages of peace and quiet, I have read every word ever committed to page. And never...never have I seen such terrible things!
And now twice in the span of a page's turn--first the wizard comes looking for his book and now you ruffians arrive to ruin my library!
Explain yourself before I condemn you all to *Infinite Jest!*
I ASSURE YOU, HE'S NOT BRINGING IT BACK.
Very well. Myrdin Wyld...the one you call Merlin...took the Eternity Book.
And he looked with great interest upon these works of the cartographer Anaximander.
They are maps of what was once your world but is now lost to time.
THESE ARE ASTONISHING. REFERENCING WORKS PREDATING THE IMAGO MUNDI.
FOCUS... WHAT WAS MERLIN LOOKING FOR, BOBO?

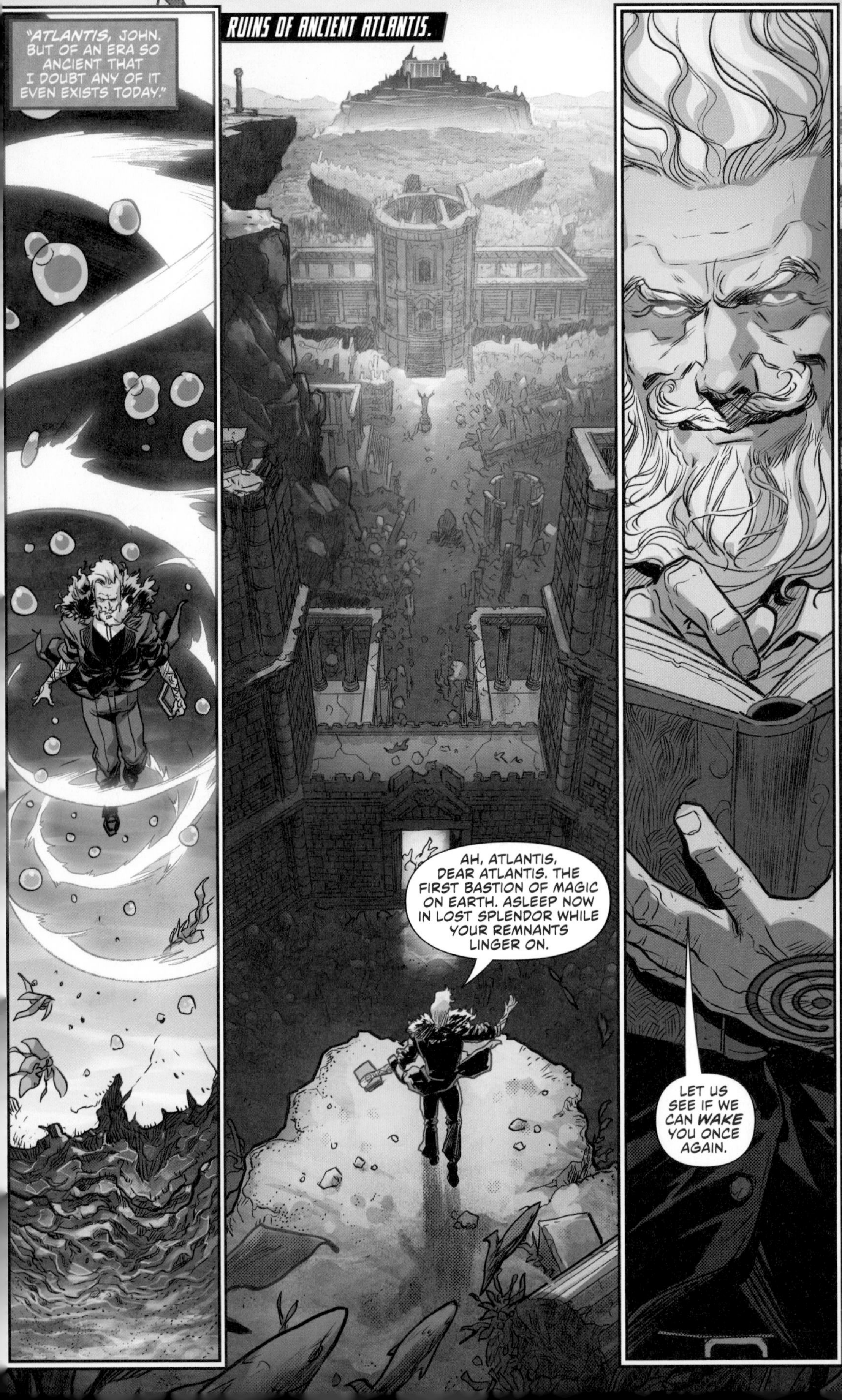
"ATLANTIS, JOHN. BUT OF AN ERA SO ANCIENT THAT I DOUBT ANY OF IT EVEN EXISTS TODAY."
RUINS OF ANCIENT ATLANTIS.
AH, ATLANTIS, DEAR ATLANTIS. THE FIRST BASTION OF MAGIC ON EARTH. ASLEEP NOW IN LOST SPLENDOR WHILE YOUR REMNANTS LINGER ON.
LET US SEE IF WE CAN WAKE YOU ONCE AGAIN.

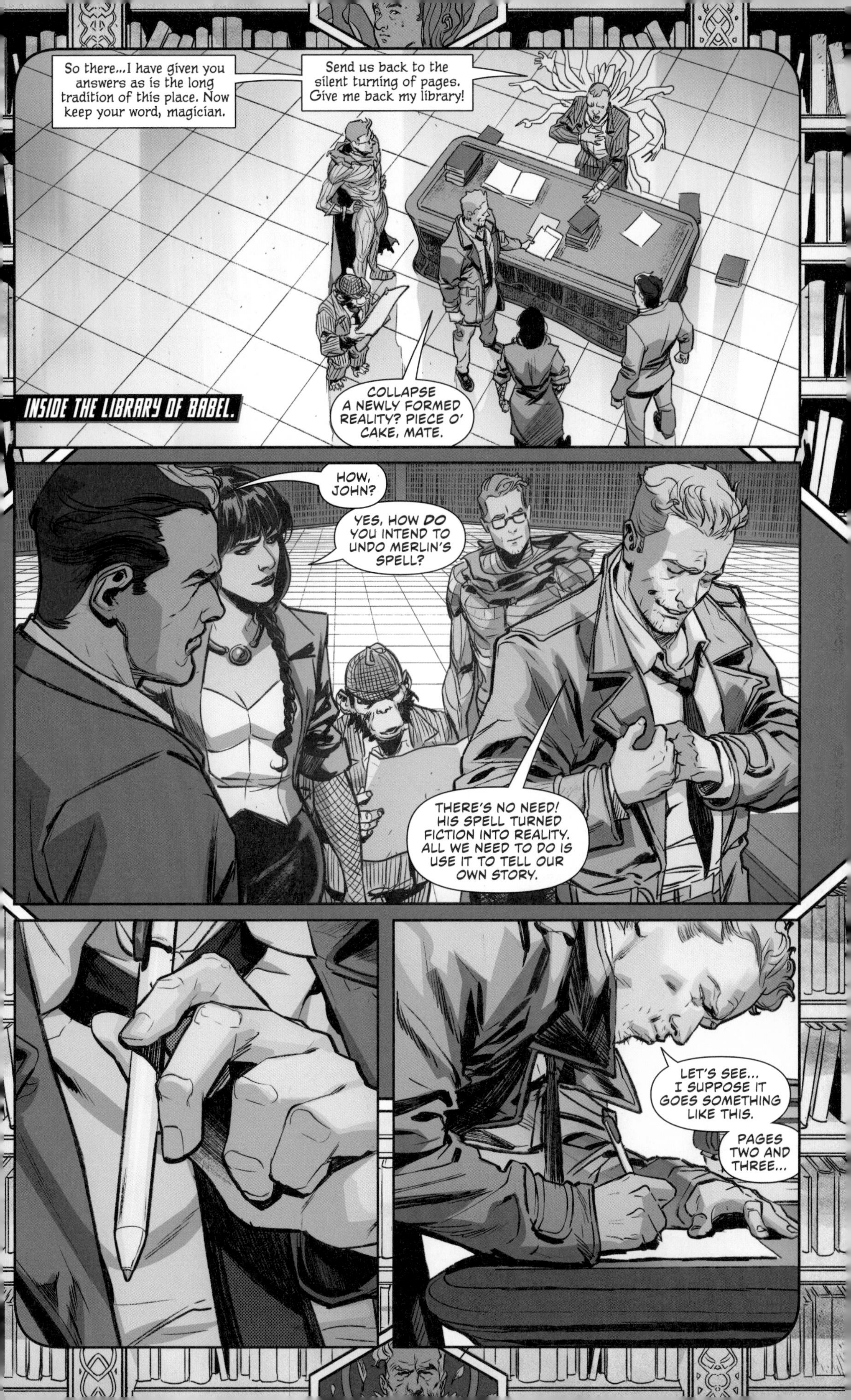
So there...I have given you answers as is the long tradition of this place. Now keep your word, magician.
Send us back to the silent turning of pages. Give me back my library!
INSIDE THE LIBRARY OF BABEL.
COLLAPSE A NEWLY FORMED REALITY? PIECE O' CAKE, MATE.
HOW, JOHN?
YES, HOW DO YOU INTEND TO UNDO MERLIN'S SPELL?
THERE'S NO NEED! HIS SPELL TURNED FICTION INTO REALITY. ALL WE NEED TO DO IS USE IT TO TELL OUR OWN STORY.
LET'S SEE... I SUPPOSE IT GOES SOMETHING LIKE THIS.
PAGES TWO AND THREE...

On this double-page spread, w

and weird. The page has no bac

put a copy of the text from his

background of the page.

HAH! IT WORKED.

YOU WEREN'T SURE?

WHAT'S THE WORST THAT COULD'VE HAPPENED?

John Constantine is writing this ve

...iting this fiction... is forcing the

conform to

METAFICTION! POSTMODERNISM!

The library and its great ~~hexagonal~~ hexa

The books and the librarians and the de

Instead there is only this text. This fic

THERE ARE ALWAYS RISKS WITH MAGIC, JOHN. SOMETIMES I REALLY WISH YOU'D REMEMBER THAT.

Merlin's spell has been used to undo itself.

to recede to just words on a page.

IT IS AN ELEGANT SOLUTION.

THERE ARE ONLY RISKS WITH MAGIC, ZEE. BUT WORTH THE COST TO SEE MERLIN'S MAGIC EATING ITS OWN TAIL, DON'T YOU RECKON?

d on top

aracters

ls, just

nces a

e'll have multiple ins

ead. the

through. Only

***

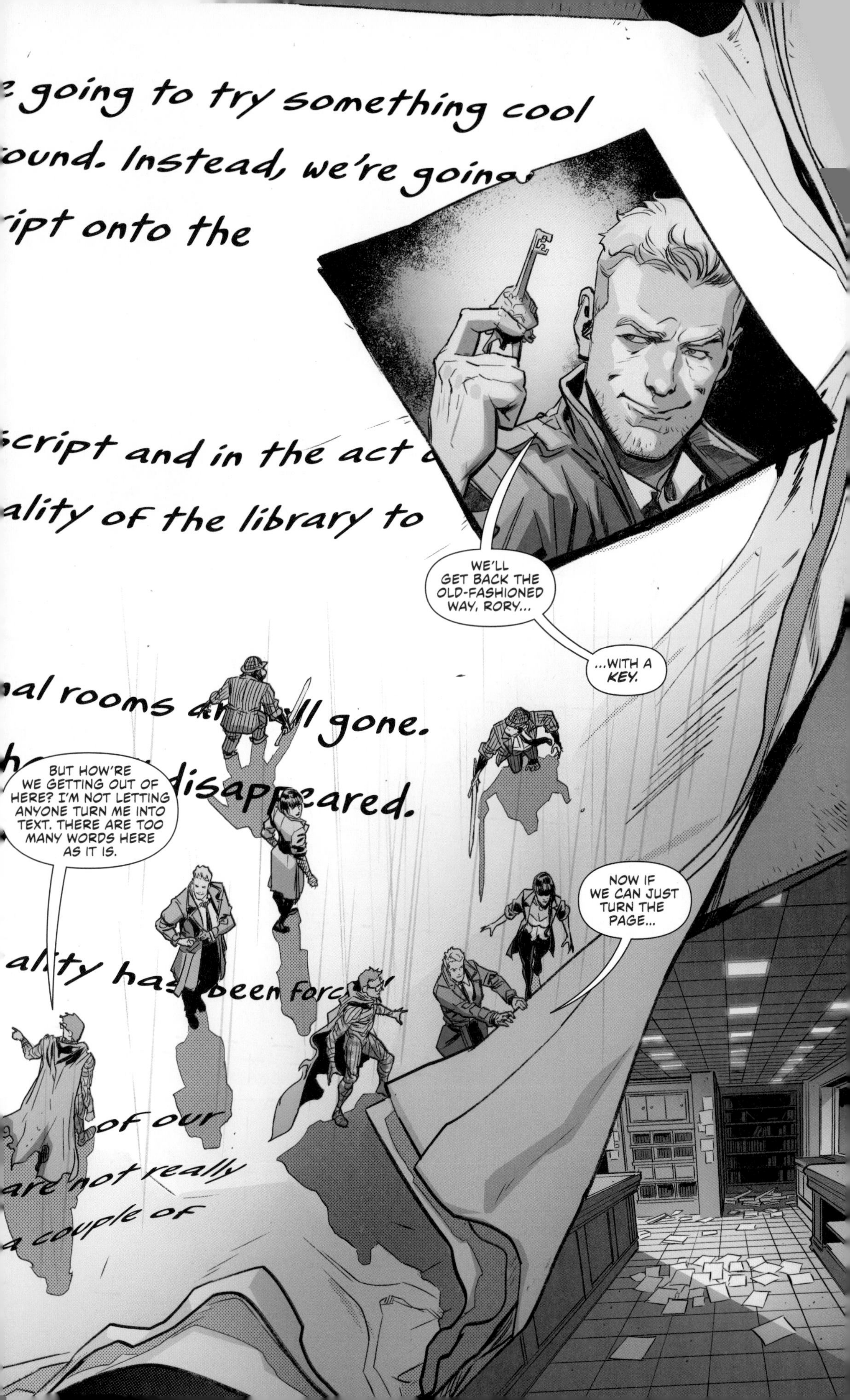

going to try something cool
ound. Instead, we're going
ript onto the
script and in the act
ality of the library to
WE'LL GET BACK THE OLD-FASHIONED WAY, RORY...
...WITH A KEY.
BUT HOW'RE WE GETTING OUT OF HERE? I'M NOT LETTING ANYONE TURN ME INTO TEXT. THERE ARE TOO MANY WORDS HERE AS IT IS.
NOW IF WE CAN JUST TURN THE PAGE...

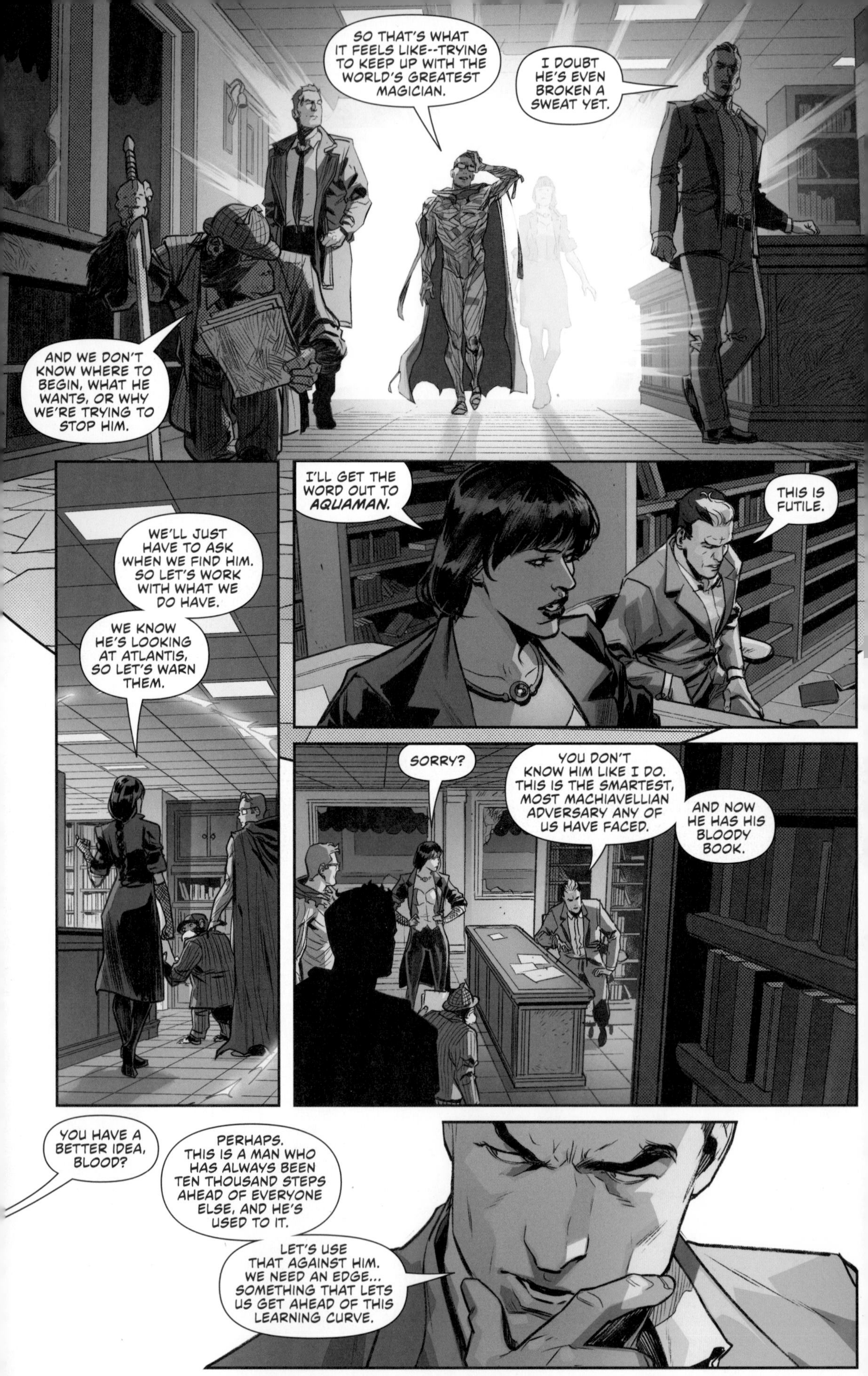
SO THAT'S WHAT IT FEELS LIKE--TRYING TO KEEP UP WITH THE WORLD'S GREATEST MAGICIAN.
I DOUBT HE'S EVEN BROKEN A SWEAT YET.
AND WE DON'T KNOW WHERE TO BEGIN, WHAT HE WANTS, OR WHY WE'RE TRYING TO STOP HIM.
WE'LL JUST HAVE TO ASK WHEN WE FIND HIM. SO LET'S WORK WITH WHAT WE DO HAVE.
WE KNOW HE'S LOOKING AT ATLANTIS, SO LET'S WARN THEM.
I'LL GET THE WORD OUT TO *AQUAMAN.*
THIS IS FUTILE.
SORRY?
YOU DON'T KNOW HIM LIKE I DO. THIS IS THE SMARTEST, MOST MACHIAVELLIAN ADVERSARY ANY OF US HAVE FACED.
AND NOW HE HAS HIS BLOODY BOOK.
YOU HAVE A BETTER IDEA, BLOOD?
PERHAPS. THIS IS A MAN WHO HAS ALWAYS BEEN TEN THOUSAND STEPS AHEAD OF EVERYONE ELSE, AND HE'S USED TO IT.
LET'S USE THAT AGAINST HIM. WE NEED AN EDGE... SOMETHING THAT LETS US GET AHEAD OF THIS LEARNING CURVE.

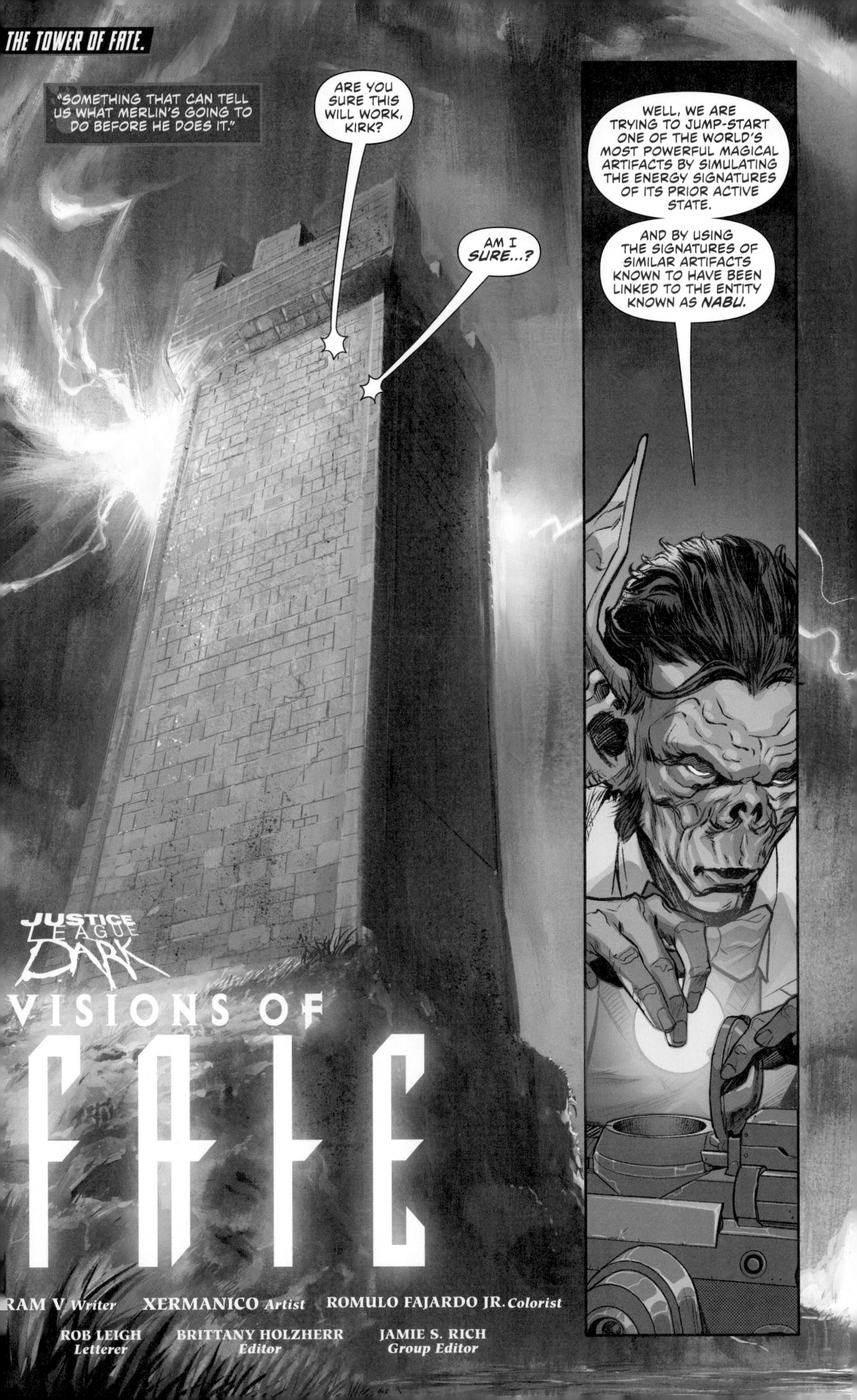
THE TOWER OF FATE.
"SOMETHING THAT CAN TELL US WHAT MERLIN'S GOING TO DO BEFORE HE DOES IT."
ARE YOU SURE THIS WILL WORK, KIRK?
AM I SURE...?
WELL, WE ARE TRYING TO JUMP-START ONE OF THE WORLD'S MOST POWERFUL MAGICAL ARTIFACTS BY SIMULATING THE ENERGY SIGNATURES OF ITS PRIOR ACTIVE STATE.
AND BY USING THE SIGNATURES OF SIMILAR ARTIFACTS KNOWN TO HAVE BEEN LINKED TO THE ENTITY KNOWN AS NABU.
JUSTICE LEAGUE DARK
VISIONS OF FATE
RAM V Writer XERMANICO Artist ROMULO FAJARDO JR. Colorist
ROB LEIGH Letterer BRITTANY HOLZHERR Editor JAMIE S. RICH Group Editor

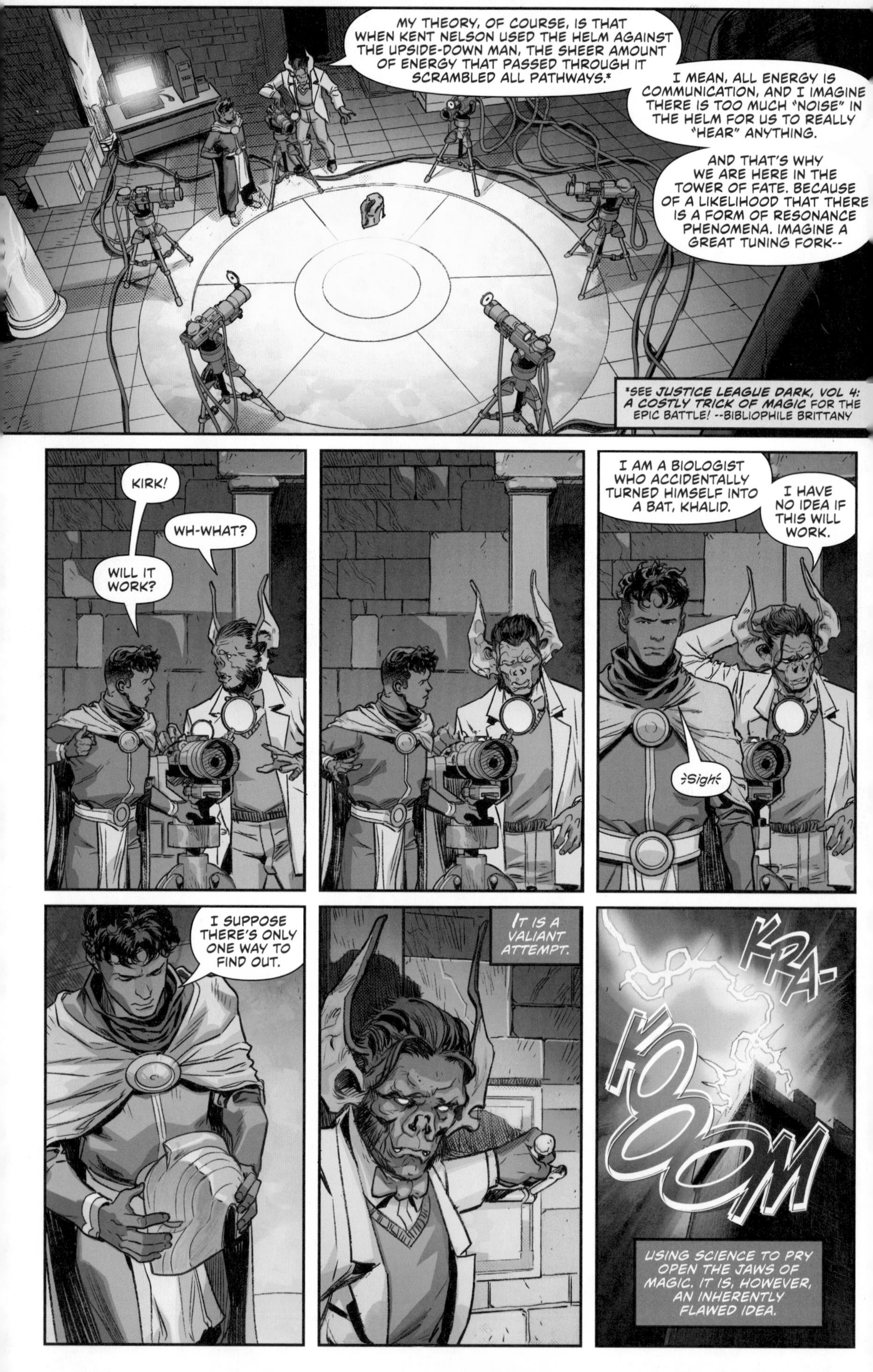
MY THEORY, OF COURSE, IS THAT WHEN KENT NELSON USED THE HELM AGAINST THE UPSIDE-DOWN MAN, THE SHEER AMOUNT OF ENERGY THAT PASSED THROUGH IT SCRAMBLED ALL PATHWAYS.*
I MEAN, ALL ENERGY IS COMMUNICATION, AND I IMAGINE THERE IS TOO MUCH "NOISE" IN THE HELM FOR US TO REALLY "HEAR" ANYTHING.
AND THAT'S WHY WE ARE HERE IN THE TOWER OF FATE. BECAUSE OF A LIKELIHOOD THAT THERE IS A FORM OF RESONANCE PHENOMENA. IMAGINE A GREAT TUNING FORK--
*SEE JUSTICE LEAGUE DARK, VOL 4: A COSTLY TRICK OF MAGIC FOR THE EPIC BATTLE! --BIBLIOPHILE BRITTANY
KIRK!
WH-WHAT?
WILL IT WORK?
I AM A BIOLOGIST WHO ACCIDENTALLY TURNED HIMSELF INTO A BAT, KHALID.
I HAVE NO IDEA IF THIS WILL WORK.
Sigh
I SUPPOSE THERE'S ONLY ONE WAY TO FIND OUT.
IT IS A VALIANT ATTEMPT.
KRA-KOOOOM
USING SCIENCE TO PRY OPEN THE JAWS OF MAGIC. IT IS, HOWEVER, AN INHERENTLY FLAWED IDEA.

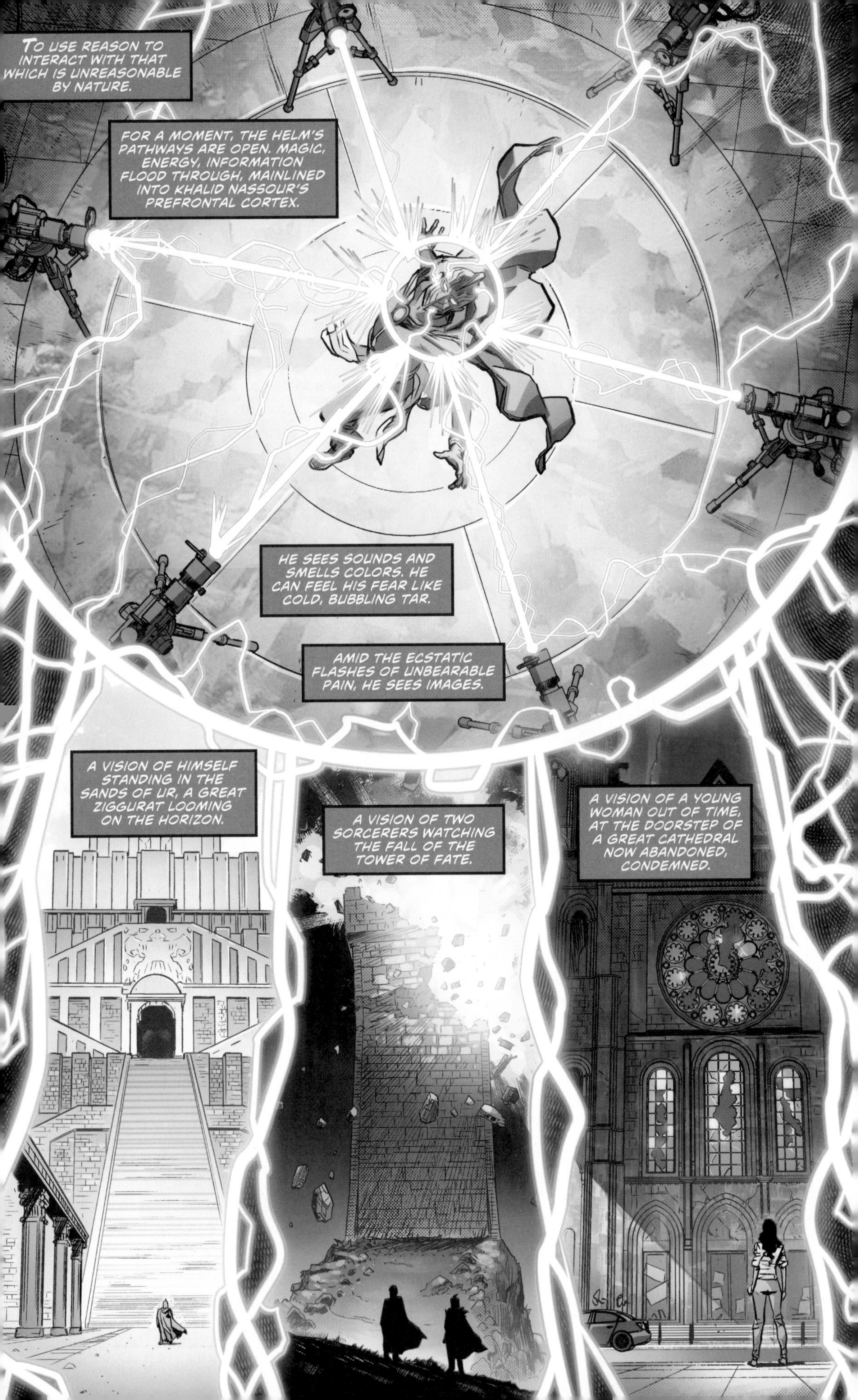
TO USE REASON TO INTERACT WITH THAT WHICH IS UNREASONABLE BY NATURE.
FOR A MOMENT, THE HELM'S PATHWAYS ARE OPEN. MAGIC, ENERGY, INFORMATION FLOOD THROUGH, MAINLINED INTO KHALID NASSOUR'S PREFRONTAL CORTEX.
HE SEES SOUNDS AND SMELLS COLORS. HE CAN FEEL HIS FEAR LIKE COLD, BUBBLING TAR.
AMID THE ECSTATIC FLASHES OF UNBEARABLE PAIN, HE SEES IMAGES.
A VISION OF HIMSELF STANDING IN THE SANDS OF UR, A GREAT ZIGGURAT LOOMING ON THE HORIZON.
A VISION OF TWO SORCERERS WATCHING THE FALL OF THE TOWER OF FATE.
A VISION OF A YOUNG WOMAN OUT OF TIME, AT THE DOORSTEP OF A GREAT CATHEDRAL NOW ABANDONED, CONDEMNED.

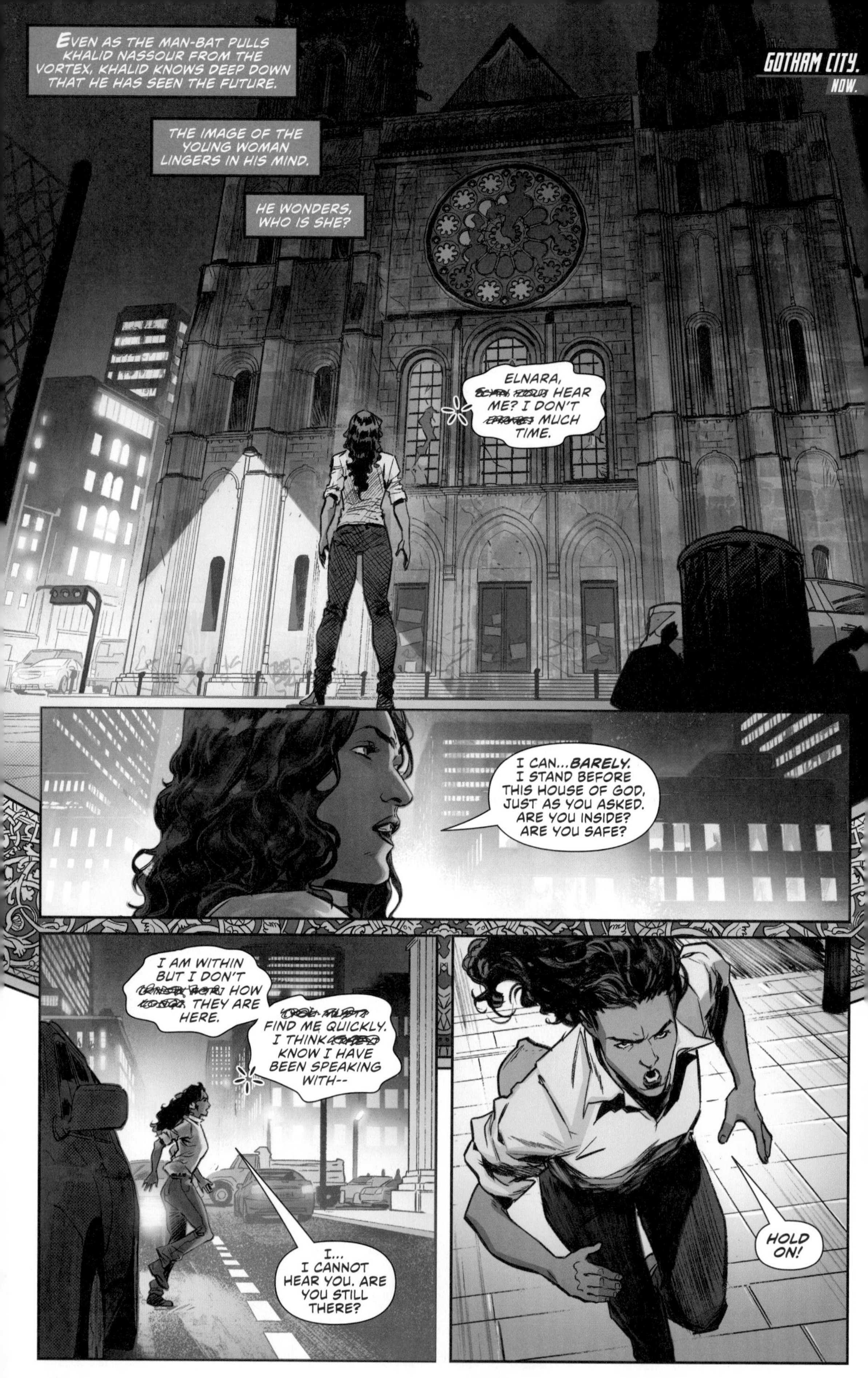

EVEN AS THE MAN-BAT PULLS KHALID NASSOUR FROM THE VORTEX, KHALID KNOWS DEEP DOWN THAT HE HAS SEEN THE FUTURE.
GOTHAM CITY.
NOW.
THE IMAGE OF THE YOUNG WOMAN LINGERS IN HIS MIND.
HE WONDERS, WHO IS SHE?
ELNARA, HEAR ME? I DON'T MUCH TIME.
I CAN...BARELY. I STAND BEFORE THIS HOUSE OF GOD, JUST AS YOU ASKED. ARE YOU INSIDE? ARE YOU SAFE?
I AM WITHIN BUT I DON'T HOW THEY ARE HERE.
FIND ME QUICKLY. I THINK KNOW I HAVE BEEN SPEAKING WITH--
I... I CANNOT HEAR YOU. ARE YOU STILL THERE?
HOLD ON!

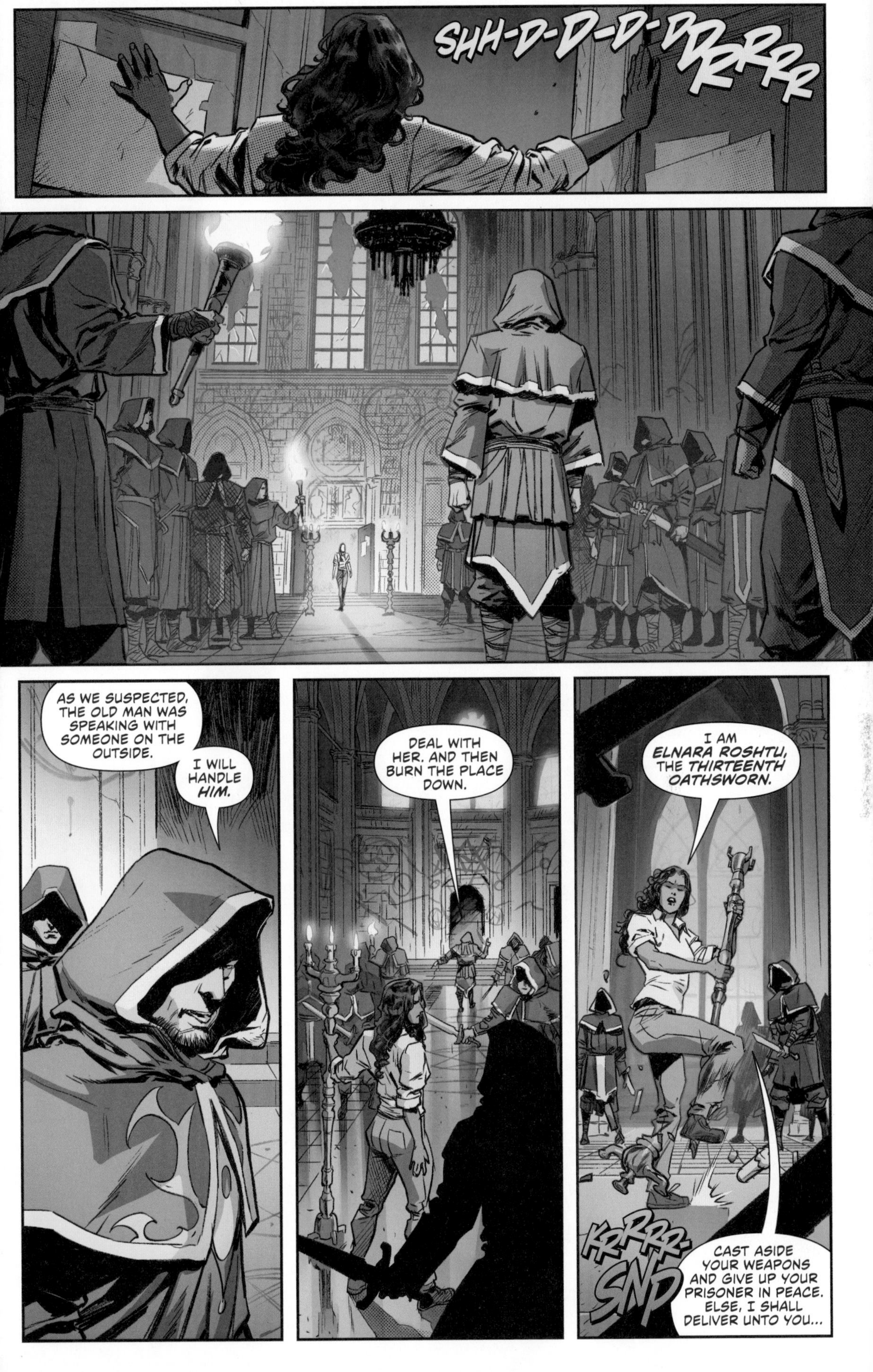
SHH-D-D-D-DDRRRRR
AS WE SUSPECTED, THE OLD MAN WAS SPEAKING WITH SOMEONE ON THE OUTSIDE.
I WILL HANDLE HIM.
DEAL WITH HER. AND THEN BURN THE PLACE DOWN.
I AM ELNARA ROSHTU, THE THIRTEENTH OATHSWORN.
KRRRR-SNP
CAST ASIDE YOUR WEAPONS AND GIVE UP YOUR PRISONER IN PEACE. ELSE, I SHALL DELIVER UNTO YOU...

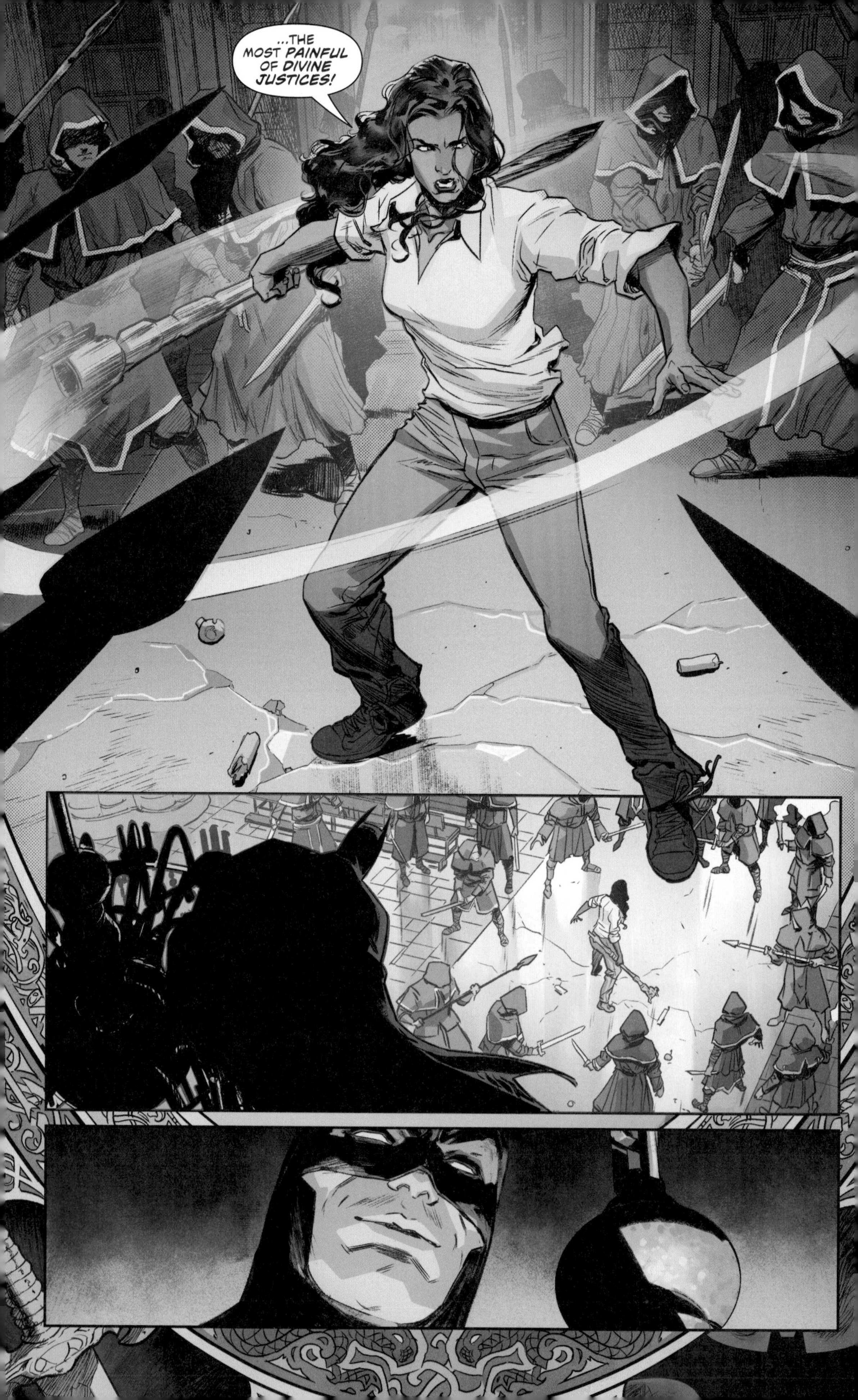
...THE MOST PAINFUL OF DIVINE JUSTICES!

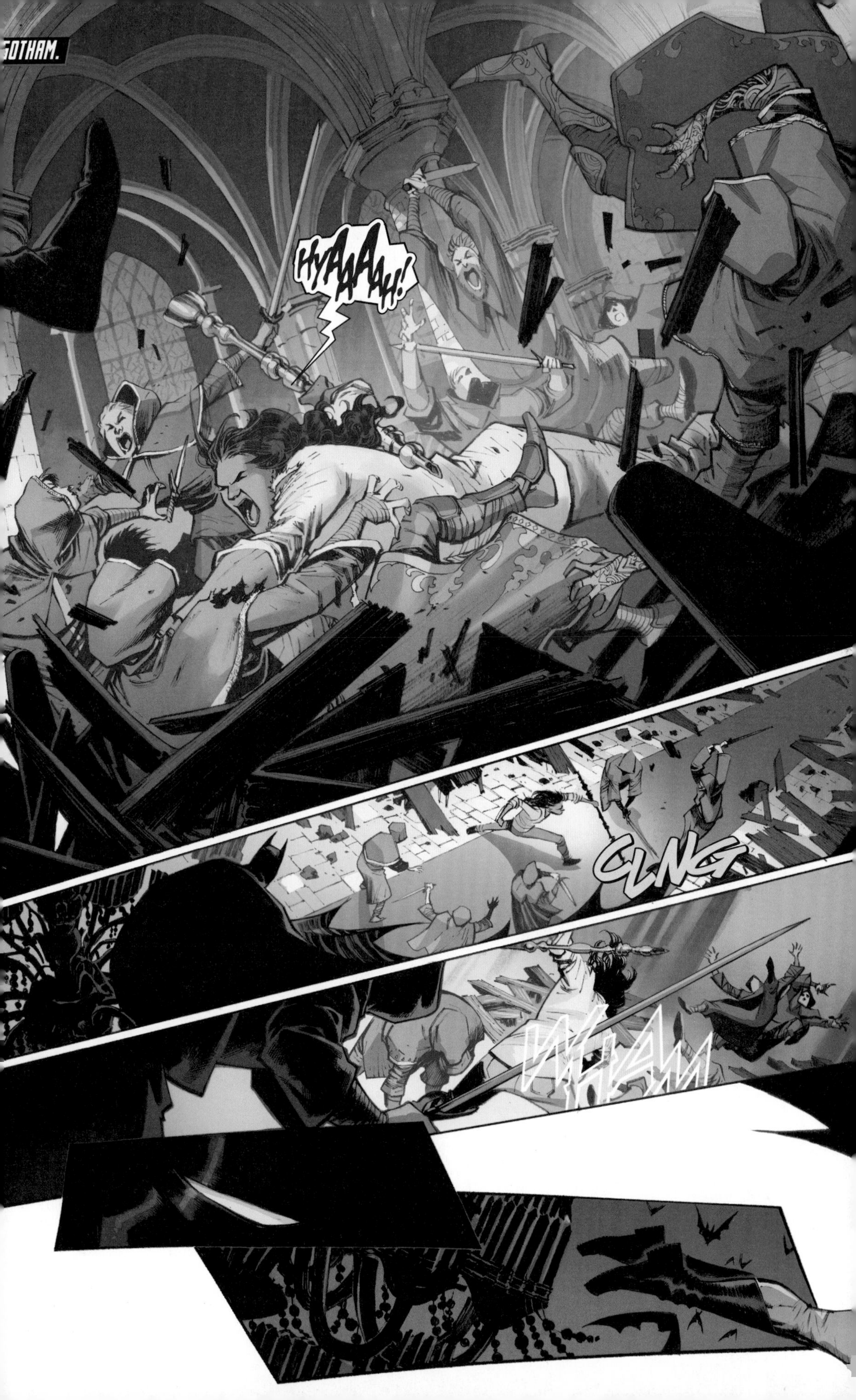
GOTHAM.
HYAAAAAH!
CLNG

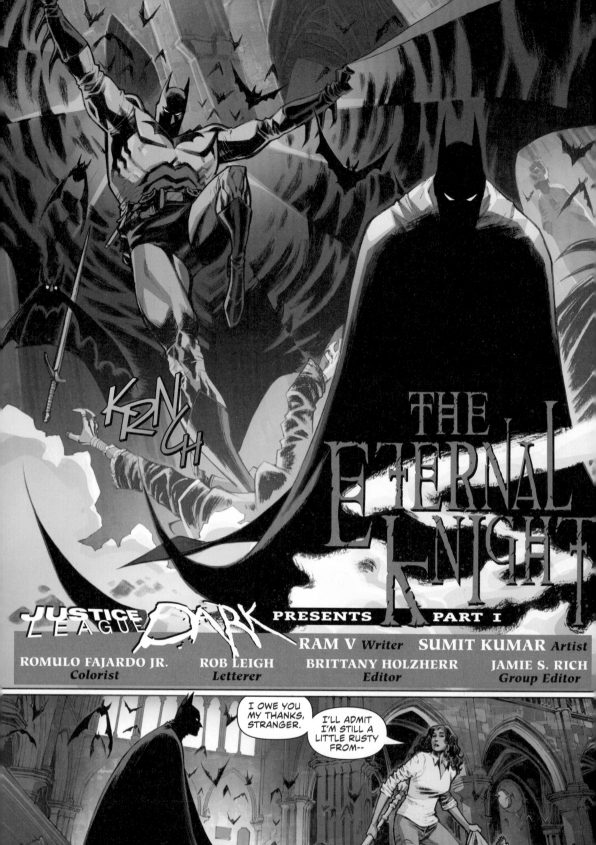

KRNCH

THE ETERNAL KNIGHT

JUSTICE LEAGUE DARK PRESENTS — PART I

RAM V *Writer*   SUMIT KUMAR *Artist*

ROMULO FAJARDO JR.
Colorist

ROB LEIGH
Letterer

BRITTANY HOLZHERR
Editor

JAMIE S. RICH
Group Editor

I OWE YOU MY THANKS, STRANGER.

I'LL ADMIT I'M STILL A LITTLE RUSTY FROM--

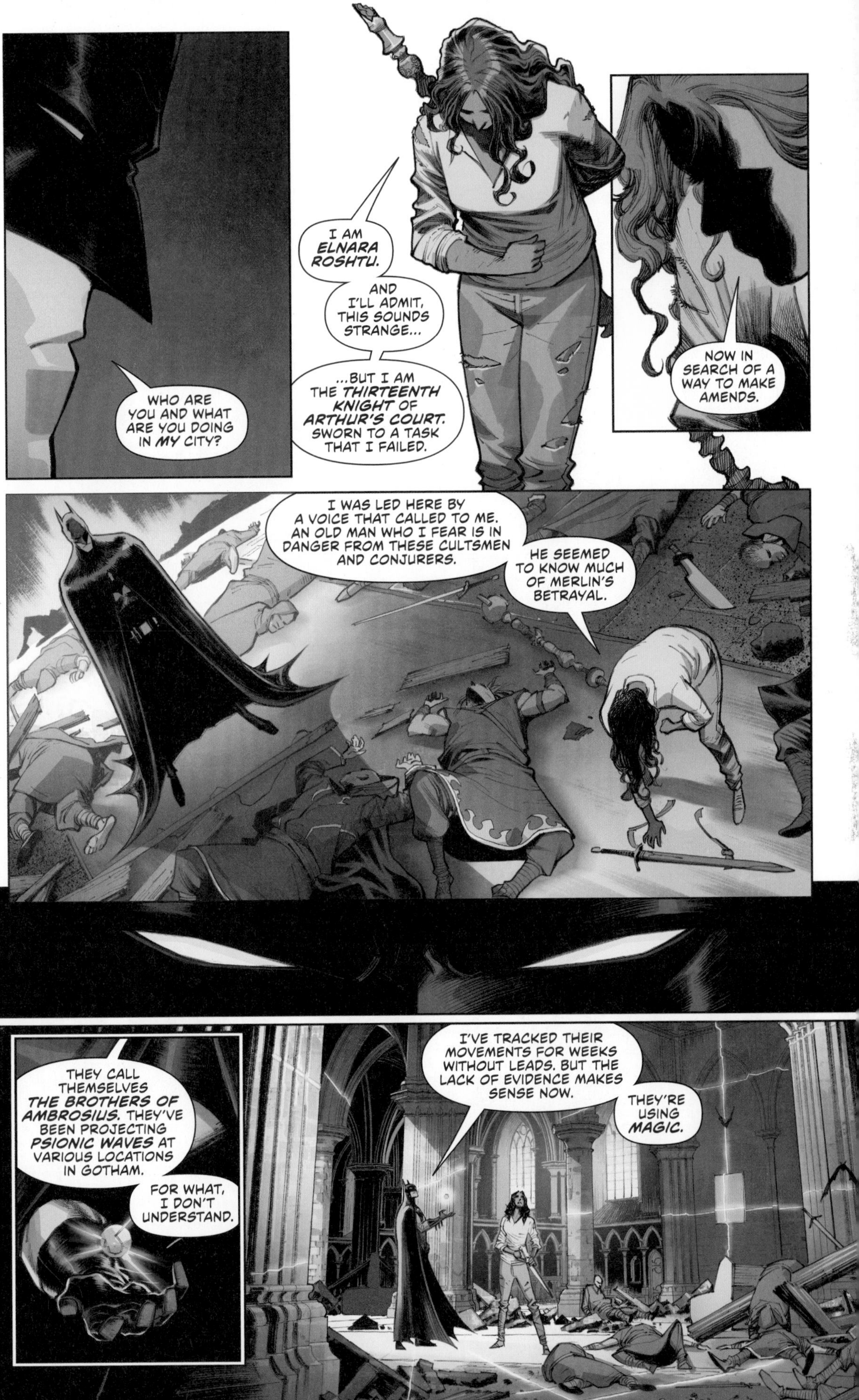
WHO ARE YOU AND WHAT ARE YOU DOING IN MY CITY?
I AM ELNARA ROSHTU.
AND I'LL ADMIT, THIS SOUNDS STRANGE...
...BUT I AM THE THIRTEENTH KNIGHT OF ARTHUR'S COURT. SWORN TO A TASK THAT I FAILED.
NOW IN SEARCH OF A WAY TO MAKE AMENDS.
I WAS LED HERE BY A VOICE THAT CALLED TO ME. AN OLD MAN WHO I FEAR IS IN DANGER FROM THESE CULTSMEN AND CONJURERS.
HE SEEMED TO KNOW MUCH OF MERLIN'S BETRAYAL.
THEY CALL THEMSELVES THE BROTHERS OF AMBROSIUS. THEY'VE BEEN PROJECTING PSIONIC WAVES AT VARIOUS LOCATIONS IN GOTHAM.
FOR WHAT, I DON'T UNDERSTAND.
I'VE TRACKED THEIR MOVEMENTS FOR WEEKS WITHOUT LEADS. BUT THE LACK OF EVIDENCE MAKES SENSE NOW.
THEY'RE USING MAGIC.

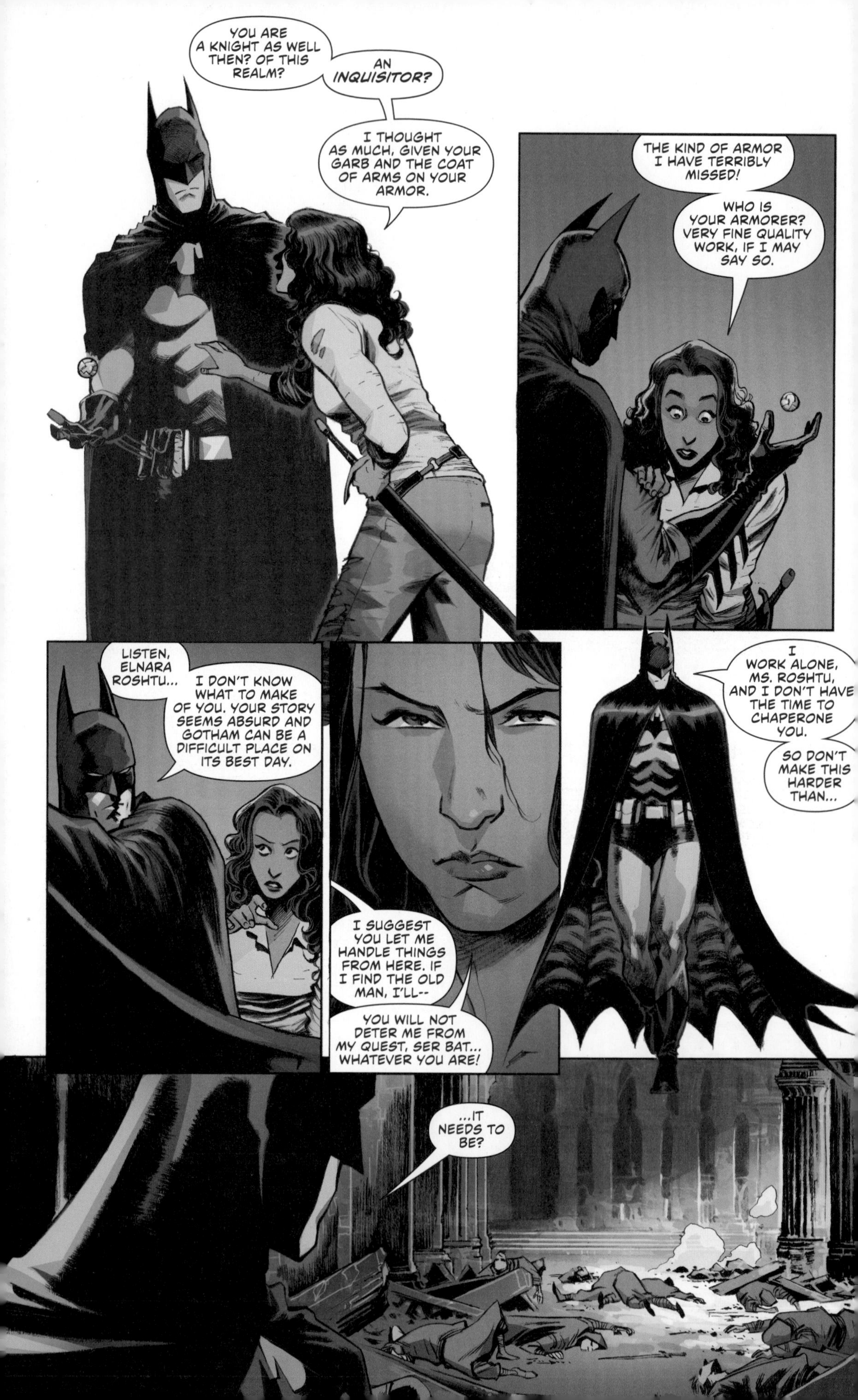
YOU ARE A KNIGHT AS WELL THEN? OF THIS REALM?
AN *INQUISITOR?*
I THOUGHT AS MUCH, GIVEN YOUR GARB AND THE COAT OF ARMS ON YOUR ARMOR.
THE KIND OF ARMOR I HAVE TERRIBLY MISSED!
WHO IS YOUR ARMORER? VERY FINE QUALITY WORK, IF I MAY SAY SO.
LISTEN, ELNARA ROSHTU...
I DON'T KNOW WHAT TO MAKE OF YOU. YOUR STORY SEEMS ABSURD AND GOTHAM CAN BE A DIFFICULT PLACE ON ITS BEST DAY.
I SUGGEST YOU LET ME HANDLE THINGS FROM HERE. IF I FIND THE OLD MAN, I'LL--
YOU WILL NOT DETER ME FROM MY QUEST, SER BAT... WHATEVER YOU ARE!
I WORK ALONE, MS. ROSHTU, AND I DON'T HAVE THE TIME TO CHAPERONE YOU.
SO DON'T MAKE THIS HARDER THAN...
...IT NEEDS TO BE?

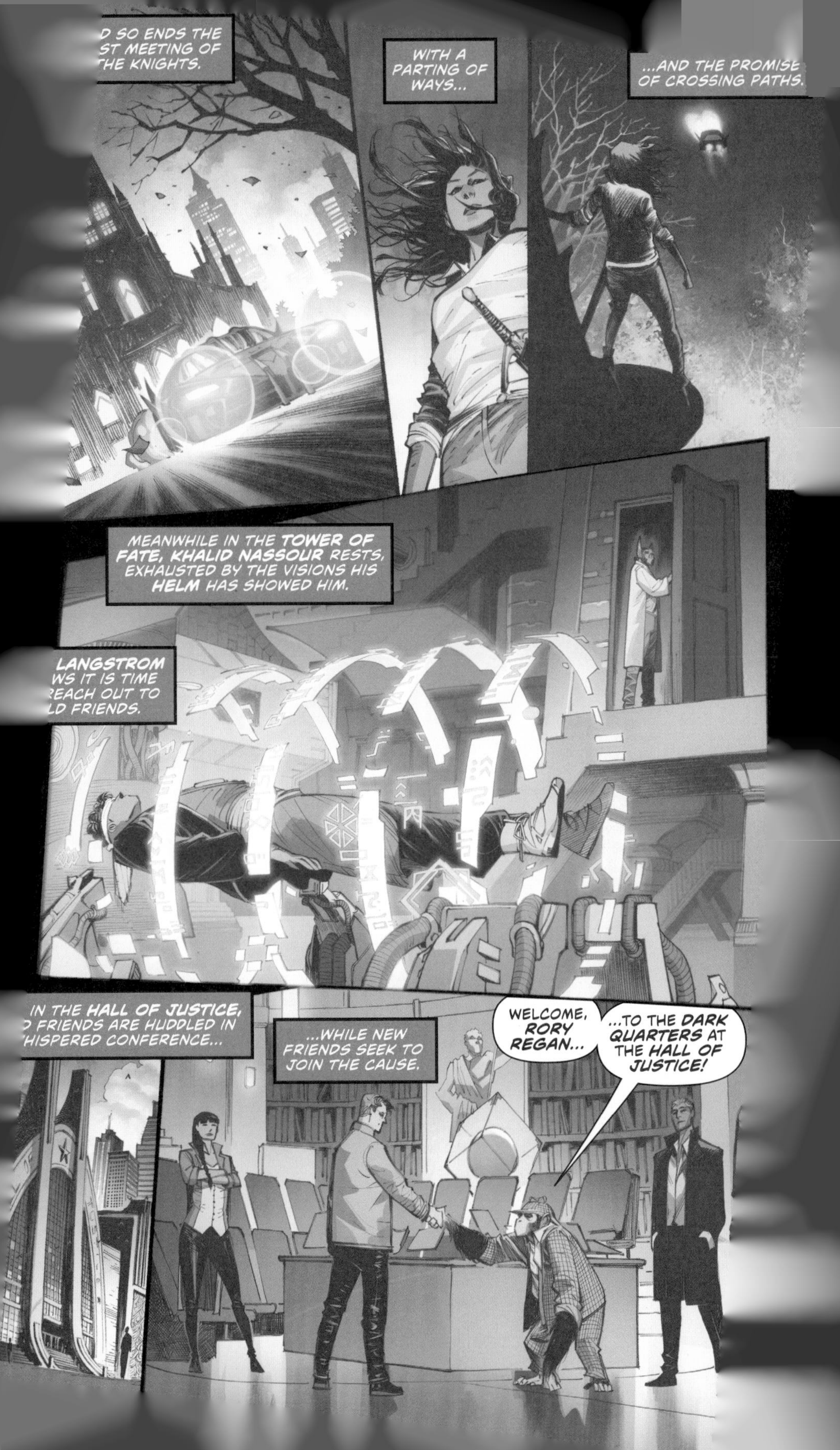
D SO ENDS THE ST MEETING OF THE KNIGHTS.
WITH A PARTING OF WAYS...
...AND THE PROMISE OF CROSSING PATHS.
MEANWHILE IN THE TOWER OF FATE, KHALID NASSOUR RESTS, EXHAUSTED BY THE VISIONS HIS HELM HAS SHOWED HIM.
LANGSTROM WS IT IS TIME REACH OUT TO LD FRIENDS.
IN THE HALL OF JUSTICE, D FRIENDS ARE HUDDLED IN HISPERED CONFERENCE...
...WHILE NEW FRIENDS SEEK TO JOIN THE CAUSE.
WELCOME, RORY REGAN...
...TO THE DARK QUARTERS AT THE HALL OF JUSTICE!

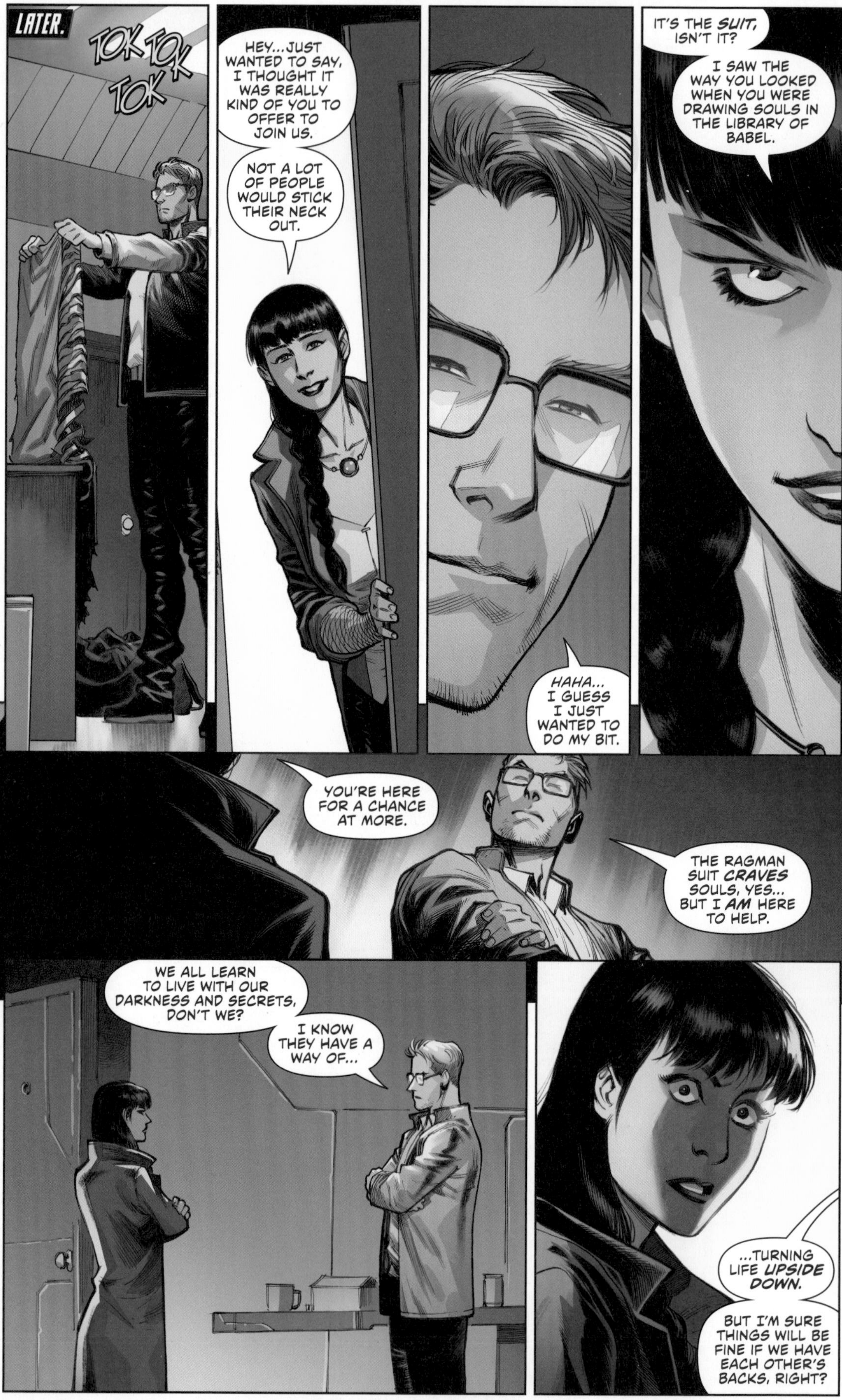
LATER.
TOK TOK TOK
HEY...JUST WANTED TO SAY, I THOUGHT IT WAS REALLY KIND OF YOU TO OFFER TO JOIN US.
NOT A LOT OF PEOPLE WOULD STICK THEIR NECK OUT.
HAHA... I GUESS I JUST WANTED TO DO MY BIT.
IT'S THE SUIT, ISN'T IT?
I SAW THE WAY YOU LOOKED WHEN YOU WERE DRAWING SOULS IN THE LIBRARY OF BABEL.
YOU'RE HERE FOR A CHANCE AT MORE.
THE RAGMAN SUIT CRAVES SOULS, YES... BUT I AM HERE TO HELP.
WE ALL LEARN TO LIVE WITH OUR DARKNESS AND SECRETS, DON'T WE?
I KNOW THEY HAVE A WAY OF...
...TURNING LIFE UPSIDE DOWN.
BUT I'M SURE THINGS WILL BE FINE IF WE HAVE EACH OTHER'S BACKS, RIGHT?

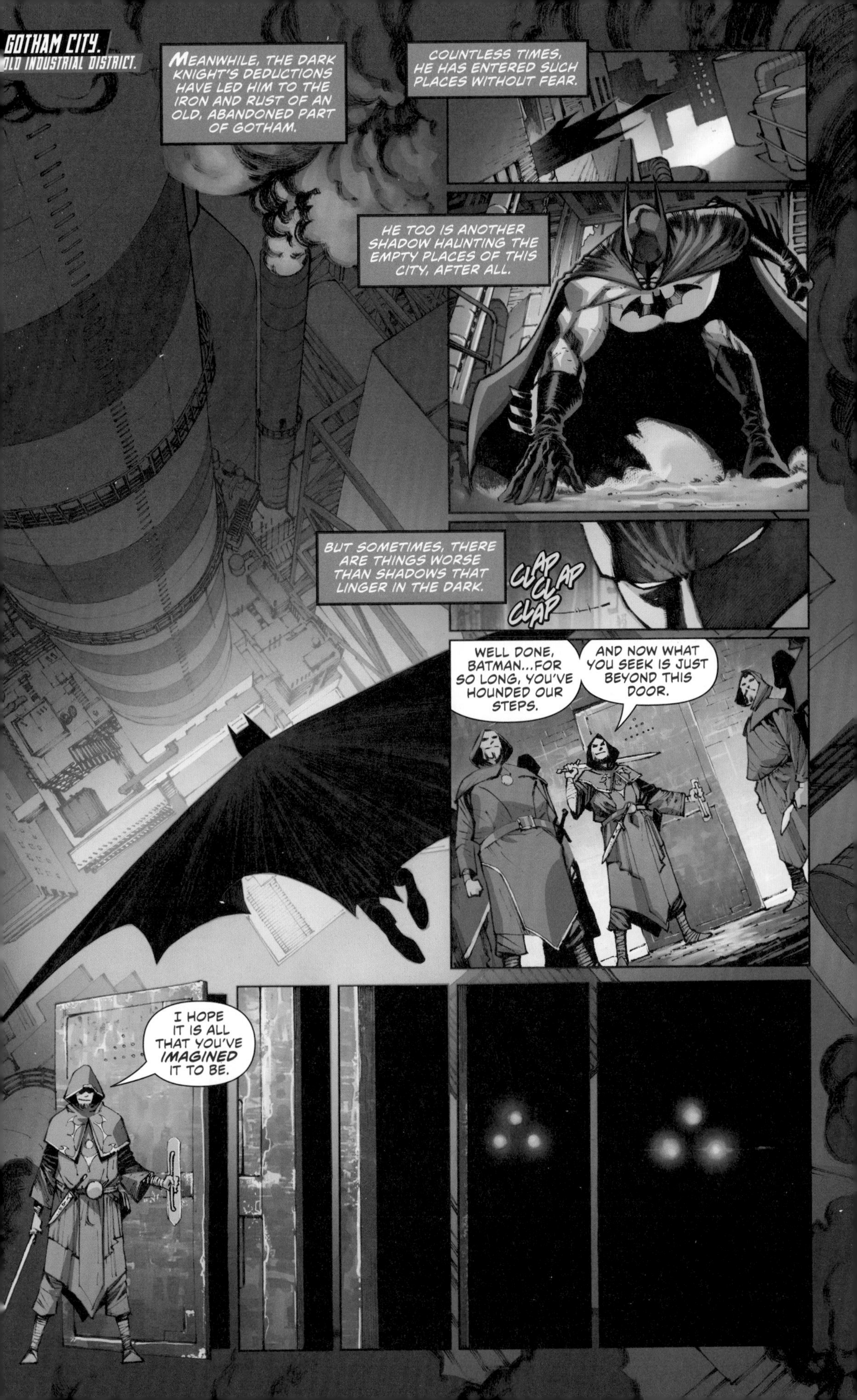
GOTHAM CITY.
OLD INDUSTRIAL DISTRICT.
MEANWHILE, THE DARK KNIGHT'S DEDUCTIONS HAVE LED HIM TO THE IRON AND RUST OF AN OLD, ABANDONED PART OF GOTHAM.
COUNTLESS TIMES, HE HAS ENTERED SUCH PLACES WITHOUT FEAR.
HE TOO IS ANOTHER SHADOW HAUNTING THE EMPTY PLACES OF THIS CITY, AFTER ALL.
BUT SOMETIMES, THERE ARE THINGS WORSE THAN SHADOWS THAT LINGER IN THE DARK.
CLAP CLAP CLAP
WELL DONE, BATMAN...FOR SO LONG, YOU'VE HOUNDED OUR STEPS.
AND NOW WHAT YOU SEEK IS JUST BEYOND THIS DOOR.
I HOPE IT IS ALL THAT YOU'VE *IMAGINED* IT TO BE.

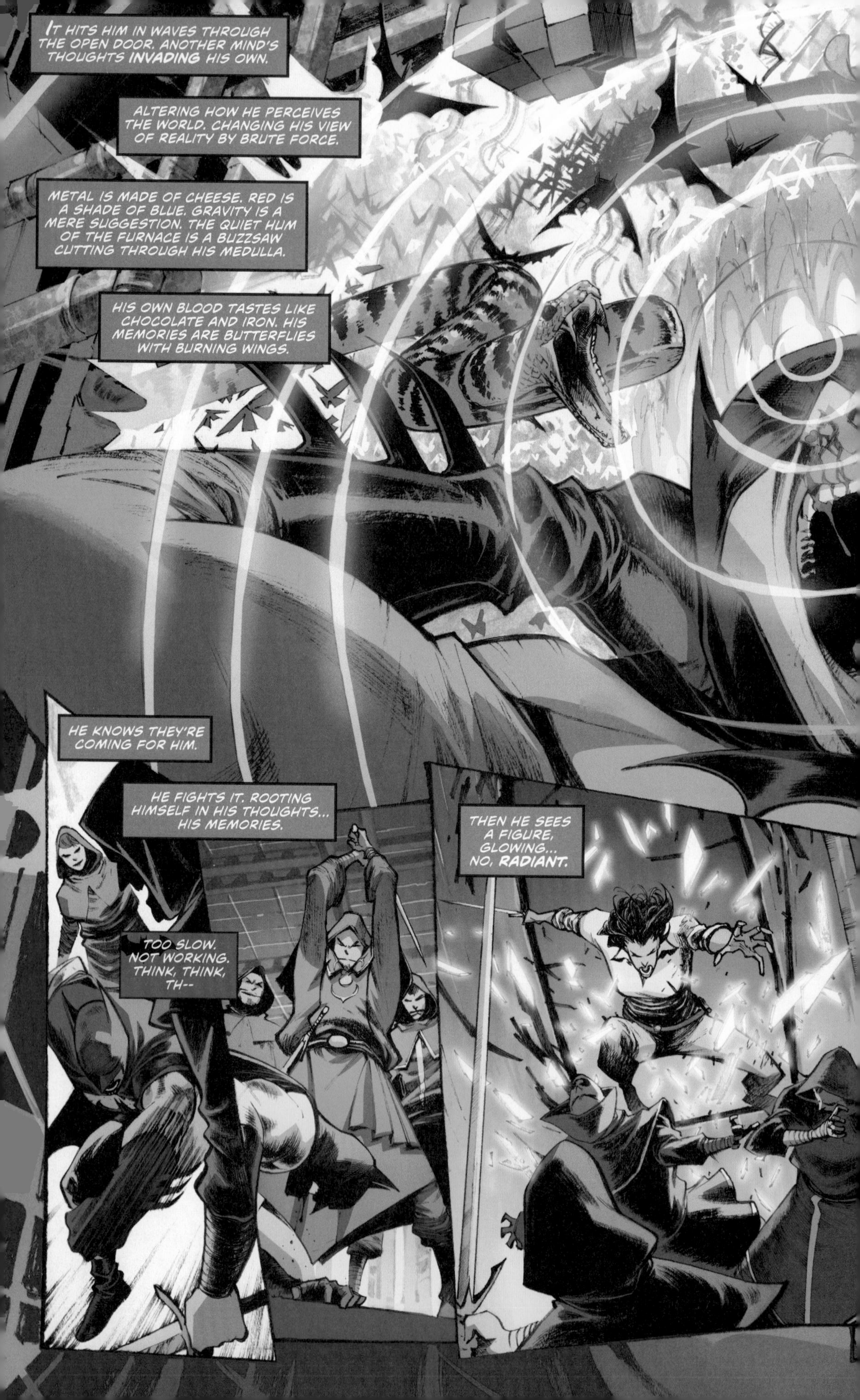
IT HITS HIM IN WAVES THROUGH THE OPEN DOOR. ANOTHER MIND'S THOUGHTS INVADING HIS OWN.
ALTERING HOW HE PERCEIVES THE WORLD. CHANGING HIS VIEW OF REALITY BY BRUTE FORCE.
METAL IS MADE OF CHEESE. RED IS A SHADE OF BLUE. GRAVITY IS A MERE SUGGESTION. THE QUIET HUM OF THE FURNACE IS A BUZZSAW CUTTING THROUGH HIS MEDULLA.
HIS OWN BLOOD TASTES LIKE CHOCOLATE AND IRON. HIS MEMORIES ARE BUTTERFLIES WITH BURNING WINGS.
HE KNOWS THEY'RE COMING FOR HIM.
HE FIGHTS IT. ROOTING HIMSELF IN HIS THOUGHTS... HIS MEMORIES.
TOO SLOW. NOT WORKING. THINK, THINK, TH--
THEN HE SEES A FIGURE, GLOWING... NO, RADIANT.

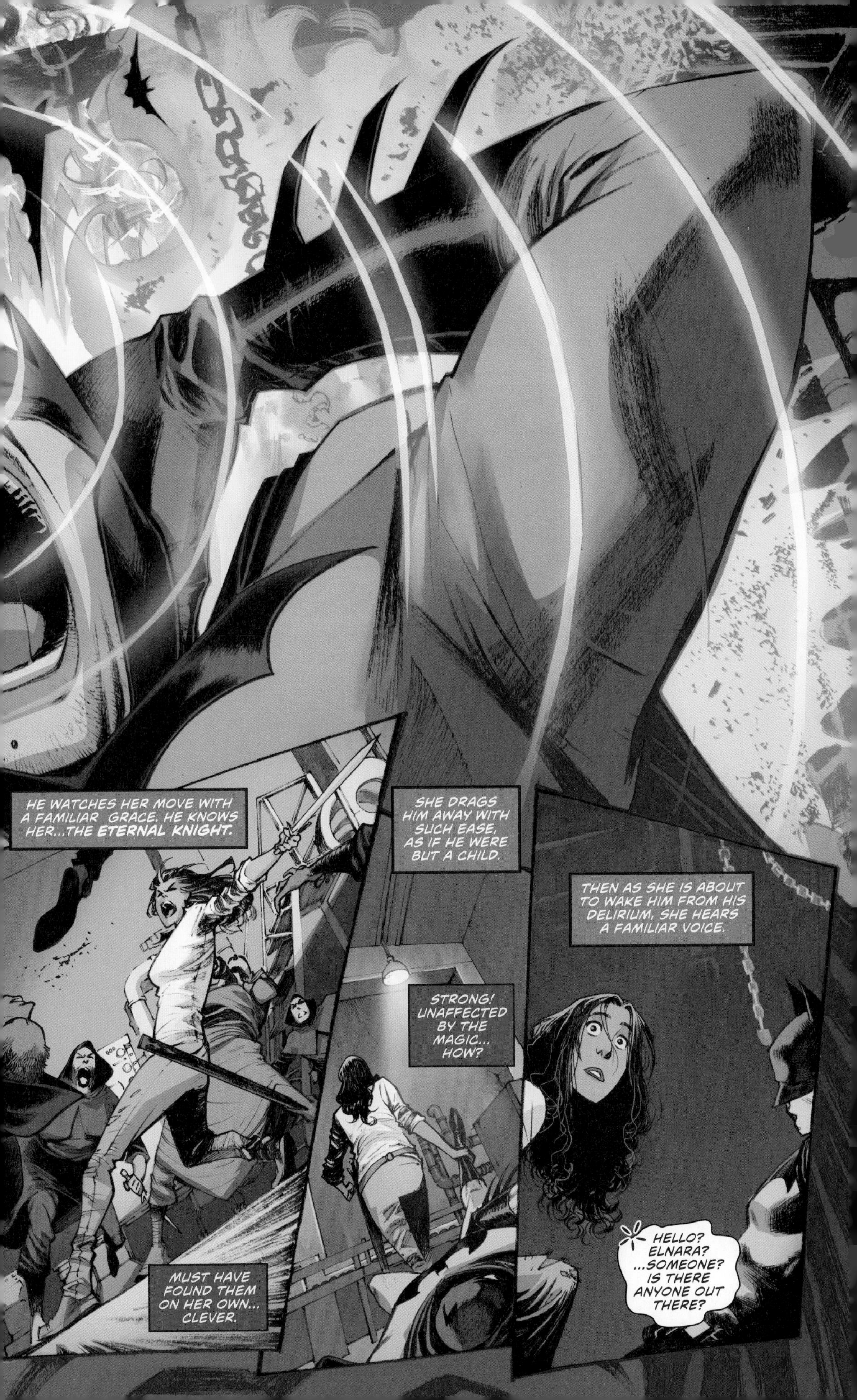
HE WATCHES HER MOVE WITH A FAMILIAR GRACE. HE KNOWS HER...THE **ETERNAL KNIGHT.**
MUST HAVE FOUND THEM ON HER OWN... CLEVER.
SHE DRAGS HIM AWAY WITH SUCH EASE, AS IF HE WERE BUT A CHILD.
STRONG! UNAFFECTED BY THE MAGIC... HOW?
THEN AS SHE IS ABOUT TO WAKE HIM FROM HIS DELIRIUM, SHE HEARS A FAMILIAR VOICE.
HELLO? ELNARA? ...SOMEONE? IS THERE ANYONE OUT THERE?

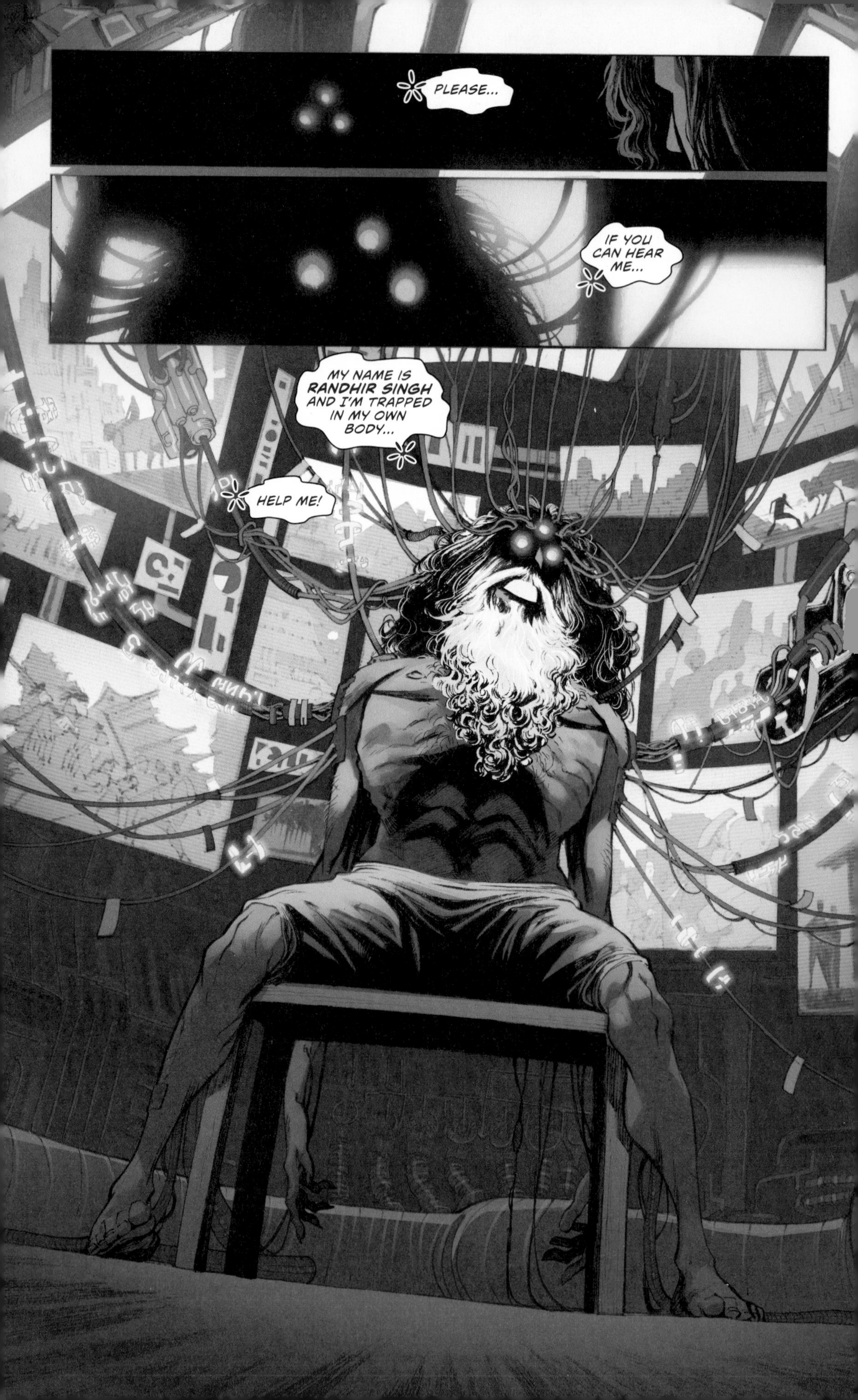
PLEASE...
IF YOU CAN HEAR ME...
MY NAME IS **RANDHIR SINGH** AND I'M TRAPPED IN MY OWN BODY...
HELP ME!

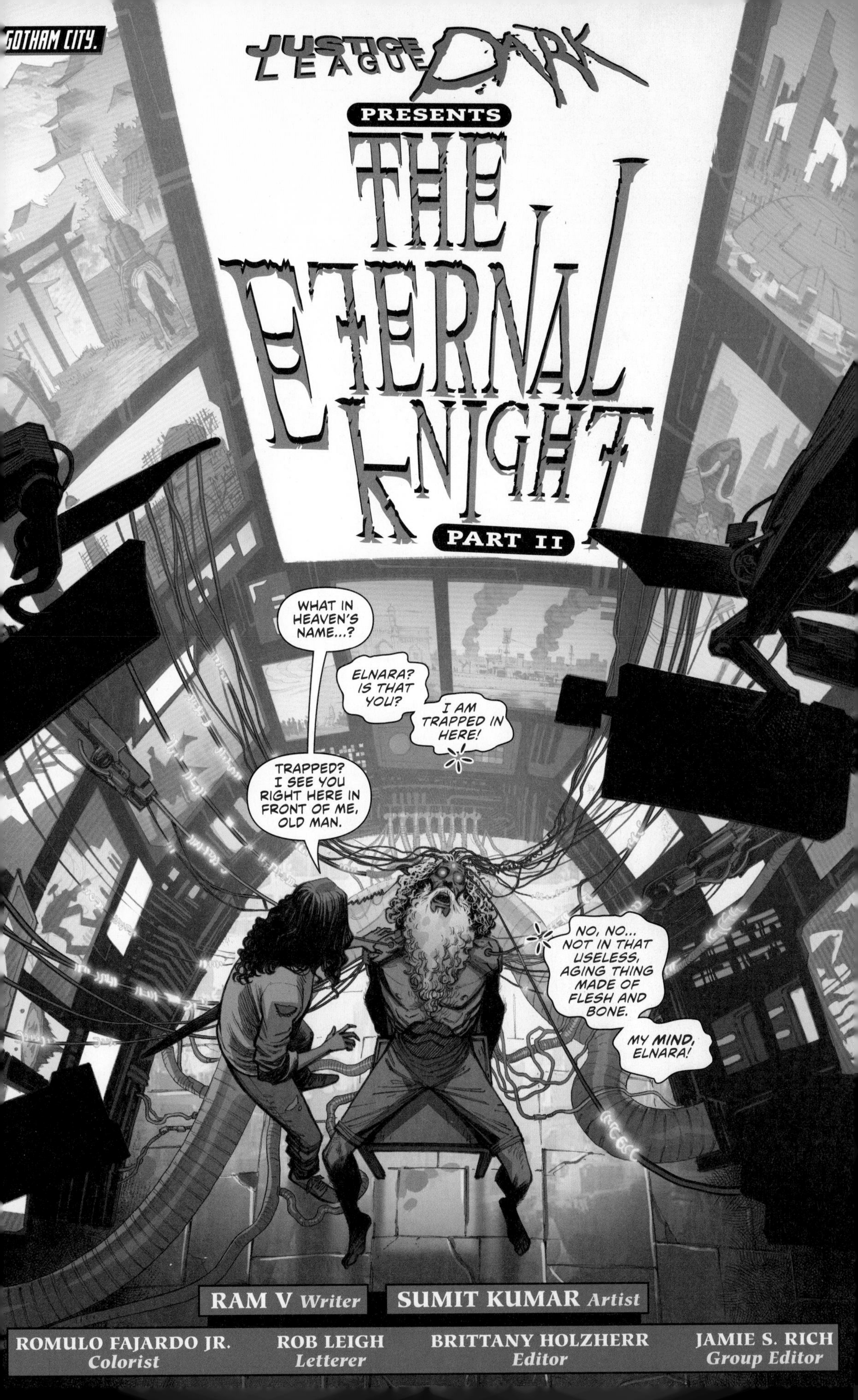
GOTHAM CITY.
JUSTICE LEAGUE DARK
PRESENTS
THE ETERNAL KNIGHT
PART II
WHAT IN HEAVEN'S NAME...?
ELNARA? IS THAT YOU?
I AM TRAPPED IN HERE!
TRAPPED? I SEE YOU RIGHT HERE IN FRONT OF ME, OLD MAN.
NO, NO... NOT IN THAT USELESS, AGING THING MADE OF FLESH AND BONE.
MY MIND, ELNARA!
RAM V Writer
SUMIT KUMAR Artist
ROMULO FAJARDO JR. Colorist
ROB LEIGH Letterer
BRITTANY HOLZHERR Editor
JAMIE S. RICH Group Editor

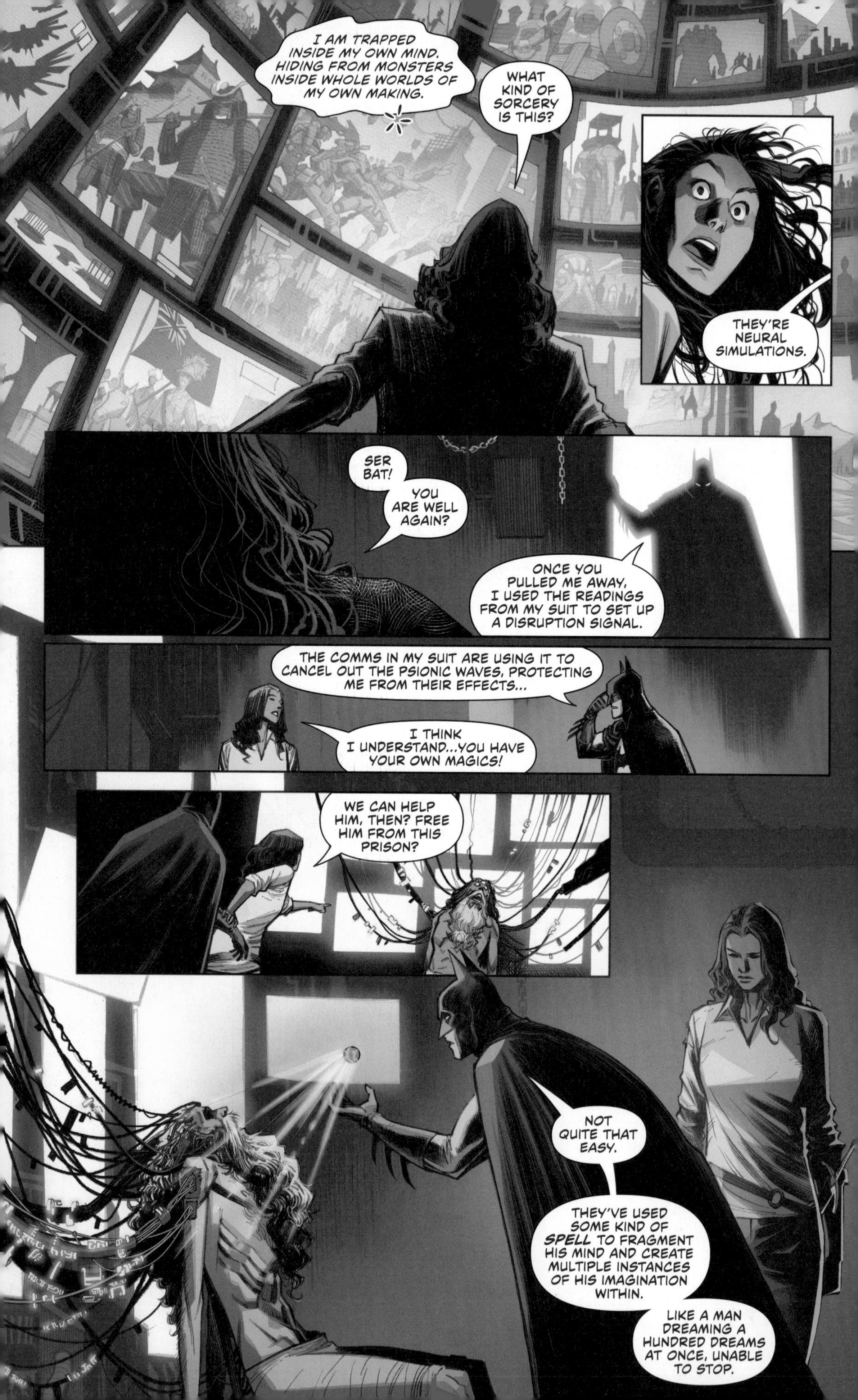
I AM TRAPPED INSIDE MY OWN MIND. HIDING FROM MONSTERS INSIDE WHOLE WORLDS OF MY OWN MAKING.
WHAT KIND OF SORCERY IS THIS?
THEY'RE NEURAL SIMULATIONS.
SER BAT!
YOU ARE WELL AGAIN?
ONCE YOU PULLED ME AWAY, I USED THE READINGS FROM MY SUIT TO SET UP A DISRUPTION SIGNAL.
THE COMMS IN MY SUIT ARE USING IT TO CANCEL OUT THE PSIONIC WAVES, PROTECTING ME FROM THEIR EFFECTS...
I THINK I UNDERSTAND...YOU HAVE YOUR OWN MAGICS!
WE CAN HELP HIM, THEN? FREE HIM FROM THIS PRISON?
NOT QUITE THAT EASY.
THEY'VE USED SOME KIND OF SPELL TO FRAGMENT HIS MIND AND CREATE MULTIPLE INSTANCES OF HIS IMAGINATION WITHIN.
LIKE A MAN DREAMING A HUNDRED DREAMS AT ONCE, UNABLE TO STOP.

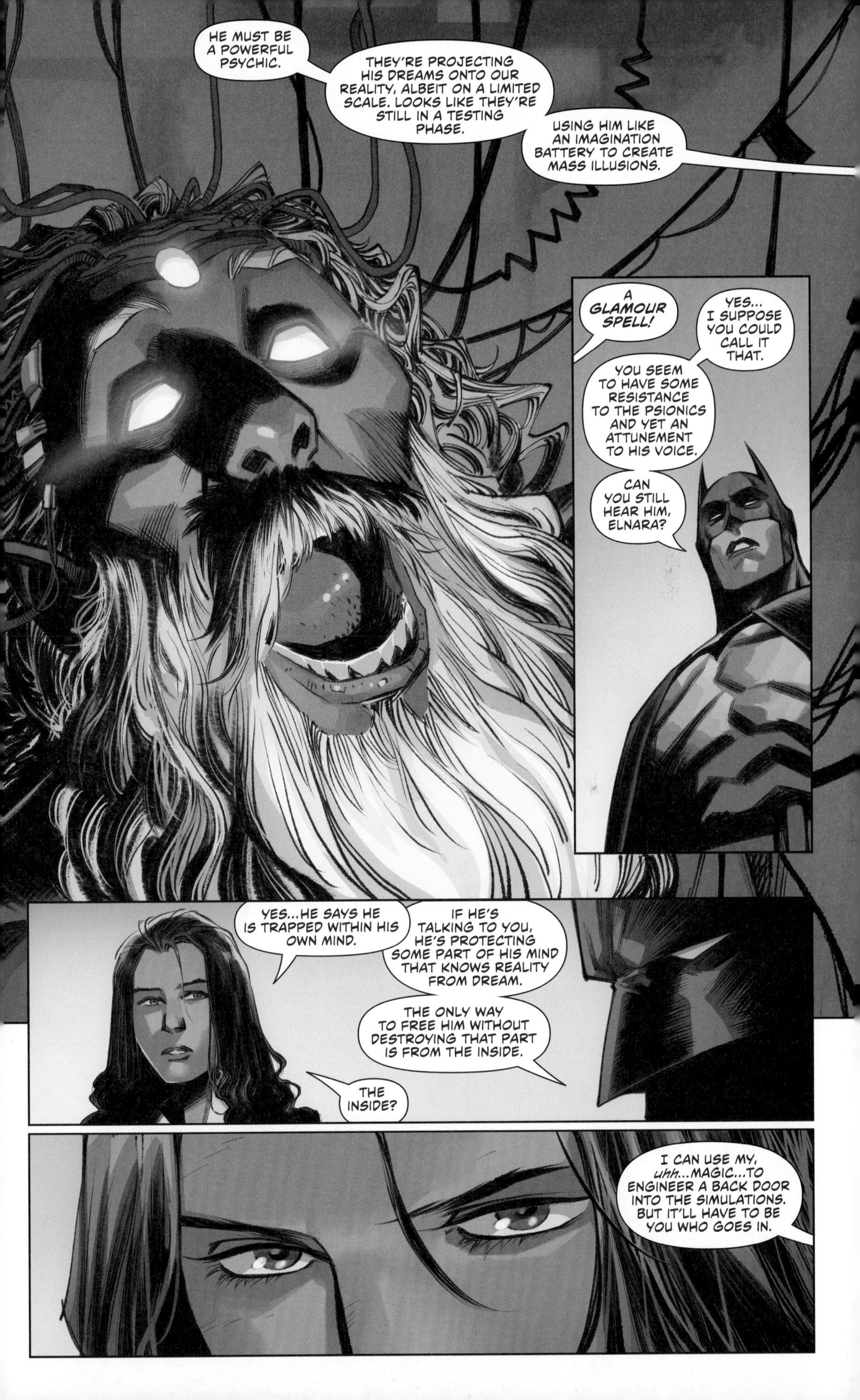
HE MUST BE A POWERFUL PSYCHIC.
THEY'RE PROJECTING HIS DREAMS ONTO OUR REALITY, ALBEIT ON A LIMITED SCALE. LOOKS LIKE THEY'RE STILL IN A TESTING PHASE.
USING HIM LIKE AN IMAGINATION BATTERY TO CREATE MASS ILLUSIONS.
A *GLAMOUR SPELL!*
YES... I SUPPOSE YOU COULD CALL IT THAT.
YOU SEEM TO HAVE SOME RESISTANCE TO THE PSIONICS AND YET AN ATTUNEMENT TO HIS VOICE.
CAN YOU STILL HEAR HIM, ELNARA?
YES...HE SAYS HE IS TRAPPED WITHIN HIS OWN MIND.
IF HE'S TALKING TO YOU, HE'S PROTECTING SOME PART OF HIS MIND THAT KNOWS REALITY FROM DREAM.
THE ONLY WAY TO FREE HIM WITHOUT DESTROYING THAT PART IS FROM THE INSIDE.
THE INSIDE?
I CAN USE MY, *uhh*...MAGIC...TO ENGINEER A BACK DOOR INTO THE SIMULATIONS. BUT IT'LL HAVE TO BE YOU WHO GOES IN.

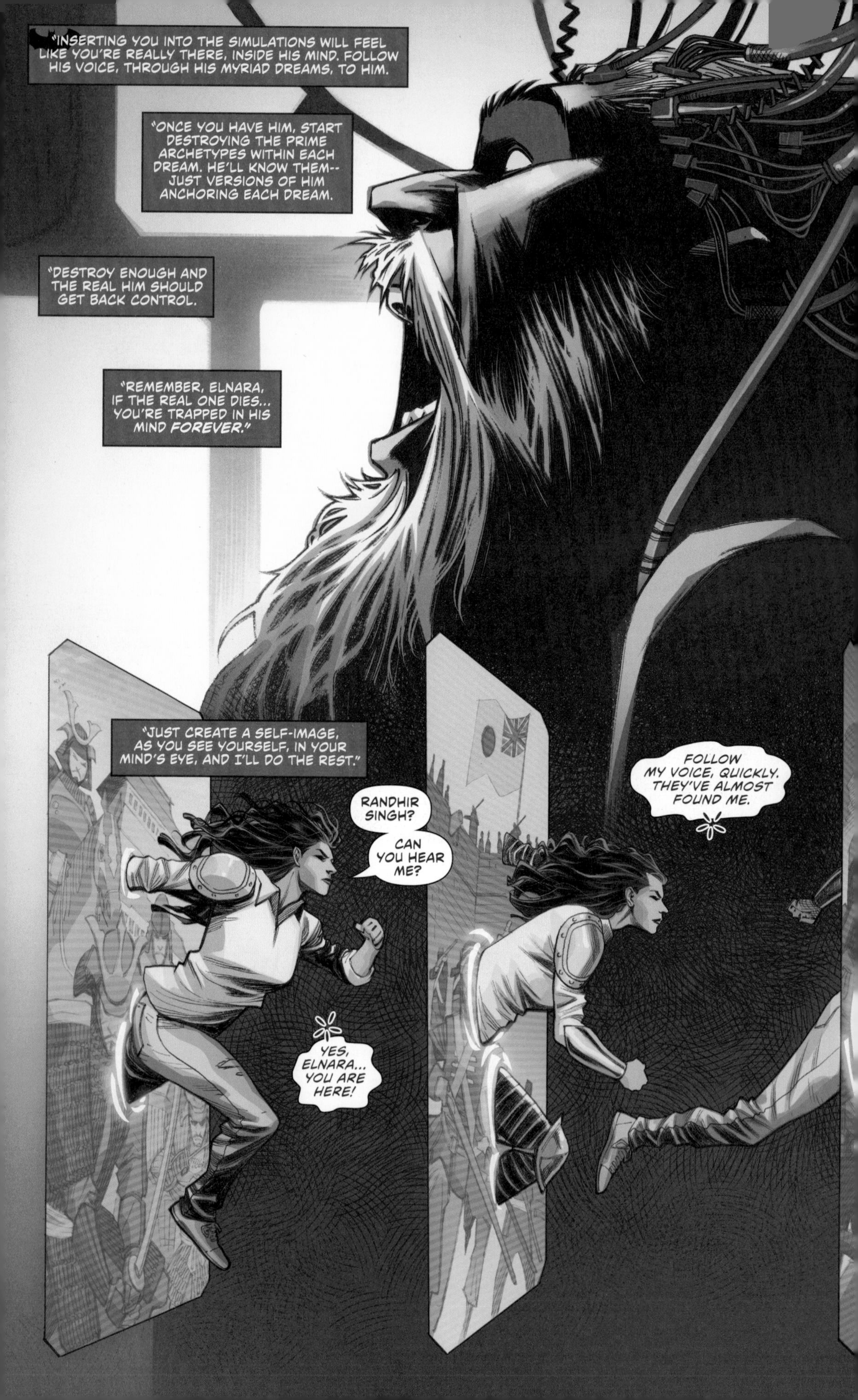
"INSERTING YOU INTO THE SIMULATIONS WILL FEEL LIKE YOU'RE REALLY THERE, INSIDE HIS MIND. FOLLOW HIS VOICE, THROUGH HIS MYRIAD DREAMS, TO HIM.
"ONCE YOU HAVE HIM, START DESTROYING THE PRIME ARCHETYPES WITHIN EACH DREAM. HE'LL KNOW THEM--JUST VERSIONS OF HIM ANCHORING EACH DREAM.
"DESTROY ENOUGH AND THE REAL HIM SHOULD GET BACK CONTROL.
"REMEMBER, ELNARA, IF THE REAL ONE DIES... YOU'RE TRAPPED IN HIS MIND *FOREVER*."
"JUST CREATE A SELF-IMAGE, AS YOU SEE YOURSELF, IN YOUR MIND'S EYE, AND I'LL DO THE REST."
RANDHIR SINGH?
CAN YOU HEAR ME?
YES, ELNARA... YOU ARE HERE!
FOLLOW MY VOICE, QUICKLY. THEY'VE ALMOST FOUND ME.

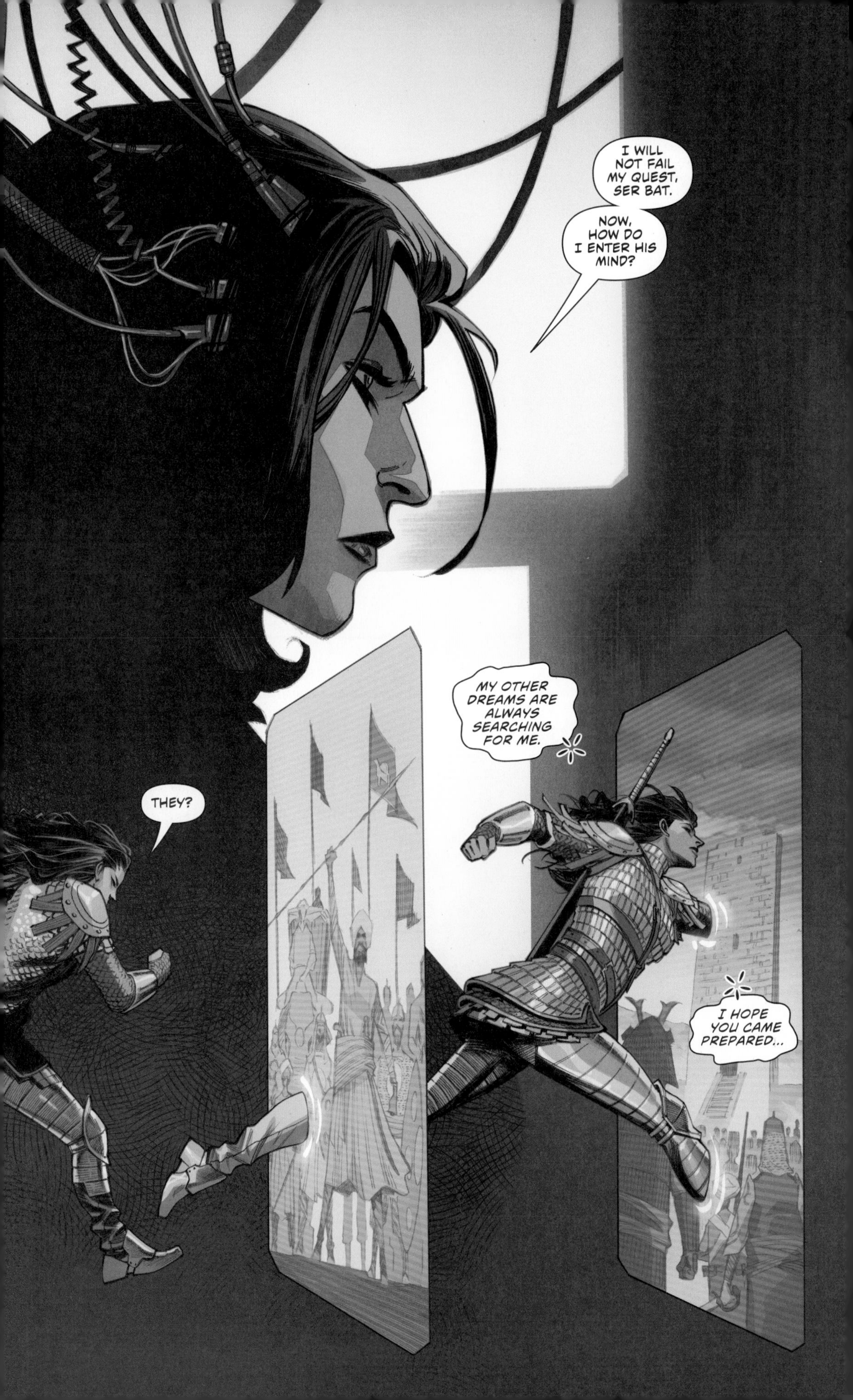
I WILL NOT FAIL MY QUEST, SER BAT.
NOW, HOW DO I ENTER HIS MIND?
THEY?
MY OTHER DREAMS ARE ALWAYS SEARCHING FOR ME.
I HOPE YOU CAME PREPARED...

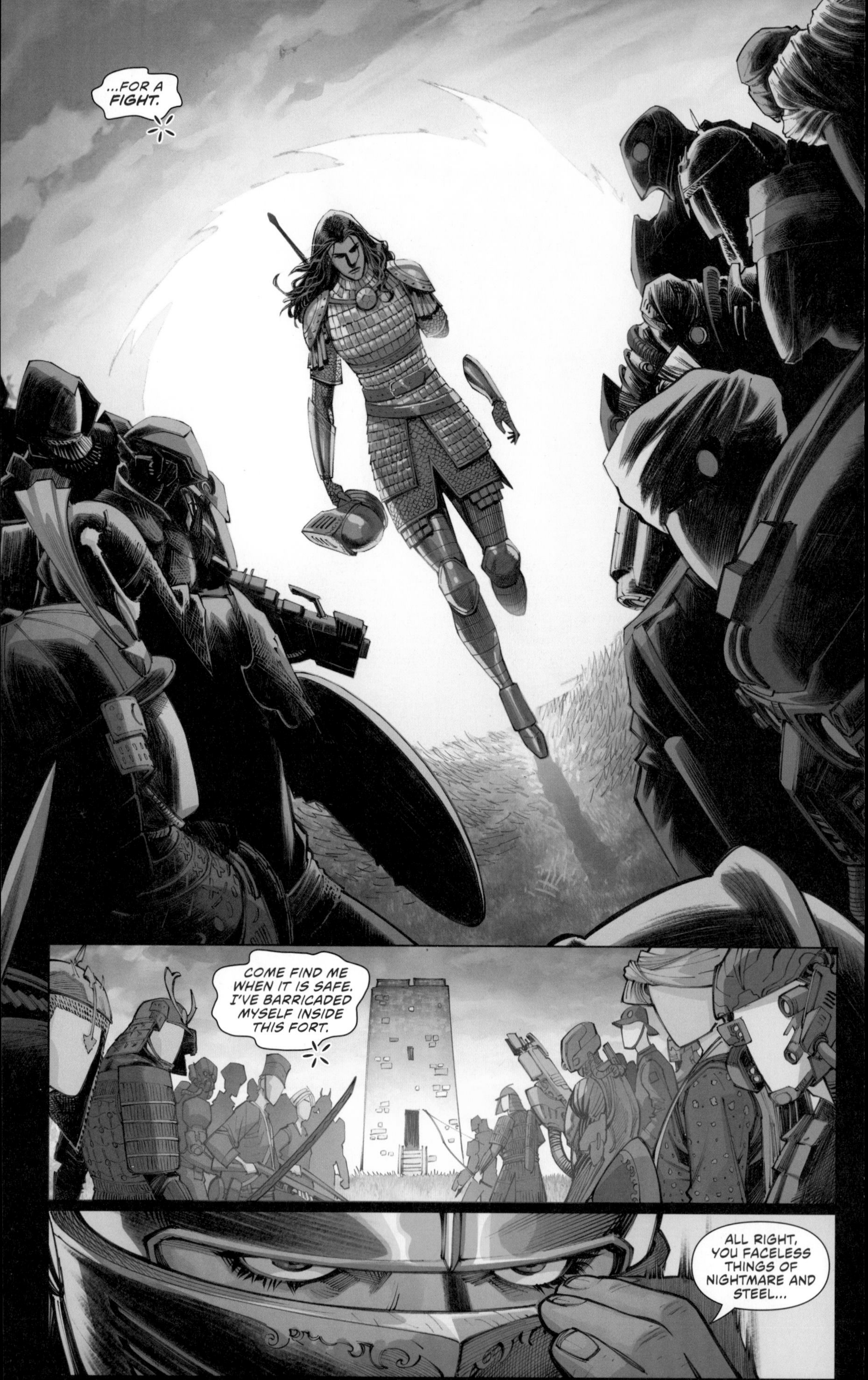
...FOR A FIGHT.
COME FIND ME WHEN IT IS SAFE. I'VE BARRICADED MYSELF INSIDE THIS FORT.
ALL RIGHT, YOU FACELESS THINGS OF NIGHTMARE AND STEEL...

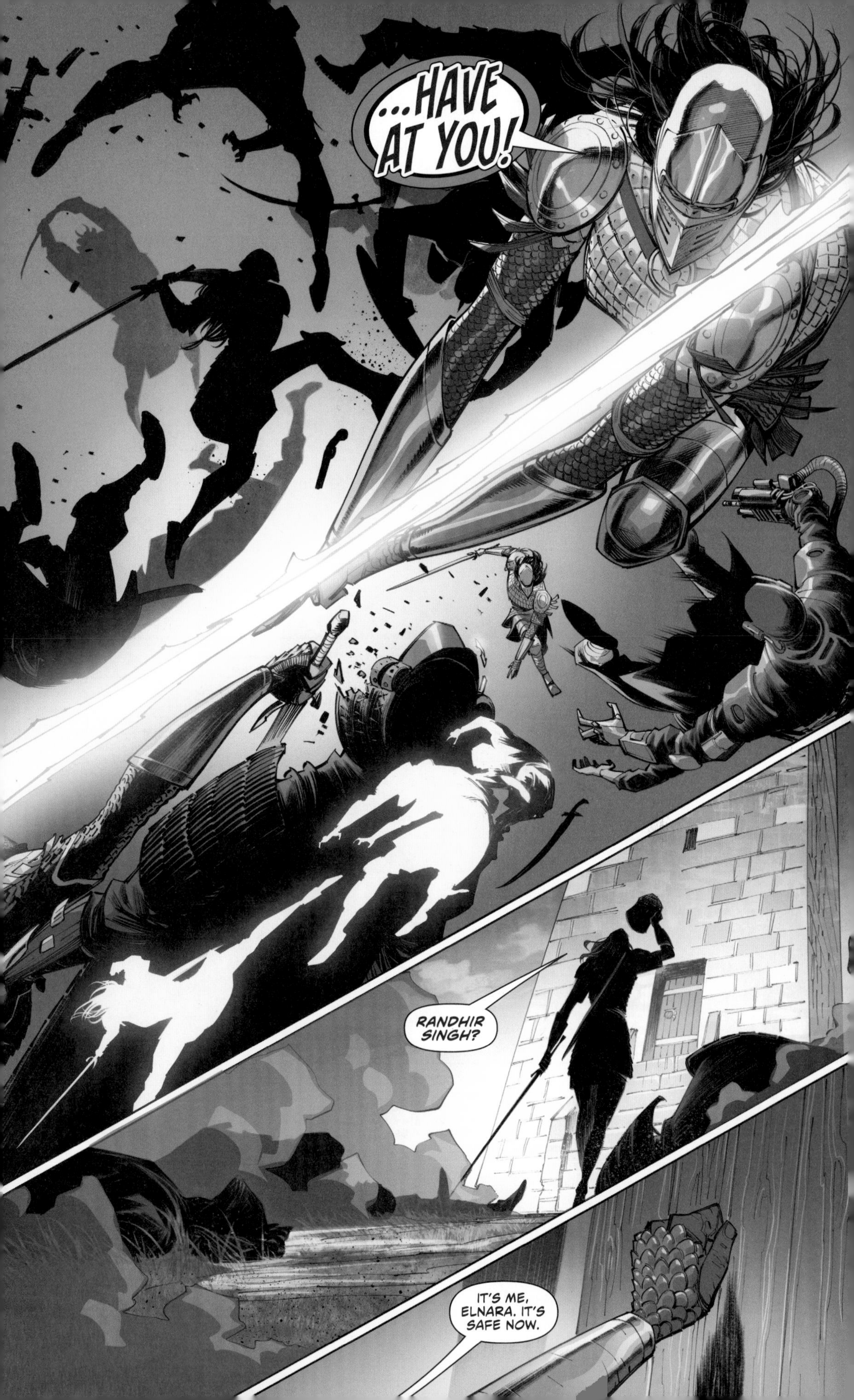
...HAVE AT YOU!
RANDHIR SINGH?
IT'S ME, ELNARA. IT'S SAFE NOW.

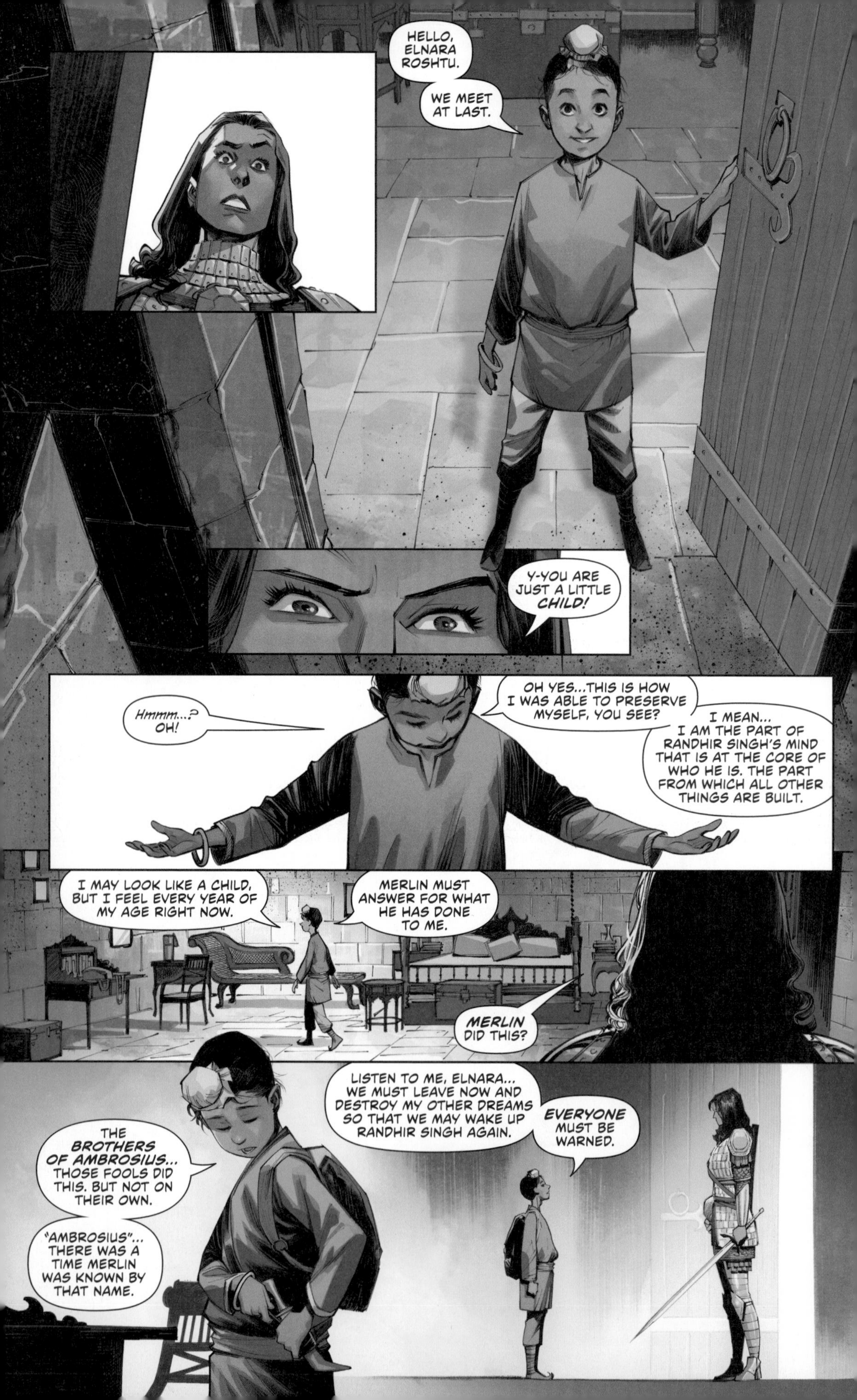
HELLO, ELNARA ROSHTU.
WE MEET AT LAST.
Y-YOU ARE JUST A LITTLE *CHILD!*
Hmmm...? OH!
OH YES...THIS IS HOW I WAS ABLE TO PRESERVE MYSELF, YOU SEE?
I MEAN... I AM THE PART OF RANDHIR SINGH'S MIND THAT IS AT THE CORE OF WHO HE IS. THE PART FROM WHICH ALL OTHER THINGS ARE BUILT.
I MAY LOOK LIKE A CHILD, BUT I FEEL EVERY YEAR OF MY AGE RIGHT NOW.
MERLIN MUST ANSWER FOR WHAT HE HAS DONE TO ME.
MERLIN DID THIS?
THE *BROTHERS OF AMBROSIUS...* THOSE FOOLS DID THIS. BUT NOT ON THEIR OWN.
"AMBROSIUS"... THERE WAS A TIME MERLIN WAS KNOWN BY THAT NAME.
LISTEN TO ME, ELNARA... WE MUST LEAVE NOW AND DESTROY MY OTHER DREAMS SO THAT WE MAY WAKE UP RANDHIR SINGH AGAIN.
EVERYONE MUST BE WARNED.

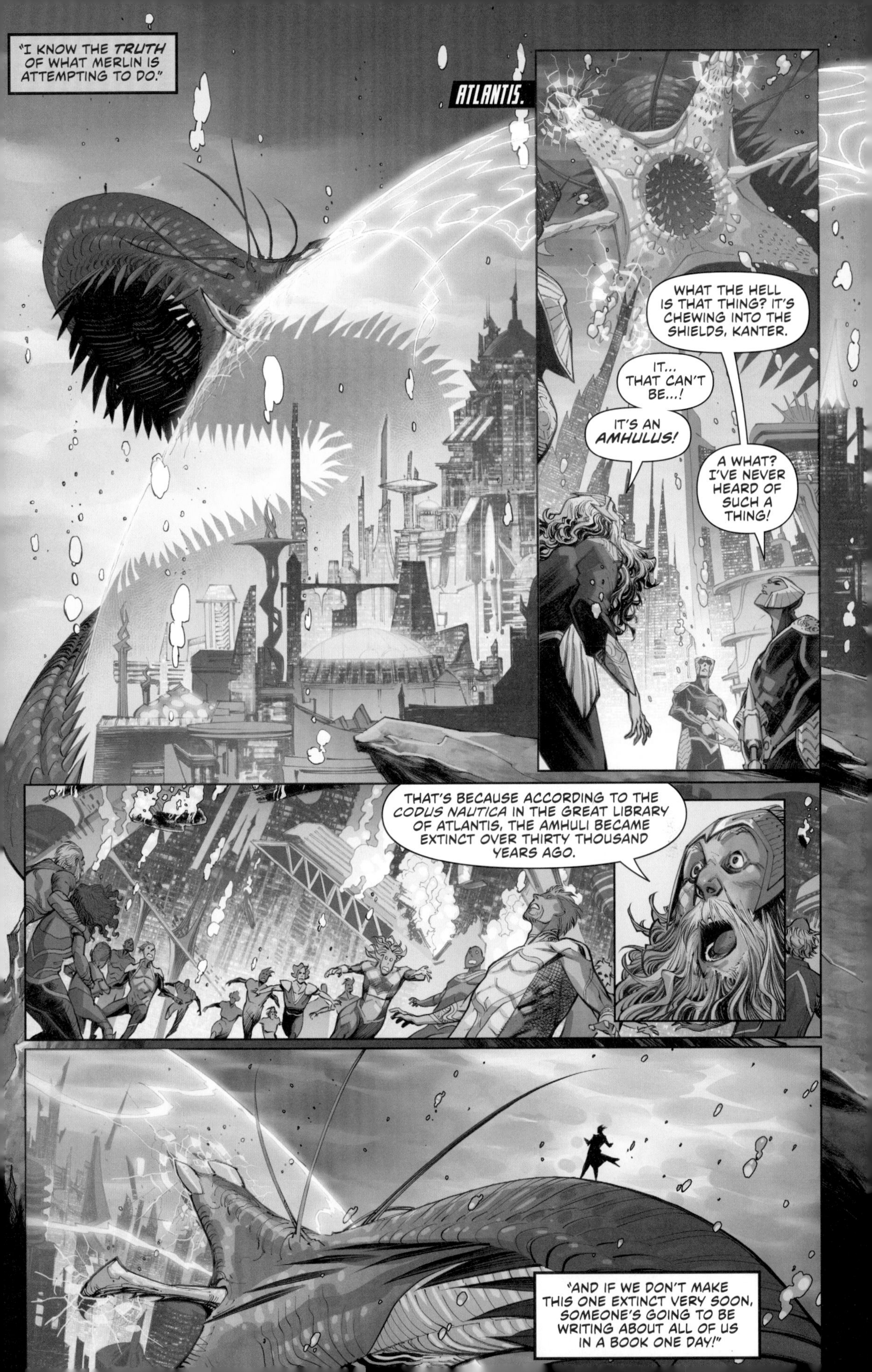
"I KNOW THE TRUTH OF WHAT MERLIN IS ATTEMPTING TO DO."
ATLANTIS.
WHAT THE HELL IS THAT THING? IT'S CHEWING INTO THE SHIELDS, KANTER.
IT... THAT CAN'T BE...!
IT'S AN AMHULUS!
A WHAT? I'VE NEVER HEARD OF SUCH A THING!
THAT'S BECAUSE ACCORDING TO THE CODUS NAUTICA IN THE GREAT LIBRARY OF ATLANTIS, THE AMHULI BECAME EXTINCT OVER THIRTY THOUSAND YEARS AGO.
"AND IF WE DON'T MAKE THIS ONE EXTINCT VERY SOON, SOMEONE'S GOING TO BE WRITING ABOUT ALL OF US IN A BOOK ONE DAY!"

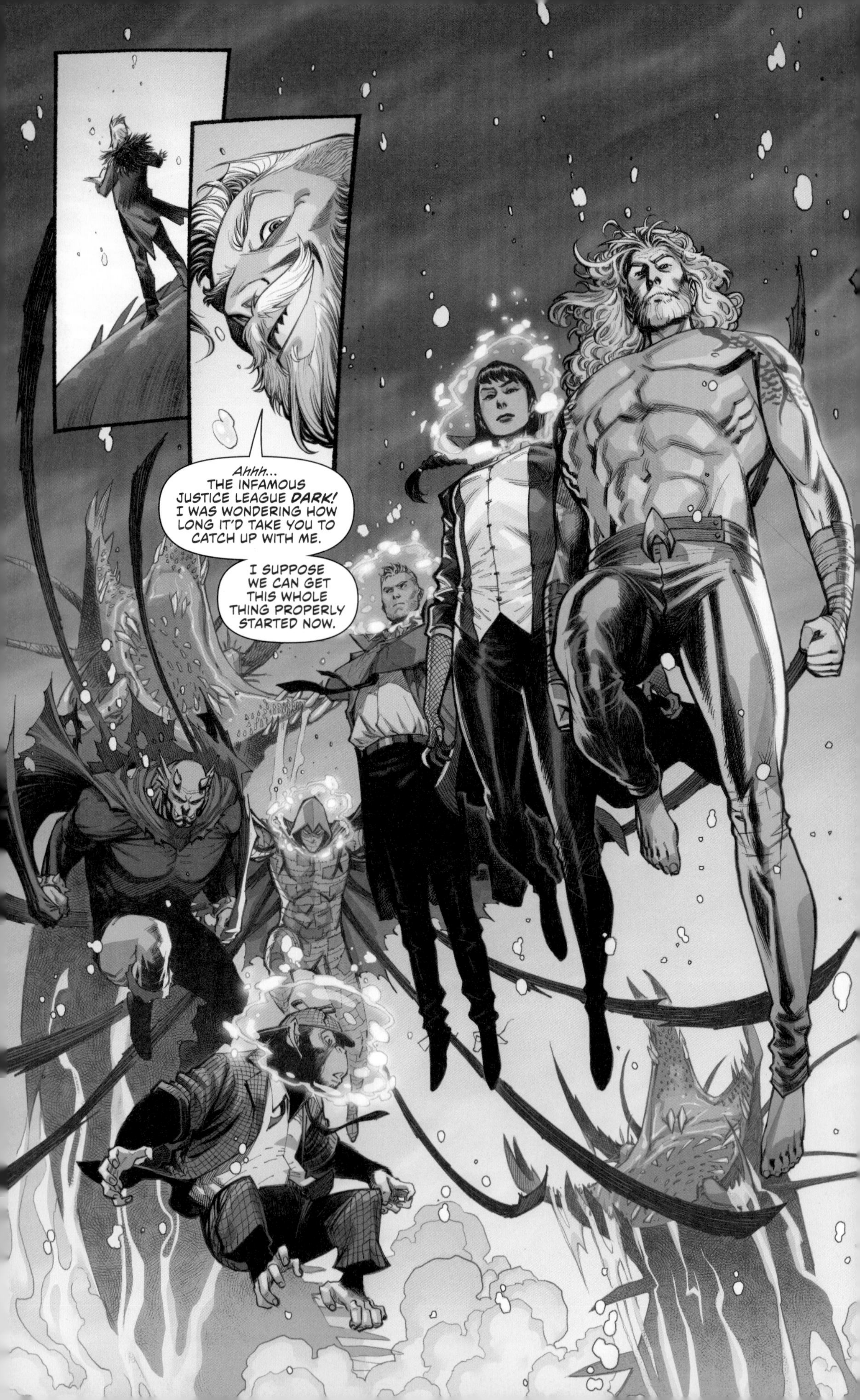

Ahhh... THE INFAMOUS JUSTICE LEAGUE **DARK!** I WAS WONDERING HOW LONG IT'D TAKE YOU TO CATCH UP WITH ME.
I SUPPOSE WE CAN GET THIS WHOLE THING PROPERLY STARTED NOW.

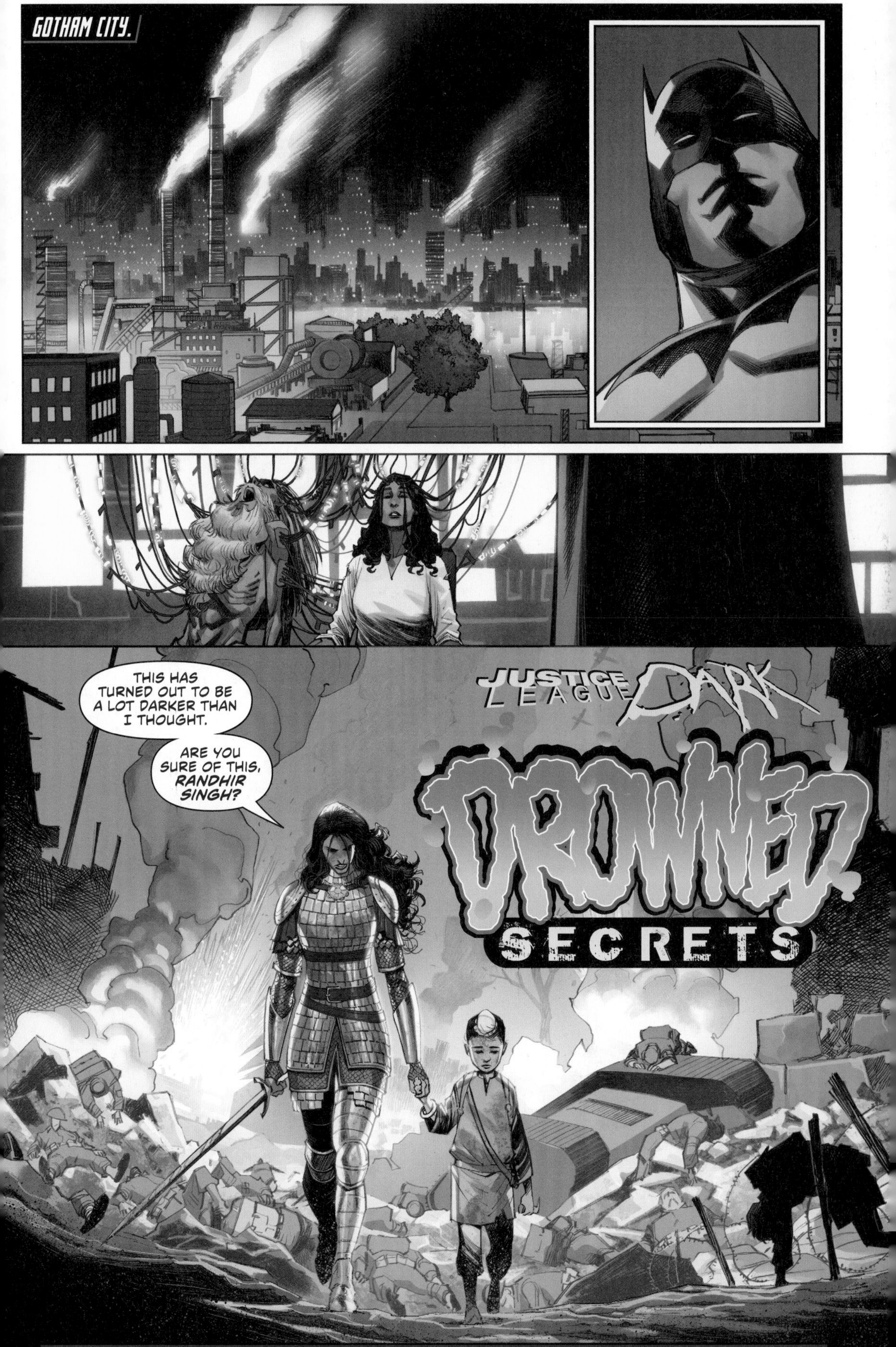
GOTHAM CITY.
THIS HAS TURNED OUT TO BE A LOT DARKER THAN I THOUGHT.
ARE YOU SURE OF THIS, RANDHIR SINGH?
JUSTICE LEAGUE DARK
DROWNED SECRETS

RAM V *Writer* | **SUMIT KUMAR** *Artist* | **ROMULO FAJARDO JR.** *Colorist* | **ROB LEIGH** *Letterer* | **BRITTANY HOLZHERR** *Editor*

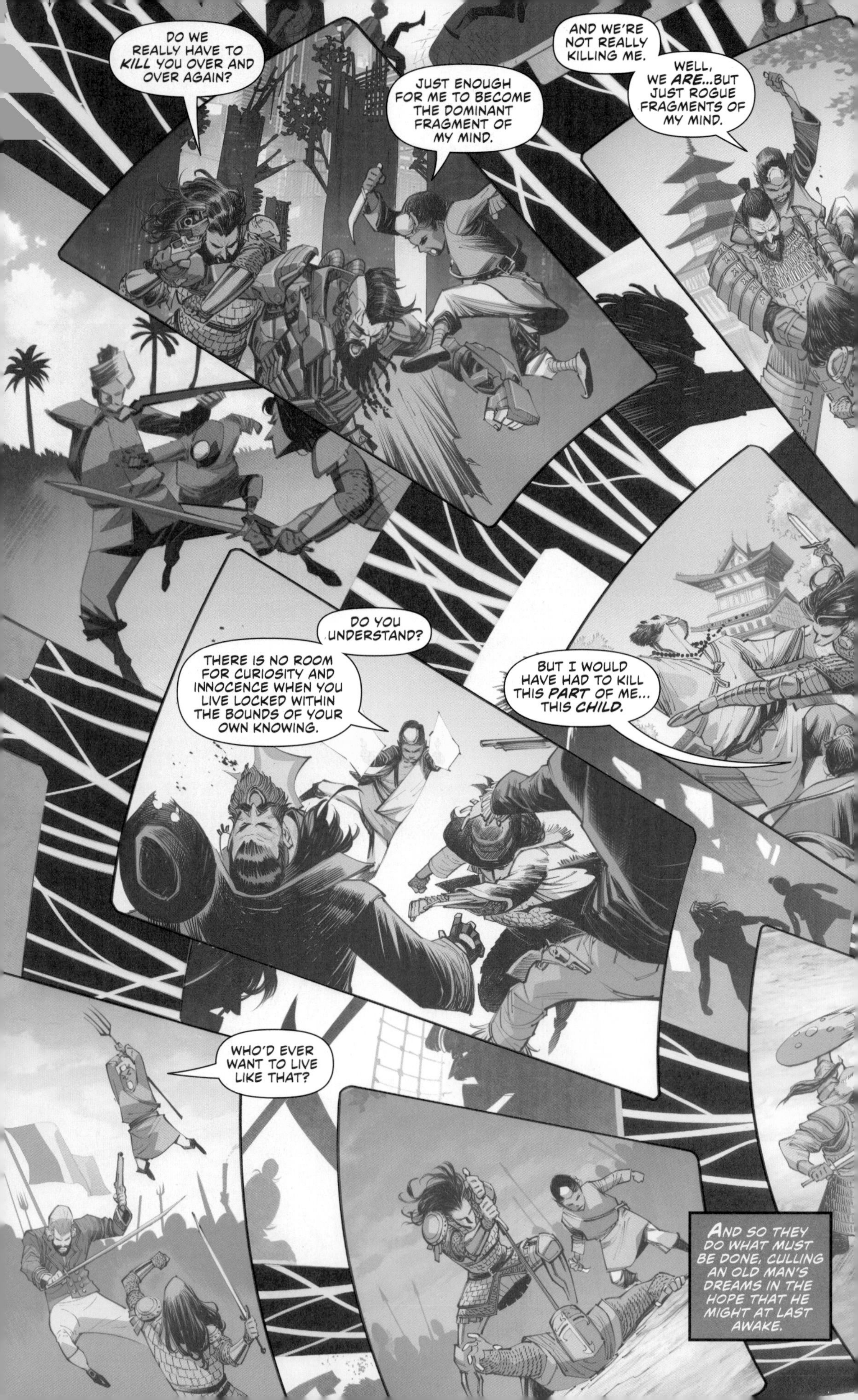
DO WE REALLY HAVE TO KILL YOU OVER AND OVER AGAIN?
JUST ENOUGH FOR ME TO BECOME THE DOMINANT FRAGMENT OF MY MIND.
AND WE'RE NOT REALLY KILLING ME.
WELL, WE ARE...BUT JUST ROGUE FRAGMENTS OF MY MIND.
DO YOU UNDERSTAND?
THERE IS NO ROOM FOR CURIOSITY AND INNOCENCE WHEN YOU LIVE LOCKED WITHIN THE BOUNDS OF YOUR OWN KNOWING.
BUT I WOULD HAVE HAD TO KILL THIS PART OF ME... THIS CHILD.
WHO'D EVER WANT TO LIVE LIKE THAT?
AND SO THEY DO WHAT MUST BE DONE, CULLING AN OLD MAN'S DREAMS IN THE HOPE THAT HE MIGHT AT LAST AWAKE.

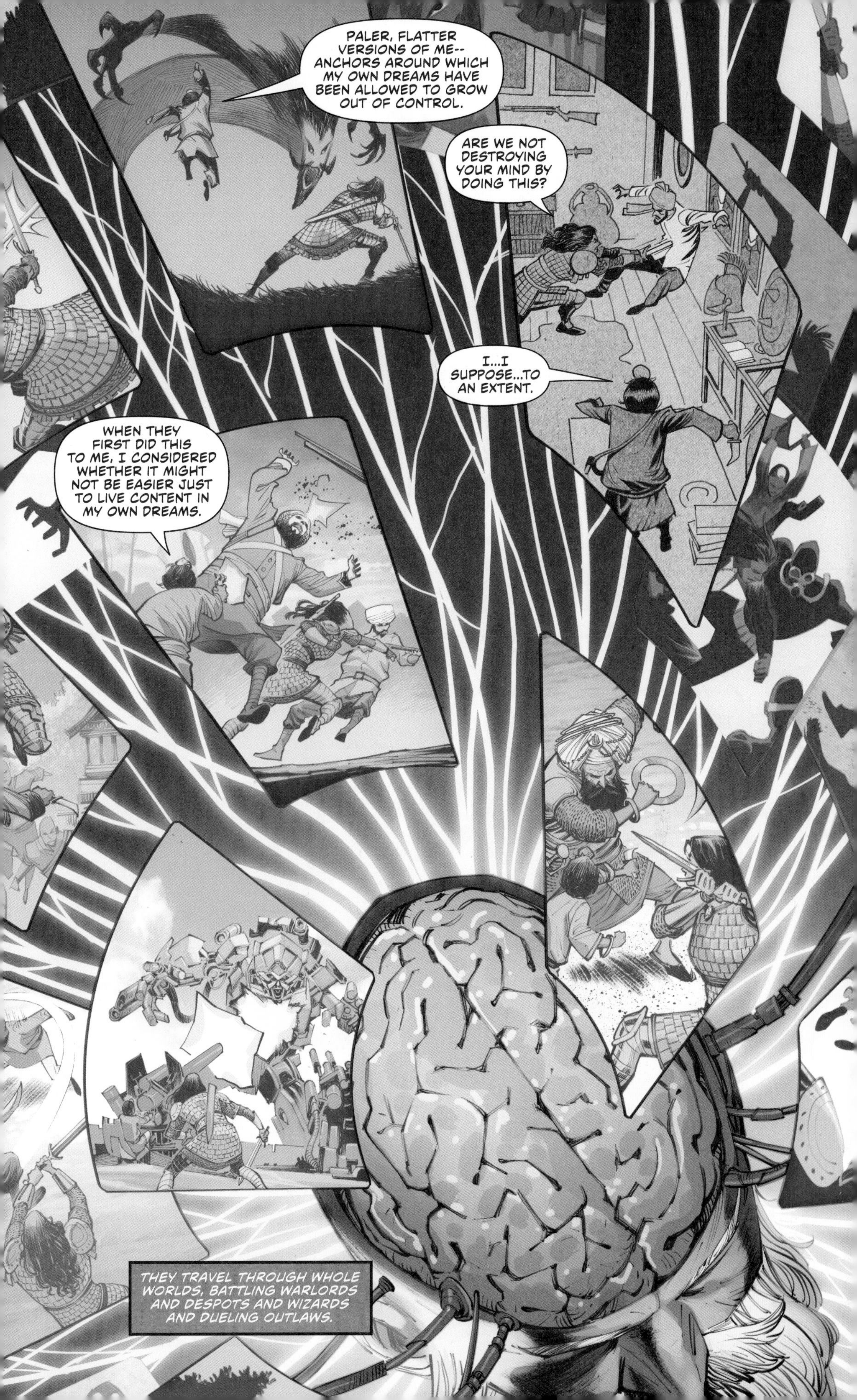
PALER, FLATTER VERSIONS OF ME-- ANCHORS AROUND WHICH MY OWN DREAMS HAVE BEEN ALLOWED TO GROW OUT OF CONTROL.
ARE WE NOT DESTROYING YOUR MIND BY DOING THIS?
I...I SUPPOSE...TO AN EXTENT.
WHEN THEY FIRST DID THIS TO ME, I CONSIDERED WHETHER IT MIGHT NOT BE EASIER JUST TO LIVE CONTENT IN MY OWN DREAMS.
THEY TRAVEL THROUGH WHOLE WORLDS, BATTLING WARLORDS AND DESPOTS AND WIZARDS AND DUELING OUTLAWS.

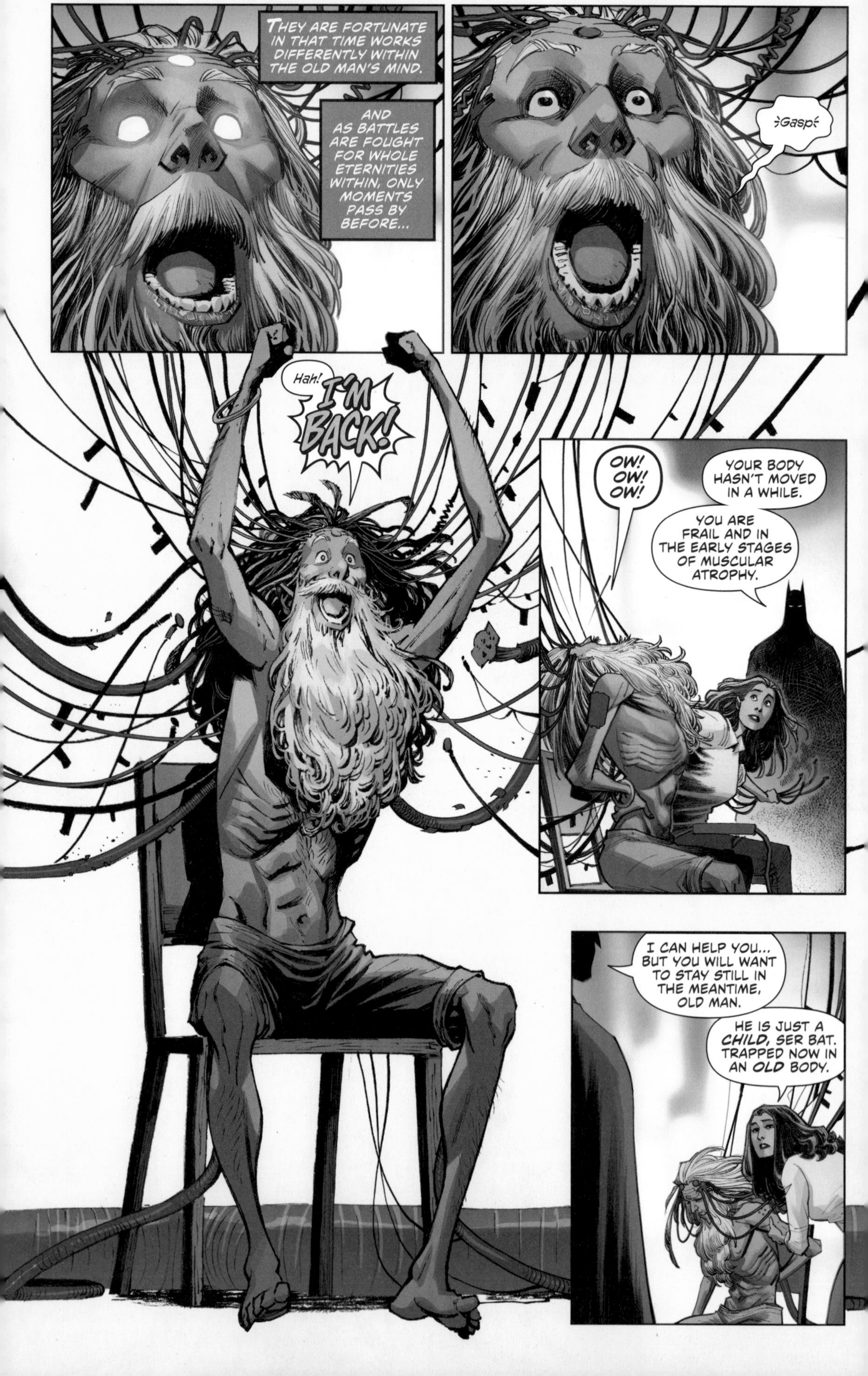

THEY ARE FORTUNATE IN THAT TIME WORKS DIFFERENTLY WITHIN THE OLD MAN'S MIND.
AND AS BATTLES ARE FOUGHT FOR WHOLE ETERNITIES WITHIN, ONLY MOMENTS PASS BY BEFORE...
Gasp
Hah!
I'M BACK!
OW! OW! OW!
YOUR BODY HASN'T MOVED IN A WHILE.
YOU ARE FRAIL AND IN THE EARLY STAGES OF MUSCULAR ATROPHY.
I CAN HELP YOU... BUT YOU WILL WANT TO STAY STILL IN THE MEANTIME, OLD MAN.
HE IS JUST A CHILD, SER BAT. TRAPPED NOW IN AN OLD BODY.

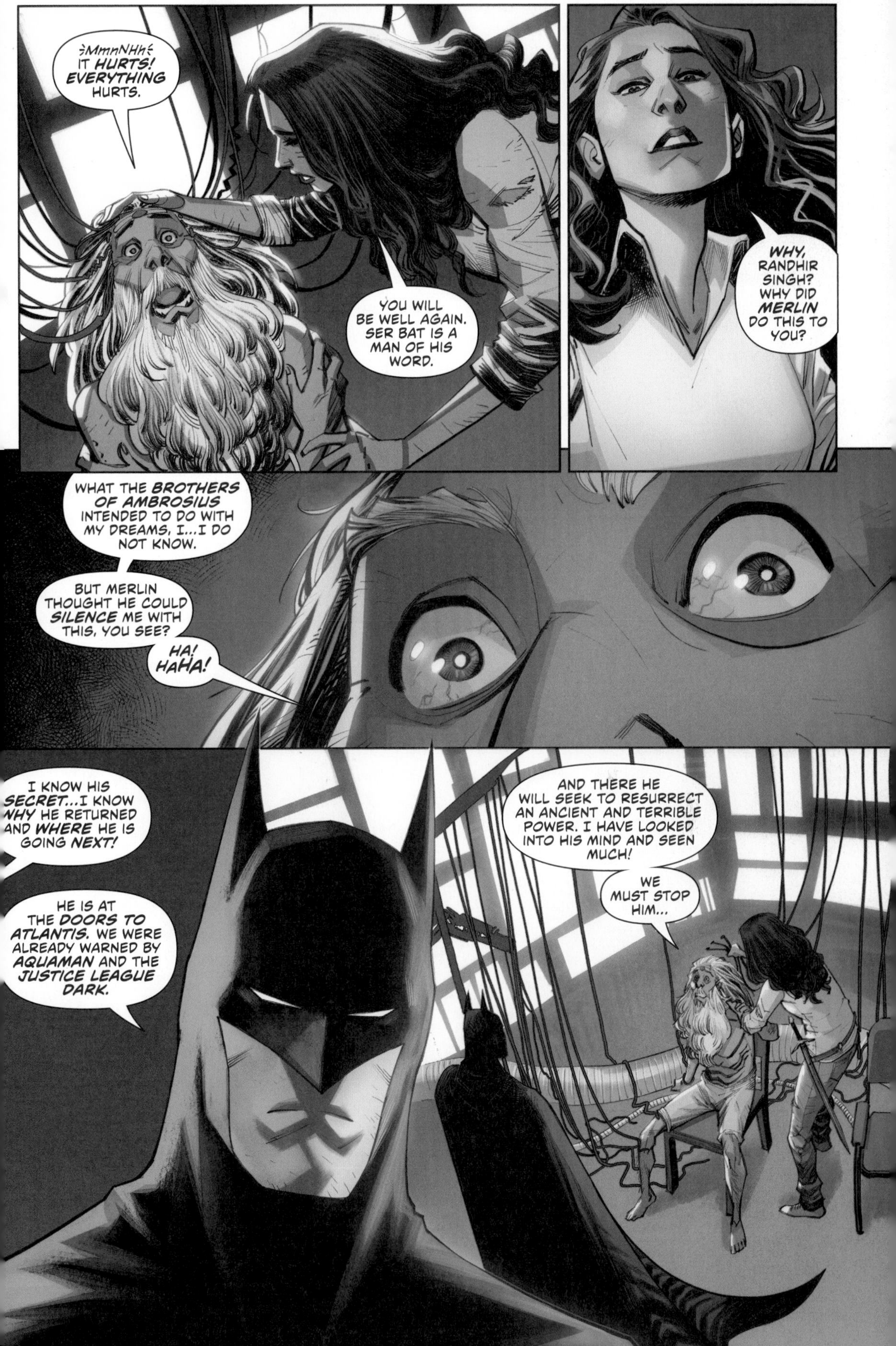
MmmNHh IT HURTS! EVERYTHING HURTS.
YOU WILL BE WELL AGAIN. SER BAT IS A MAN OF HIS WORD.
WHY, RANDHIR SINGH? WHY DID MERLIN DO THIS TO YOU?
WHAT THE BROTHERS OF AMBROSIUS INTENDED TO DO WITH MY DREAMS, I...I DO NOT KNOW.
BUT MERLIN THOUGHT HE COULD SILENCE ME WITH THIS, YOU SEE?
HA! HAHA!
I KNOW HIS SECRET...I KNOW WHY HE RETURNED AND WHERE HE IS GOING NEXT!
AND THERE HE WILL SEEK TO RESURRECT AN ANCIENT AND TERRIBLE POWER. I HAVE LOOKED INTO HIS MIND AND SEEN MUCH!
WE MUST STOP HIM...
HE IS AT THE DOORS TO ATLANTIS. WE WERE ALREADY WARNED BY AQUAMAN AND THE JUSTICE LEAGUE DARK.

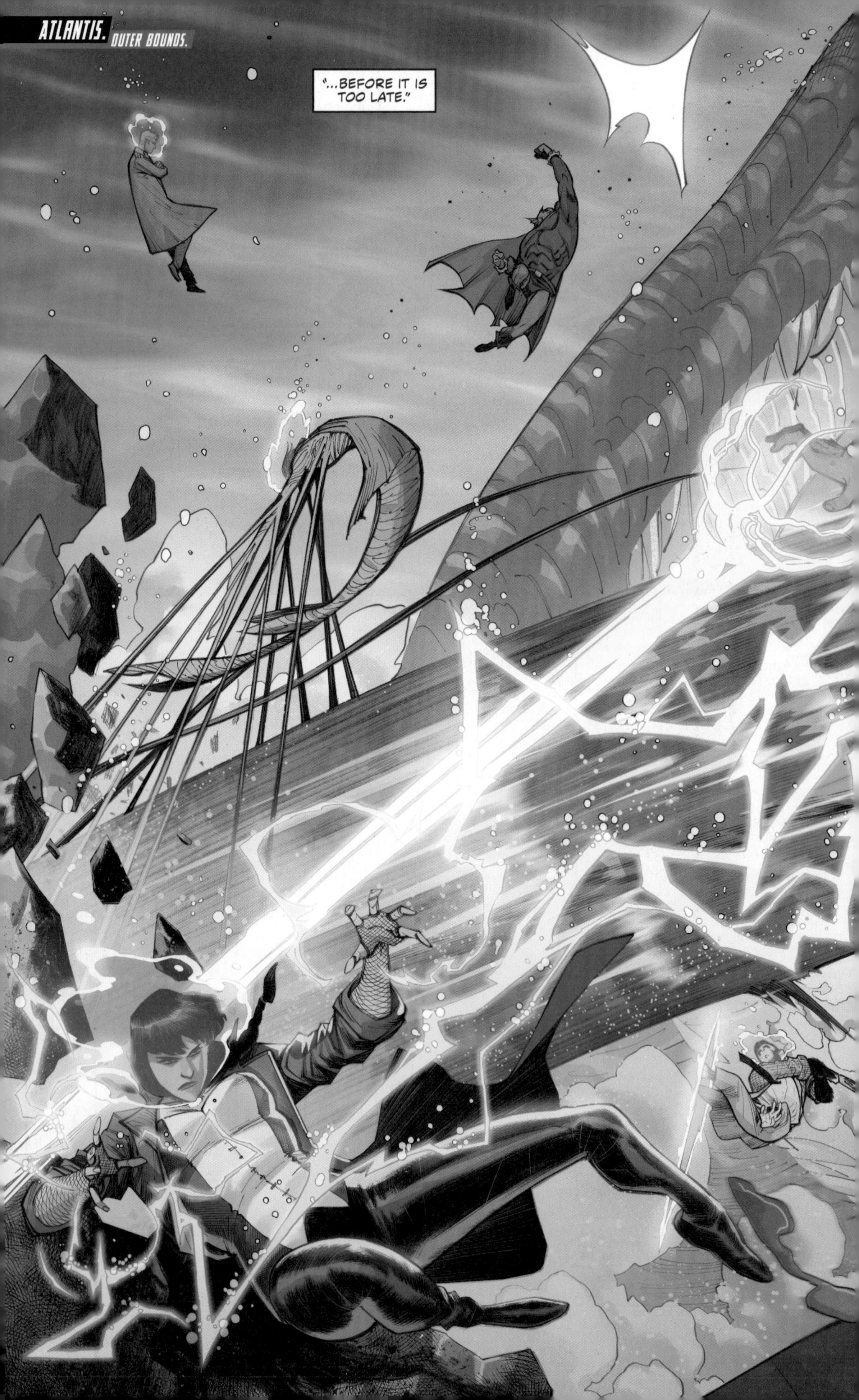
ATLANTIS. OUTER BOUNDS.
"...BEFORE IT IS TOO LATE."

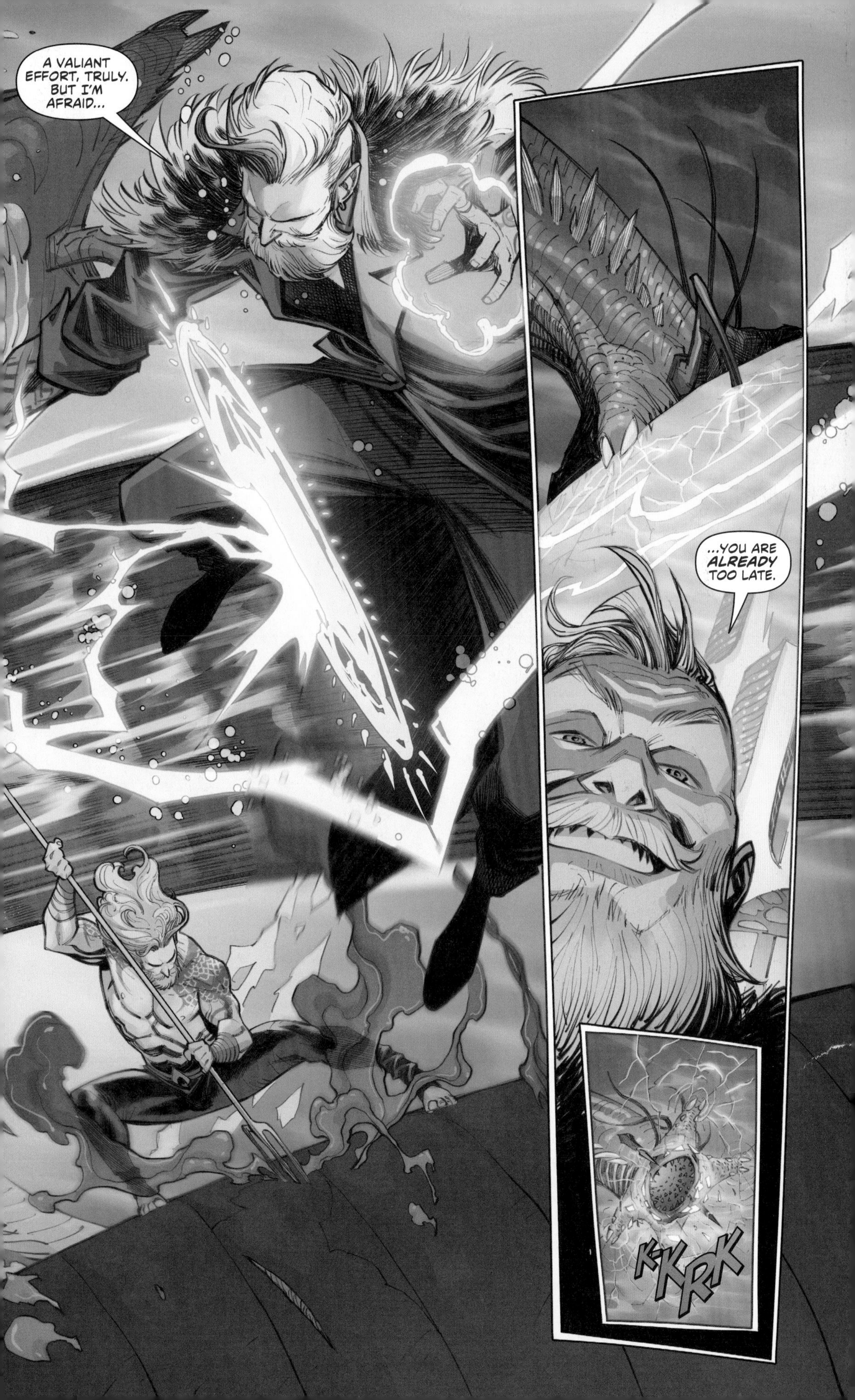
A VALIANT EFFORT, TRULY. BUT I'M AFRAID...
...YOU ARE ALREADY TOO LATE.
KKRK

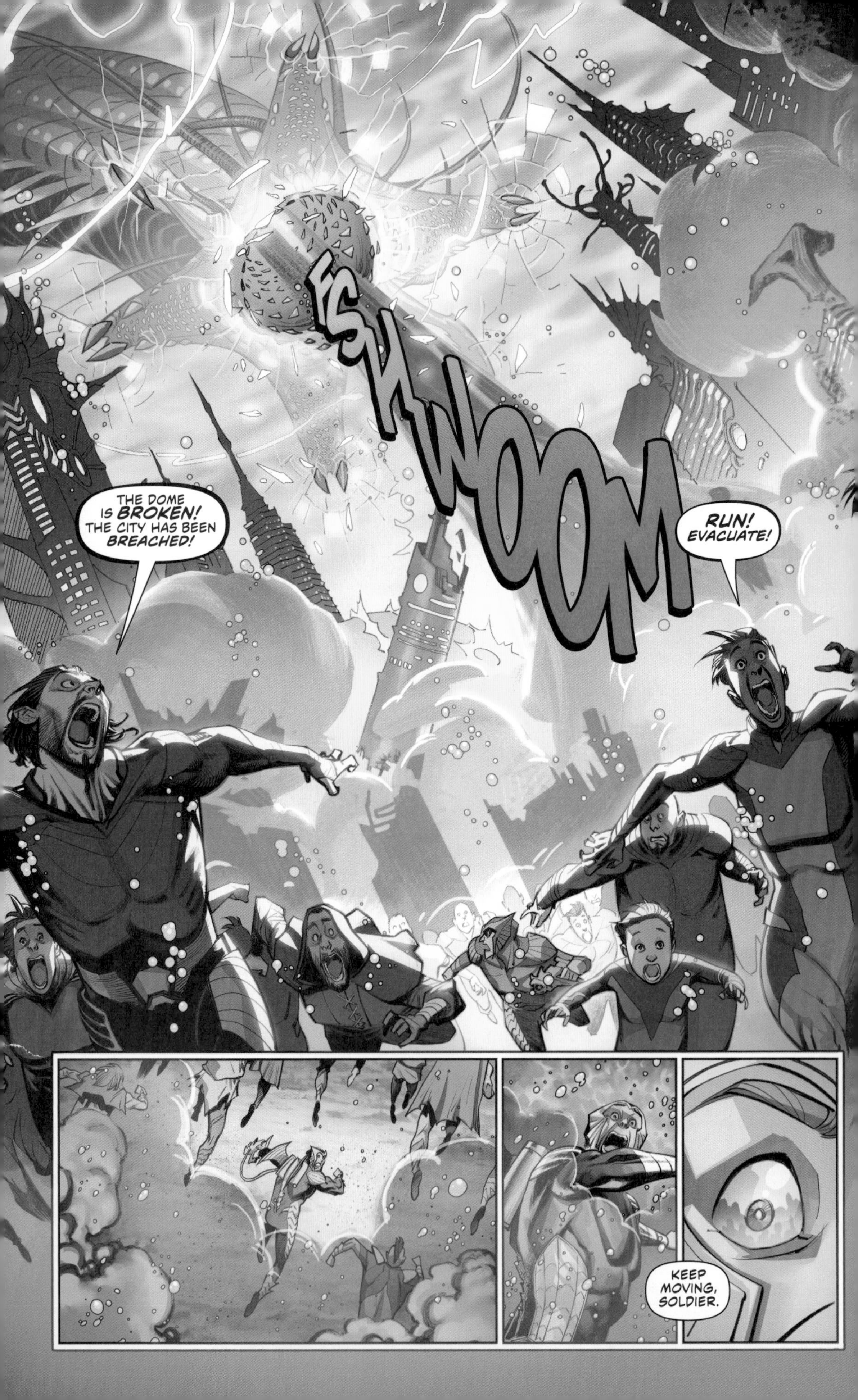
FSHWOOM
THE DOME IS BROKEN! THE CITY HAS BEEN BREACHED!
RUN! EVACUATE!
KEEP MOVING, SOLDIER.

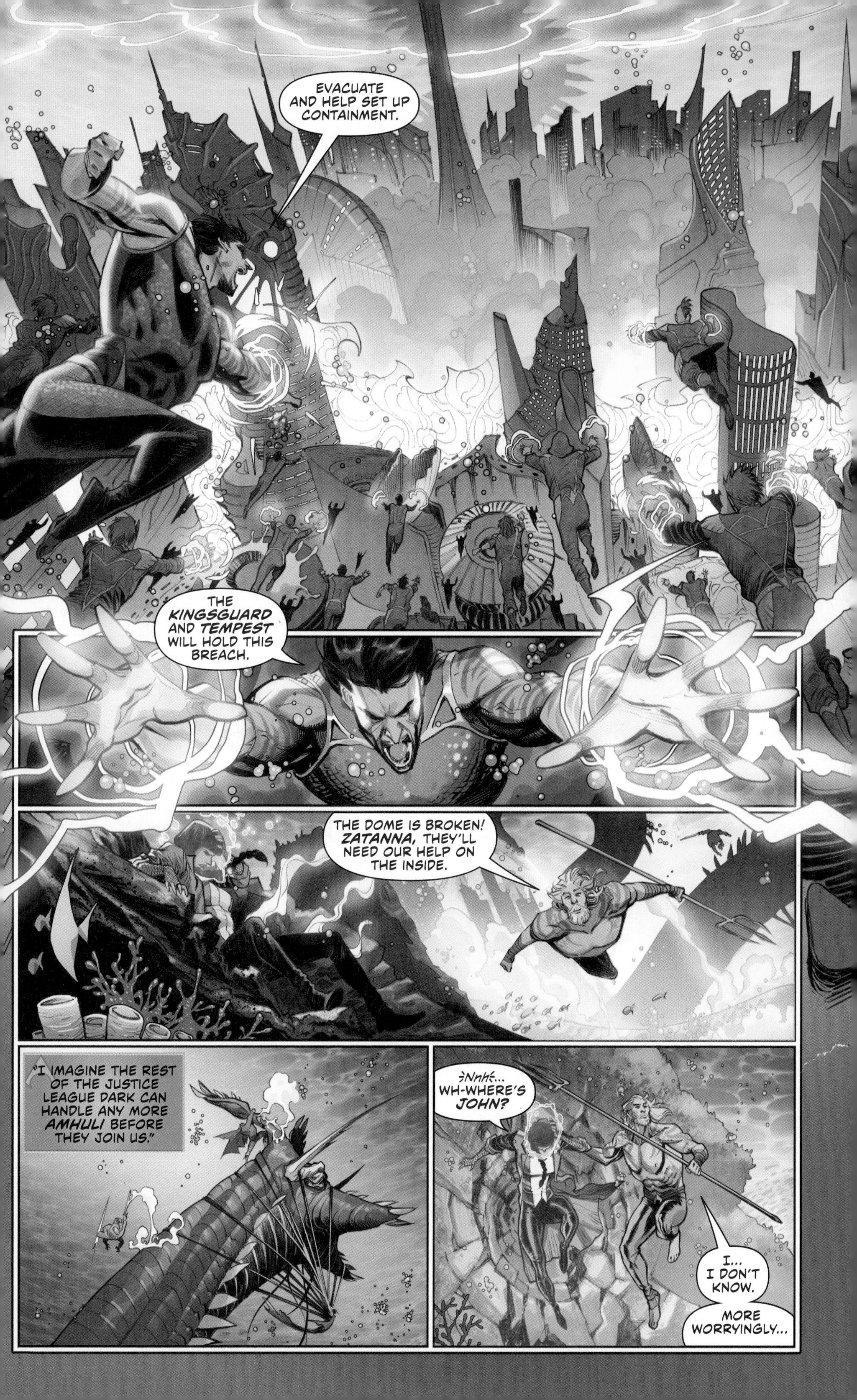
EVACUATE AND HELP SET UP CONTAINMENT.
THE KINGSGUARD AND TEMPEST WILL HOLD THIS BREACH.
THE DOME IS BROKEN! ZATANNA, THEY'LL NEED OUR HELP ON THE INSIDE.
"I IMAGINE THE REST OF THE JUSTICE LEAGUE DARK CAN HANDLE ANY MORE AMHULI BEFORE THEY JOIN US."
Nnh... WH-WHERE'S JOHN?
I... I DON'T KNOW.
MORE WORRYINGLY...

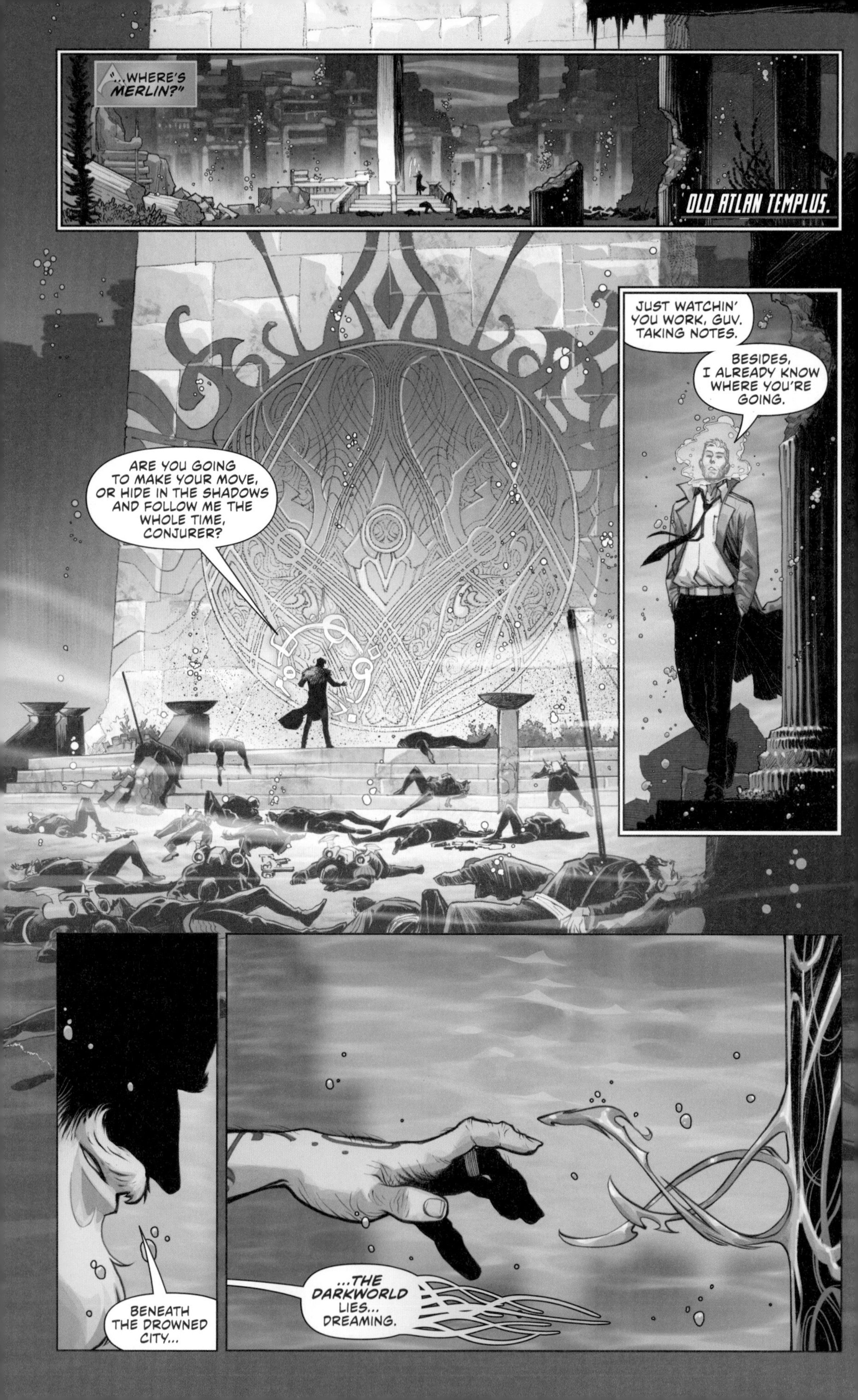
"...WHERE'S MERLIN?"
OLD ATLAN TEMPLUS.
ARE YOU GOING TO MAKE YOUR MOVE, OR HIDE IN THE SHADOWS AND FOLLOW ME THE WHOLE TIME, CONJURER?
JUST WATCHIN' YOU WORK, GUV. TAKING NOTES.
BESIDES, I ALREADY KNOW WHERE YOU'RE GOING.
BENEATH THE DROWNED CITY...
...THE DARKWORLD LIES... DREAMING.

"...Consciousness was manifested, perhaps, in shapes and forms long since withdrawn before the tide of advancing humanity... forms of which poetry and legend alone have caught a flying memory and called them gods, monsters, mythical beings..."

—*Algernon Blackwood*

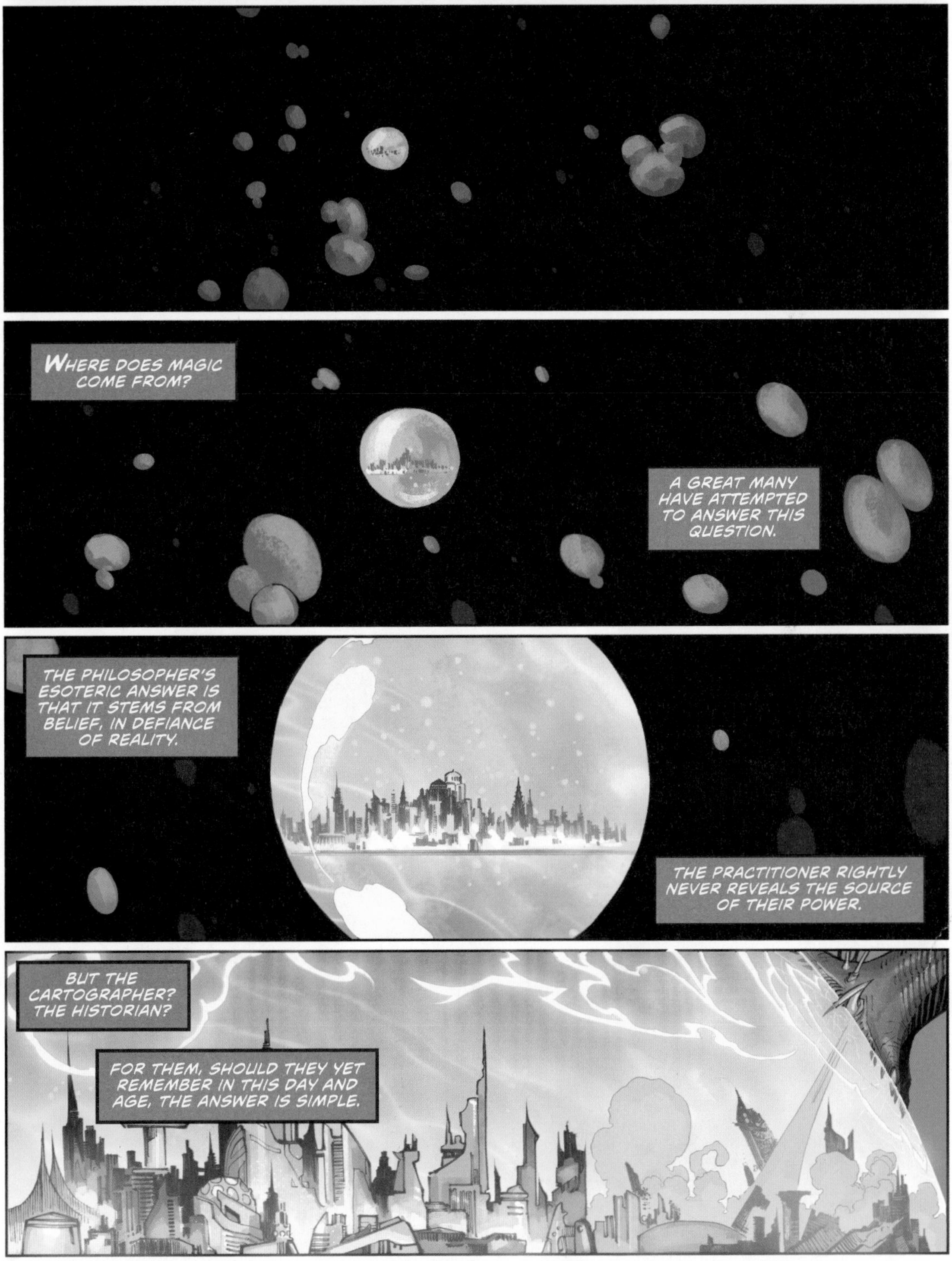
WHERE DOES MAGIC COME FROM?
A GREAT MANY HAVE ATTEMPTED TO ANSWER THIS QUESTION.
THE PHILOSOPHER'S ESOTERIC ANSWER IS THAT IT STEMS FROM BELIEF, IN DEFIANCE OF REALITY.
THE PRACTITIONER RIGHTLY NEVER REVEALS THE SOURCE OF THEIR POWER.
BUT THE CARTOGRAPHER? THE HISTORIAN?
FOR THEM, SHOULD THEY YET REMEMBER IN THIS DAY AND AGE, THE ANSWER IS SIMPLE.

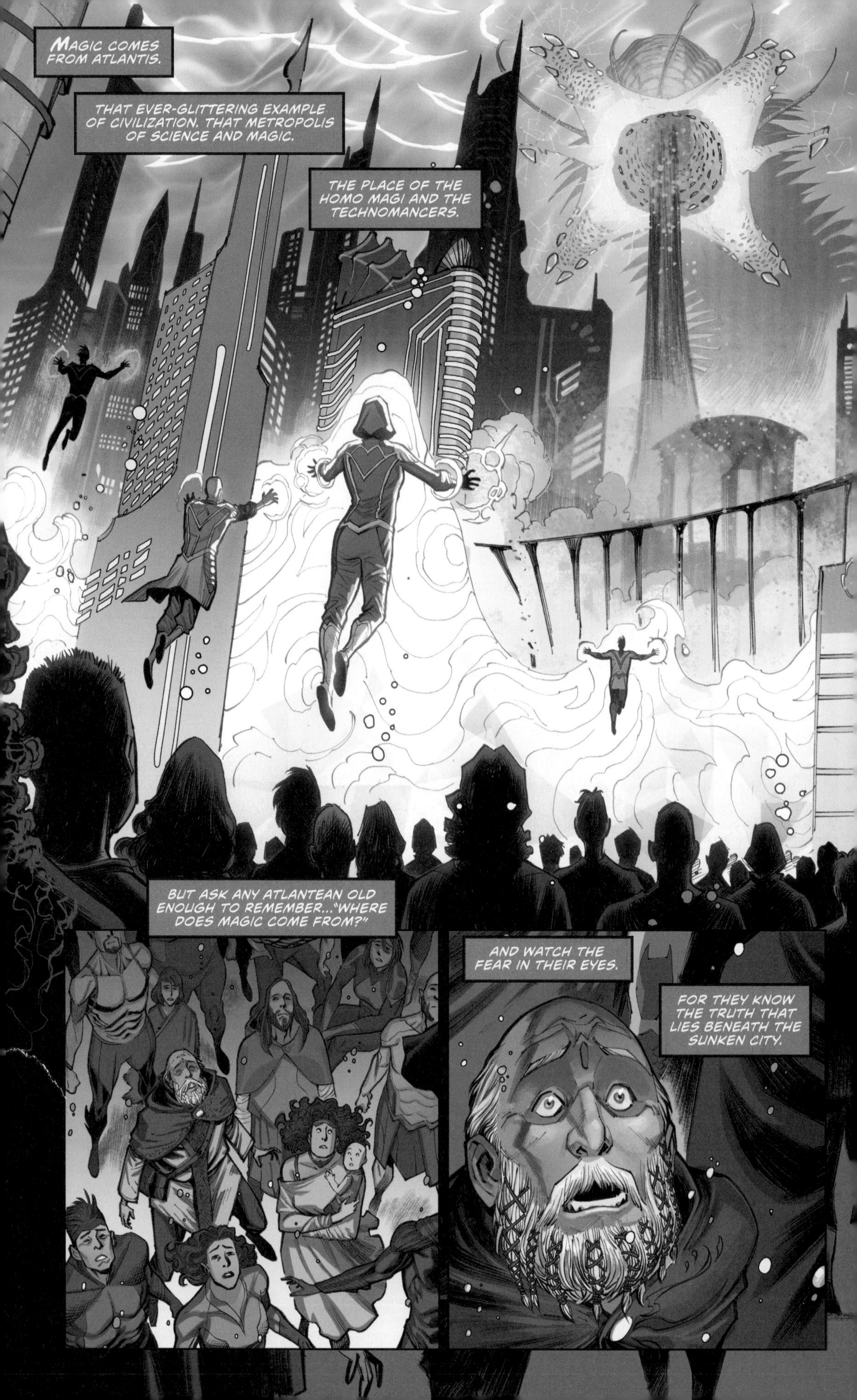
MAGIC COMES FROM ATLANTIS.
THAT EVER-GLITTERING EXAMPLE OF CIVILIZATION. THAT METROPOLIS OF SCIENCE AND MAGIC.
THE PLACE OF THE HOMO MAGI AND THE TECHNOMANCERS.
BUT ASK ANY ATLANTEAN OLD ENOUGH TO REMEMBER..."WHERE DOES MAGIC COME FROM?"
AND WATCH THE FEAR IN THEIR EYES.
FOR THEY KNOW THE TRUTH THAT LIES BENEATH THE SUNKEN CITY.

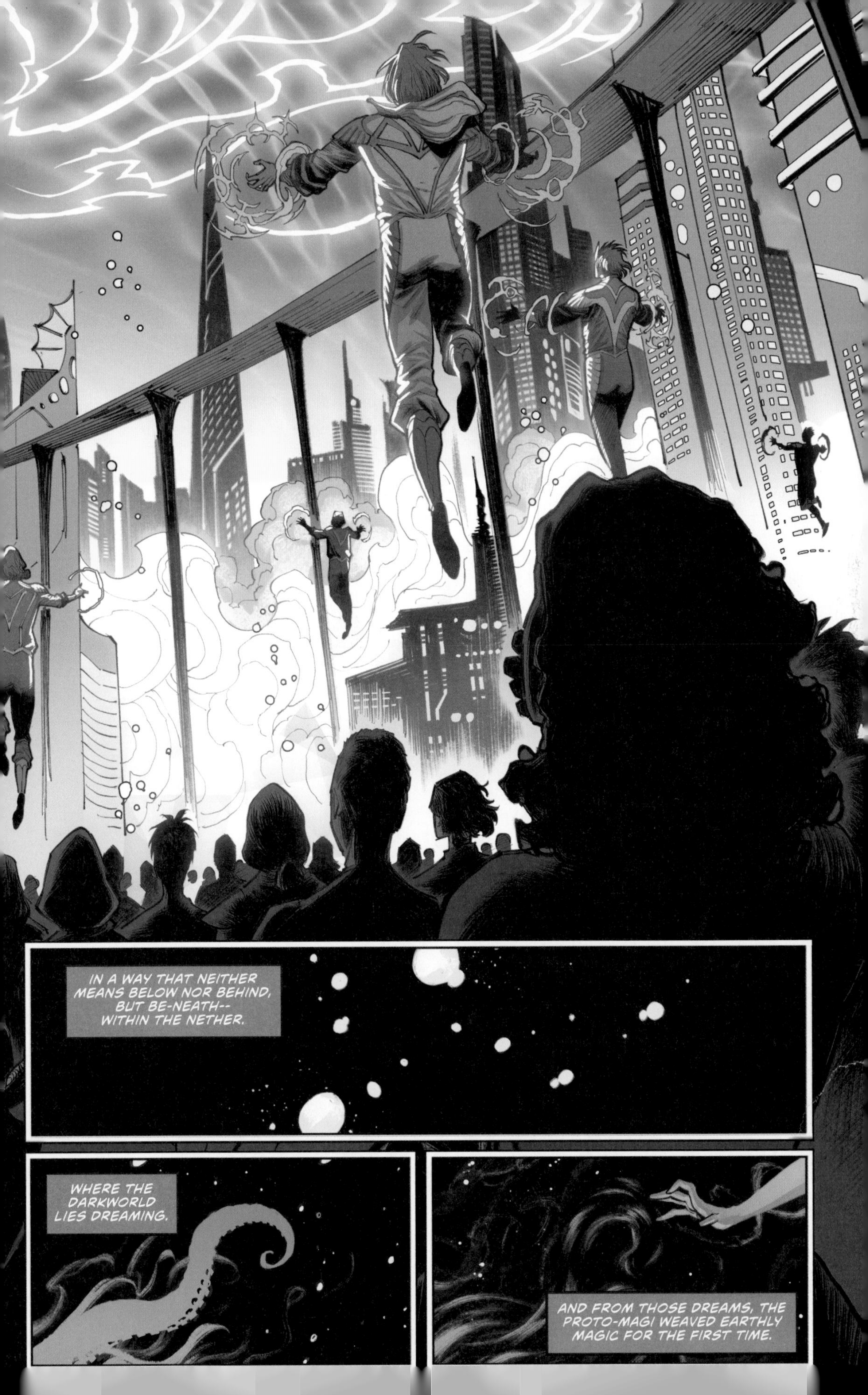
IN A WAY THAT NEITHER MEANS BELOW NOR BEHIND, BUT BE-NEATH-- WITHIN THE NETHER.
WHERE THE DARKWORLD LIES DREAMING.
AND FROM THOSE DREAMS, THE PROTO-MAGI WEAVED EARTHLY MAGIC FOR THE FIRST TIME.

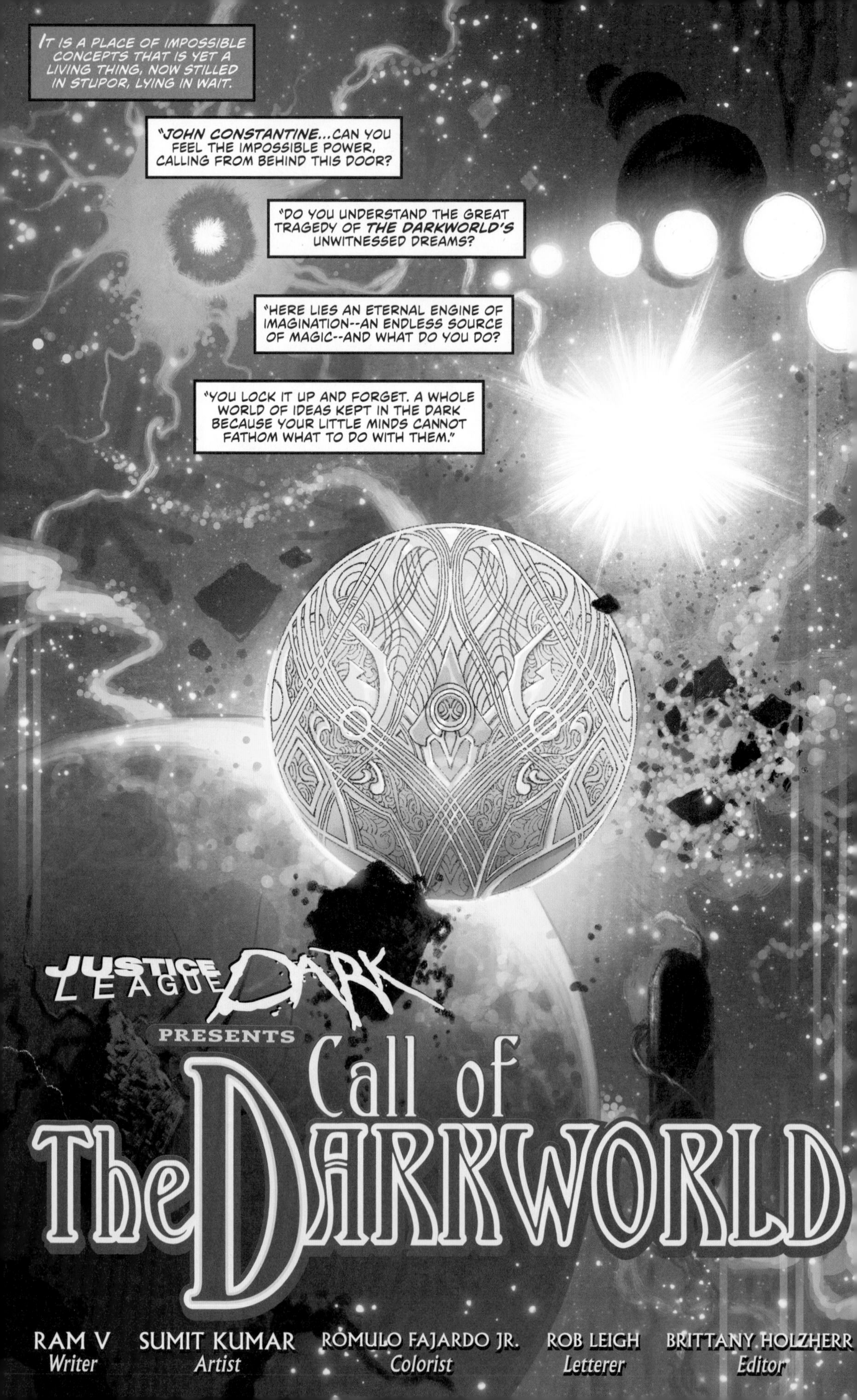
IT IS A PLACE OF IMPOSSIBLE CONCEPTS THAT IS YET A LIVING THING, NOW STILLED IN STUPOR, LYING IN WAIT.
"JOHN CONSTANTINE...CAN YOU FEEL THE IMPOSSIBLE POWER, CALLING FROM BEHIND THIS DOOR?
"DO YOU UNDERSTAND THE GREAT TRAGEDY OF THE DARKWORLD'S UNWITNESSED DREAMS?
"HERE LIES AN ETERNAL ENGINE OF IMAGINATION--AN ENDLESS SOURCE OF MAGIC--AND WHAT DO YOU DO?
"YOU LOCK IT UP AND FORGET. A WHOLE WORLD OF IDEAS KEPT IN THE DARK BECAUSE YOUR LITTLE MINDS CANNOT FATHOM WHAT TO DO WITH THEM."
JUSTICE LEAGUE DARK
PRESENTS
Call of The DARKWORLD
RAM V Writer
SUMIT KUMAR Artist
ROMULO FAJARDO JR. Colorist
ROB LEIGH Letterer
BRITTANY HOLZHERR Editor

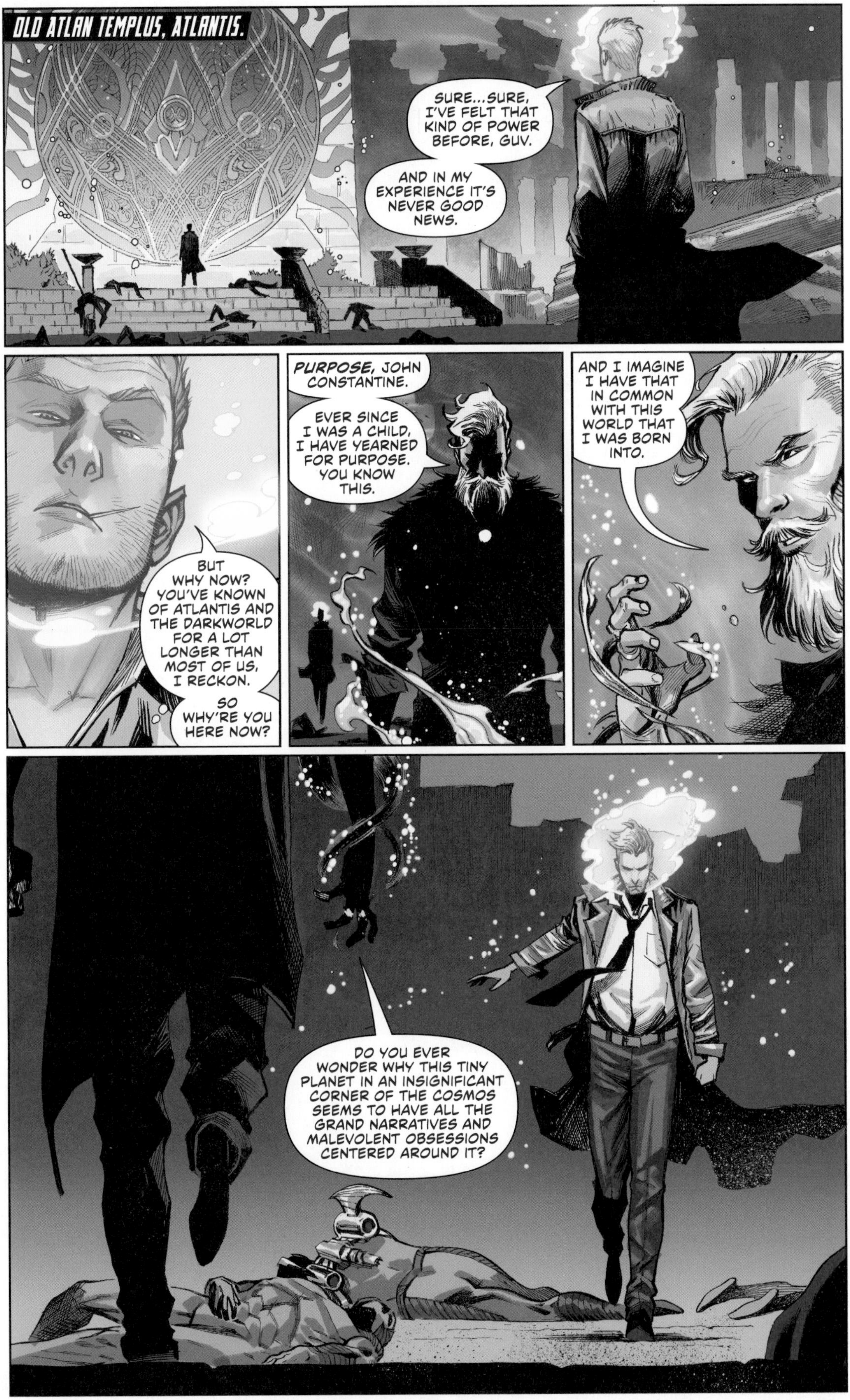

OLD ATLAN TEMPLUS, ATLANTIS.
SURE...SURE, I'VE FELT THAT KIND OF POWER BEFORE, GUV.
AND IN MY EXPERIENCE IT'S NEVER GOOD NEWS.
BUT WHY NOW? YOU'VE KNOWN OF ATLANTIS AND THE DARKWORLD FOR A LOT LONGER THAN MOST OF US, I RECKON.
SO WHY'RE YOU HERE NOW?
PURPOSE, JOHN CONSTANTINE.
EVER SINCE I WAS A CHILD, I HAVE YEARNED FOR PURPOSE. YOU KNOW THIS.
AND I IMAGINE I HAVE THAT IN COMMON WITH THIS WORLD THAT I WAS BORN INTO.
DO YOU EVER WONDER WHY THIS TINY PLANET IN AN INSIGNIFICANT CORNER OF THE COSMOS SEEMS TO HAVE ALL THE GRAND NARRATIVES AND MALEVOLENT OBSESSIONS CENTERED AROUND IT?

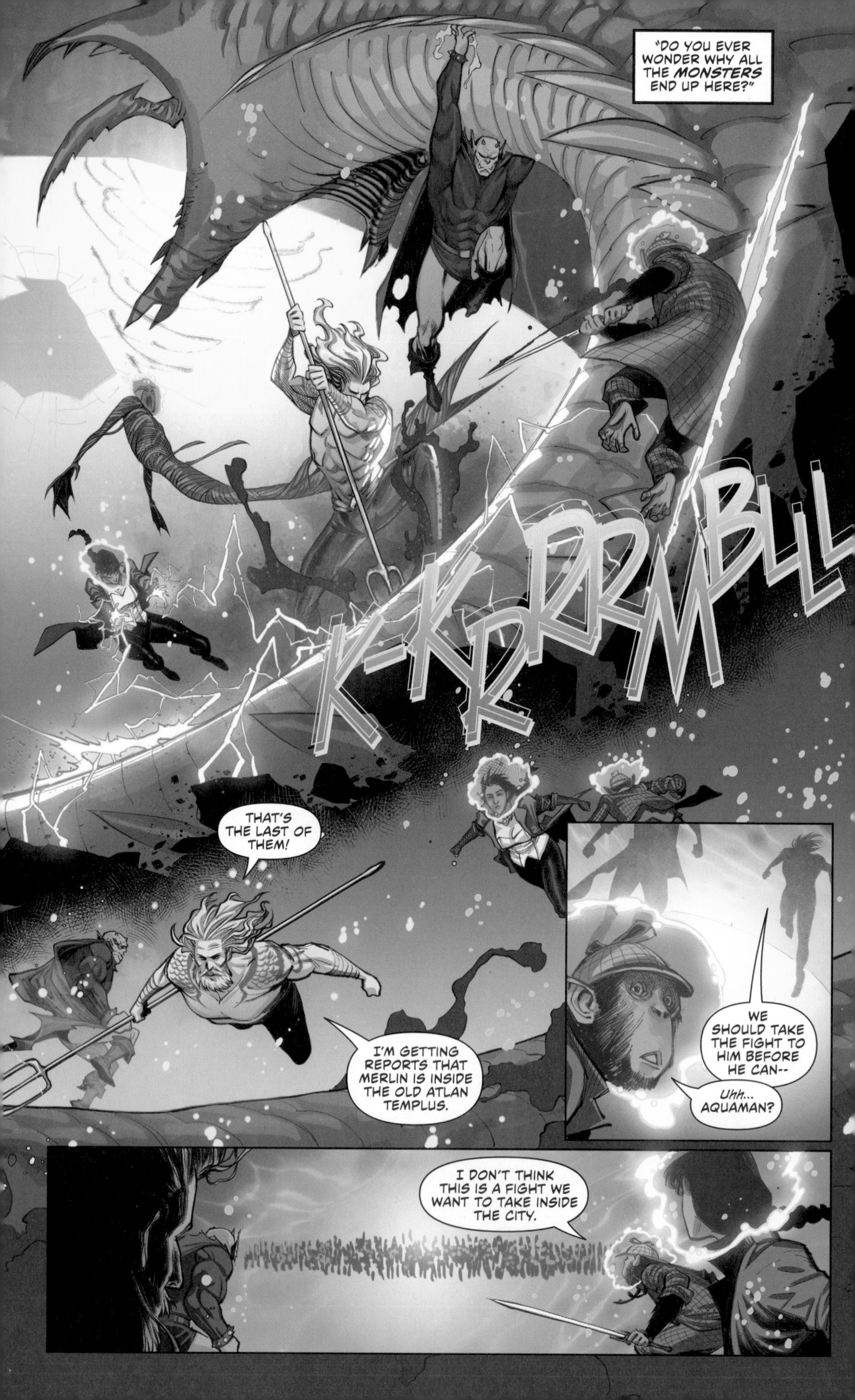
"DO YOU EVER WONDER WHY ALL THE *MONSTERS* END UP HERE?"
K-KRRRMBLLL
THAT'S THE LAST OF THEM!
I'M GETTING REPORTS THAT MERLIN IS INSIDE THE OLD ATLAN TEMPLUS.
WE SHOULD TAKE THE FIGHT TO HIM BEFORE HE CAN--
Uhh... AQUAMAN?
I DON'T THINK THIS IS A FIGHT WE WANT TO TAKE INSIDE THE CITY.

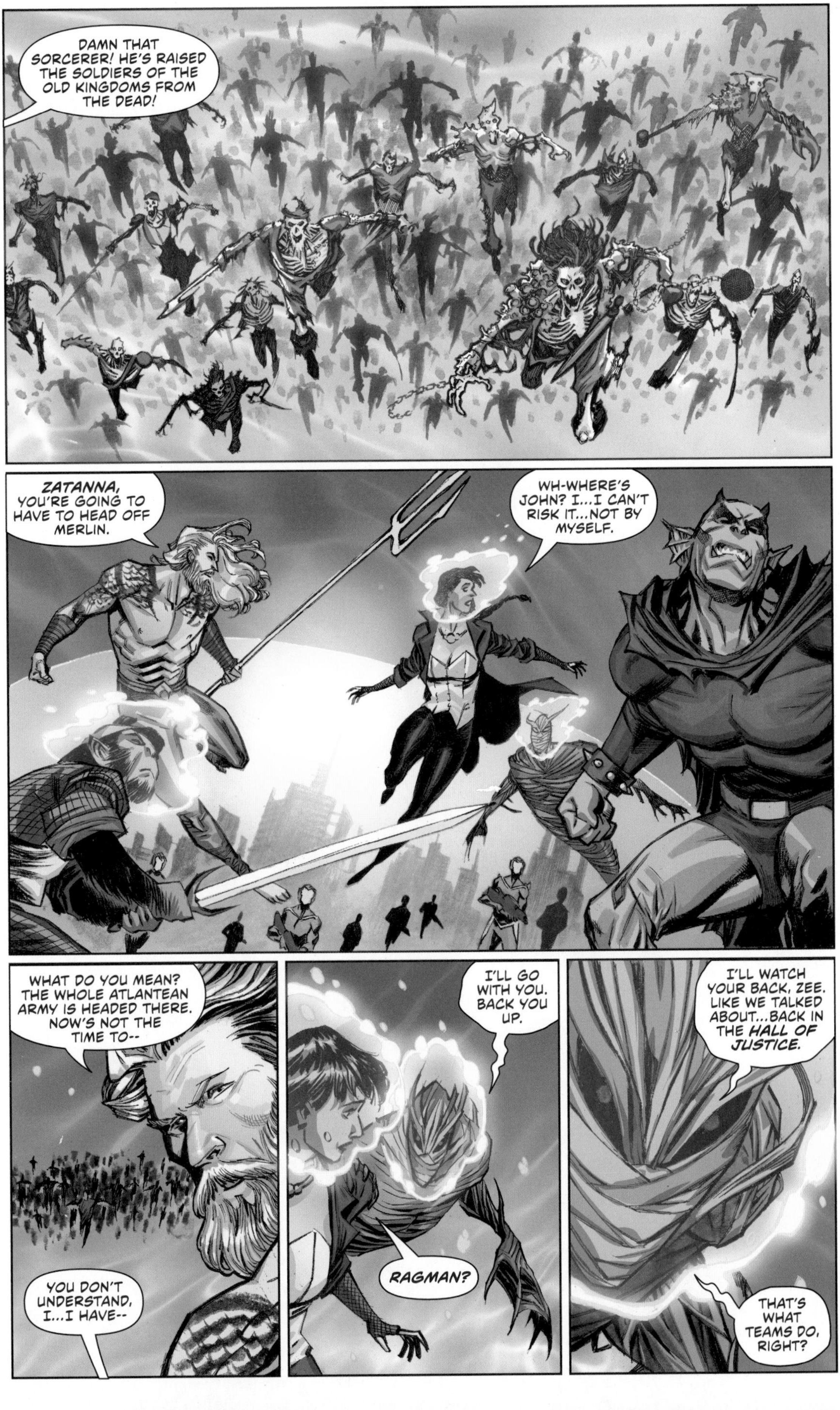
DAMN THAT SORCERER! HE'S RAISED THE SOLDIERS OF THE OLD KINGDOMS FROM THE DEAD!
ZATANNA, YOU'RE GOING TO HAVE TO HEAD OFF MERLIN.
WH-WHERE'S JOHN? I...I CAN'T RISK IT...NOT BY MYSELF.
WHAT DO YOU MEAN? THE WHOLE ATLANTEAN ARMY IS HEADED THERE. NOW'S NOT THE TIME TO--
YOU DON'T UNDERSTAND, I...I HAVE--
I'LL GO WITH YOU. BACK YOU UP.
RAGMAN?
I'LL WATCH YOUR BACK, ZEE. LIKE WE TALKED ABOUT...BACK IN THE HALL OF JUSTICE.
THAT'S WHAT TEAMS DO, RIGHT?

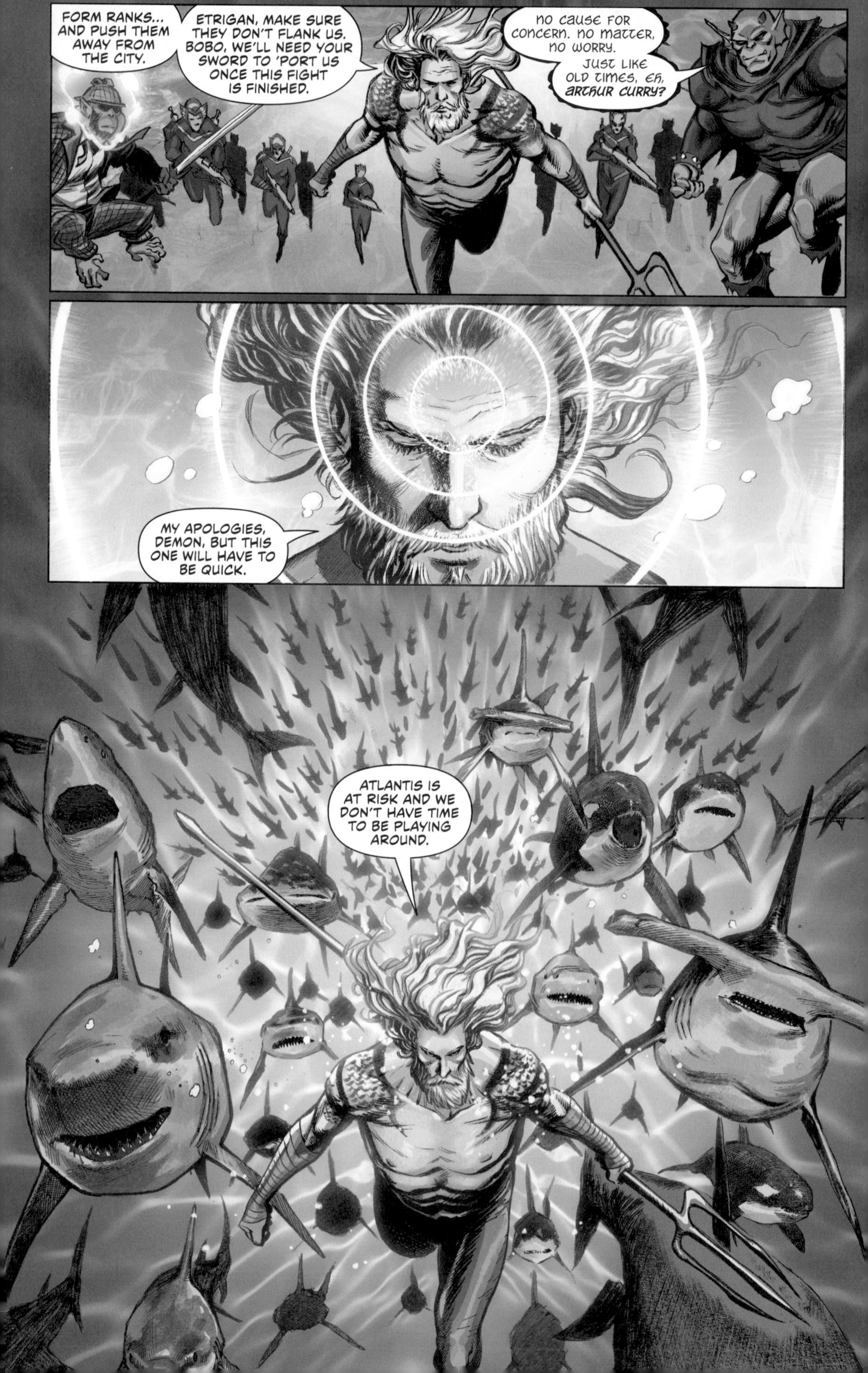
FORM RANKS... AND PUSH THEM AWAY FROM THE CITY.
ETRIGAN, MAKE SURE THEY DON'T FLANK US. BOBO, WE'LL NEED YOUR SWORD TO 'PORT US ONCE THIS FIGHT IS FINISHED.
NO CAUSE FOR CONCERN. NO MATTER, NO WORRY.
JUST LIKE OLD TIMES, EH, ARTHUR CURRY?
MY APOLOGIES, DEMON, BUT THIS ONE WILL HAVE TO BE QUICK.
ATLANTIS IS AT RISK AND WE DON'T HAVE TIME TO BE PLAYING AROUND.

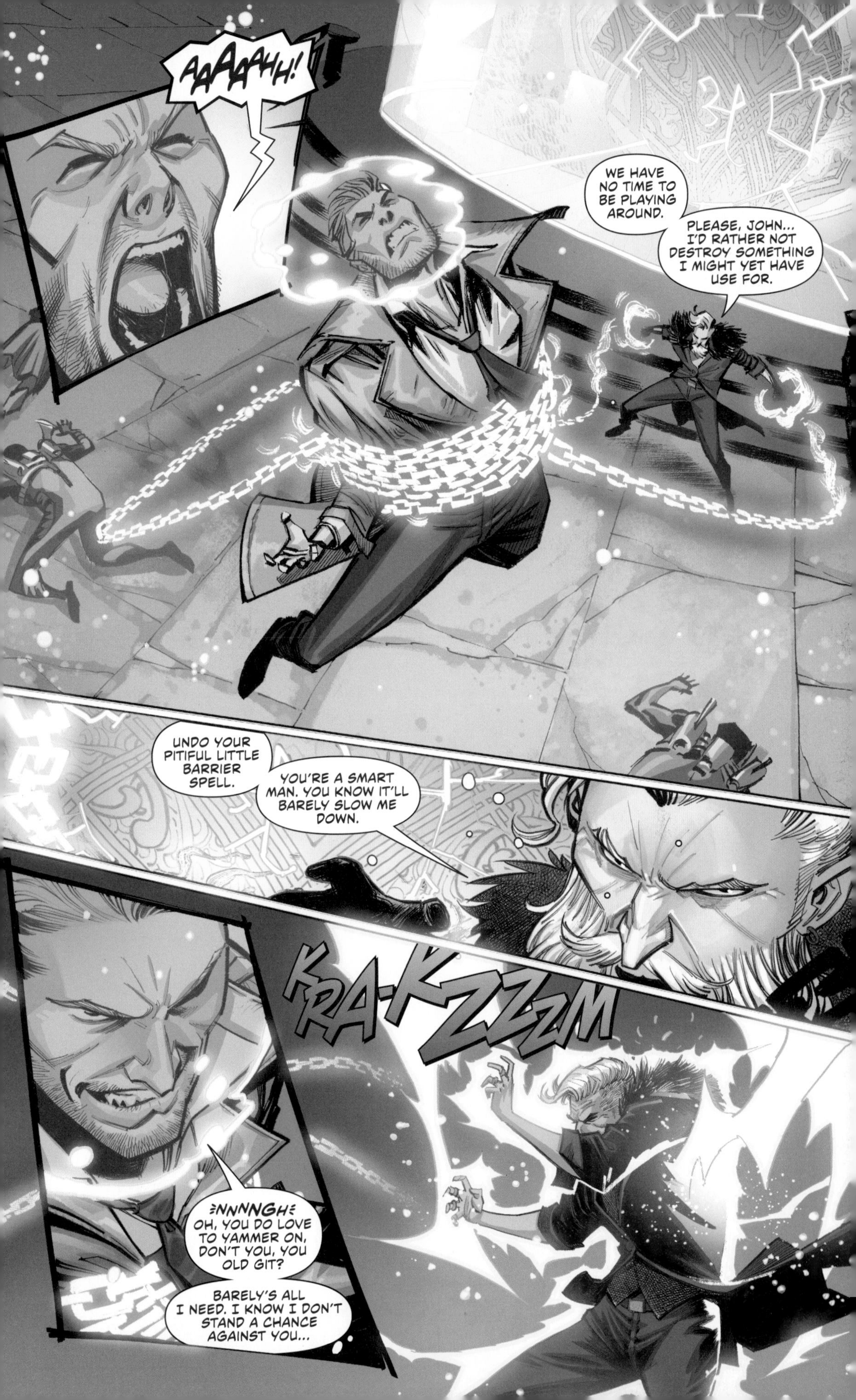
AAAAAHH!
WE HAVE NO TIME TO BE PLAYING AROUND.
PLEASE, JOHN... I'D RATHER NOT DESTROY SOMETHING I MIGHT YET HAVE USE FOR.
UNDO YOUR PITIFUL LITTLE BARRIER SPELL.
YOU'RE A SMART MAN. YOU KNOW IT'LL BARELY SLOW ME DOWN.
KRA-KZZZM
NNNNGH
OH, YOU DO LOVE TO YAMMER ON, DON'T YOU, YOU OLD GIT?
BARELY'S ALL I NEED. I KNOW I DON'T STAND A CHANCE AGAINST YOU...

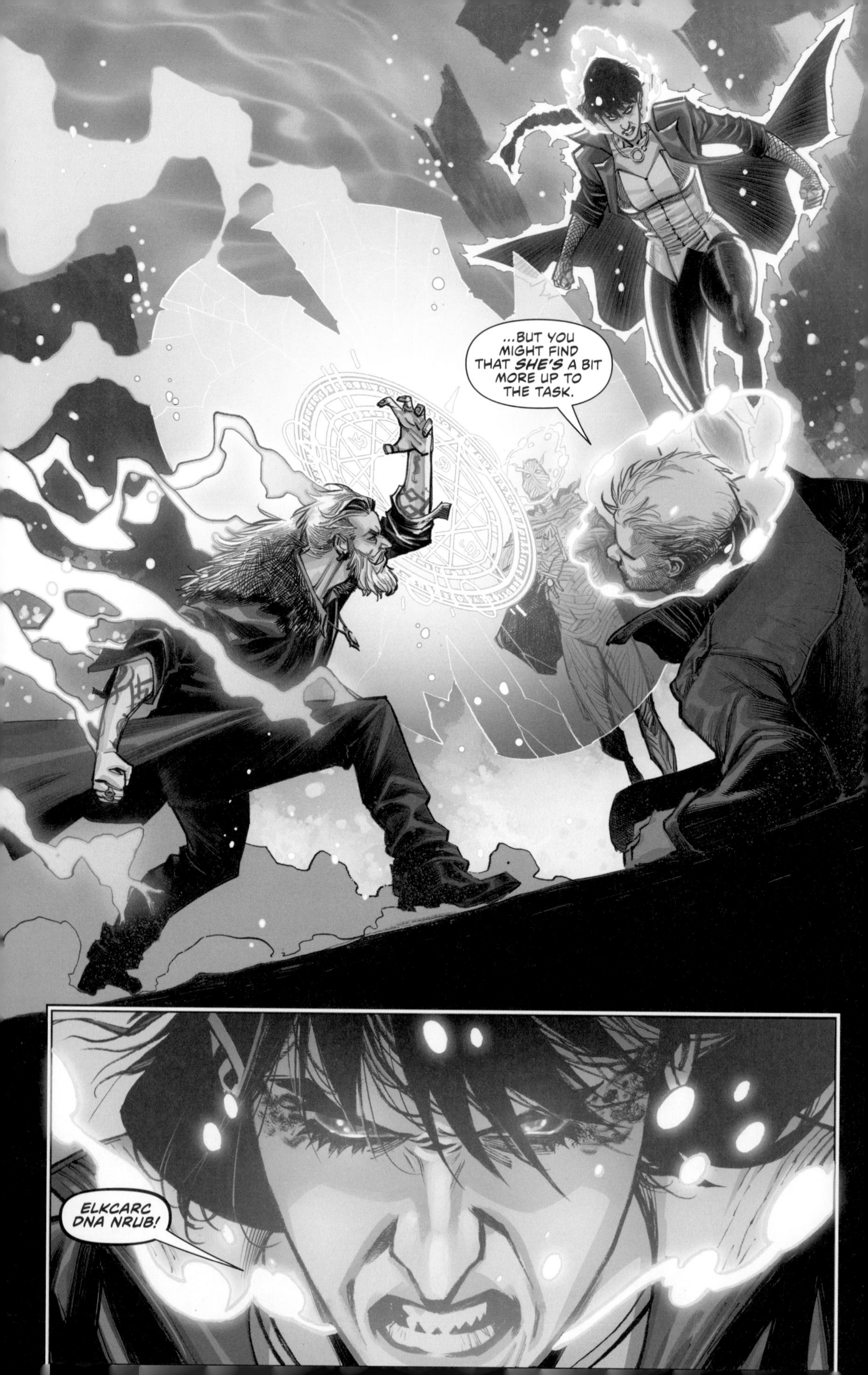
...BUT YOU MIGHT FIND THAT SHE'S A BIT MORE UP TO THE TASK.
ELKCARC DNA NRUB!

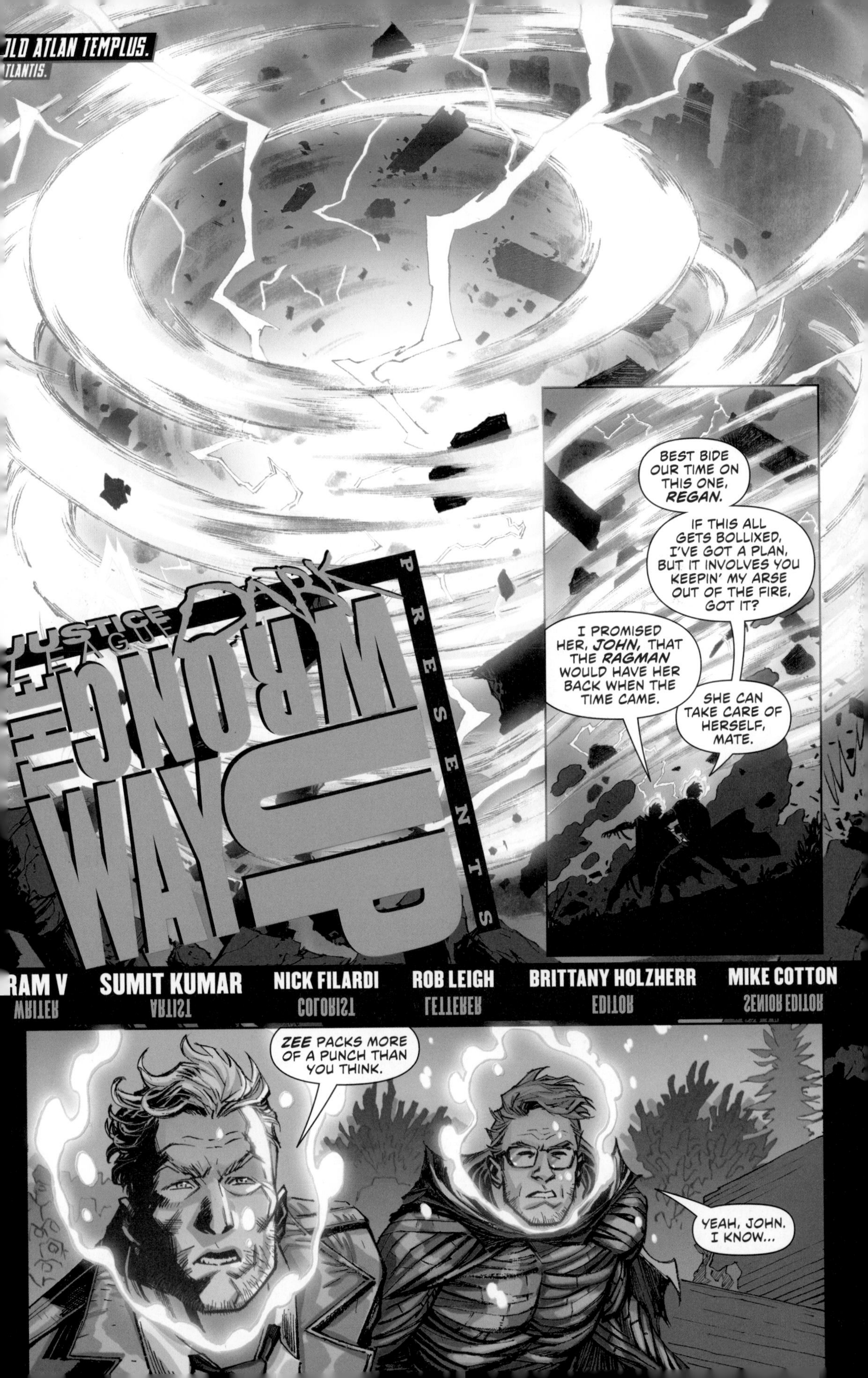

LD ATLAN TEMPLUS.
TLANTIS.
JUSTICE LEAGUE DARK PRESENTS
THE WRONG WAY UP
BEST BIDE OUR TIME ON THIS ONE, REGAN.
IF THIS ALL GETS BOLLIXED, I'VE GOT A PLAN, BUT IT INVOLVES YOU KEEPIN' MY ARSE OUT OF THE FIRE, GOT IT?
I PROMISED HER, JOHN, THAT THE RAGMAN WOULD HAVE HER BACK WHEN THE TIME CAME.
SHE CAN TAKE CARE OF HERSELF, MATE.
RAM V WRITER
SUMIT KUMAR ARTIST
NICK FILARDI COLORIST
ROB LEIGH LETTERER
BRITTANY HOLZHERR EDITOR
MIKE COTTON SENIOR EDITOR
ZEE PACKS MORE OF A PUNCH THAN YOU THINK.
YEAH, JOHN. I KNOW...

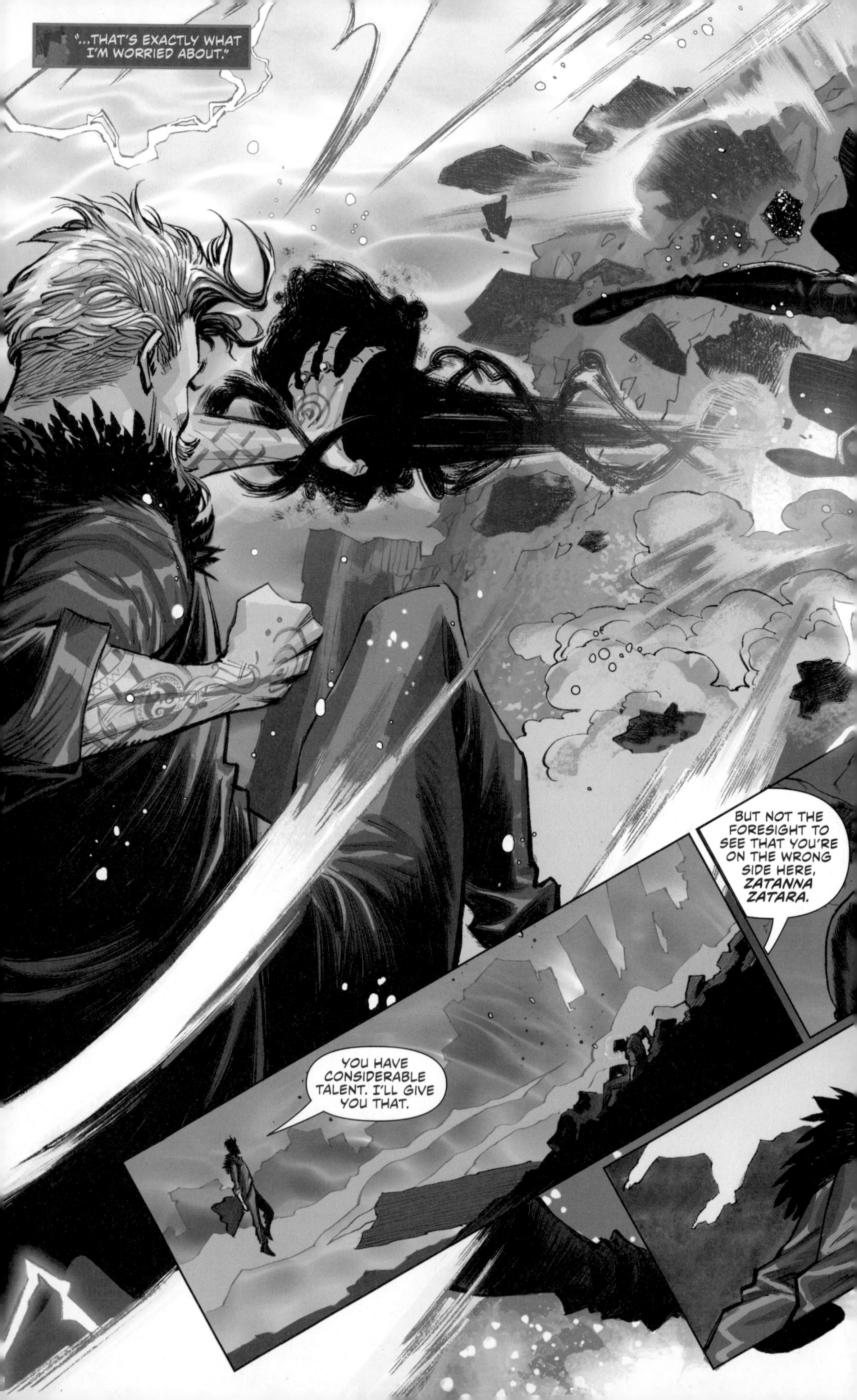
"...THAT'S EXACTLY WHAT I'M WORRIED ABOUT."
YOU HAVE CONSIDERABLE TALENT. I'LL GIVE YOU THAT.
BUT NOT THE FORESIGHT TO SEE THAT YOU'RE ON THE WRONG SIDE HERE, ZATANNA ZATARA.

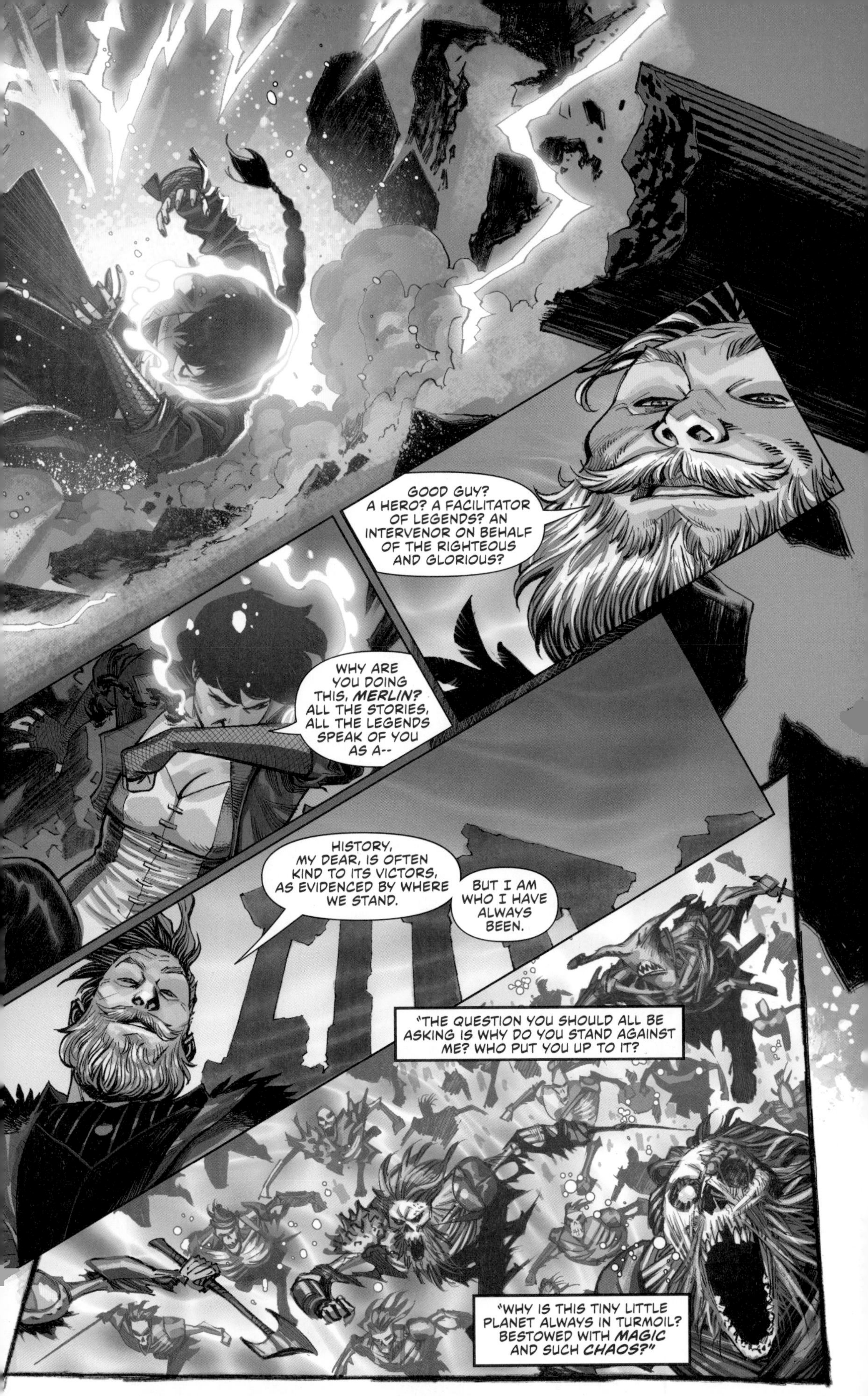

WHY ARE YOU DOING THIS, MERLIN? ALL THE STORIES, ALL THE LEGENDS SPEAK OF YOU AS A--
GOOD GUY? A HERO? A FACILITATOR OF LEGENDS? AN INTERVENOR ON BEHALF OF THE RIGHTEOUS AND GLORIOUS?
HISTORY, MY DEAR, IS OFTEN KIND TO ITS VICTORS, AS EVIDENCED BY WHERE WE STAND.
BUT I AM WHO I HAVE ALWAYS BEEN.
"THE QUESTION YOU SHOULD ALL BE ASKING IS WHY DO YOU STAND AGAINST ME? WHO PUT YOU UP TO IT?
"WHY IS THIS TINY LITTLE PLANET ALWAYS IN TURMOIL? BESTOWED WITH MAGIC AND SUCH CHAOS?"

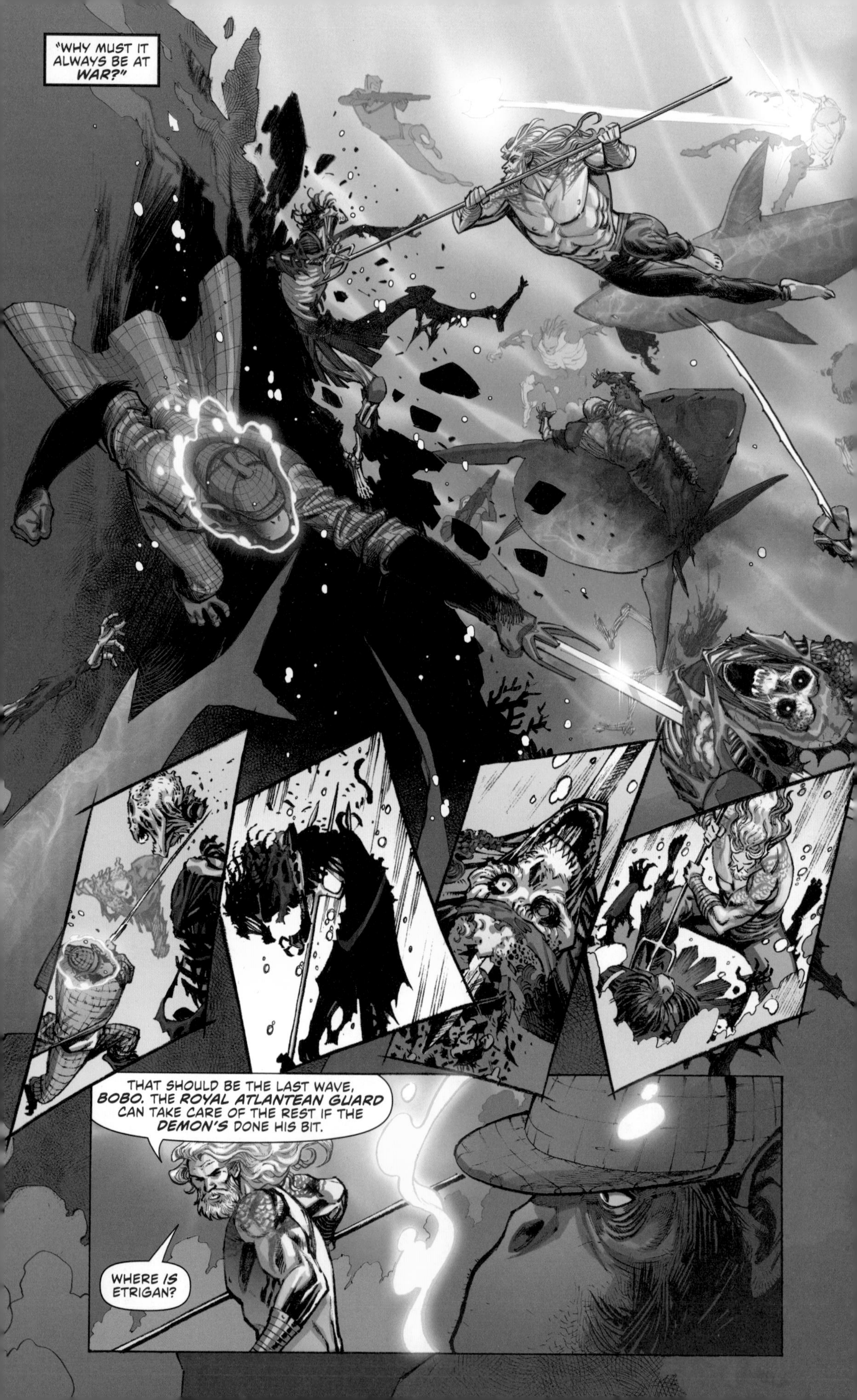
"WHY MUST IT ALWAYS BE AT WAR?"
THAT SHOULD BE THE LAST WAVE, BOBO. THE ROYAL ATLANTEAN GUARD CAN TAKE CARE OF THE REST IF THE DEMON'S DONE HIS BIT.
WHERE IS ETRIGAN?

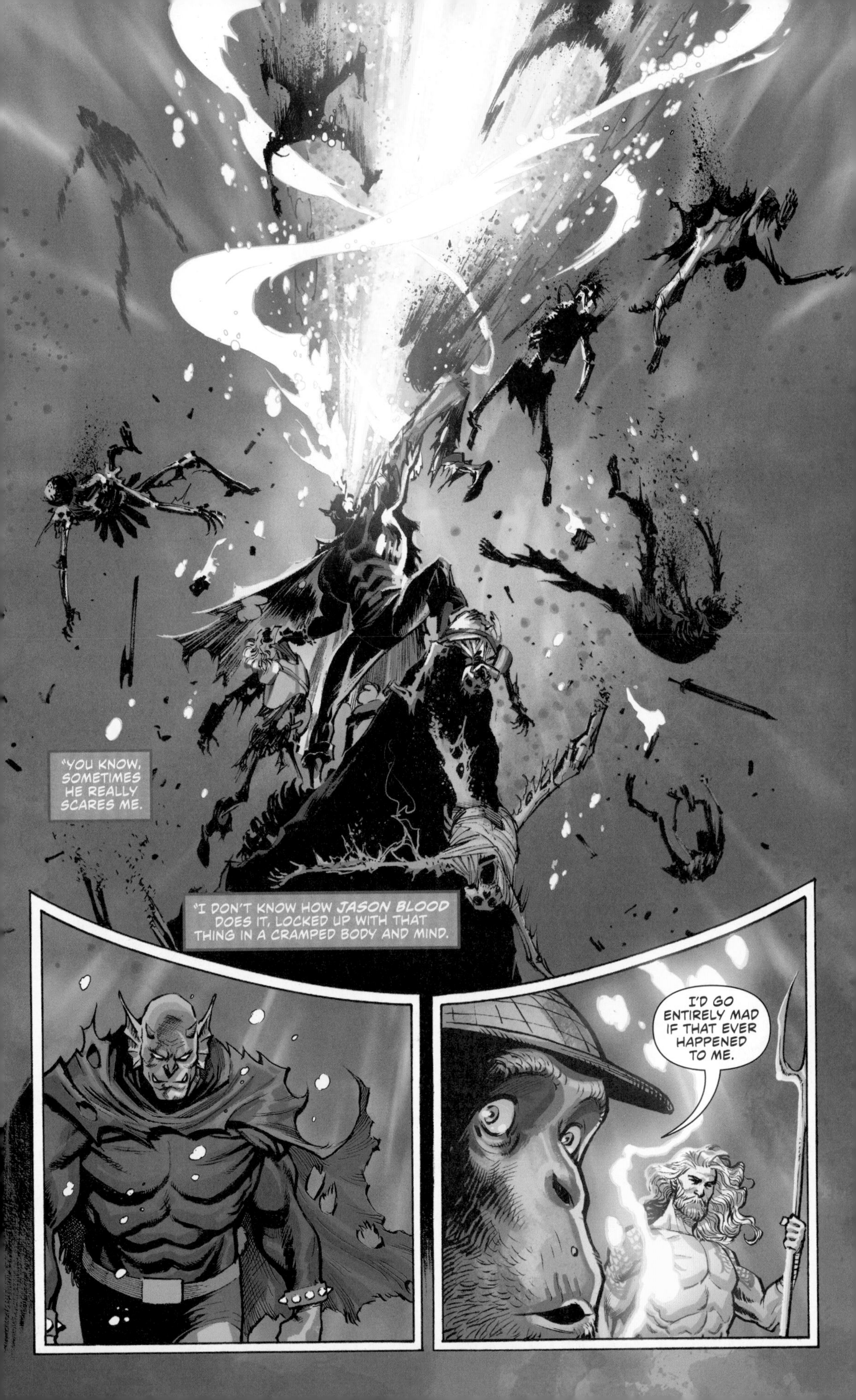
"YOU KNOW, SOMETIMES HE REALLY SCARES ME.
"I DON'T KNOW HOW JASON BLOOD DOES IT, LOCKED UP WITH THAT THING IN A CRAMPED BODY AND MIND.
I'D GO ENTIRELY MAD IF THAT EVER HAPPENED TO ME.

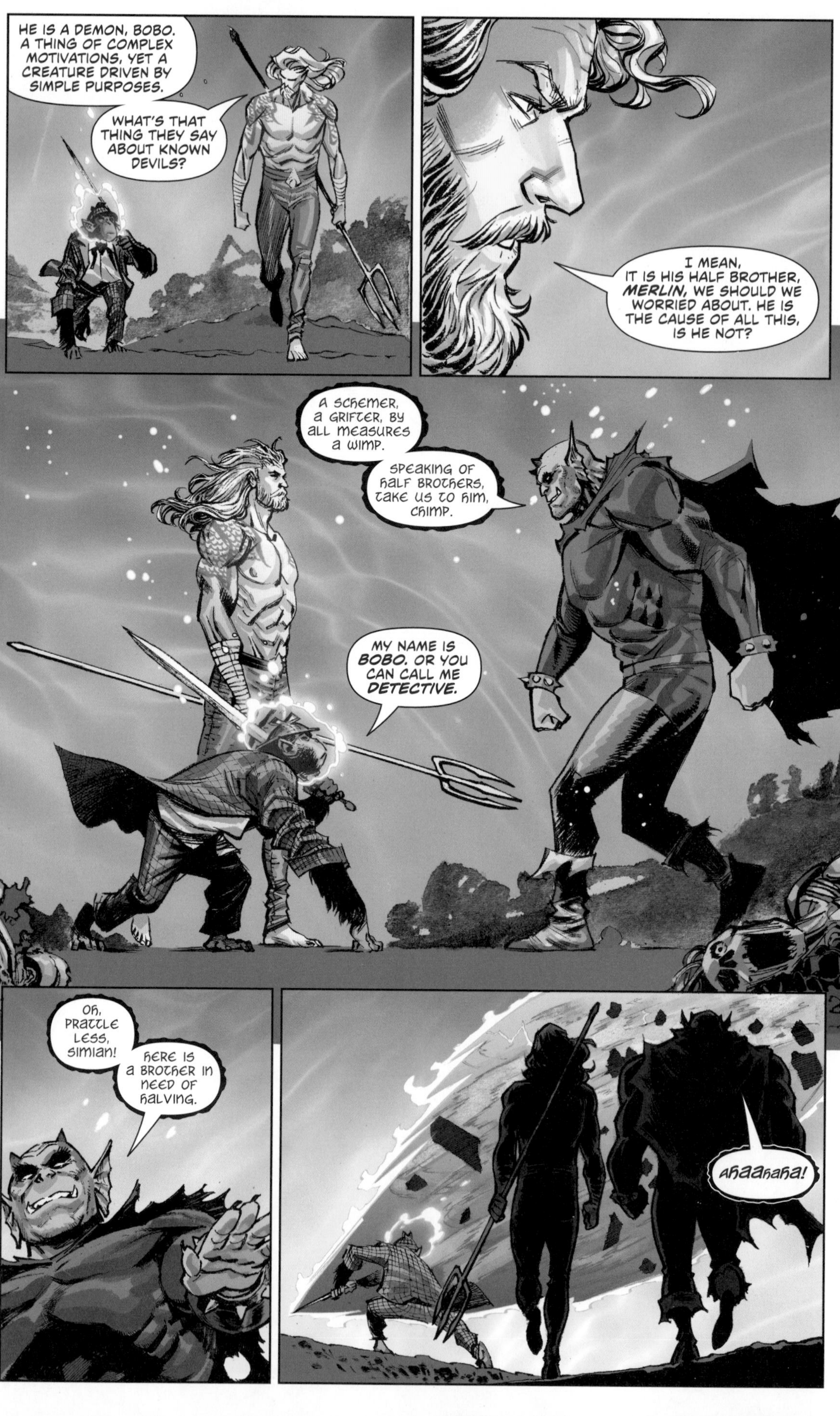

HE IS A DEMON, BOBO. A THING OF COMPLEX MOTIVATIONS, YET A CREATURE DRIVEN BY SIMPLE PURPOSES.
WHAT'S THAT THING THEY SAY ABOUT KNOWN DEVILS?
I MEAN, IT IS HIS HALF BROTHER, MERLIN, WE SHOULD WE WORRIED ABOUT. HE IS THE CAUSE OF ALL THIS, IS HE NOT?
A SCHEMER, A GRIFTER, BY ALL MEASURES A WIMP.
SPEAKING OF HALF BROTHERS, TAKE US TO HIM, CHIMP.
MY NAME IS BOBO. OR YOU CAN CALL ME DETECTIVE.
OH, PRATTLE LESS, SIMIAN!
HERE IS A BROTHER IN NEED OF HALVING.
AHAAHAHA!

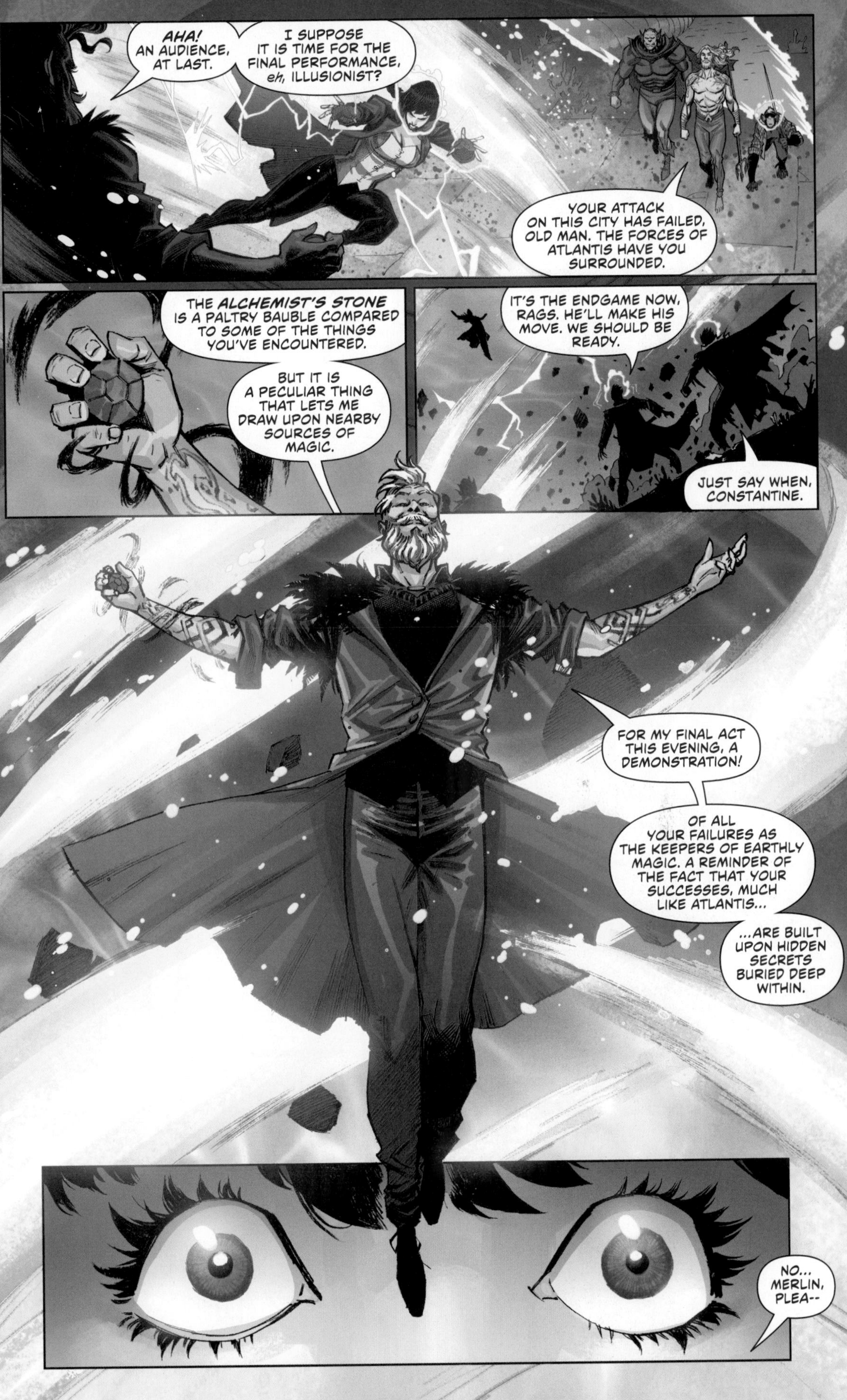
AHA! AN AUDIENCE, AT LAST.
I SUPPOSE IT IS TIME FOR THE FINAL PERFORMANCE, *eh,* ILLUSIONIST?
YOUR ATTACK ON THIS CITY HAS FAILED, OLD MAN. THE FORCES OF ATLANTIS HAVE YOU SURROUNDED.
THE *ALCHEMIST'S STONE* IS A PALTRY BAUBLE COMPARED TO SOME OF THE THINGS YOU'VE ENCOUNTERED.
BUT IT IS A PECULIAR THING THAT LETS ME DRAW UPON NEARBY SOURCES OF MAGIC.
IT'S THE ENDGAME NOW, RAGS. HE'LL MAKE HIS MOVE. WE SHOULD BE READY.
JUST SAY WHEN, CONSTANTINE.
FOR MY FINAL ACT THIS EVENING, A DEMONSTRATION!
OF ALL YOUR FAILURES AS THE KEEPERS OF EARTHLY MAGIC. A REMINDER OF THE FACT THAT YOUR SUCCESSES, MUCH LIKE ATLANTIS...
...ARE BUILT UPON HIDDEN SECRETS BURIED DEEP WITHIN.
NO... MERLIN, PLEA--

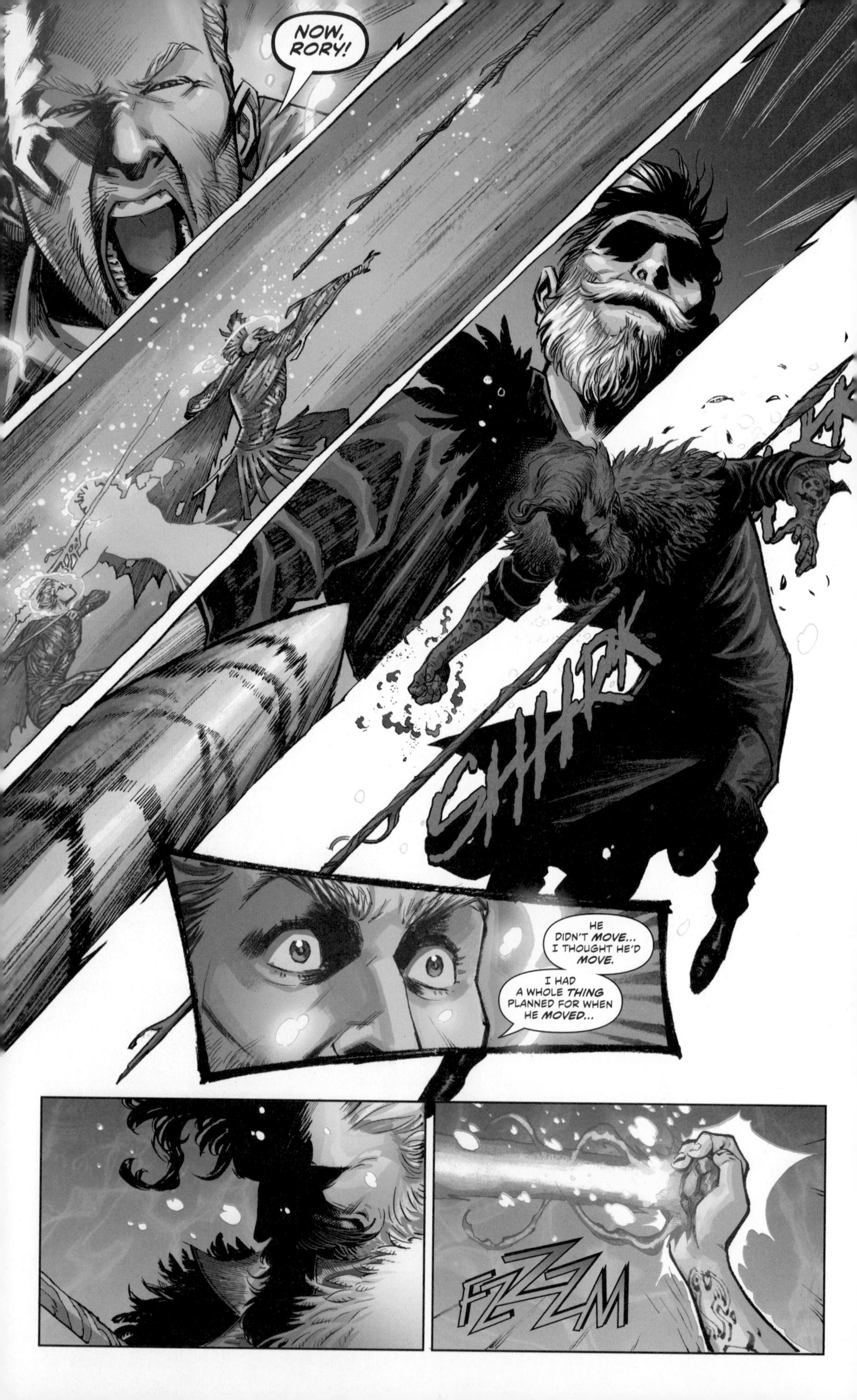
NOW, RORY!
SHHRK
HE DIDN'T MOVE... I THOUGHT HE'D MOVE.
I HAD A WHOLE THING PLANNED FOR WHEN HE MOVED...
FZZZM

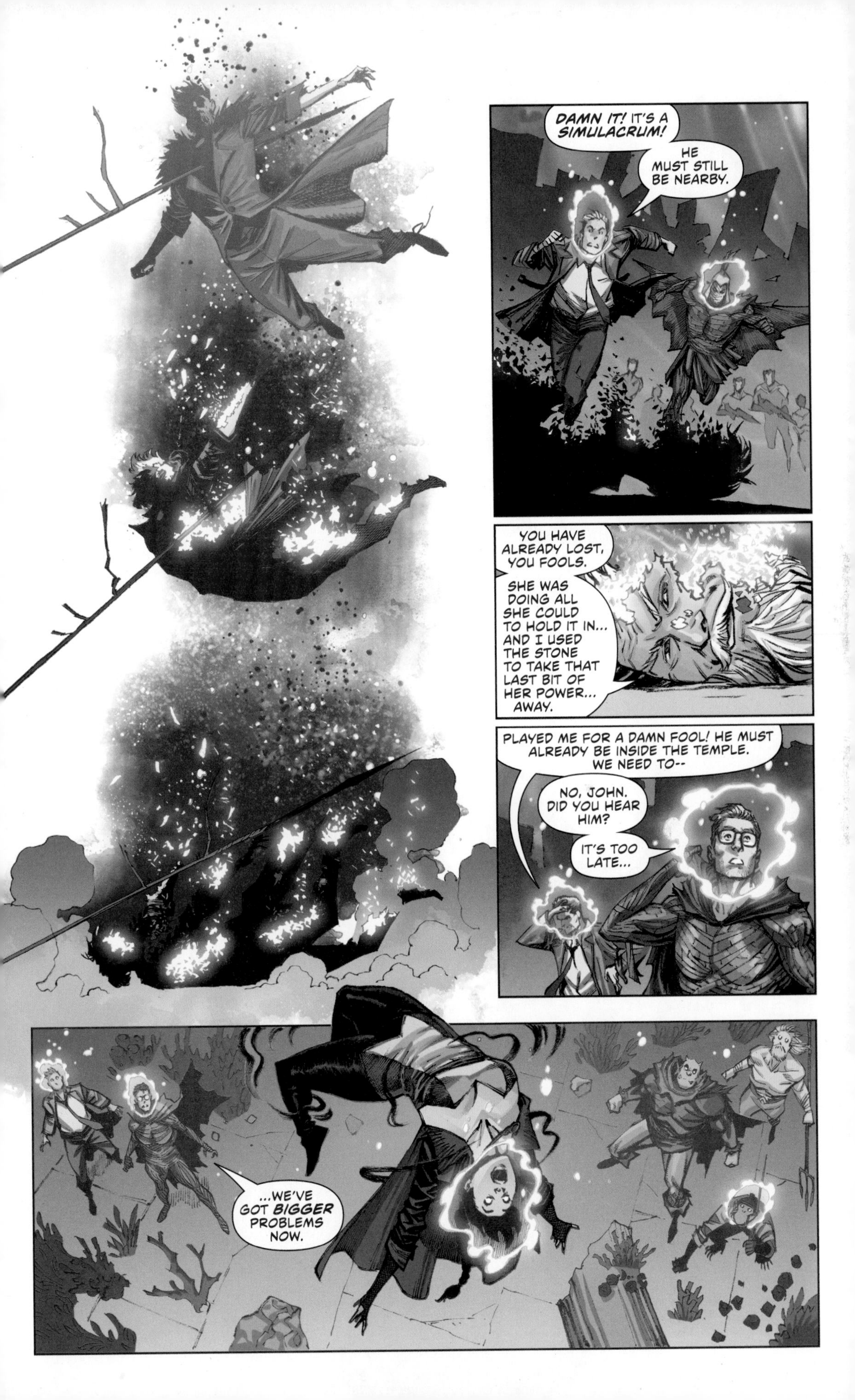
DAMN IT! IT'S A SIMULACRUM!
HE MUST STILL BE NEARBY.
YOU HAVE ALREADY LOST, YOU FOOLS.
SHE WAS DOING ALL SHE COULD TO HOLD IT IN... AND I USED THE STONE TO TAKE THAT LAST BIT OF HER POWER... AWAY.
PLAYED ME FOR A DAMN FOOL! HE MUST ALREADY BE INSIDE THE TEMPLE. WE NEED TO--
NO, JOHN. DID YOU HEAR HIM?
IT'S TOO LATE...
...WE'VE GOT BIGGER PROBLEMS NOW.

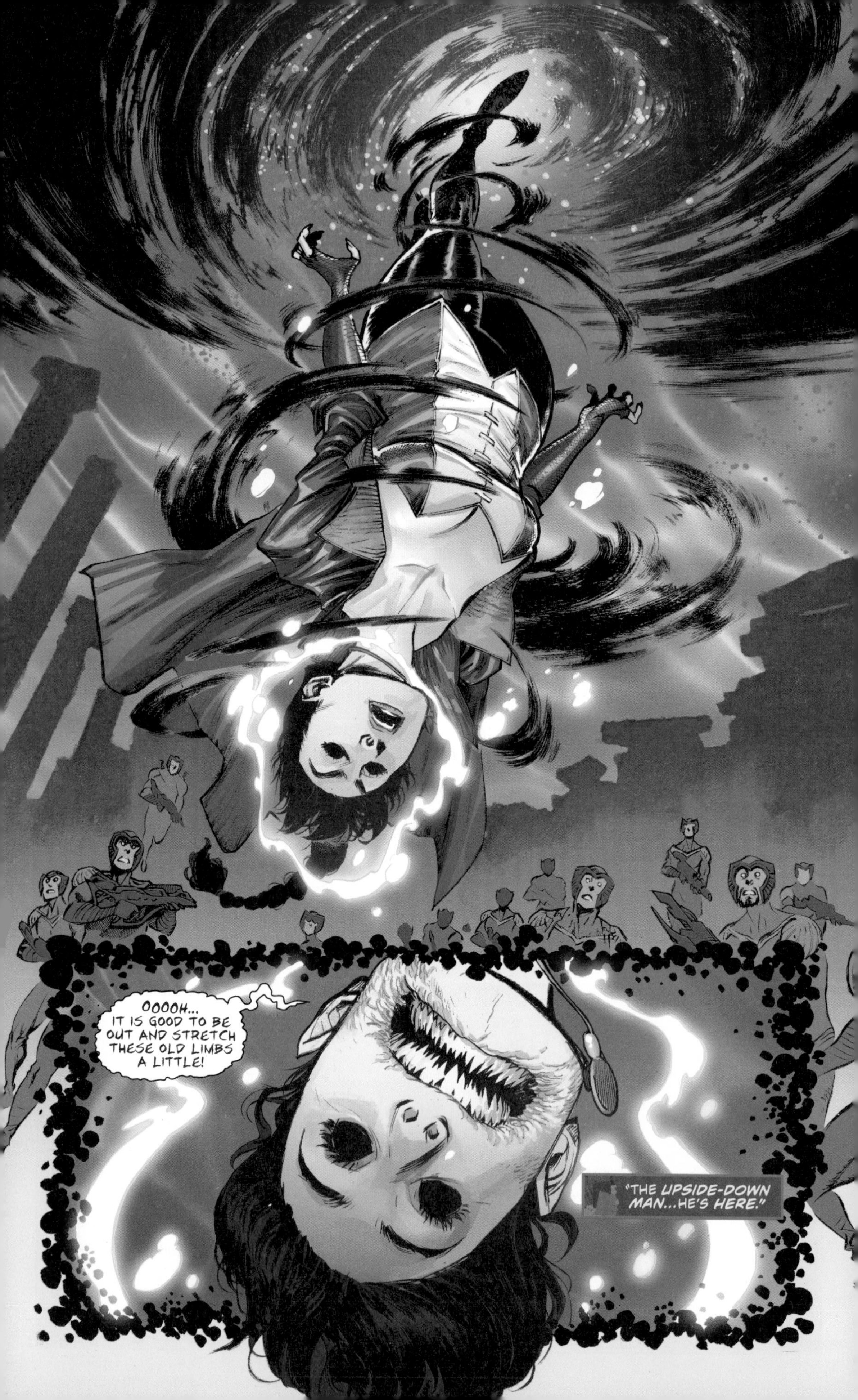
OOOOH... IT IS GOOD TO BE OUT AND STRETCH THESE OLD LIMBS A LITTLE!
"THE UPSIDE-DOWN MAN...HE'S HERE."

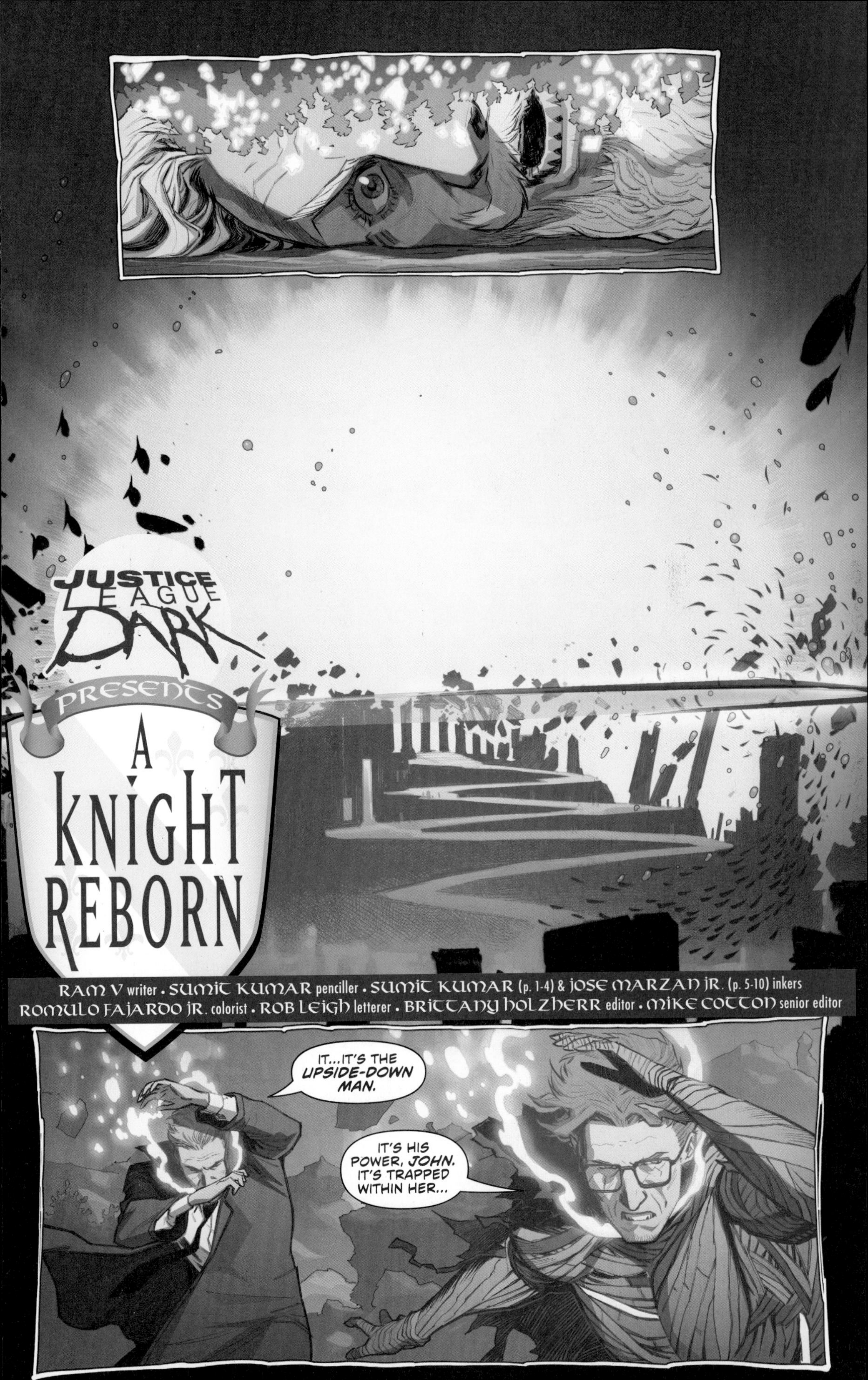
JUSTICE LEAGUE DARK
PRESENTS
A KNIGHT REBORN
RAM V writer • SUMIT KUMAR penciller • SUMIT KUMAR (p. 1-4) & JOSE MARZAN JR. (p. 5-10) inkers
ROMULO FAJARDO JR. colorist • ROB LEIGH letterer • BRITTANY HOLZHERR editor • MIKE COTTON senior editor
IT...IT'S THE UPSIDE-DOWN MAN.
IT'S HIS POWER, JOHN. IT'S TRAPPED WITHIN HER...

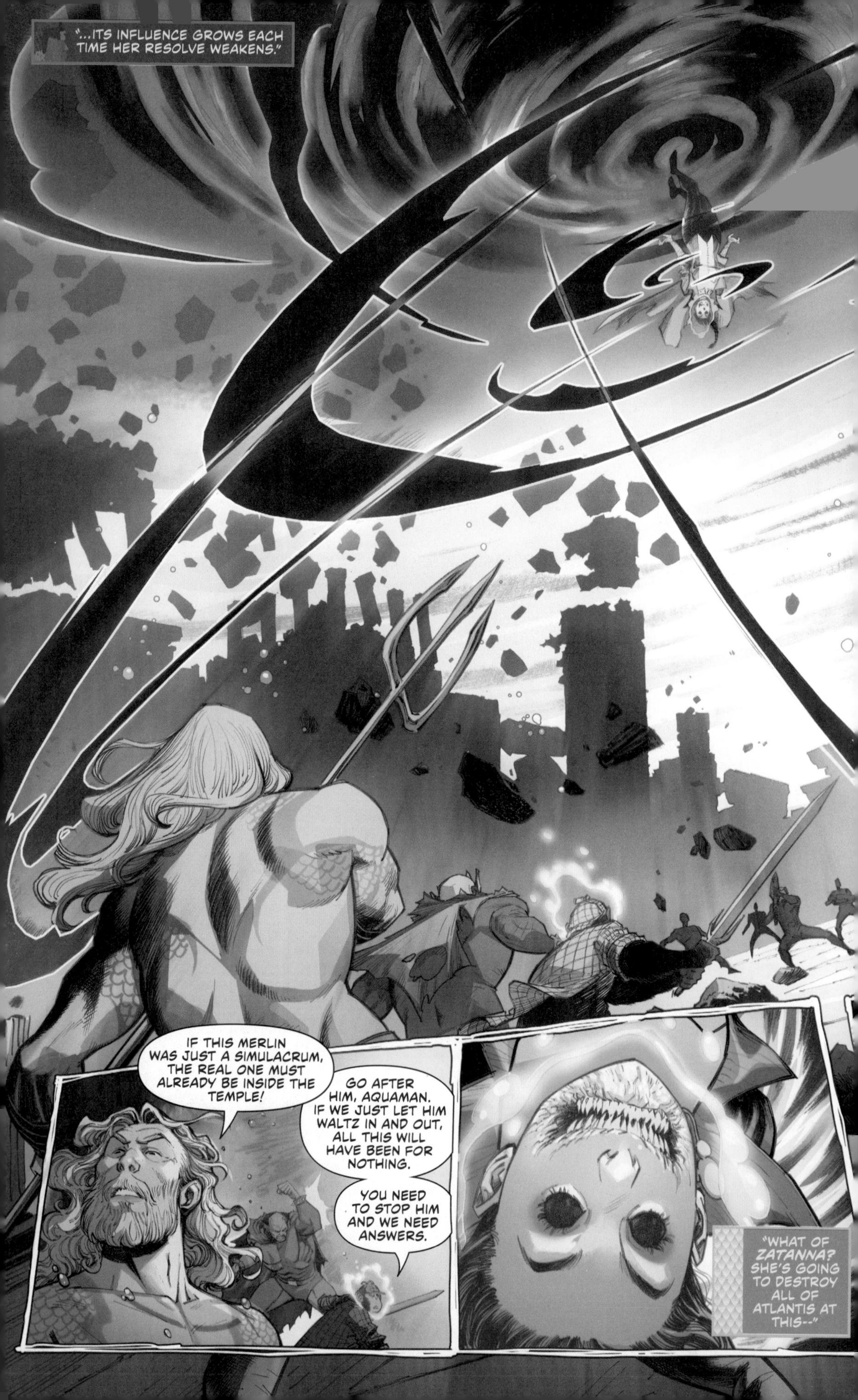

"...ITS INFLUENCE GROWS EACH TIME HER RESOLVE WEAKENS."
IF THIS MERLIN WAS JUST A SIMULACRUM, THE REAL ONE MUST ALREADY BE INSIDE THE TEMPLE!
GO AFTER HIM, AQUAMAN. IF WE JUST LET HIM WALTZ IN AND OUT, ALL THIS WILL HAVE BEEN FOR NOTHING.
YOU NEED TO STOP HIM AND WE NEED ANSWERS.
"WHAT OF *ZATANNA?* SHE'S GOING TO DESTROY ALL OF ATLANTIS AT THIS--"

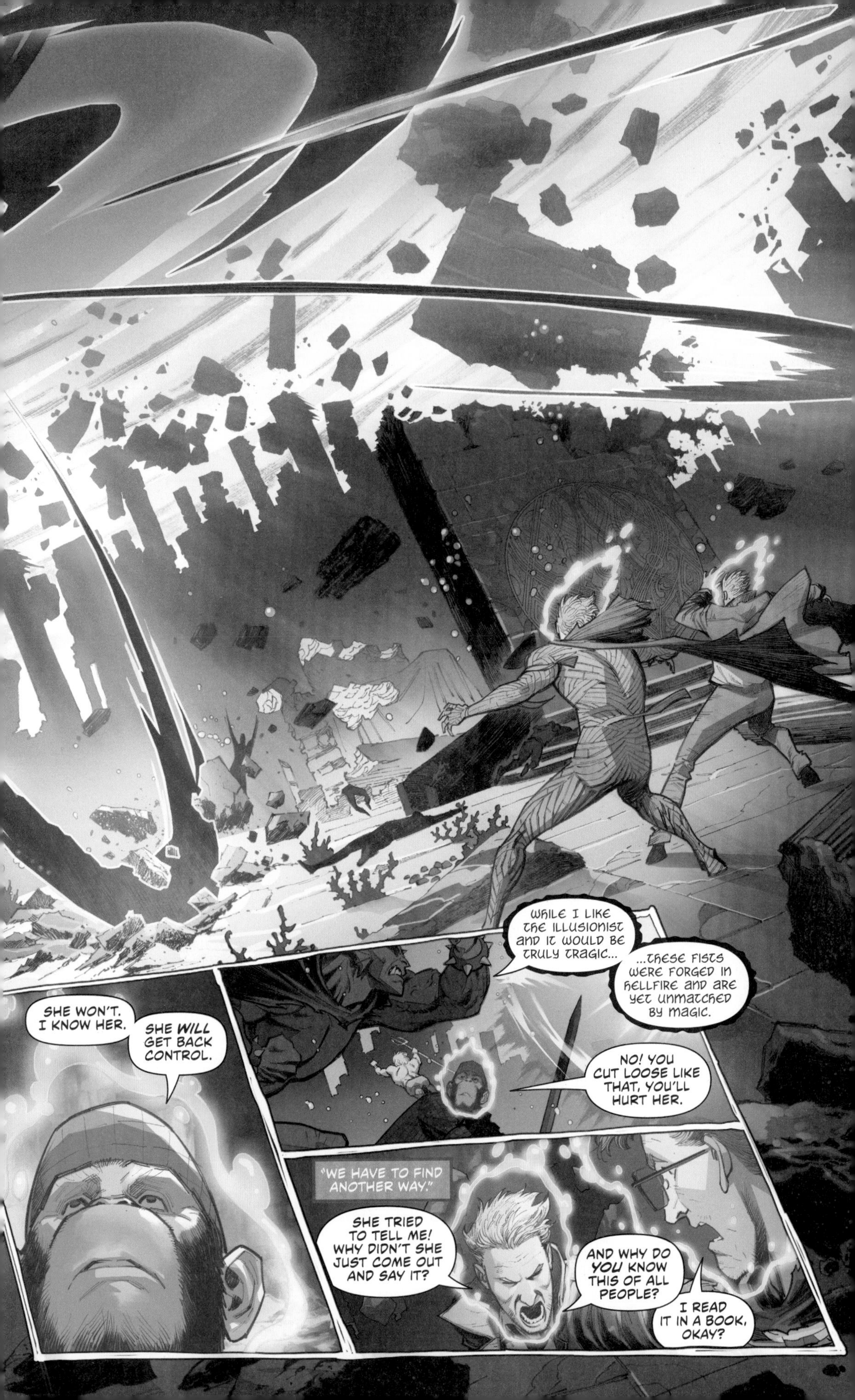

WHILE I LIKE THE ILLUSIONIST AND IT WOULD BE TRULY TRAGIC...
...THESE FISTS WERE FORGED IN HELLFIRE AND ARE YET UNMATCHED BY MAGIC.
SHE WON'T. I KNOW HER.
SHE WILL GET BACK CONTROL.
NO! YOU CUT LOOSE LIKE THAT, YOU'LL HURT HER.
"WE HAVE TO FIND ANOTHER WAY."
SHE TRIED TO TELL ME! WHY DIDN'T SHE JUST COME OUT AND SAY IT?
AND WHY DO YOU KNOW THIS OF ALL PEOPLE?
I READ IT IN A BOOK, OKAY?

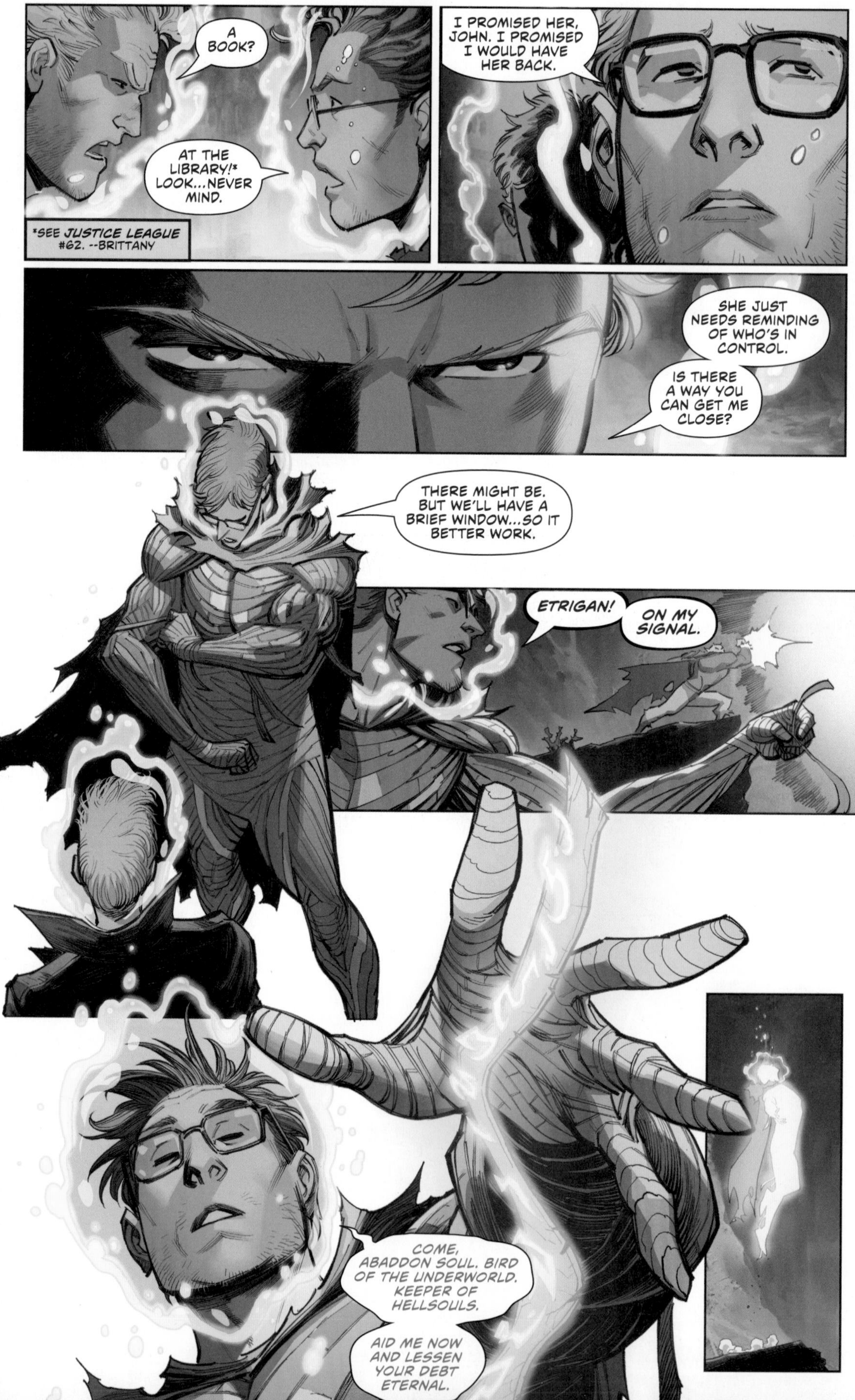
A BOOK?
AT THE LIBRARY!* LOOK...NEVER MIND.
*SEE JUSTICE LEAGUE #62. --BRITTANY
I PROMISED HER, JOHN. I PROMISED I WOULD HAVE HER BACK.
SHE JUST NEEDS REMINDING OF WHO'S IN CONTROL.
IS THERE A WAY YOU CAN GET ME CLOSE?
THERE MIGHT BE. BUT WE'LL HAVE A BRIEF WINDOW...SO IT BETTER WORK.
ETRIGAN!
ON MY SIGNAL.
COME, ABADDON SOUL. BIRD OF THE UNDERWORLD. KEEPER OF HELLSOULS.
AID ME NOW AND LESSEN YOUR DEBT ETERNAL.

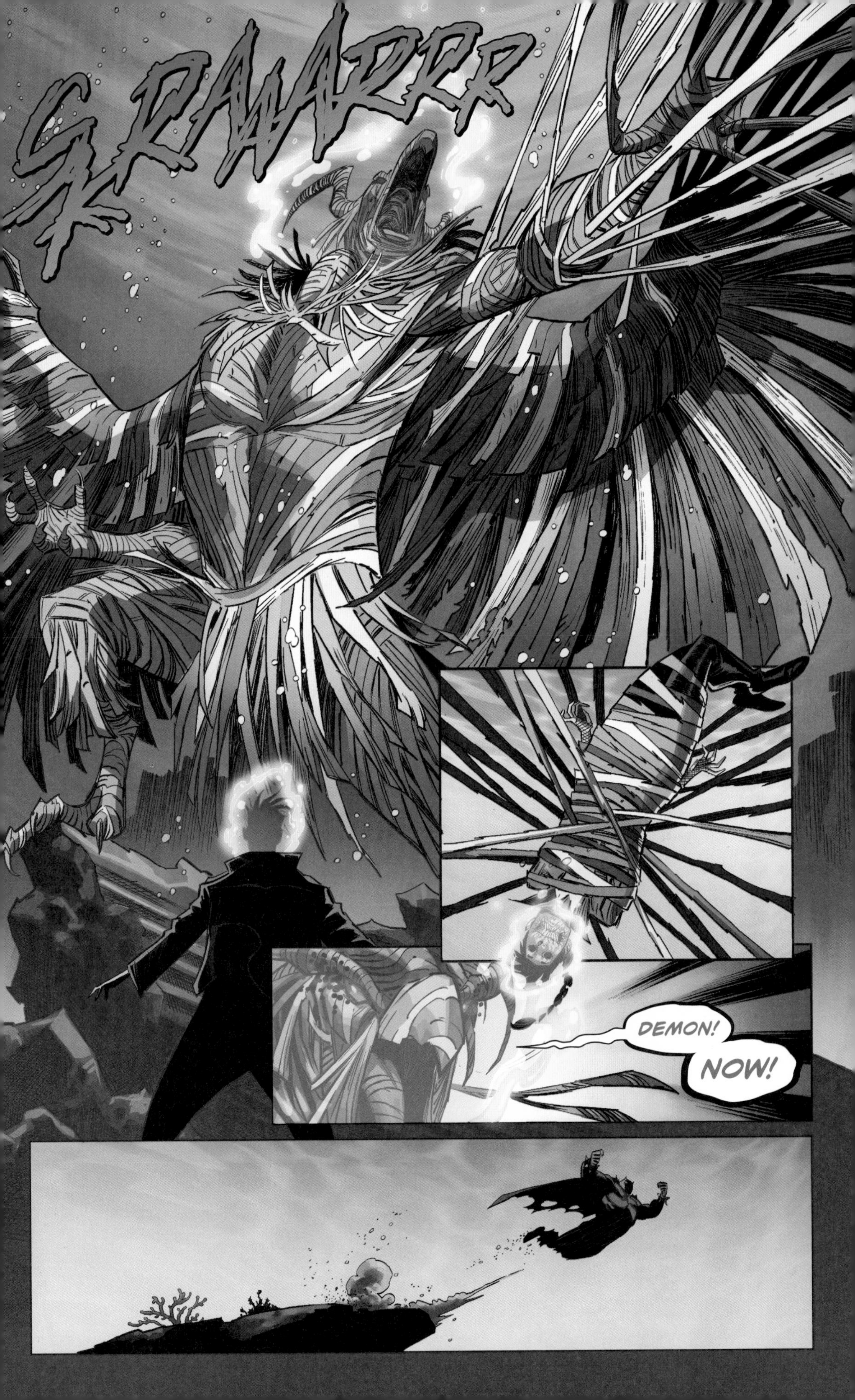
SKRAWRRR
DEMON!
NOW!

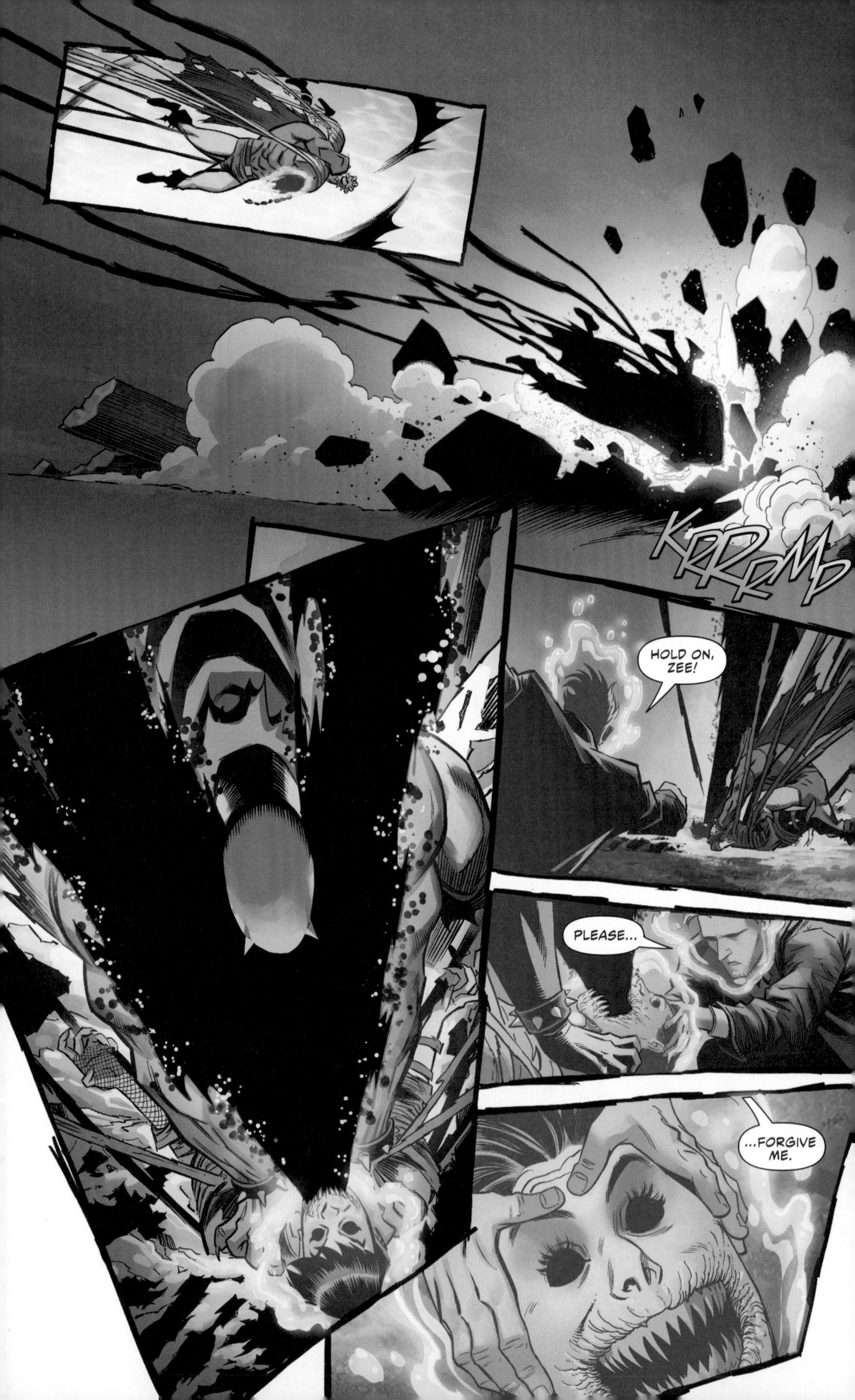
KRRRRMP
HOLD ON, ZEE!
PLEASE...
...FORGIVE ME.

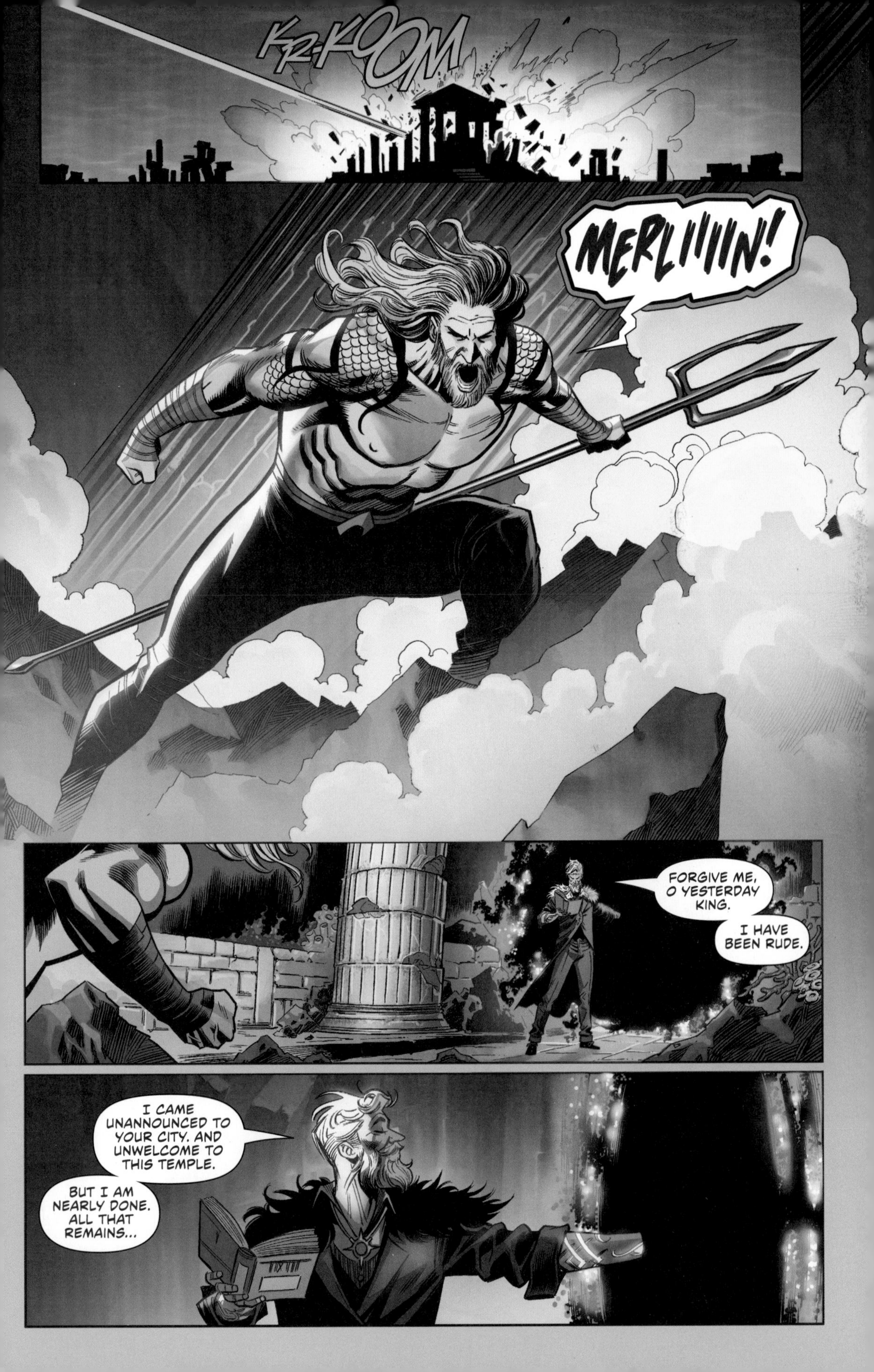
KR-KOOM
MERLIIIIN!
FORGIVE ME, O YESTERDAY KING.
I HAVE BEEN RUDE.
I CAME UNANNOUNCED TO YOUR CITY. AND UNWELCOME TO THIS TEMPLE.
BUT I AM NEARLY DONE. ALL THAT REMAINS...

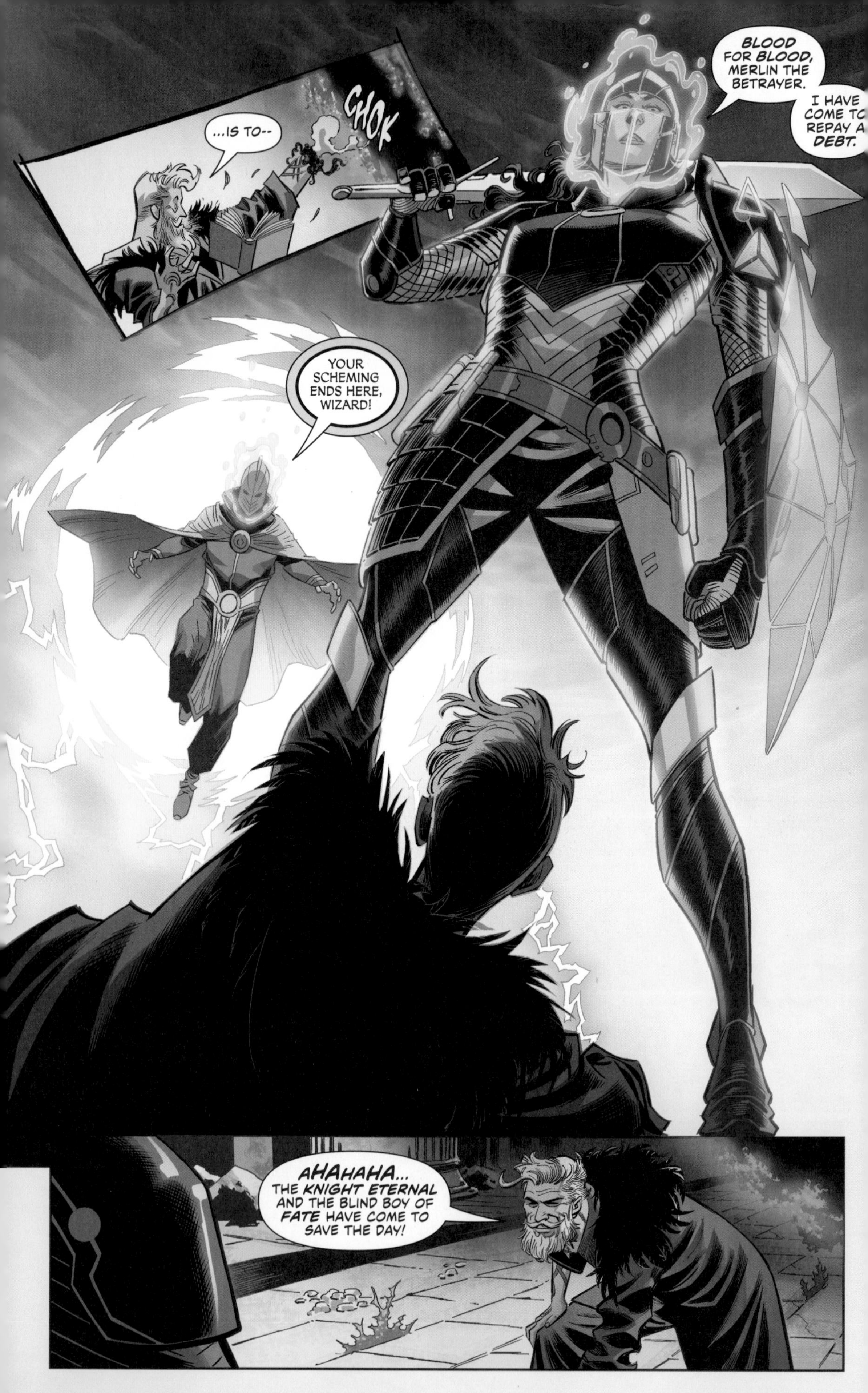
...IS TO--
CHOK
BLOOD FOR BLOOD, MERLIN THE BETRAYER.
I HAVE COME TO REPAY A DEBT.
YOUR SCHEMING ENDS HERE, WIZARD!
AHAHAHA... THE KNIGHT ETERNAL AND THE BLIND BOY OF FATE HAVE COME TO SAVE THE DAY!

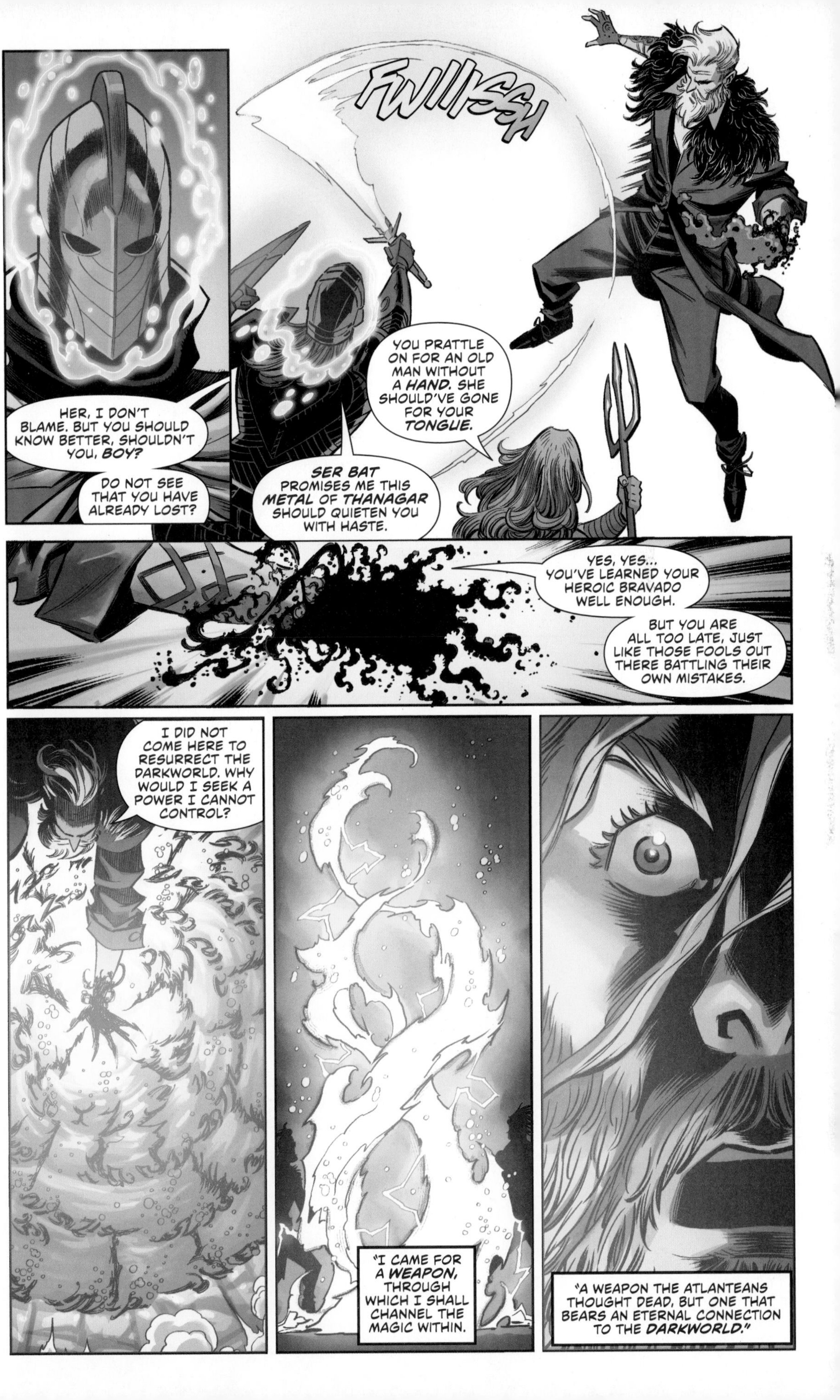
FWIIISSH
HER, I DON'T BLAME. BUT YOU SHOULD KNOW BETTER, SHOULDN'T YOU, BOY?
DO NOT SEE THAT YOU HAVE ALREADY LOST?
SER BAT PROMISES ME THIS METAL OF THANAGAR SHOULD QUIETEN YOU WITH HASTE.
YOU PRATTLE ON FOR AN OLD MAN WITHOUT A HAND. SHE SHOULD'VE GONE FOR YOUR TONGUE.
YES, YES... YOU'VE LEARNED YOUR HEROIC BRAVADO WELL ENOUGH.
BUT YOU ARE ALL TOO LATE, JUST LIKE THOSE FOOLS OUT THERE BATTLING THEIR OWN MISTAKES.
I DID NOT COME HERE TO RESURRECT THE DARKWORLD. WHY WOULD I SEEK A POWER I CANNOT CONTROL?
"I CAME FOR A WEAPON, THROUGH WHICH I SHALL CHANNEL THE MAGIC WITHIN.
"A WEAPON THE ATLANTEANS THOUGHT DEAD, BUT ONE THAT BEARS AN ETERNAL CONNECTION TO THE DARKWORLD."

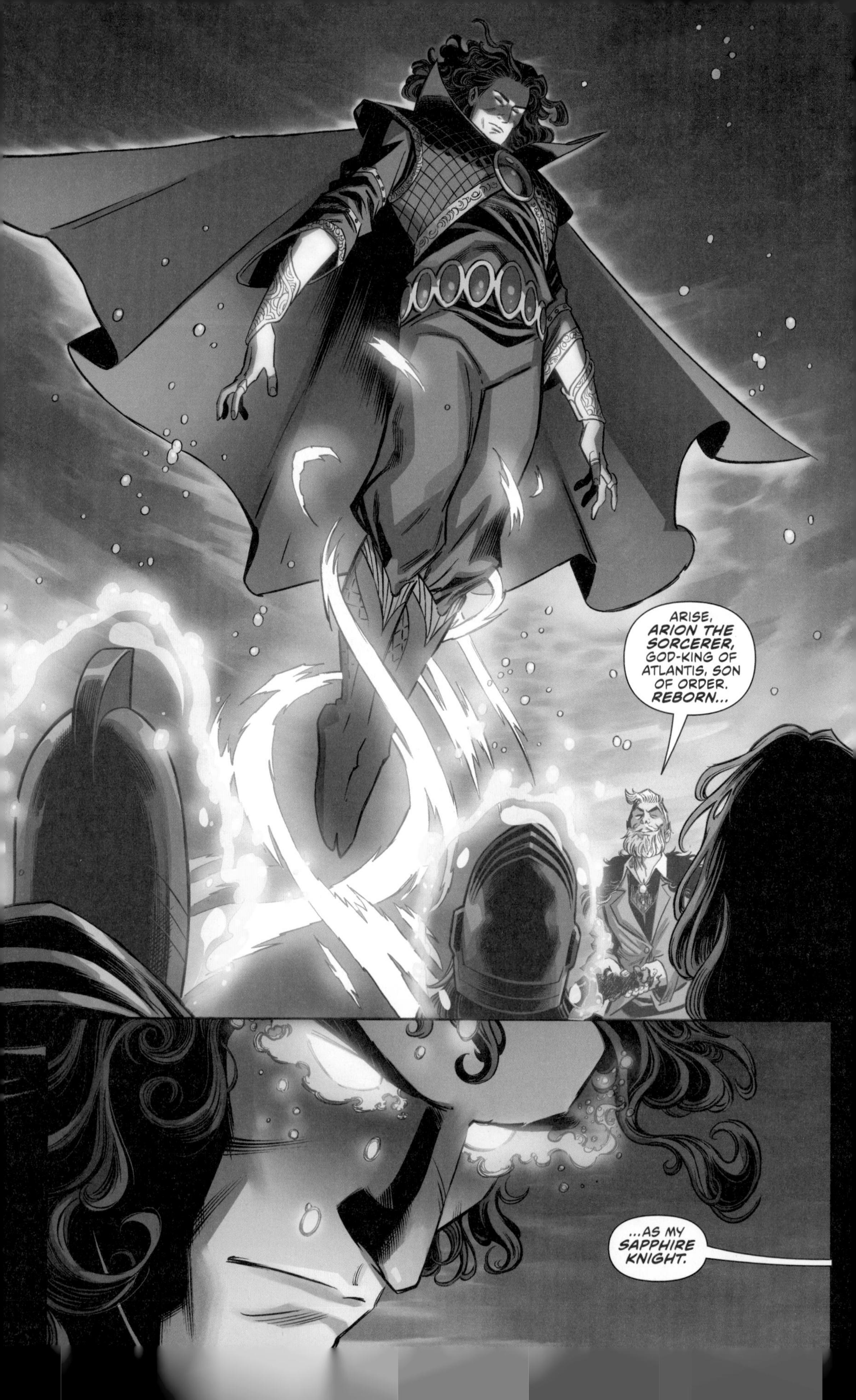
ARISE, ARION THE SORCERER, GOD-KING OF ATLANTIS, SON OF ORDER. REBORN...
...AS MY SAPPHIRE KNIGHT.

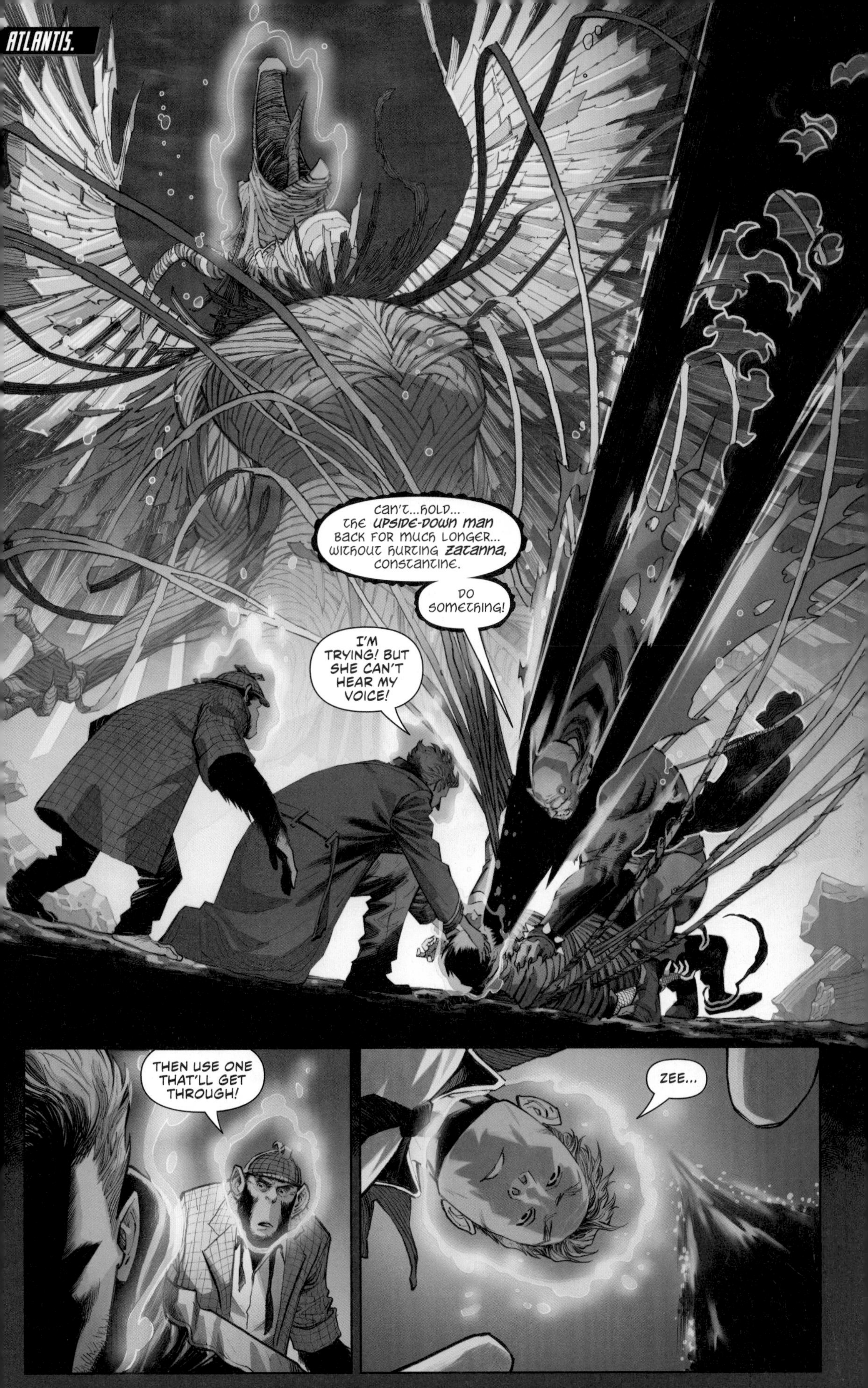
ATLANTIS.
CAN'T...HOLD... THE UPSIDE-DOWN MAN BACK FOR MUCH LONGER... WITHOUT HURTING ZATANNA, CONSTANTINE.
DO SOMETHING!
I'M TRYING! BUT SHE CAN'T HEAR MY VOICE!
THEN USE ONE THAT'LL GET THROUGH!
ZEE...

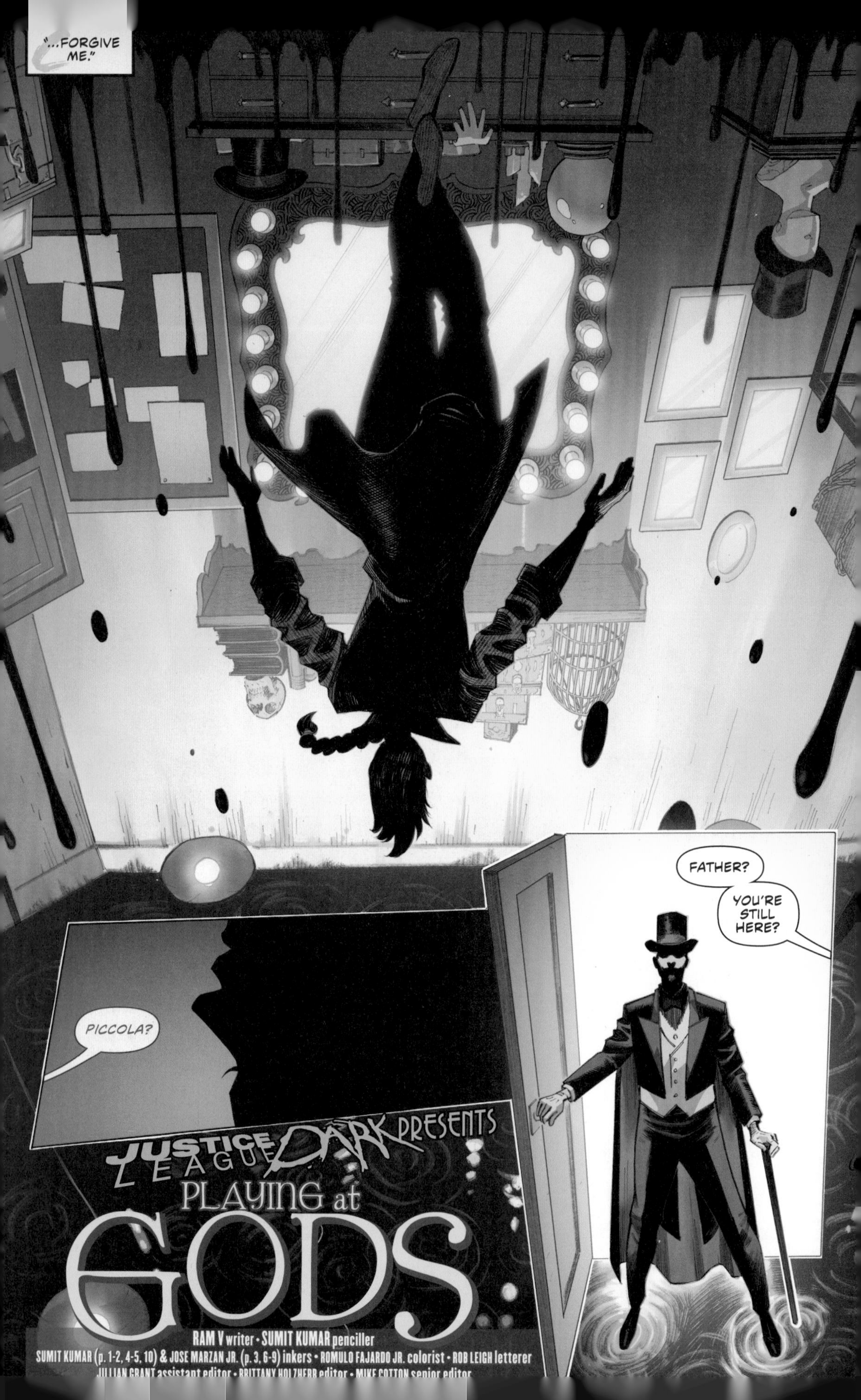

"...FORGIVE ME."
FATHER?
YOU'RE STILL HERE?
PICCOLA?
JUSTICE LEAGUE DARK PRESENTS
PLAYING at GODS
RAM V writer • SUMIT KUMAR penciller
SUMIT KUMAR (p. 1-2, 4-5, 10) & JOSE MARZAN JR. (p. 3, 6-9) inkers • ROMULO FAJARDO JR. colorist • ROB LEIGH letterer
JILLIAN GRANT assistant editor • BRITTANY HOLZHERR editor • MIKE COTTON senior editor

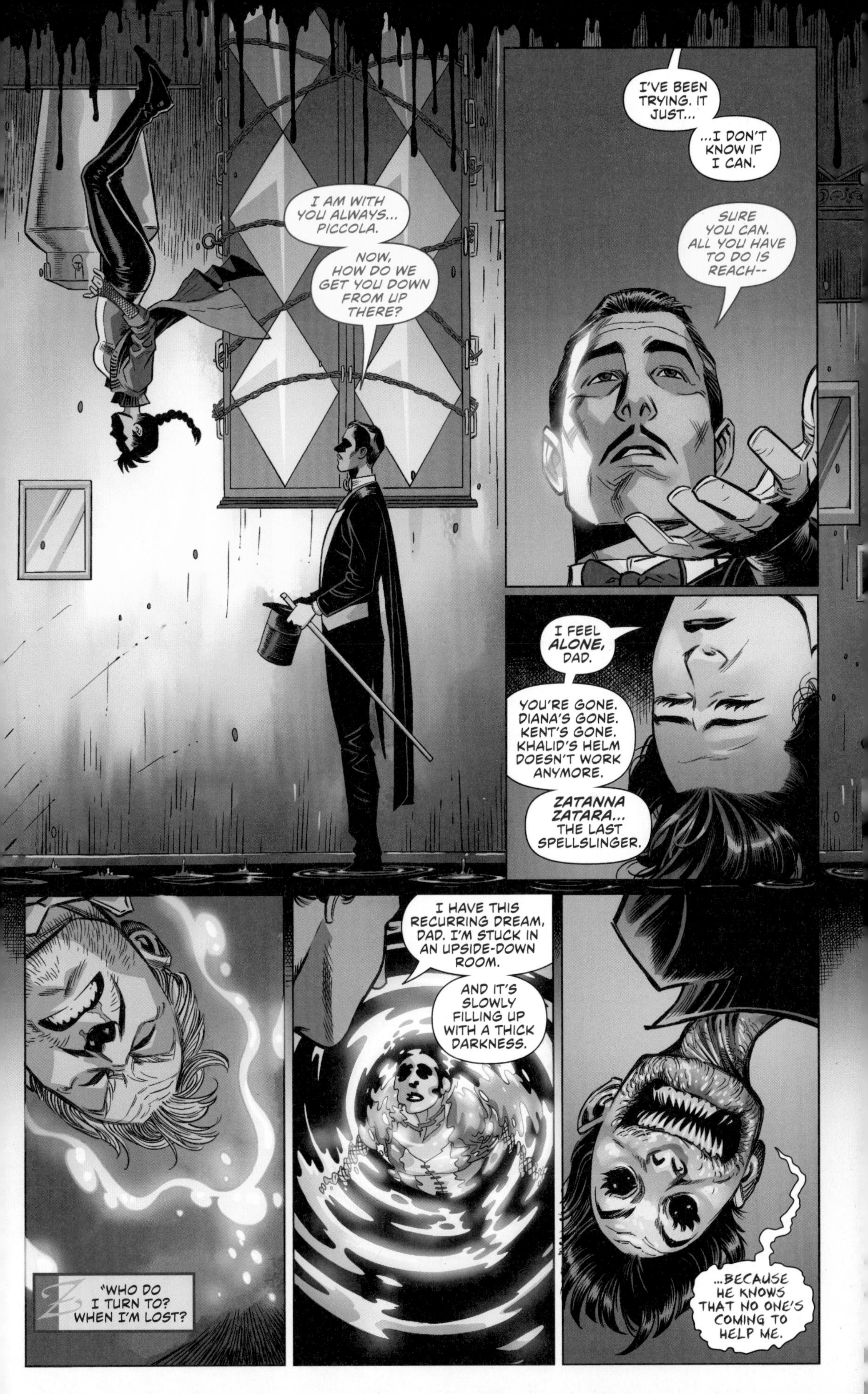
I AM WITH YOU ALWAYS... PICCOLA.
NOW, HOW DO WE GET YOU DOWN FROM UP THERE?
I'VE BEEN TRYING. IT JUST...
...I DON'T KNOW IF I CAN.
SURE YOU CAN. ALL YOU HAVE TO DO IS REACH--
I FEEL ALONE, DAD.
YOU'RE GONE. DIANA'S GONE. KENT'S GONE. KHALID'S HELM DOESN'T WORK ANYMORE.
ZATANNA ZATARA... THE LAST SPELLSLINGER.
"WHO DO I TURN TO? WHEN I'M LOST?
I HAVE THIS RECURRING DREAM, DAD. I'M STUCK IN AN UPSIDE-DOWN ROOM.
AND IT'S SLOWLY FILLING UP WITH A THICK DARKNESS.
...BECAUSE HE KNOWS THAT NO ONE'S COMING TO HELP ME.

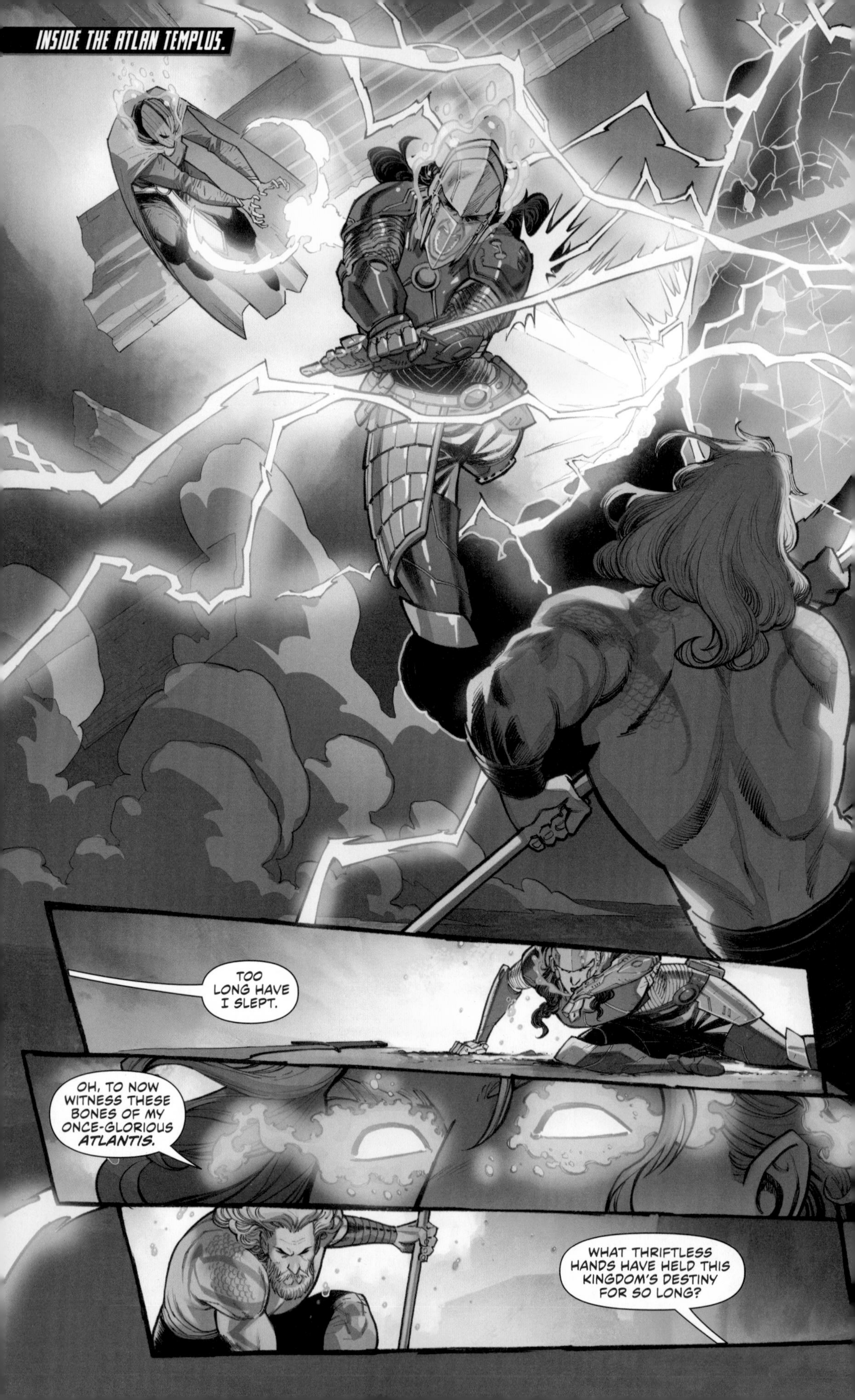
INSIDE THE ATLAN TEMPLUS.
TOO LONG HAVE I SLEPT.
OH, TO NOW WITNESS THESE BONES OF MY ONCE-GLORIOUS *ATLANTIS.*
WHAT THRIFTLESS HANDS HAVE HELD THIS KINGDOM'S DESTINY FOR SO LONG?

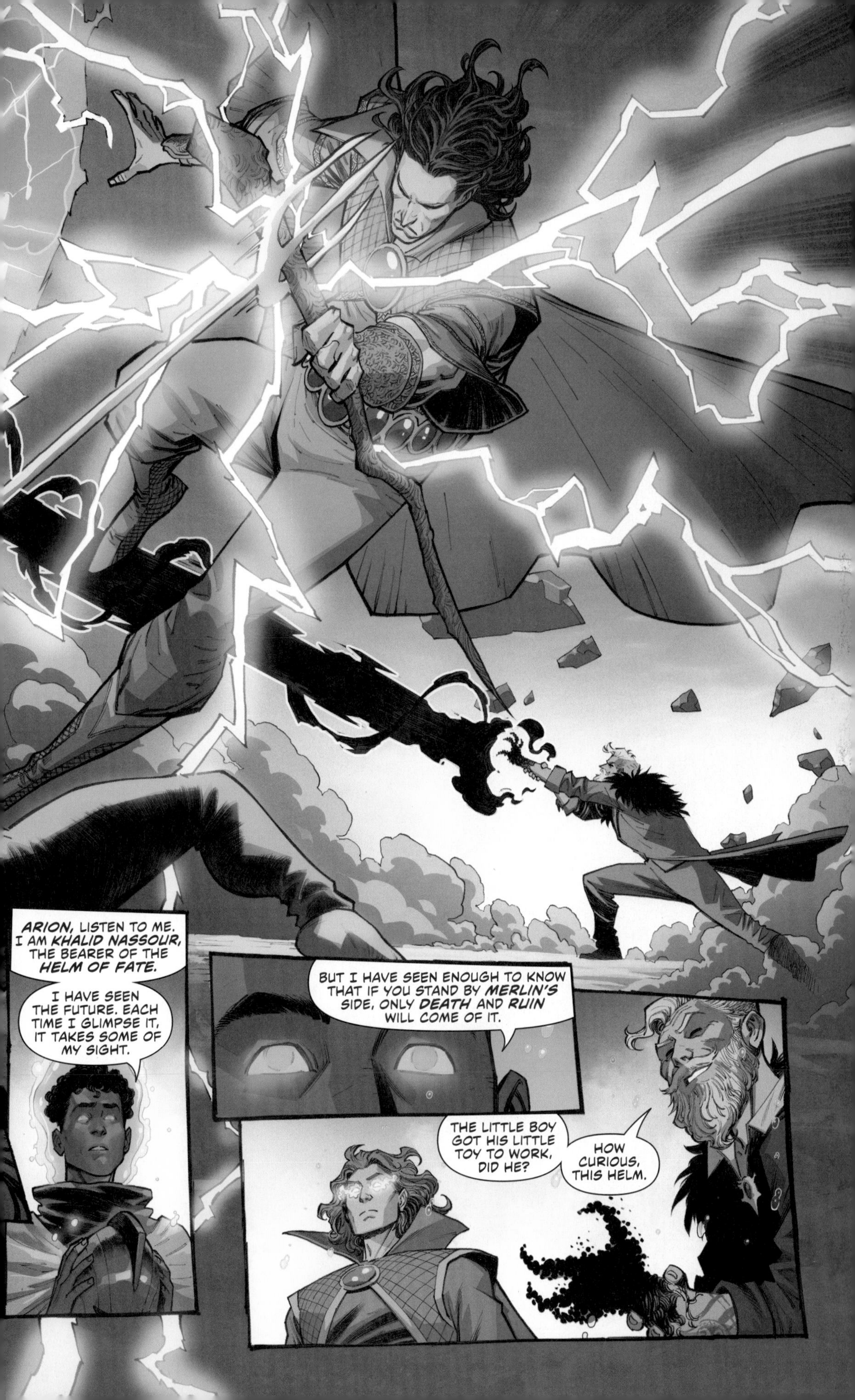
ARION, LISTEN TO ME. I AM KHALID NASSOUR, THE BEARER OF THE HELM OF FATE.
I HAVE SEEN THE FUTURE. EACH TIME I GLIMPSE IT, IT TAKES SOME OF MY SIGHT.
BUT I HAVE SEEN ENOUGH TO KNOW THAT IF YOU STAND BY MERLIN'S SIDE, ONLY DEATH AND RUIN WILL COME OF IT.
THE LITTLE BOY GOT HIS LITTLE TOY TO WORK, DID HE?
HOW CURIOUS, THIS HELM.

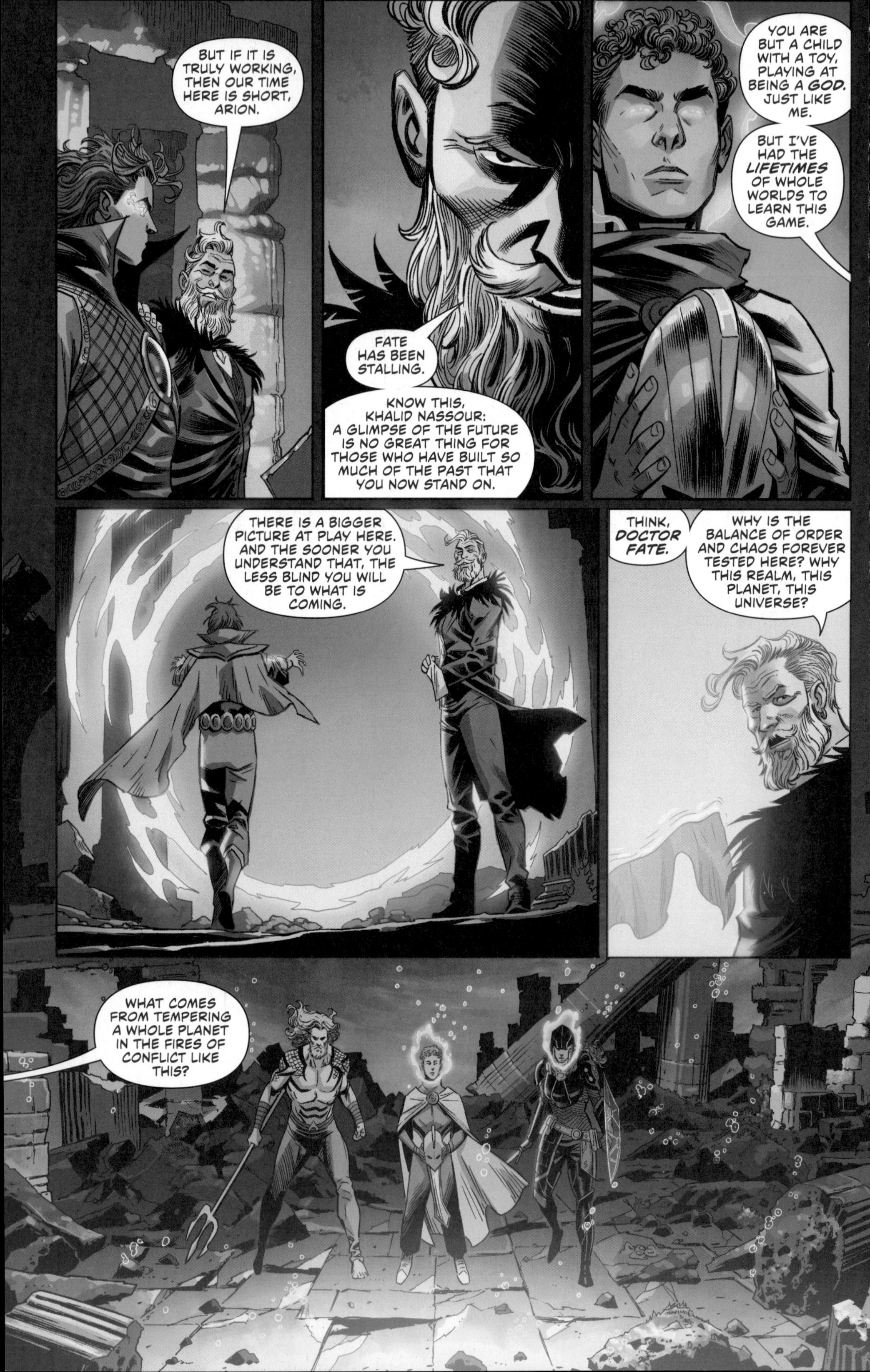
BUT IF IT IS TRULY WORKING, THEN OUR TIME HERE IS SHORT, ARION.
FATE HAS BEEN STALLING.
KNOW THIS, KHALID NASSOUR: A GLIMPSE OF THE FUTURE IS NO GREAT THING FOR THOSE WHO HAVE BUILT SO MUCH OF THE PAST THAT YOU NOW STAND ON.
YOU ARE BUT A CHILD WITH A TOY, PLAYING AT BEING A *GOD.* JUST LIKE ME.
BUT I'VE HAD THE *LIFETIMES* OF WHOLE WORLDS TO LEARN THIS GAME.
THERE IS A BIGGER PICTURE AT PLAY HERE. AND THE SOONER YOU UNDERSTAND THAT, THE LESS BLIND YOU WILL BE TO WHAT IS COMING.
THINK, *DOCTOR FATE.*
WHY IS THE BALANCE OF ORDER AND CHAOS FOREVER TESTED HERE? WHY THIS REALM, THIS PLANET, THIS UNIVERSE?
WHAT COMES FROM TEMPERING A WHOLE PLANET IN THE FIRES OF CONFLICT LIKE THIS?

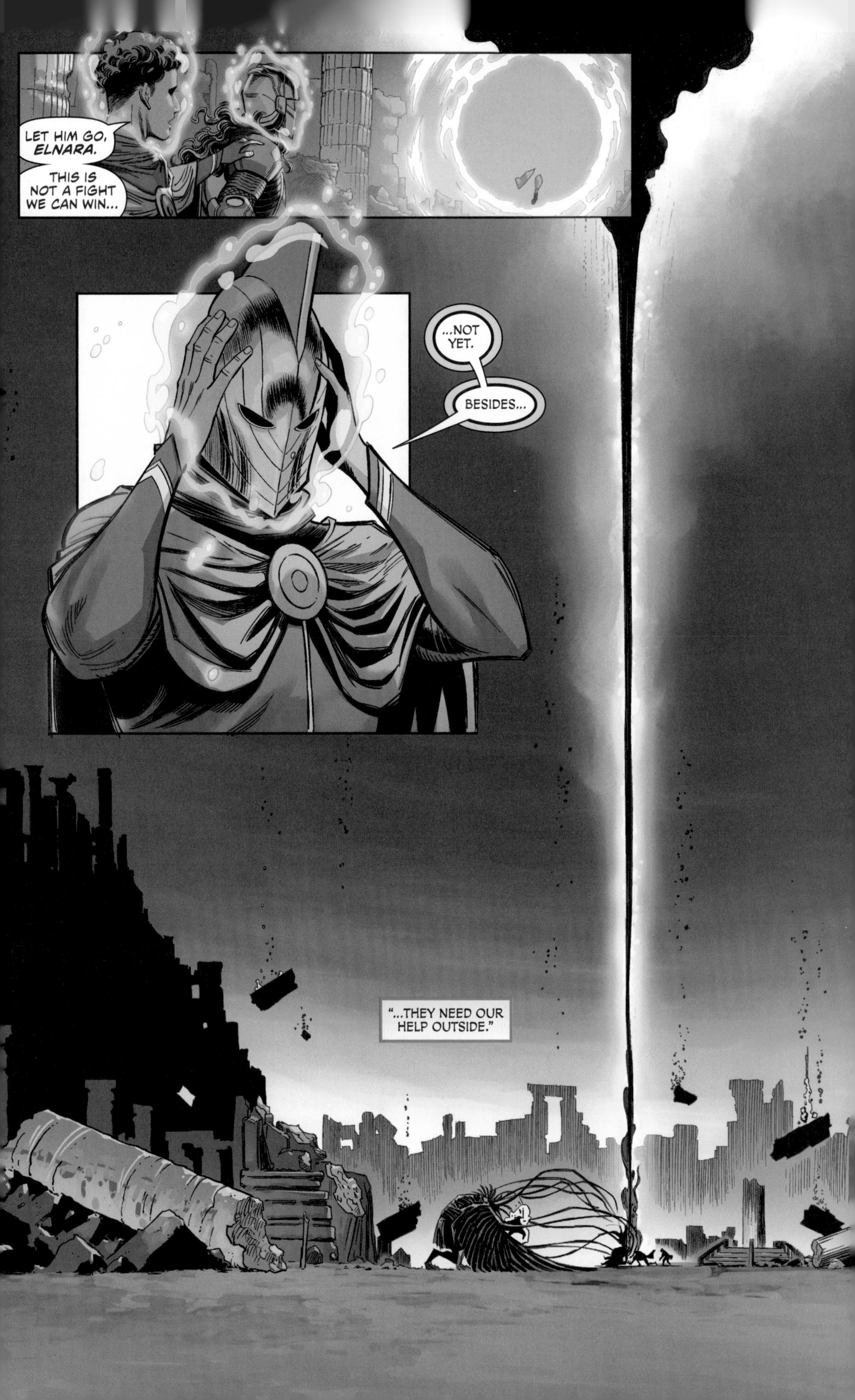
LET HIM GO, ELNARA.
THIS IS NOT A FIGHT WE CAN WIN...
...NOT YET.
BESIDES...
"...THEY NEED OUR HELP OUTSIDE."

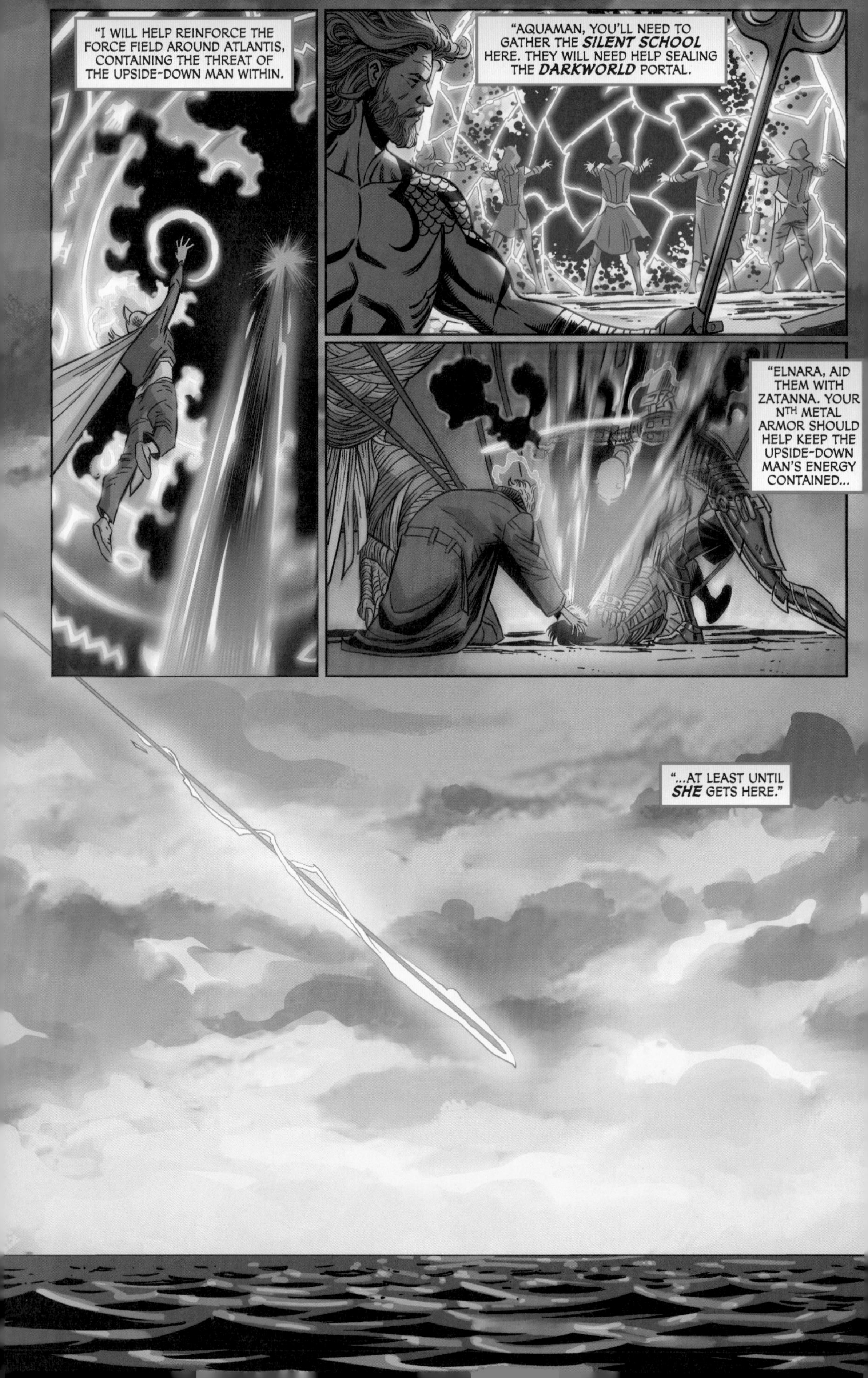
"I WILL HELP REINFORCE THE FORCE FIELD AROUND ATLANTIS, CONTAINING THE THREAT OF THE UPSIDE-DOWN MAN WITHIN.
"AQUAMAN, YOU'LL NEED TO GATHER THE SILENT SCHOOL HERE. THEY WILL NEED HELP SEALING THE DARKWORLD PORTAL.
"ELNARA, AID THEM WITH ZATANNA. YOUR Nth METAL ARMOR SHOULD HELP KEEP THE UPSIDE-DOWN MAN'S ENERGY CONTAINED...
"...AT LEAST UNTIL SHE GETS HERE."

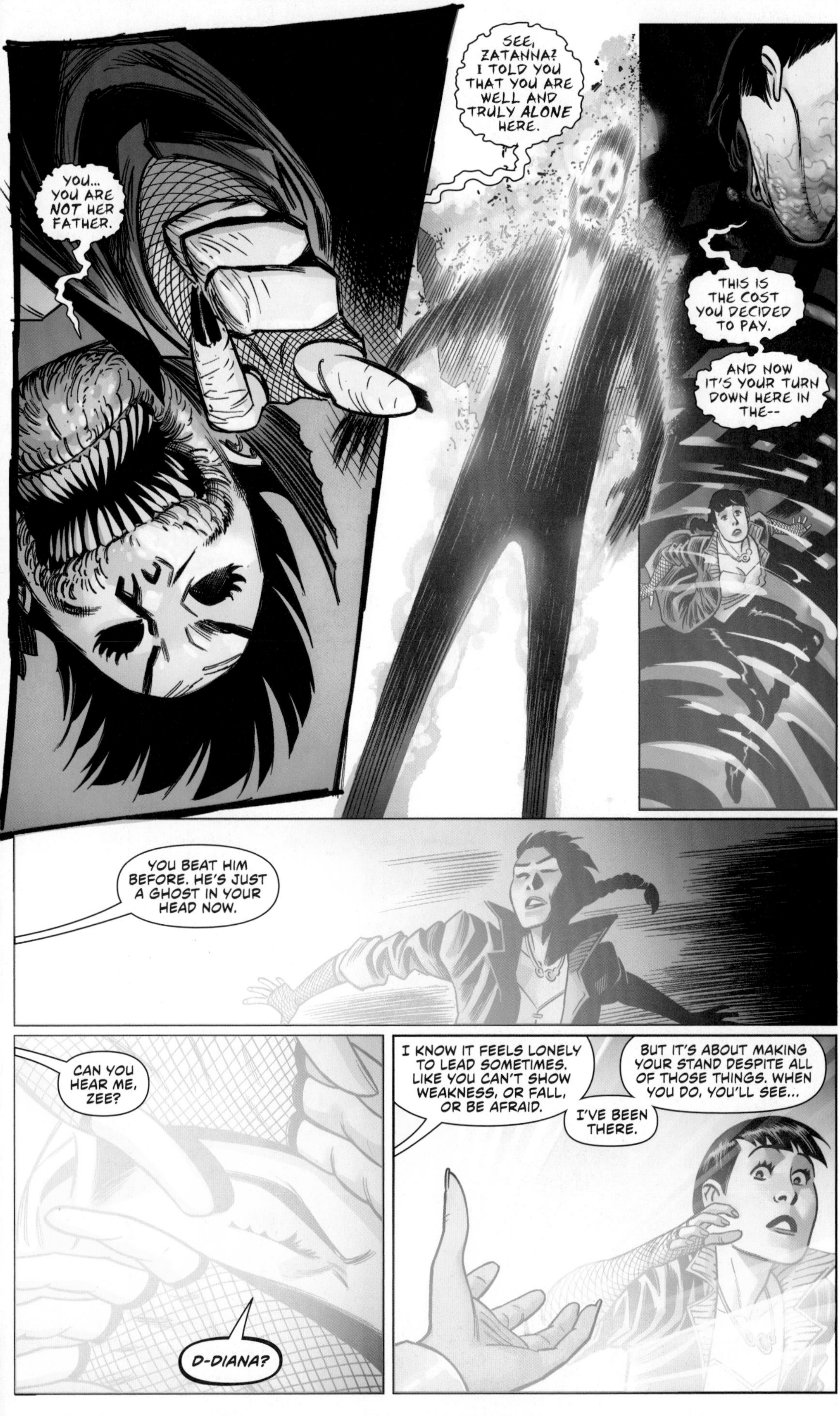
YOU... YOU ARE NOT HER FATHER.
SEE, ZATANNA? I TOLD YOU THAT YOU ARE WELL AND TRULY ALONE HERE.
THIS IS THE COST YOU DECIDED TO PAY.
AND NOW IT'S YOUR TURN DOWN HERE IN THE--
YOU BEAT HIM BEFORE. HE'S JUST A GHOST IN YOUR HEAD NOW.
CAN YOU HEAR ME, ZEE?
D-DIANA?
I KNOW IT FEELS LONELY TO LEAD SOMETIMES. LIKE YOU CAN'T SHOW WEAKNESS, OR FALL, OR BE AFRAID.
I'VE BEEN THERE.
BUT IT'S ABOUT MAKING YOUR STAND DESPITE ALL OF THOSE THINGS. WHEN YOU DO, YOU'LL SEE...

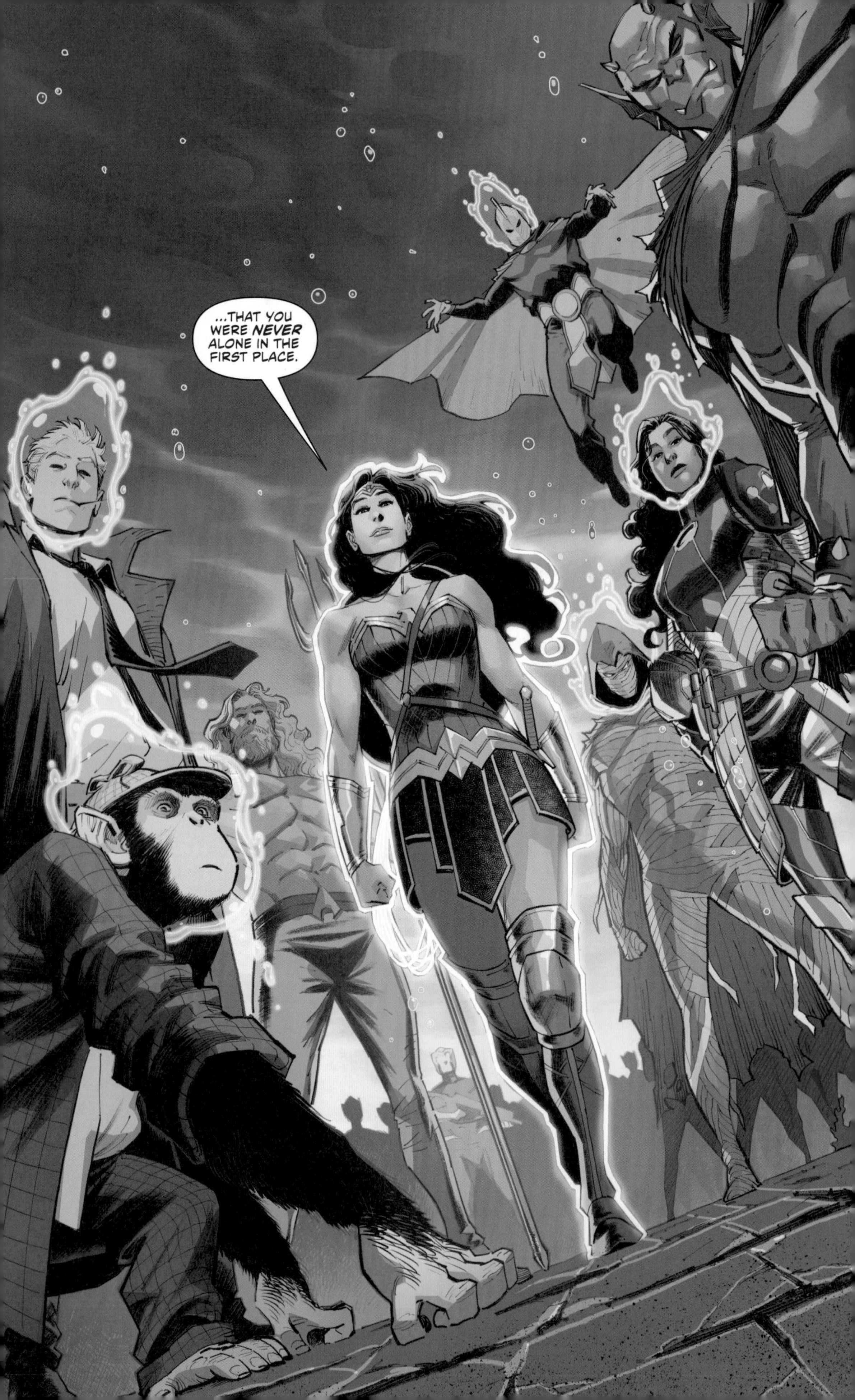
...THAT YOU WERE NEVER ALONE IN THE FIRST PLACE.

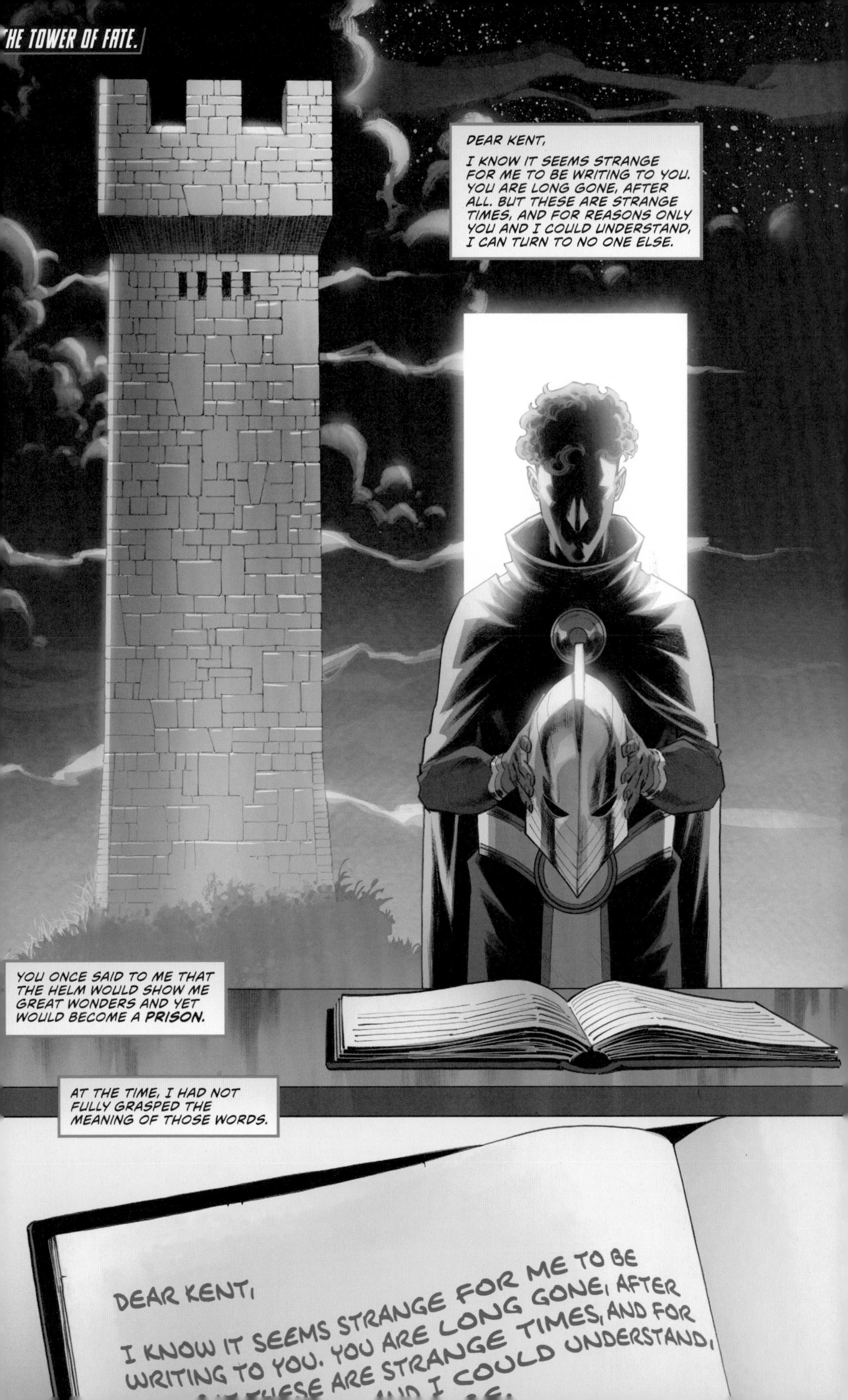
HE TOWER OF FATE.
DEAR KENT,
I KNOW IT SEEMS STRANGE FOR ME TO BE WRITING TO YOU. YOU ARE LONG GONE, AFTER ALL. BUT THESE ARE STRANGE TIMES, AND FOR REASONS ONLY YOU AND I COULD UNDERSTAND, I CAN TURN TO NO ONE ELSE.
YOU ONCE SAID TO ME THAT THE HELM WOULD SHOW ME GREAT WONDERS AND YET WOULD BECOME A **PRISON**.
AT THE TIME, I HAD NOT FULLY GRASPED THE MEANING OF THOSE WORDS.
DEAR KENT,
I KNOW IT SEEMS STRANGE FOR ME TO BE
WRITING TO YOU. YOU ARE LONG GONE, AFTER
THESE ARE STRANGE TIMES, AND FOR
I COULD UNDERSTAND,

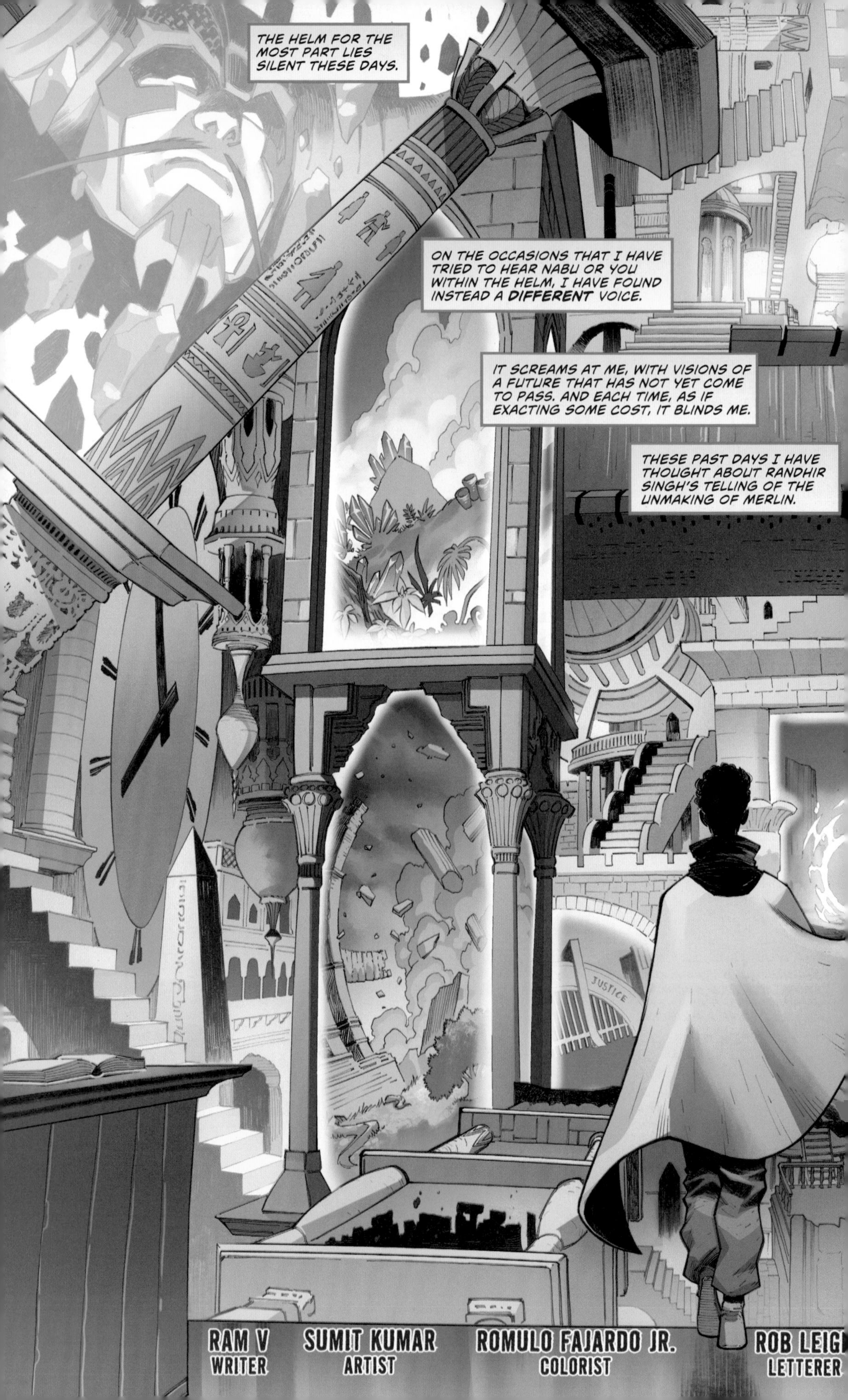
THE HELM FOR THE MOST PART LIES SILENT THESE DAYS.
ON THE OCCASIONS THAT I HAVE TRIED TO HEAR NABU OR YOU WITHIN THE HELM, I HAVE FOUND INSTEAD A DIFFERENT VOICE.
IT SCREAMS AT ME, WITH VISIONS OF A FUTURE THAT HAS NOT YET COME TO PASS. AND EACH TIME, AS IF EXACTING SOME COST, IT BLINDS ME.
THESE PAST DAYS I HAVE THOUGHT ABOUT RANDHIR SINGH'S TELLING OF THE UNMAKING OF MERLIN.
JUSTICE
RAM V WRITER
SUMIT KUMAR ARTIST
ROMULO FAJARDO JR. COLORIST
ROB LEIG LETTERER

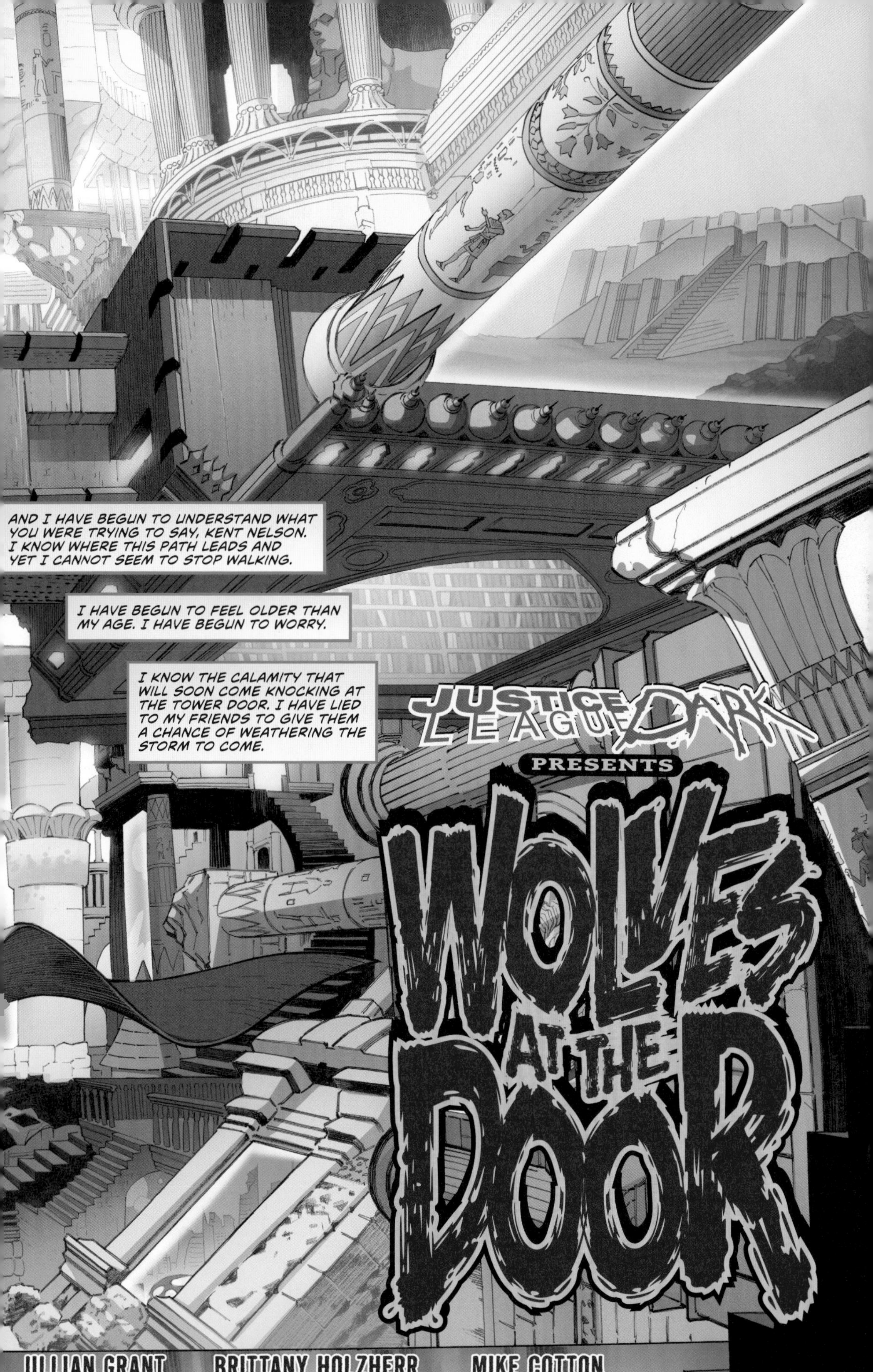
AND I HAVE BEGUN TO UNDERSTAND WHAT YOU WERE TRYING TO SAY, KENT NELSON. I KNOW WHERE THIS PATH LEADS AND YET I CANNOT SEEM TO STOP WALKING.
I HAVE BEGUN TO FEEL OLDER THAN MY AGE. I HAVE BEGUN TO WORRY.
I KNOW THE CALAMITY THAT WILL SOON COME KNOCKING AT THE TOWER DOOR. I HAVE LIED TO MY FRIENDS TO GIVE THEM A CHANCE OF WEATHERING THE STORM TO COME.
JUSTICE LEAGUE DARK
PRESENTS
WOLVES AT THE DOOR

JILLIAN GRANT ASSISTANT EDITOR · BRITTANY HOLZHERR EDITOR · MIKE COTTON SENIOR EDITOR

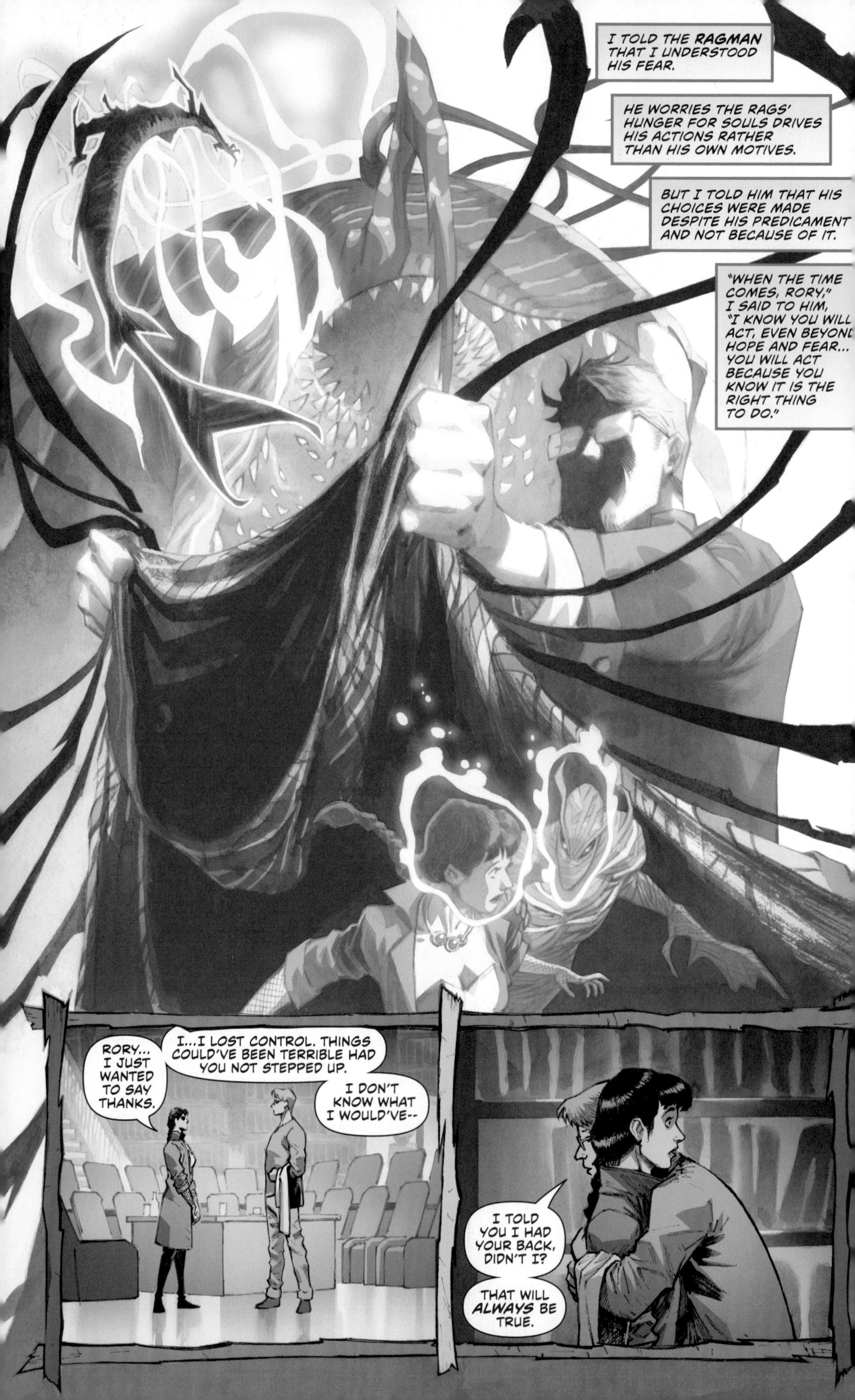
I TOLD THE RAGMAN THAT I UNDERSTOOD HIS FEAR.
HE WORRIES THE RAGS' HUNGER FOR SOULS DRIVES HIS ACTIONS RATHER THAN HIS OWN MOTIVES.
BUT I TOLD HIM THAT HIS CHOICES WERE MADE DESPITE HIS PREDICAMENT AND NOT BECAUSE OF IT.
"WHEN THE TIME COMES, RORY," I SAID TO HIM, "I KNOW YOU WILL ACT, EVEN BEYOND HOPE AND FEAR... YOU WILL ACT BECAUSE YOU KNOW IT IS THE RIGHT THING TO DO."
RORY... I JUST WANTED TO SAY THANKS.
I...I LOST CONTROL. THINGS COULD'VE BEEN TERRIBLE HAD YOU NOT STEPPED UP.
I DON'T KNOW WHAT I WOULD'VE--
I TOLD YOU I HAD YOUR BACK, DIDN'T I?
THAT WILL ALWAYS BE TRUE.

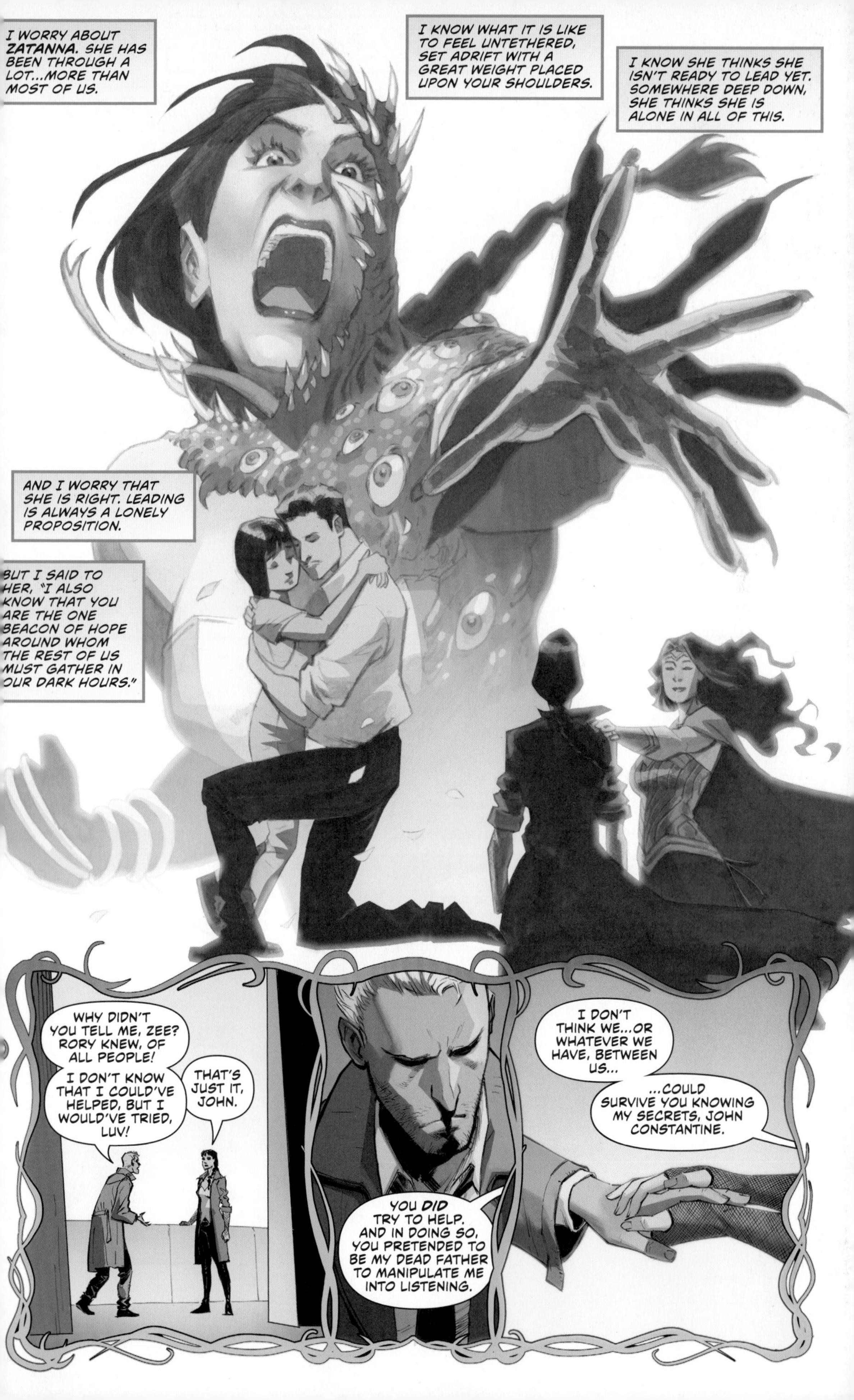
I WORRY ABOUT ZATANNA. SHE HAS BEEN THROUGH A LOT...MORE THAN MOST OF US.
I KNOW WHAT IT IS LIKE TO FEEL UNTETHERED, SET ADRIFT WITH A GREAT WEIGHT PLACED UPON YOUR SHOULDERS.
I KNOW SHE THINKS SHE ISN'T READY TO LEAD YET. SOMEWHERE DEEP DOWN, SHE THINKS SHE IS ALONE IN ALL OF THIS.
AND I WORRY THAT SHE IS RIGHT. LEADING IS ALWAYS A LONELY PROPOSITION.
BUT I SAID TO HER, "I ALSO KNOW THAT YOU ARE THE ONE BEACON OF HOPE AROUND WHOM THE REST OF US MUST GATHER IN OUR DARK HOURS."
WHY DIDN'T YOU TELL ME, ZEE? RORY KNEW, OF ALL PEOPLE!
I DON'T KNOW THAT I COULD'VE HELPED, BUT I WOULD'VE TRIED, LUV!
THAT'S JUST IT, JOHN.
YOU DID TRY TO HELP. AND IN DOING SO, YOU PRETENDED TO BE MY DEAD FATHER TO MANIPULATE ME INTO LISTENING.
I DON'T THINK WE...OR WHATEVER WE HAVE, BETWEEN US...
...COULD SURVIVE YOU KNOWING MY SECRETS, JOHN CONSTANTINE.

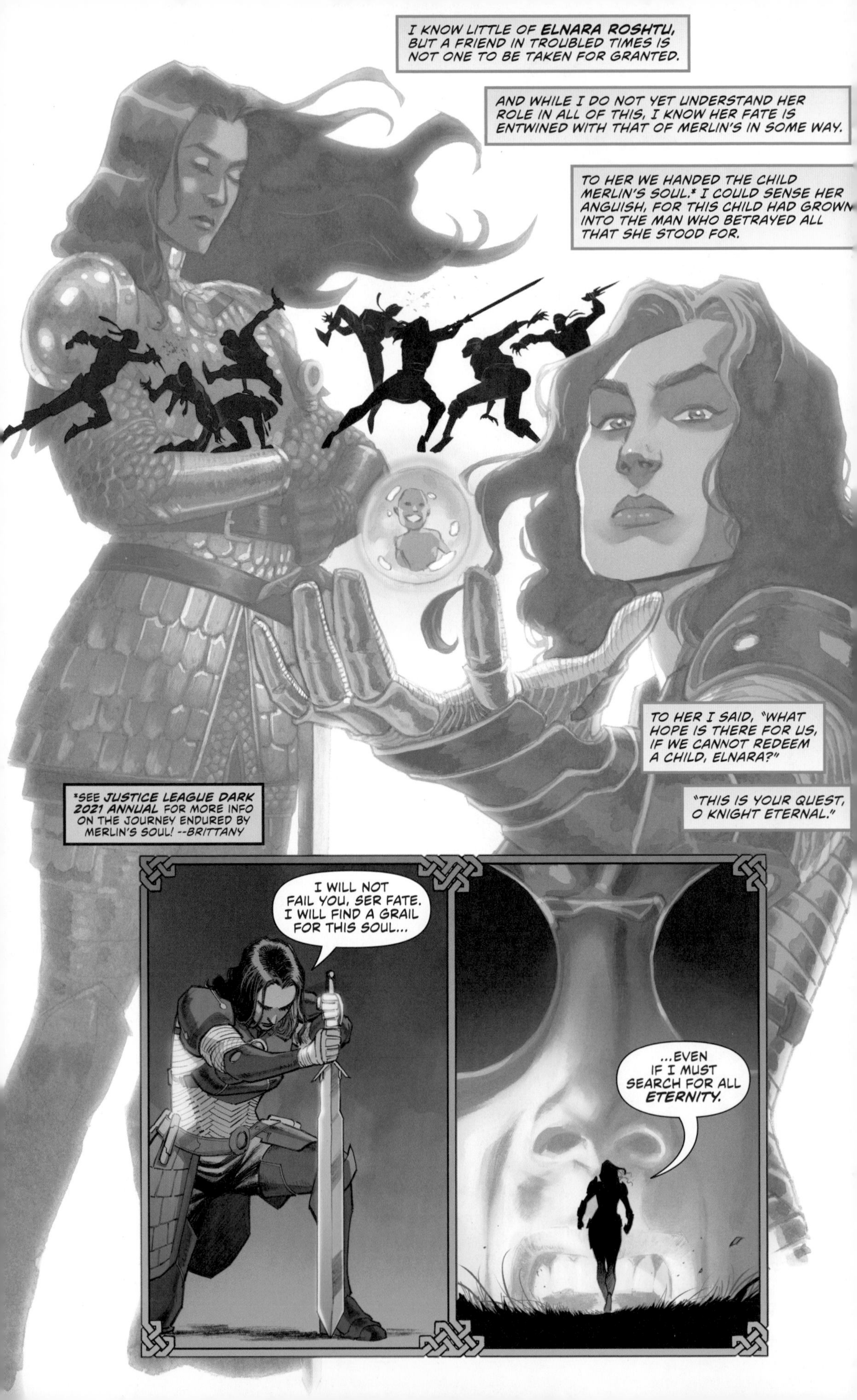

I KNOW LITTLE OF **ELNARA ROSHTU**, BUT A FRIEND IN TROUBLED TIMES IS NOT ONE TO BE TAKEN FOR GRANTED.
AND WHILE I DO NOT YET UNDERSTAND HER ROLE IN ALL OF THIS, I KNOW HER FATE IS ENTWINED WITH THAT OF MERLIN'S IN SOME WAY.
TO HER WE HANDED THE CHILD MERLIN'S SOUL.* I COULD SENSE HER ANGUISH, FOR THIS CHILD HAD GROWN INTO THE MAN WHO BETRAYED ALL THAT SHE STOOD FOR.
TO HER I SAID, "WHAT HOPE IS THERE FOR US, IF WE CANNOT REDEEM A CHILD, ELNARA?"
"THIS IS YOUR QUEST, O KNIGHT ETERNAL."
*SEE ***JUSTICE LEAGUE DARK 2021 ANNUAL*** FOR MORE INFO ON THE JOURNEY ENDURED BY MERLIN'S SOUL! --BRITTANY
I WILL NOT FAIL YOU, SER FATE. I WILL FIND A GRAIL FOR THIS SOUL...
...EVEN IF I MUST SEARCH FOR ALL ***ETERNITY.***

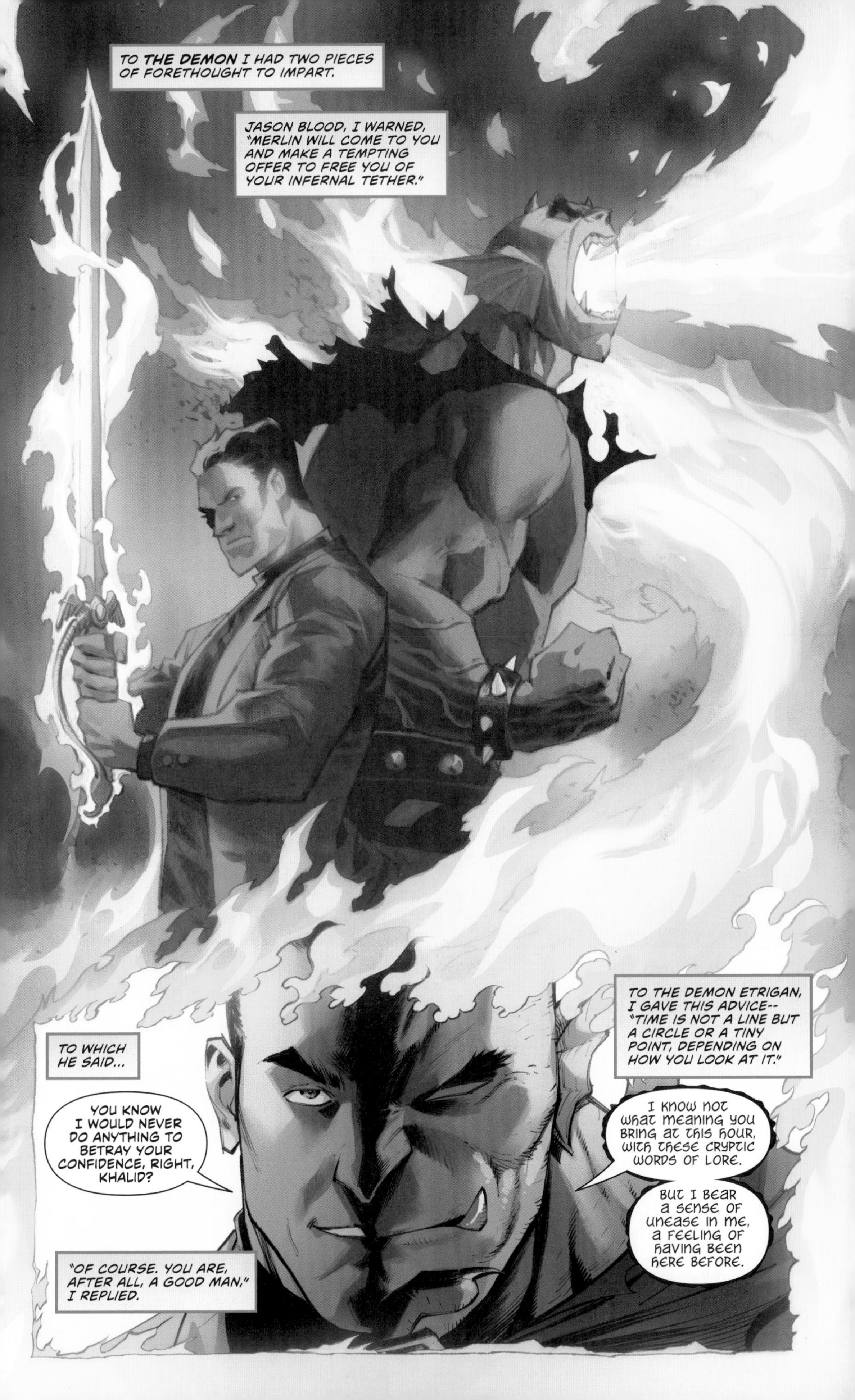
TO THE DEMON I HAD TWO PIECES OF FORETHOUGHT TO IMPART.
JASON BLOOD, I WARNED, "MERLIN WILL COME TO YOU AND MAKE A TEMPTING OFFER TO FREE YOU OF YOUR INFERNAL TETHER."
TO WHICH HE SAID...
YOU KNOW I WOULD NEVER DO ANYTHING TO BETRAY YOUR CONFIDENCE, RIGHT, KHALID?
"OF COURSE. YOU ARE, AFTER ALL, A GOOD MAN," I REPLIED.
TO THE DEMON ETRIGAN, I GAVE THIS ADVICE-- "TIME IS NOT A LINE BUT A CIRCLE OR A TINY POINT, DEPENDING ON HOW YOU LOOK AT IT."
I KNOW NOT WHAT MEANING YOU BRING AT THIS HOUR, WITH THESE CRYPTIC WORDS OF LORE.
BUT I BEAR A SENSE OF UNEASE IN ME, A FEELING OF HAVING BEEN HERE BEFORE.

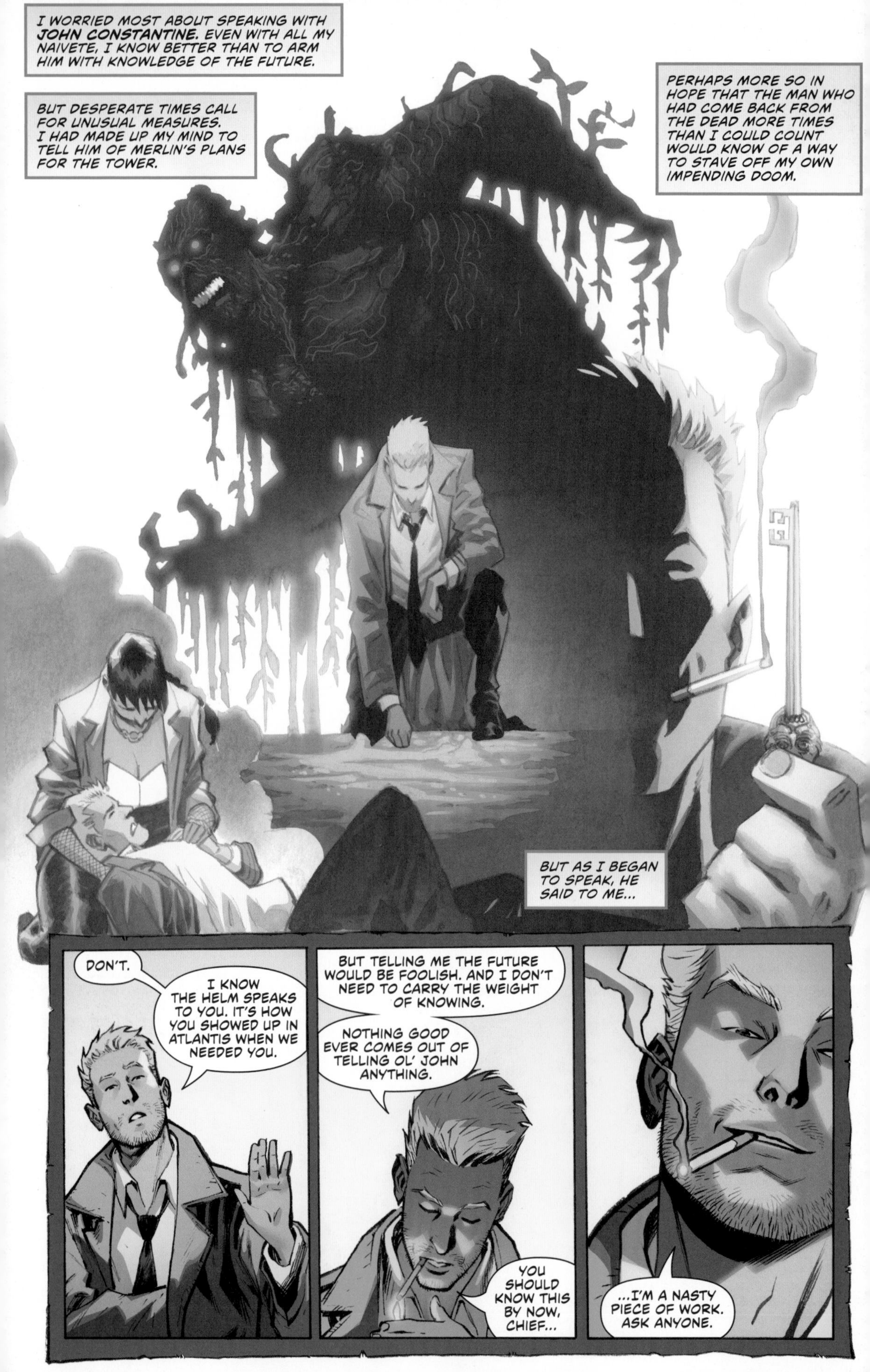
I WORRIED MOST ABOUT SPEAKING WITH JOHN CONSTANTINE. EVEN WITH ALL MY NAIVETE, I KNOW BETTER THAN TO ARM HIM WITH KNOWLEDGE OF THE FUTURE.
BUT DESPERATE TIMES CALL FOR UNUSUAL MEASURES. I HAD MADE UP MY MIND TO TELL HIM OF MERLIN'S PLANS FOR THE TOWER.
PERHAPS MORE SO IN HOPE THAT THE MAN WHO HAD COME BACK FROM THE DEAD MORE TIMES THAN I COULD COUNT WOULD KNOW OF A WAY TO STAVE OFF MY OWN IMPENDING DOOM.
BUT AS I BEGAN TO SPEAK, HE SAID TO ME...
DON'T.
I KNOW THE HELM SPEAKS TO YOU. IT'S HOW YOU SHOWED UP IN ATLANTIS WHEN WE NEEDED YOU.
BUT TELLING ME THE FUTURE WOULD BE FOOLISH. AND I DON'T NEED TO CARRY THE WEIGHT OF KNOWING.
NOTHING GOOD EVER COMES OUT OF TELLING OL' JOHN ANYTHING.
YOU SHOULD KNOW THIS BY NOW, CHIEF...
...I'M A NASTY PIECE OF WORK. ASK ANYONE.

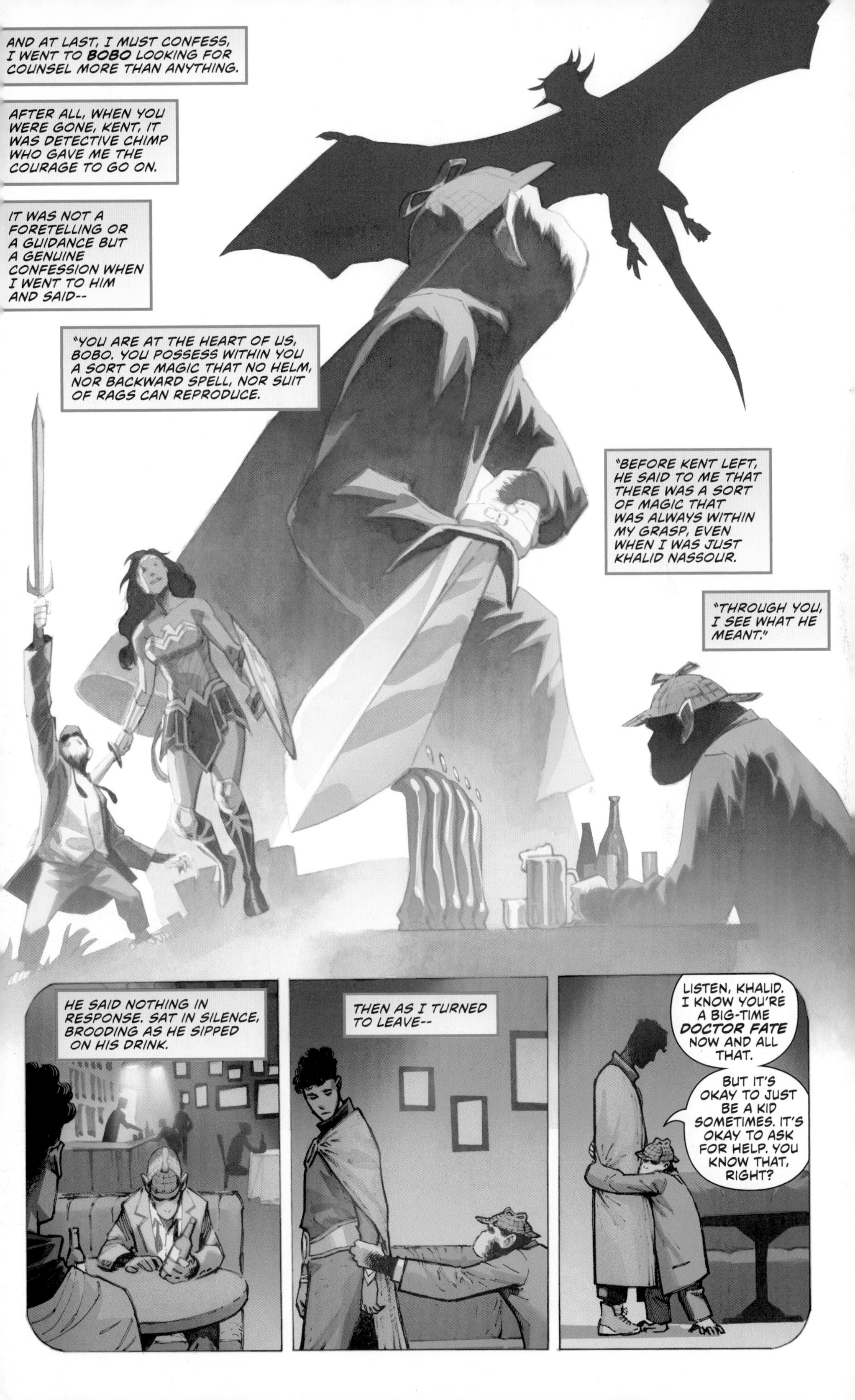
AND AT LAST, I MUST CONFESS, I WENT TO BOBO LOOKING FOR COUNSEL MORE THAN ANYTHING.
AFTER ALL, WHEN YOU WERE GONE, KENT, IT WAS DETECTIVE CHIMP WHO GAVE ME THE COURAGE TO GO ON.
IT WAS NOT A FORETELLING OR A GUIDANCE BUT A GENUINE CONFESSION WHEN I WENT TO HIM AND SAID--
"YOU ARE AT THE HEART OF US, BOBO. YOU POSSESS WITHIN YOU A SORT OF MAGIC THAT NO HELM, NOR BACKWARD SPELL, NOR SUIT OF RAGS CAN REPRODUCE.
"BEFORE KENT LEFT, HE SAID TO ME THAT THERE WAS A SORT OF MAGIC THAT WAS ALWAYS WITHIN MY GRASP, EVEN WHEN I WAS JUST KHALID NASSOUR.
"THROUGH YOU, I SEE WHAT HE MEANT."
HE SAID NOTHING IN RESPONSE. SAT IN SILENCE, BROODING AS HE SIPPED ON HIS DRINK.
THEN AS I TURNED TO LEAVE--
LISTEN, KHALID. I KNOW YOU'RE A BIG-TIME DOCTOR FATE NOW AND ALL THAT.
BUT IT'S OKAY TO JUST BE A KID SOMETIMES. IT'S OKAY TO ASK FOR HELP. YOU KNOW THAT, RIGHT?

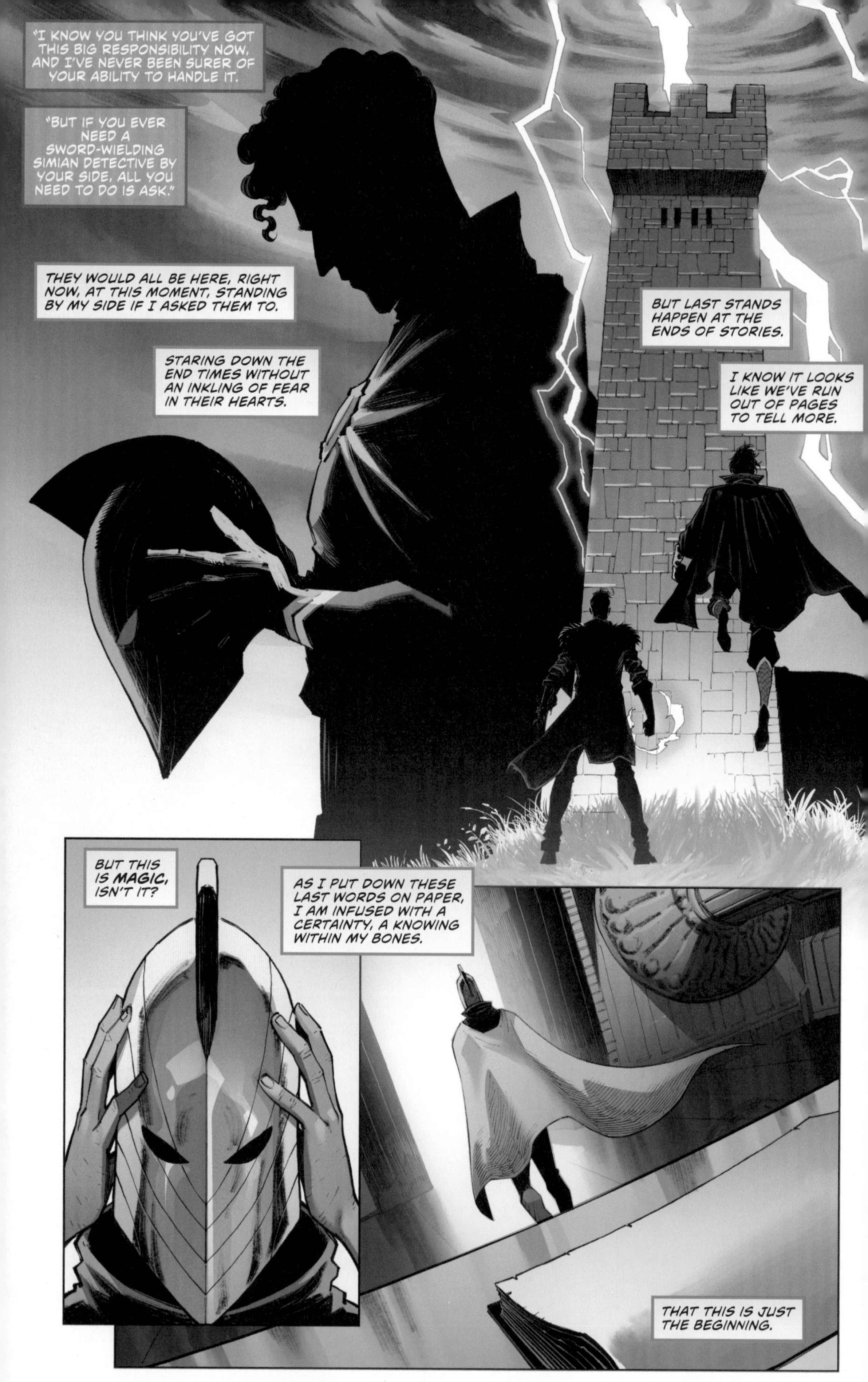
"I KNOW YOU THINK YOU'VE GOT THIS BIG RESPONSIBILITY NOW, AND I'VE NEVER BEEN SURER OF YOUR ABILITY TO HANDLE IT.
"BUT IF YOU EVER NEED A SWORD-WIELDING SIMIAN DETECTIVE BY YOUR SIDE, ALL YOU NEED TO DO IS ASK."
THEY WOULD ALL BE HERE, RIGHT NOW, AT THIS MOMENT, STANDING BY MY SIDE IF I ASKED THEM TO.
STARING DOWN THE END TIMES WITHOUT AN INKLING OF FEAR IN THEIR HEARTS.
BUT LAST STANDS HAPPEN AT THE ENDS OF STORIES.
I KNOW IT LOOKS LIKE WE'VE RUN OUT OF PAGES TO TELL MORE.
BUT THIS IS MAGIC, ISN'T IT?
AS I PUT DOWN THESE LAST WORDS ON PAPER, I AM INFUSED WITH A CERTAINTY, A KNOWING WITHIN MY BONES.
THAT THIS IS JUST THE BEGINNING.

Justice League Dark 2021 Annual #1 cover
by SEBASTIAN FIUMARA

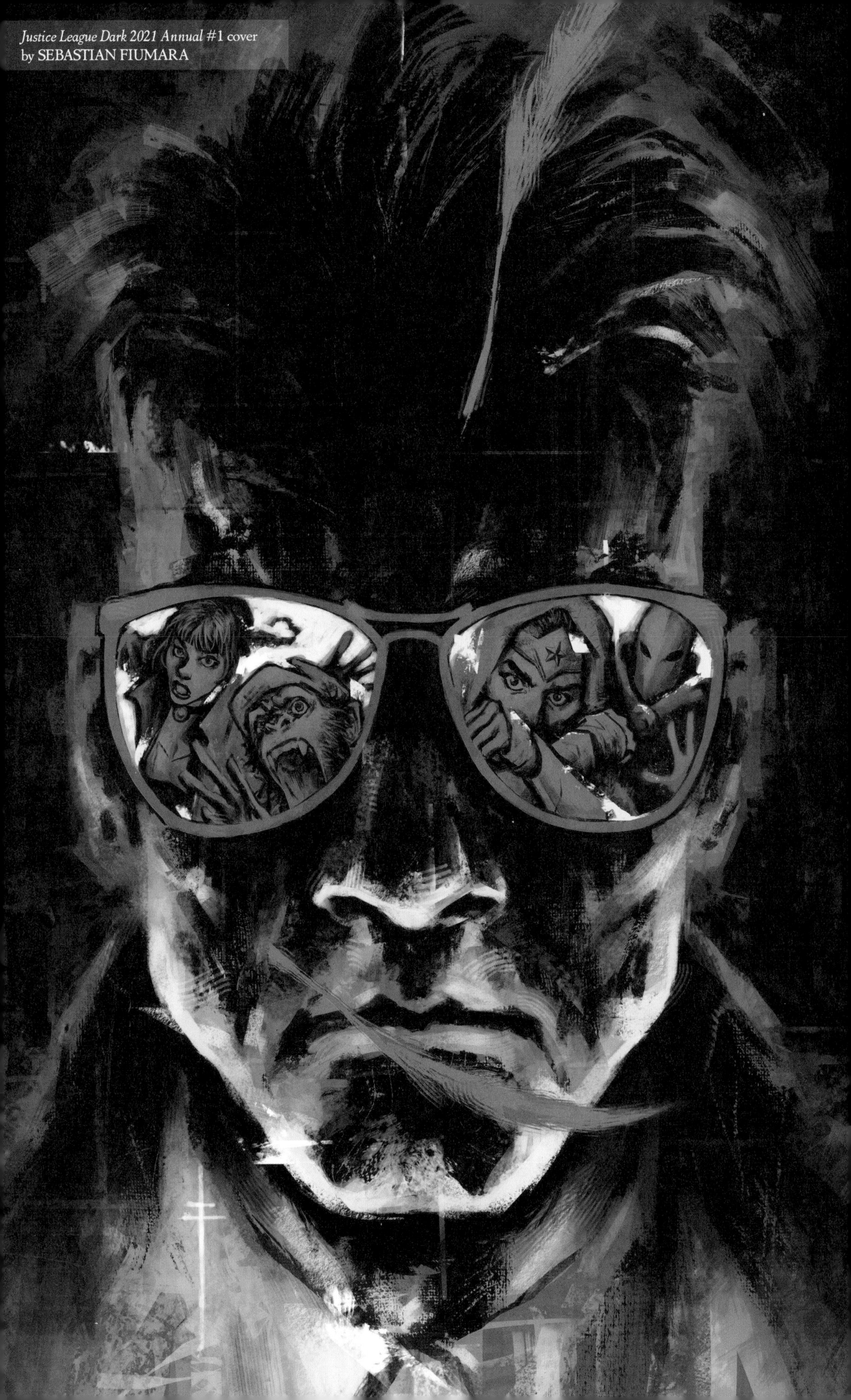

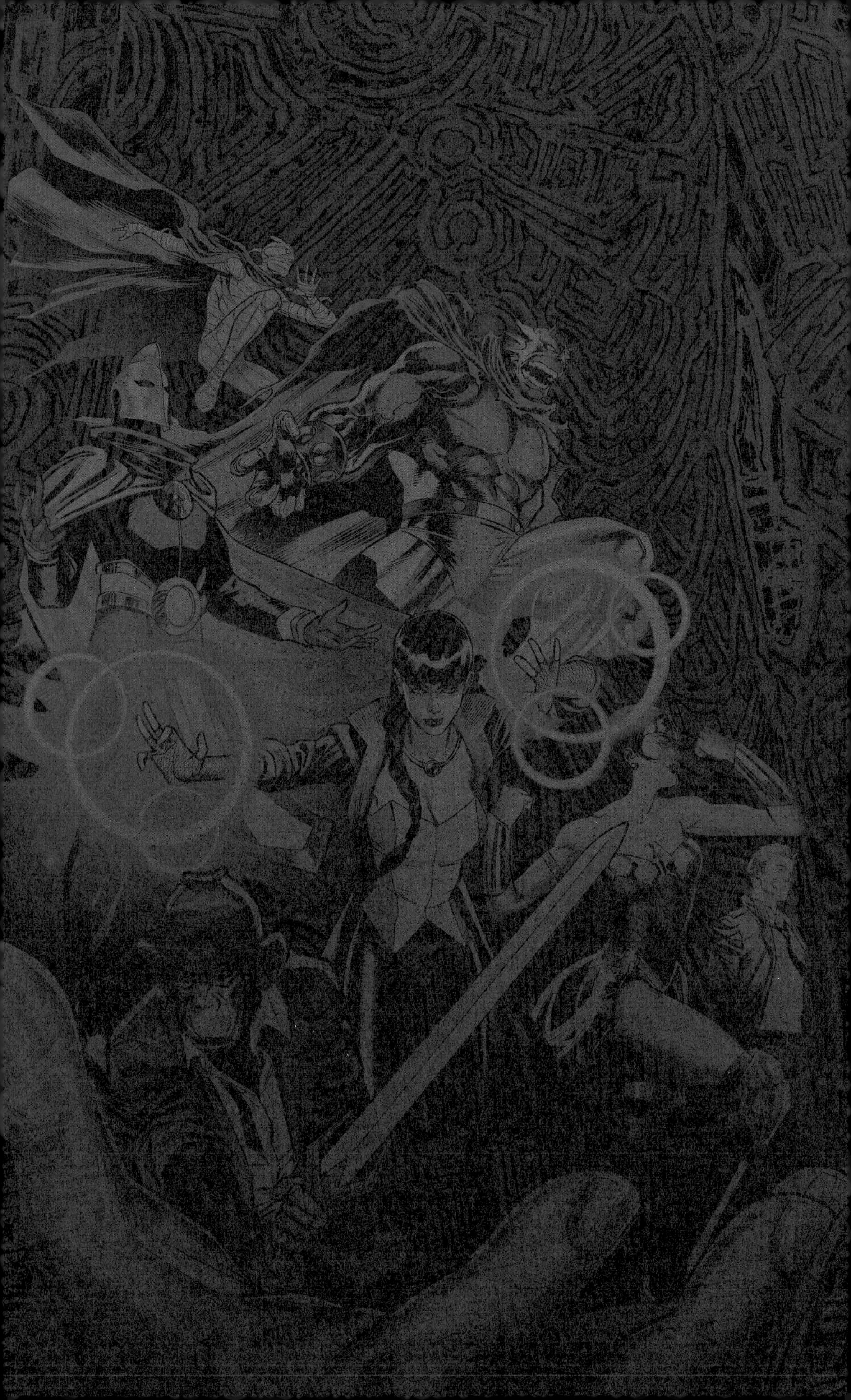

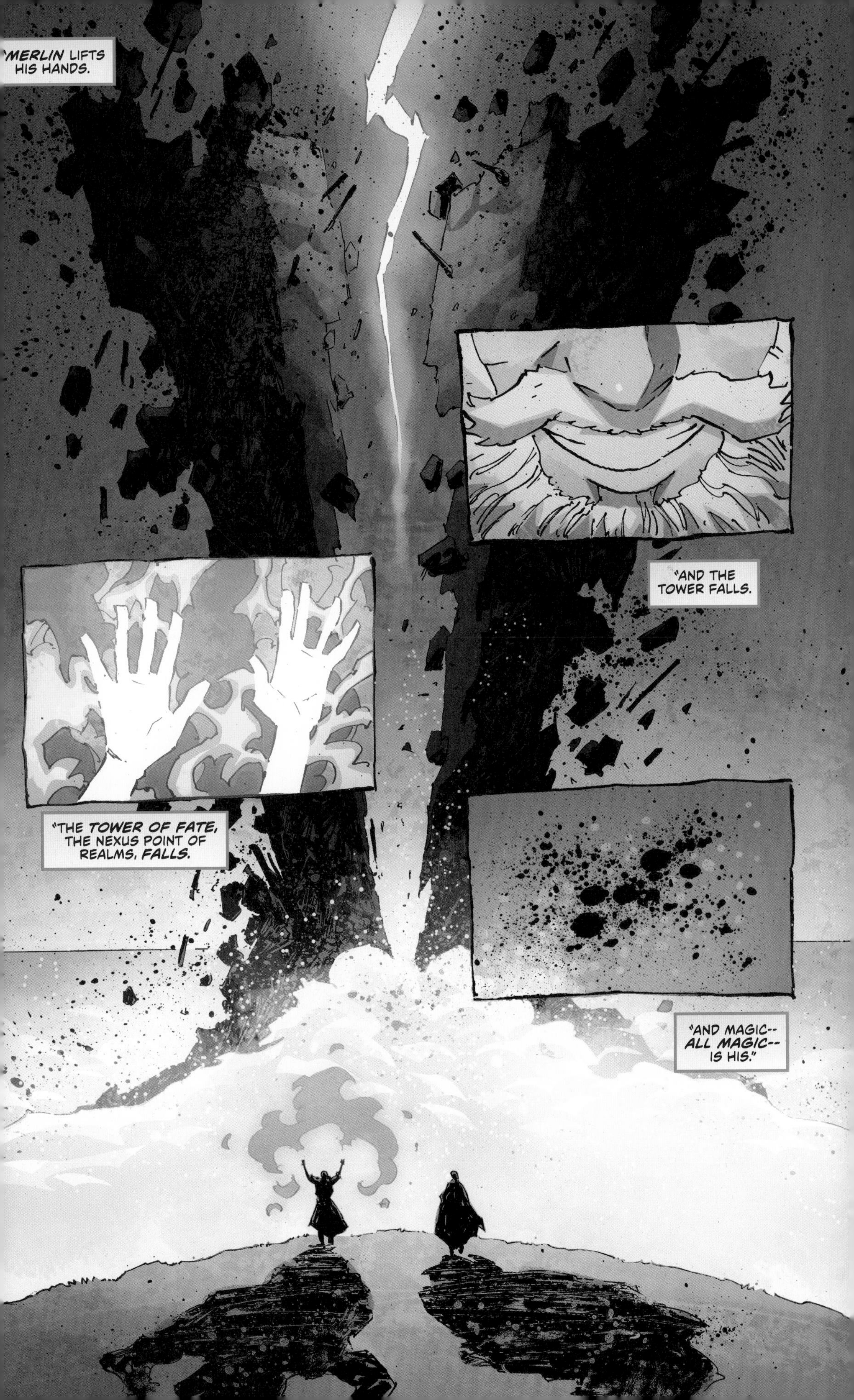
"MERLIN LIFTS HIS HANDS.
"AND THE TOWER FALLS.
"THE TOWER OF FATE, THE NEXUS POINT OF REALMS, FALLS.
"AND MAGIC-- ALL MAGIC-- IS HIS."

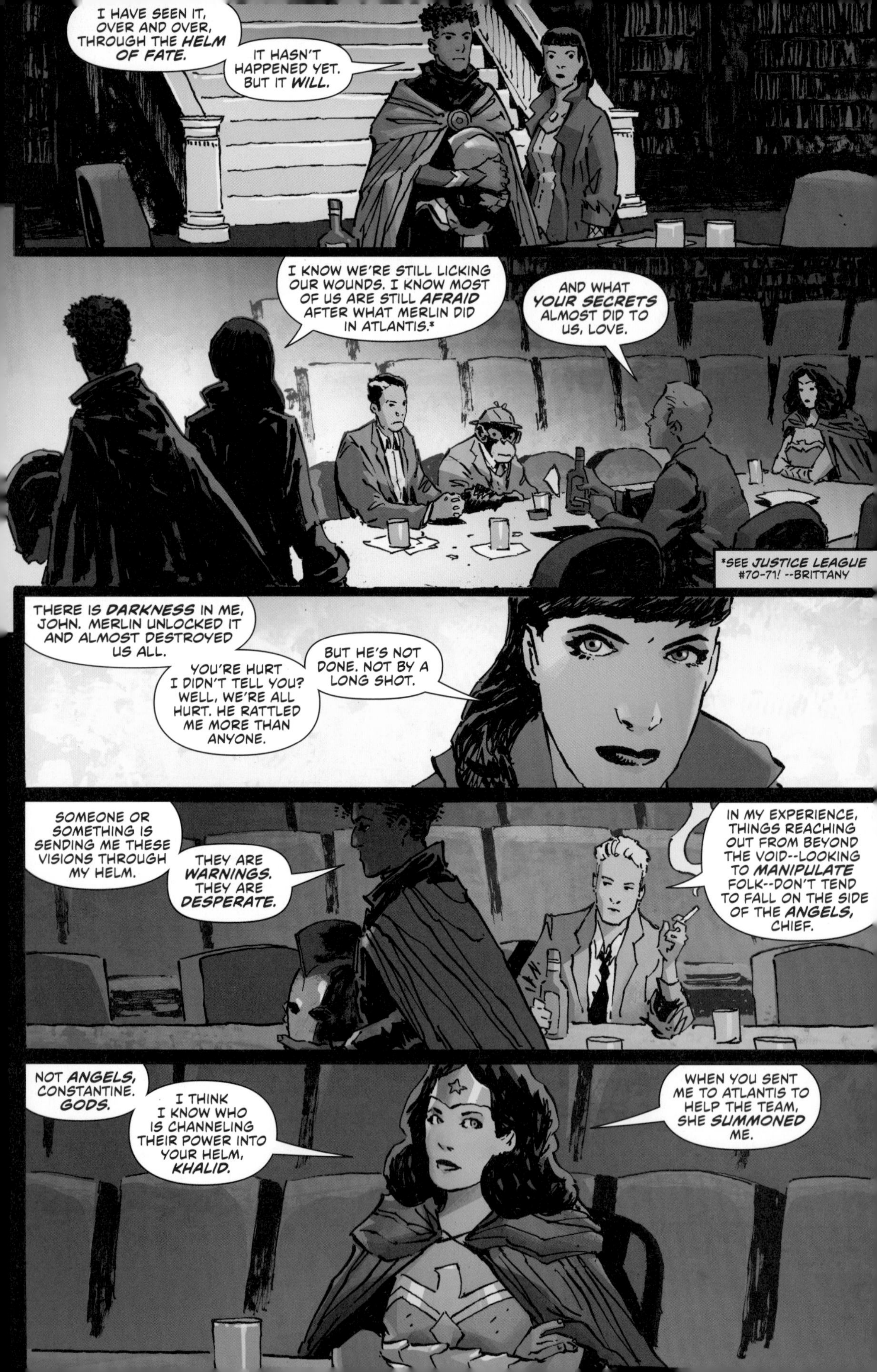

I HAVE SEEN IT, OVER AND OVER, THROUGH THE HELM OF FATE.
IT HASN'T HAPPENED YET. BUT IT WILL.
I KNOW WE'RE STILL LICKING OUR WOUNDS. I KNOW MOST OF US ARE STILL AFRAID AFTER WHAT MERLIN DID IN ATLANTIS.*
AND WHAT YOUR SECRETS ALMOST DID TO US, LOVE.
*SEE JUSTICE LEAGUE #70-71! --BRITTANY
THERE IS DARKNESS IN ME, JOHN. MERLIN UNLOCKED IT AND ALMOST DESTROYED US ALL.
YOU'RE HURT I DIDN'T TELL YOU? WELL, WE'RE ALL HURT. HE RATTLED ME MORE THAN ANYONE.
BUT HE'S NOT DONE. NOT BY A LONG SHOT.
SOMEONE OR SOMETHING IS SENDING ME THESE VISIONS THROUGH MY HELM.
THEY ARE WARNINGS. THEY ARE DESPERATE.
IN MY EXPERIENCE, THINGS REACHING OUT FROM BEYOND THE VOID--LOOKING TO MANIPULATE FOLK--DON'T TEND TO FALL ON THE SIDE OF THE ANGELS, CHIEF.
NOT ANGELS, CONSTANTINE. GODS.
I THINK I KNOW WHO IS CHANNELING THEIR POWER INTO YOUR HELM, KHALID.
WHEN YOU SENT ME TO ATLANTIS TO HELP THE TEAM, SHE SUMMONED ME.

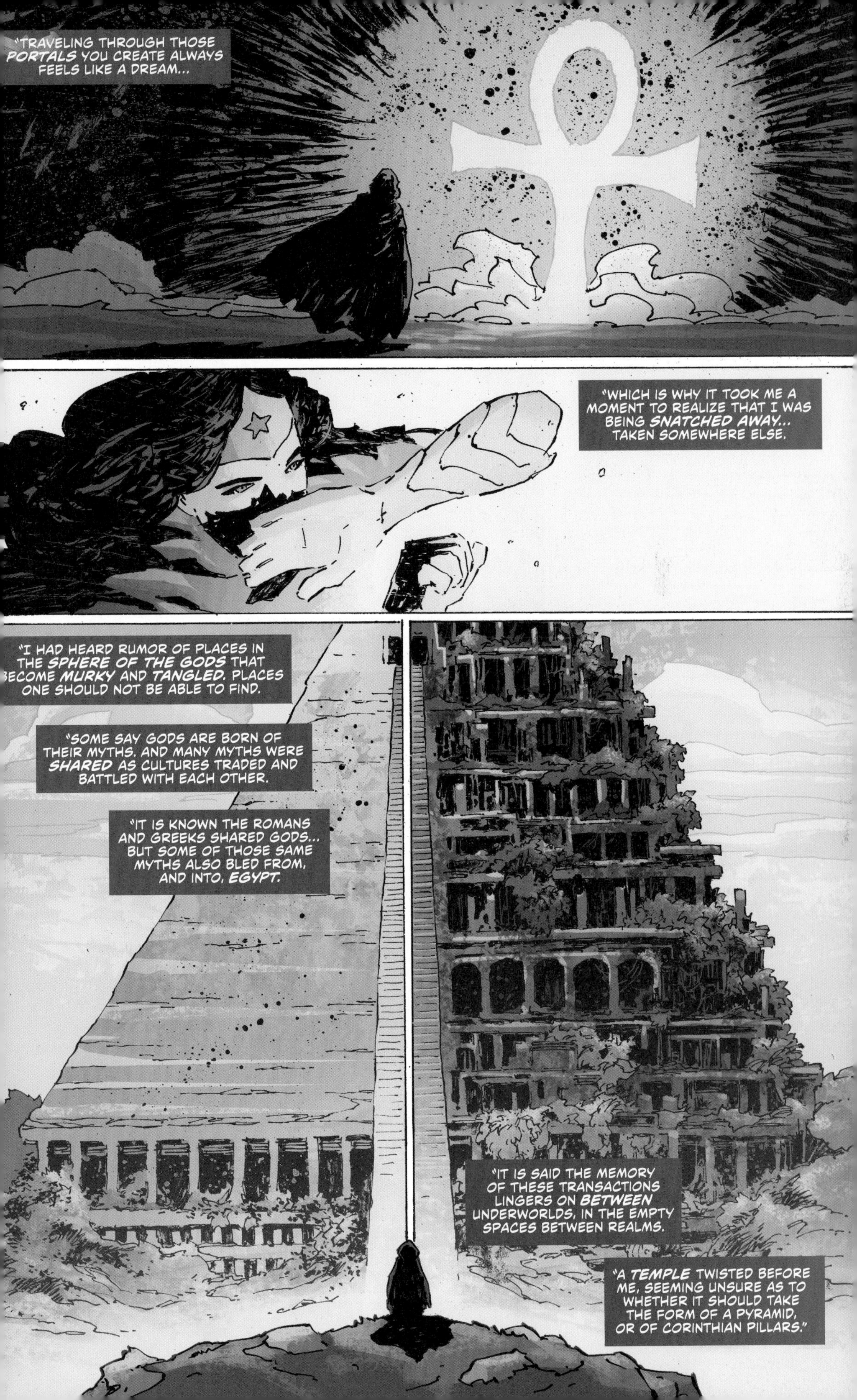
"TRAVELING THROUGH THOSE PORTALS YOU CREATE ALWAYS FEELS LIKE A DREAM...
"WHICH IS WHY IT TOOK ME A MOMENT TO REALIZE THAT I WAS BEING SNATCHED AWAY... TAKEN SOMEWHERE ELSE.
"I HAD HEARD RUMOR OF PLACES IN THE SPHERE OF THE GODS THAT BECOME MURKY AND TANGLED. PLACES ONE SHOULD NOT BE ABLE TO FIND.
"SOME SAY GODS ARE BORN OF THEIR MYTHS. AND MANY MYTHS WERE SHARED AS CULTURES TRADED AND BATTLED WITH EACH OTHER.
"IT IS KNOWN THE ROMANS AND GREEKS SHARED GODS... BUT SOME OF THOSE SAME MYTHS ALSO BLED FROM, AND INTO, EGYPT.
"IT IS SAID THE MEMORY OF THESE TRANSACTIONS LINGERS ON BETWEEN UNDERWORLDS, IN THE EMPTY SPACES BETWEEN REALMS.
"A TEMPLE TWISTED BEFORE ME, SEEMING UNSURE AS TO WHETHER IT SHOULD TAKE THE FORM OF A PYRAMID, OR OF CORINTHIAN PILLARS."

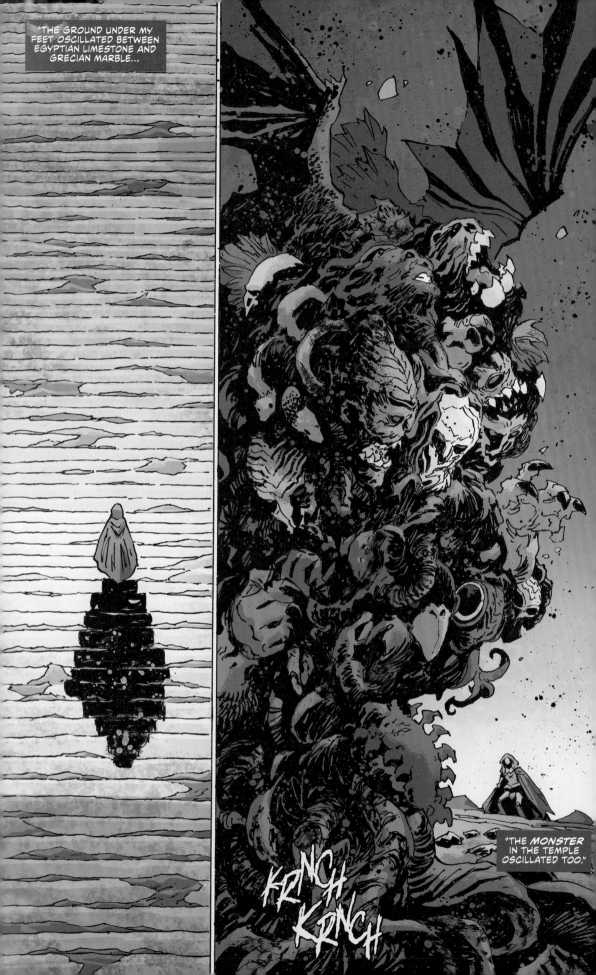

"THE GROUND UNDER MY FEET OSCILLATED BETWEEN EGYPTIAN LIMESTONE AND GRECIAN MARBLE...

"THE *MONSTER* IN THE TEMPLE OSCILLATED TOO."

KRNCH KRNCH

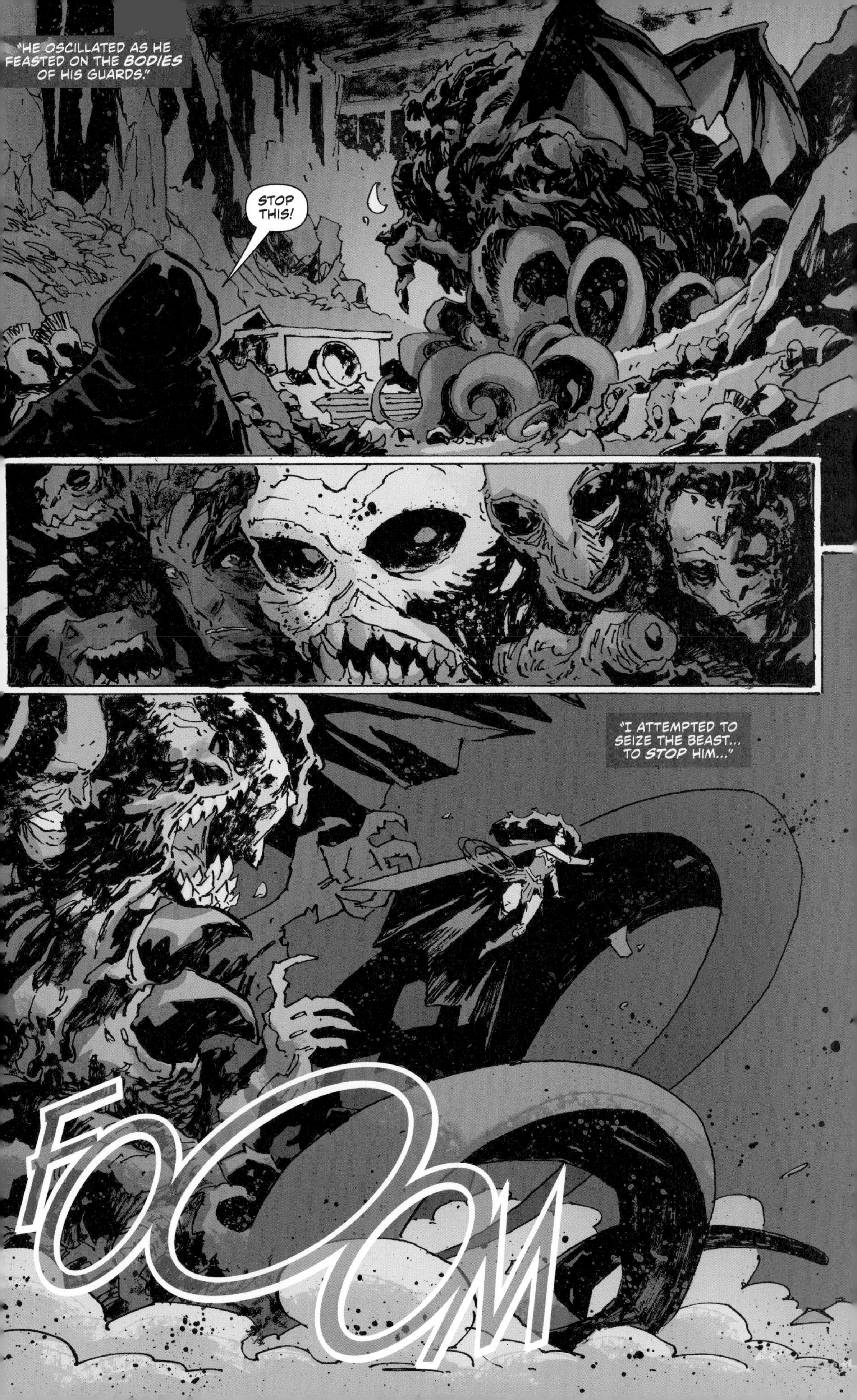
"HE OSCILLATED AS HE FEASTED ON THE BODIES OF HIS GUARDS."
STOP THIS!
"I ATTEMPTED TO SEIZE THE BEAST... TO STOP HIM..."
FOOOM

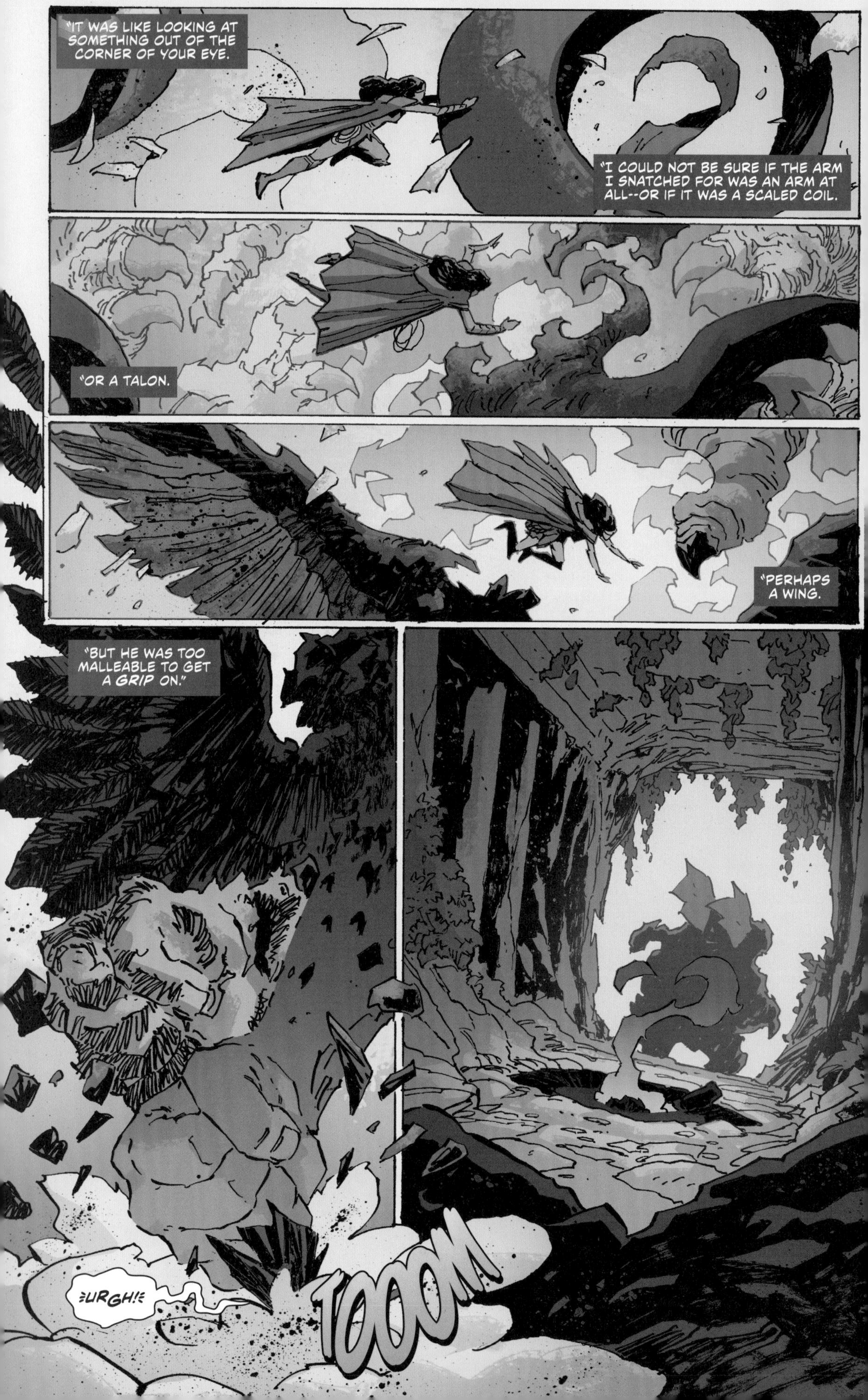
"IT WAS LIKE LOOKING AT SOMETHING OUT OF THE CORNER OF YOUR EYE.
"I COULD NOT BE SURE IF THE ARM I SNATCHED FOR WAS AN ARM AT ALL--OR IF IT WAS A SCALED COIL.
"OR A TALON.
"PERHAPS A WING.
"BUT HE WAS TOO MALLEABLE TO GET A GRIP ON."
URGH!
TOOOM

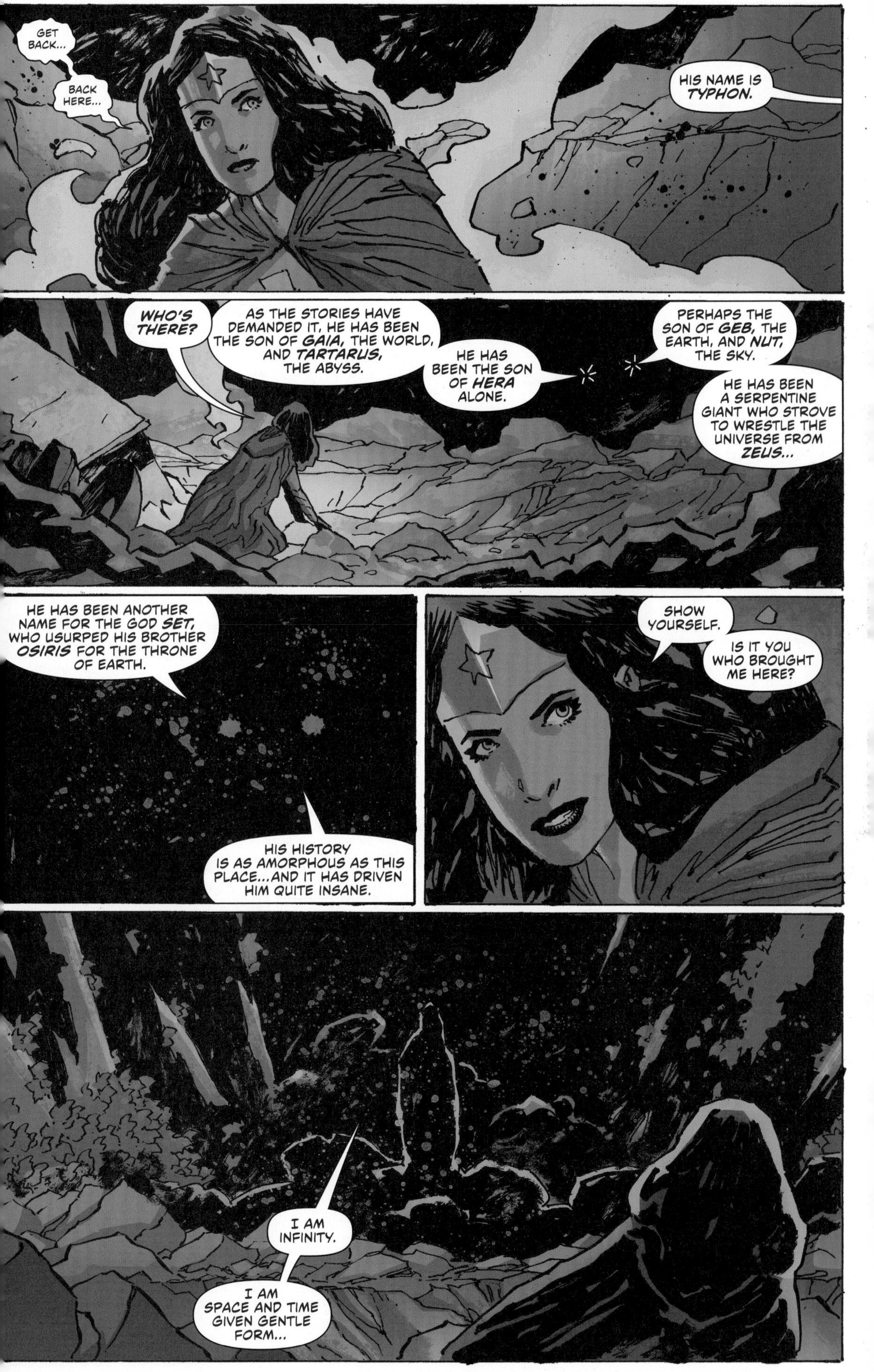
GET BACK...
BACK HERE...
HIS NAME IS TYPHON.
WHO'S THERE?
AS THE STORIES HAVE DEMANDED IT, HE HAS BEEN THE SON OF GAIA, THE WORLD, AND TARTARUS, THE ABYSS.
HE HAS BEEN THE SON OF HERA ALONE.
PERHAPS THE SON OF GEB, THE EARTH, AND NUT, THE SKY.
HE HAS BEEN A SERPENTINE GIANT WHO STROVE TO WRESTLE THE UNIVERSE FROM ZEUS...
HE HAS BEEN ANOTHER NAME FOR THE GOD SET, WHO USURPED HIS BROTHER OSIRIS FOR THE THRONE OF EARTH.
HIS HISTORY IS AS AMORPHOUS AS THIS PLACE...AND IT HAS DRIVEN HIM QUITE INSANE.
SHOW YOURSELF.
IS IT YOU WHO BROUGHT ME HERE?
I AM INFINITY.
I AM SPACE AND TIME GIVEN GENTLE FORM...

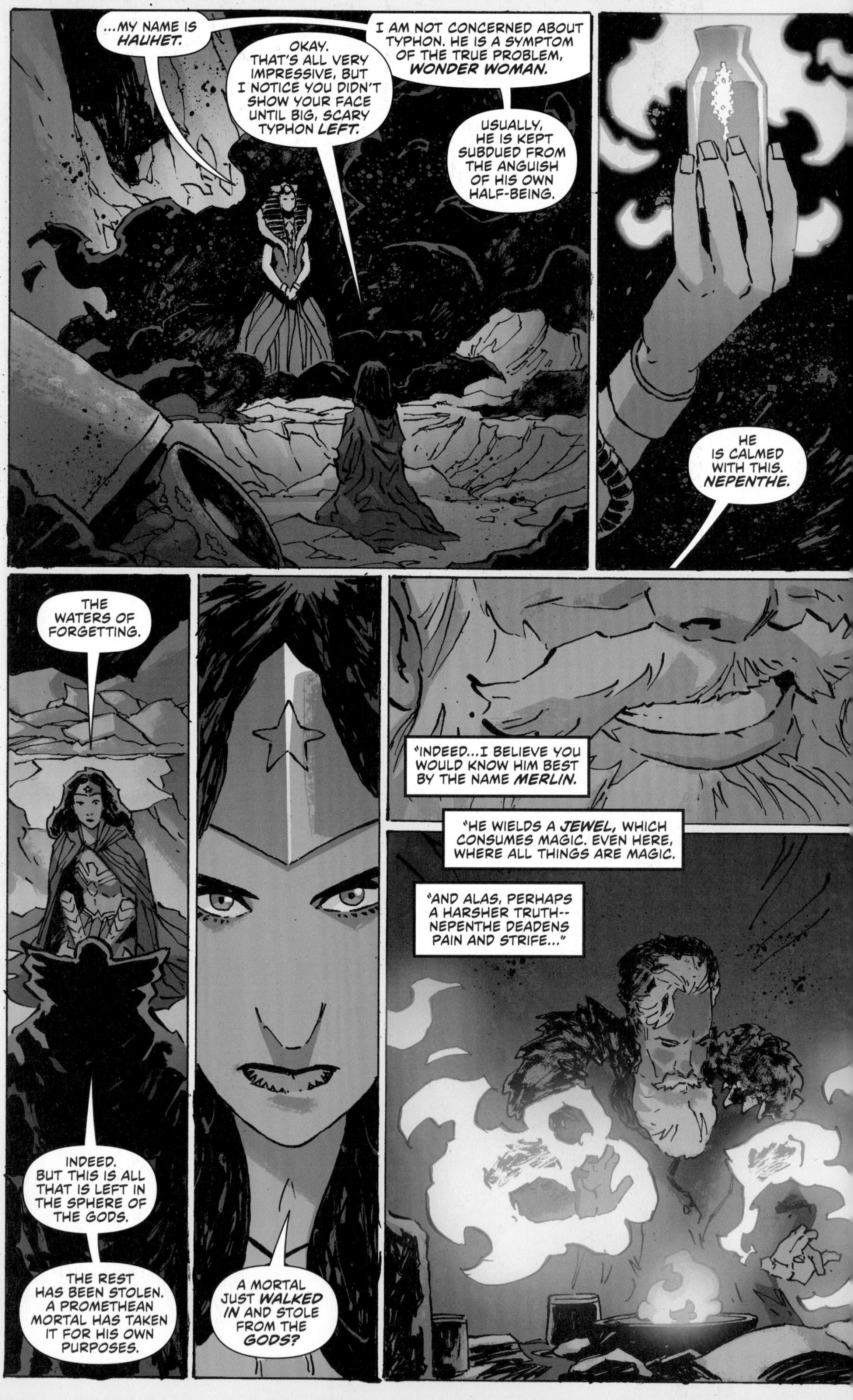
...MY NAME IS HAUHET.
OKAY. THAT'S ALL VERY IMPRESSIVE, BUT I NOTICE YOU DIDN'T SHOW YOUR FACE UNTIL BIG, SCARY TYPHON LEFT.
I AM NOT CONCERNED ABOUT TYPHON. HE IS A SYMPTOM OF THE TRUE PROBLEM, WONDER WOMAN.
USUALLY, HE IS KEPT SUBDUED FROM THE ANGUISH OF HIS OWN HALF-BEING.
HE IS CALMED WITH THIS. NEPENTHE.
THE WATERS OF FORGETTING.
INDEED. BUT THIS IS ALL THAT IS LEFT IN THE SPHERE OF THE GODS.
THE REST HAS BEEN STOLEN. A PROMETHEAN MORTAL HAS TAKEN IT FOR HIS OWN PURPOSES.
A MORTAL JUST WALKED IN AND STOLE FROM THE GODS?
"INDEED...I BELIEVE YOU WOULD KNOW HIM BEST BY THE NAME MERLIN.
"HE WIELDS A JEWEL, WHICH CONSUMES MAGIC. EVEN HERE, WHERE ALL THINGS ARE MAGIC.
"AND ALAS, PERHAPS A HARSHER TRUTH-- NEPENTHE DEADENS PAIN AND STRIFE..."

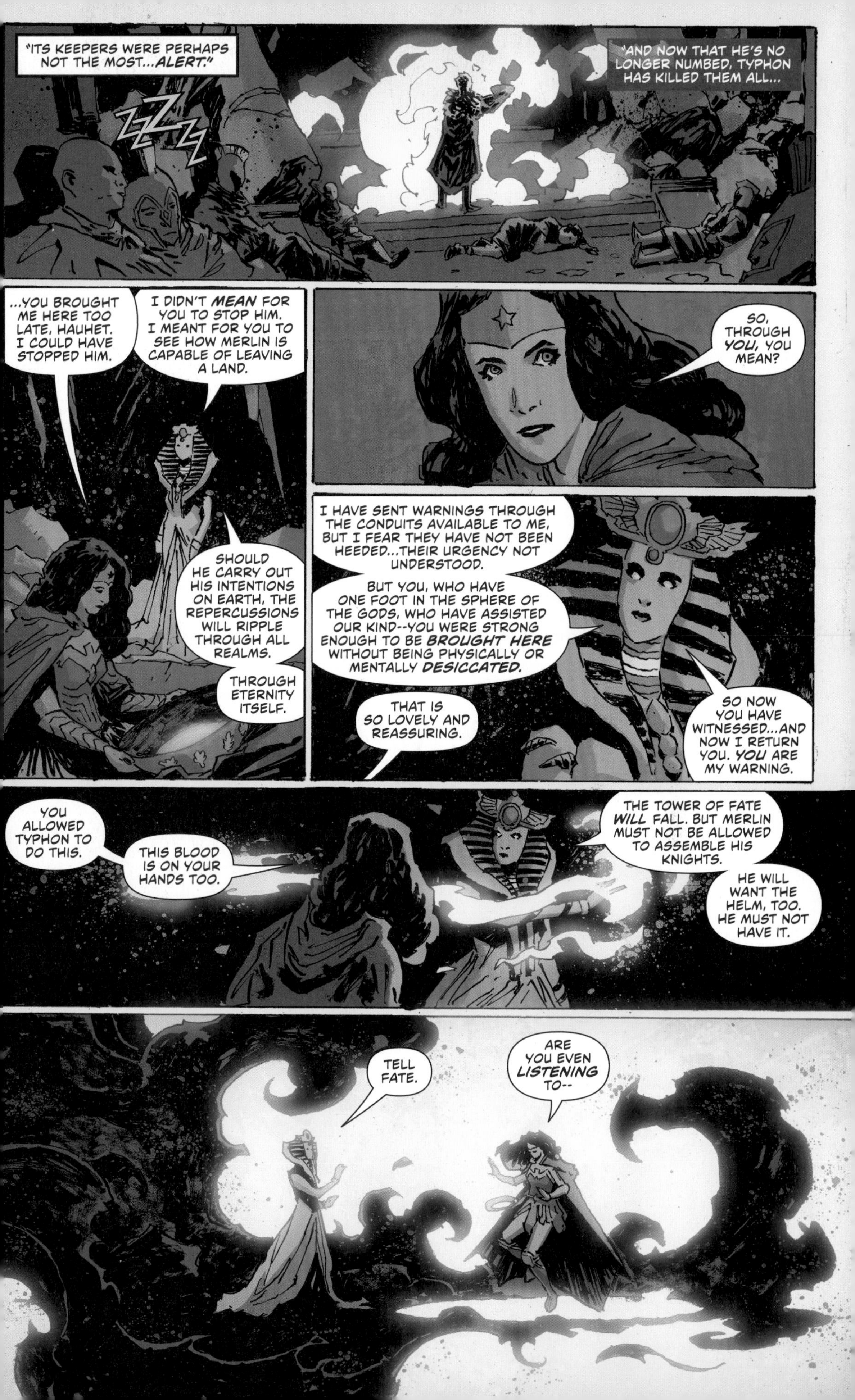
"ITS KEEPERS WERE PERHAPS NOT THE MOST...ALERT."
ZZZZ
"AND NOW THAT HE'S NO LONGER NUMBED, TYPHON HAS KILLED THEM ALL...
...YOU BROUGHT ME HERE TOO LATE, HAUHET. I COULD HAVE STOPPED HIM.
I DIDN'T MEAN FOR YOU TO STOP HIM. I MEANT FOR YOU TO SEE HOW MERLIN IS CAPABLE OF LEAVING A LAND.
SHOULD HE CARRY OUT HIS INTENTIONS ON EARTH, THE REPERCUSSIONS WILL RIPPLE THROUGH ALL REALMS.
THROUGH ETERNITY ITSELF.
SO, THROUGH YOU, YOU MEAN?
I HAVE SENT WARNINGS THROUGH THE CONDUITS AVAILABLE TO ME, BUT I FEAR THEY HAVE NOT BEEN HEEDED...THEIR URGENCY NOT UNDERSTOOD.
BUT YOU, WHO HAVE ONE FOOT IN THE SPHERE OF THE GODS, WHO HAVE ASSISTED OUR KIND--YOU WERE STRONG ENOUGH TO BE BROUGHT HERE WITHOUT BEING PHYSICALLY OR MENTALLY DESICCATED.
THAT IS SO LOVELY AND REASSURING.
SO NOW YOU HAVE WITNESSED...AND NOW I RETURN YOU. YOU ARE MY WARNING.
YOU ALLOWED TYPHON TO DO THIS.
THIS BLOOD IS ON YOUR HANDS TOO.
THE TOWER OF FATE WILL FALL. BUT MERLIN MUST NOT BE ALLOWED TO ASSEMBLE HIS KNIGHTS.
HE WILL WANT THE HELM, TOO. HE MUST NOT HAVE IT.
TELL FATE.
ARE YOU EVEN LISTENING TO--

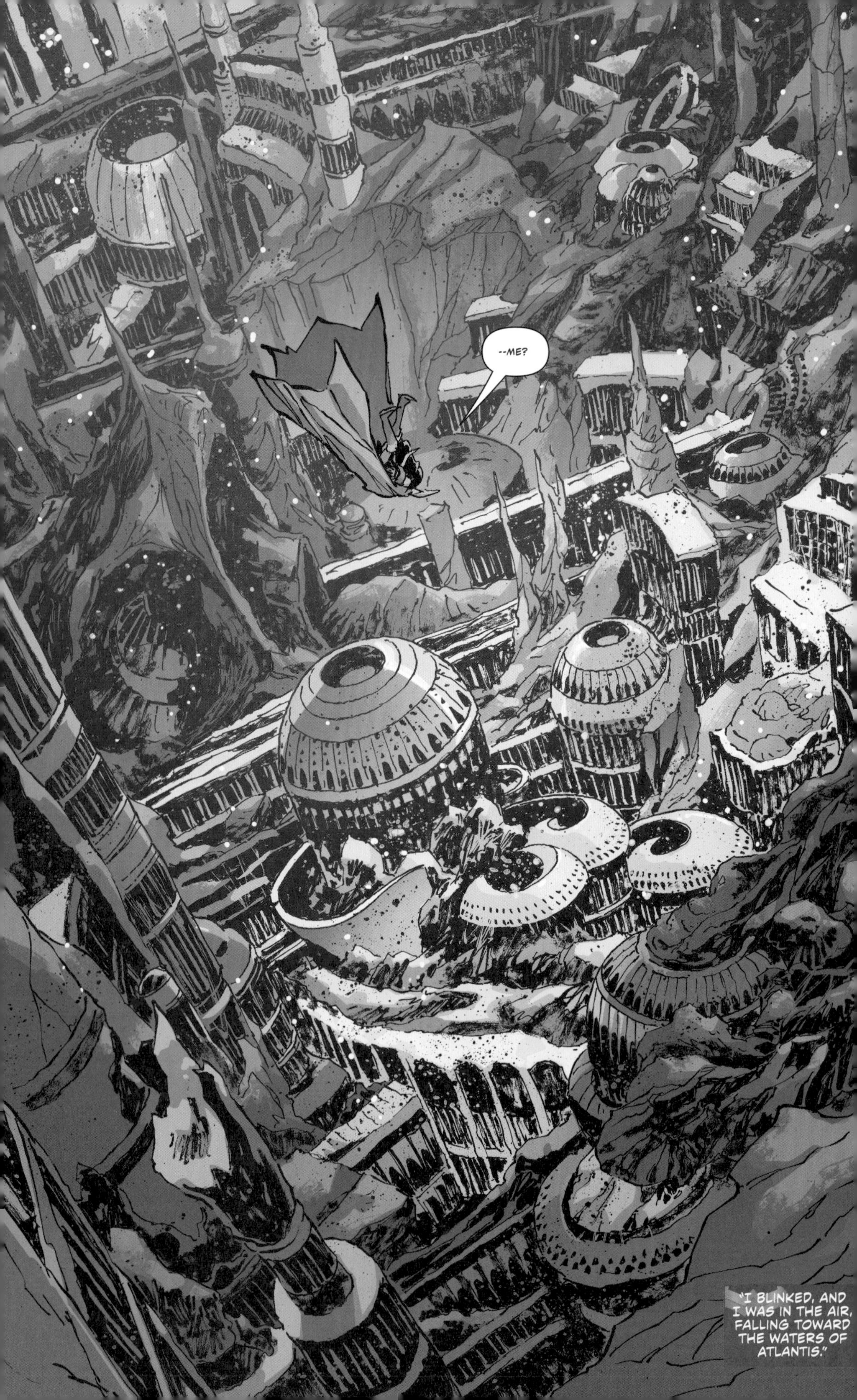
--ME?
"I BLINKED, AND I WAS IN THE AIR, FALLING TOWARD THE WATERS OF ATLANTIS."

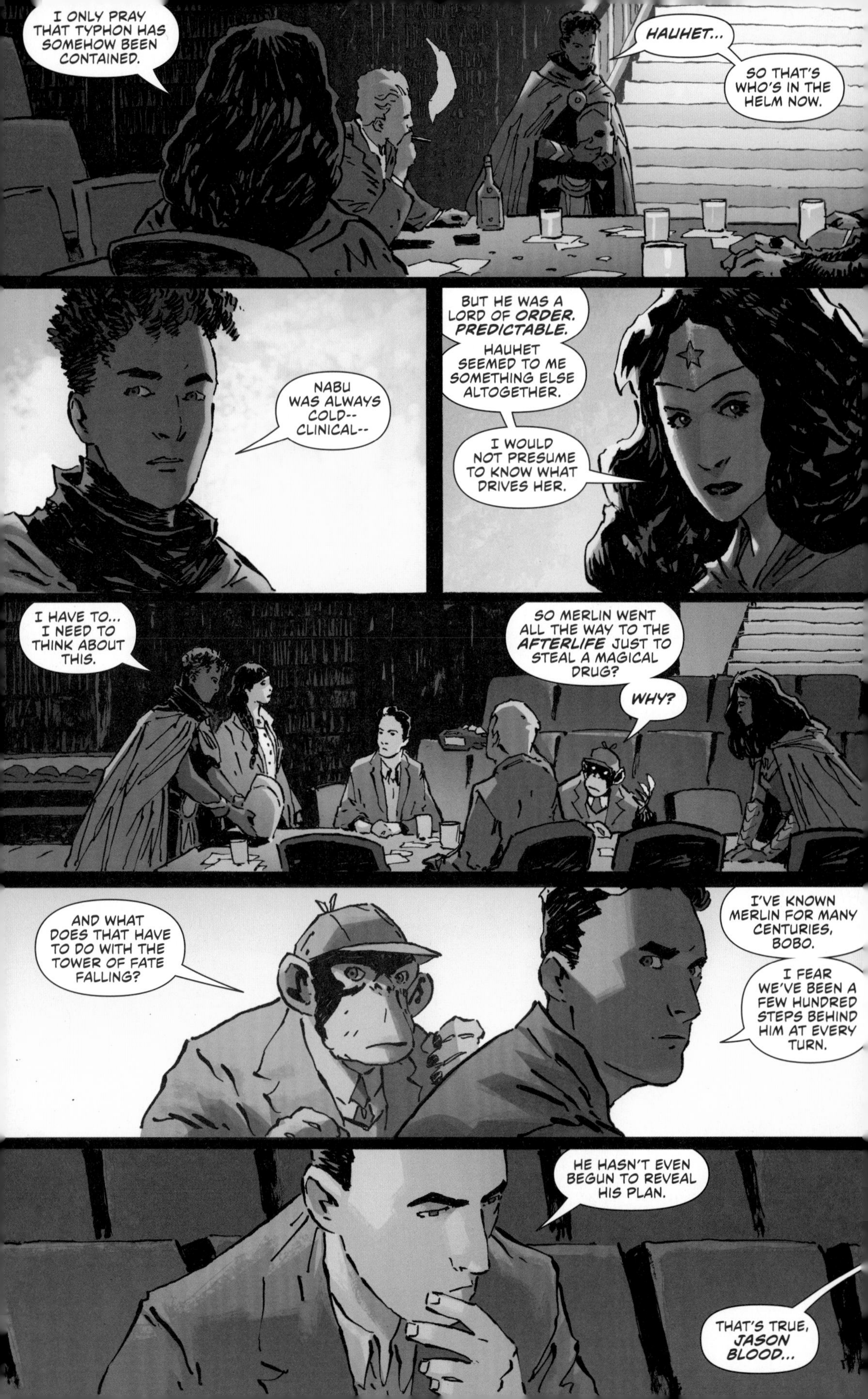
I ONLY PRAY THAT TYPHON HAS SOMEHOW BEEN CONTAINED.
HAUHET...
SO THAT'S WHO'S IN THE HELM NOW.
NABU WAS ALWAYS COLD-- CLINICAL--
BUT HE WAS A LORD OF ORDER. PREDICTABLE.
HAUHET SEEMED TO ME SOMETHING ELSE ALTOGETHER.
I WOULD NOT PRESUME TO KNOW WHAT DRIVES HER.
I HAVE TO... I NEED TO THINK ABOUT THIS.
SO MERLIN WENT ALL THE WAY TO THE AFTERLIFE JUST TO STEAL A MAGICAL DRUG?
WHY?
AND WHAT DOES THAT HAVE TO DO WITH THE TOWER OF FATE FALLING?
I'VE KNOWN MERLIN FOR MANY CENTURIES, BOBO.
I FEAR WE'VE BEEN A FEW HUNDRED STEPS BEHIND HIM AT EVERY TURN.
HE HASN'T EVEN BEGUN TO REVEAL HIS PLAN.
THAT'S TRUE, JASON BLOOD...

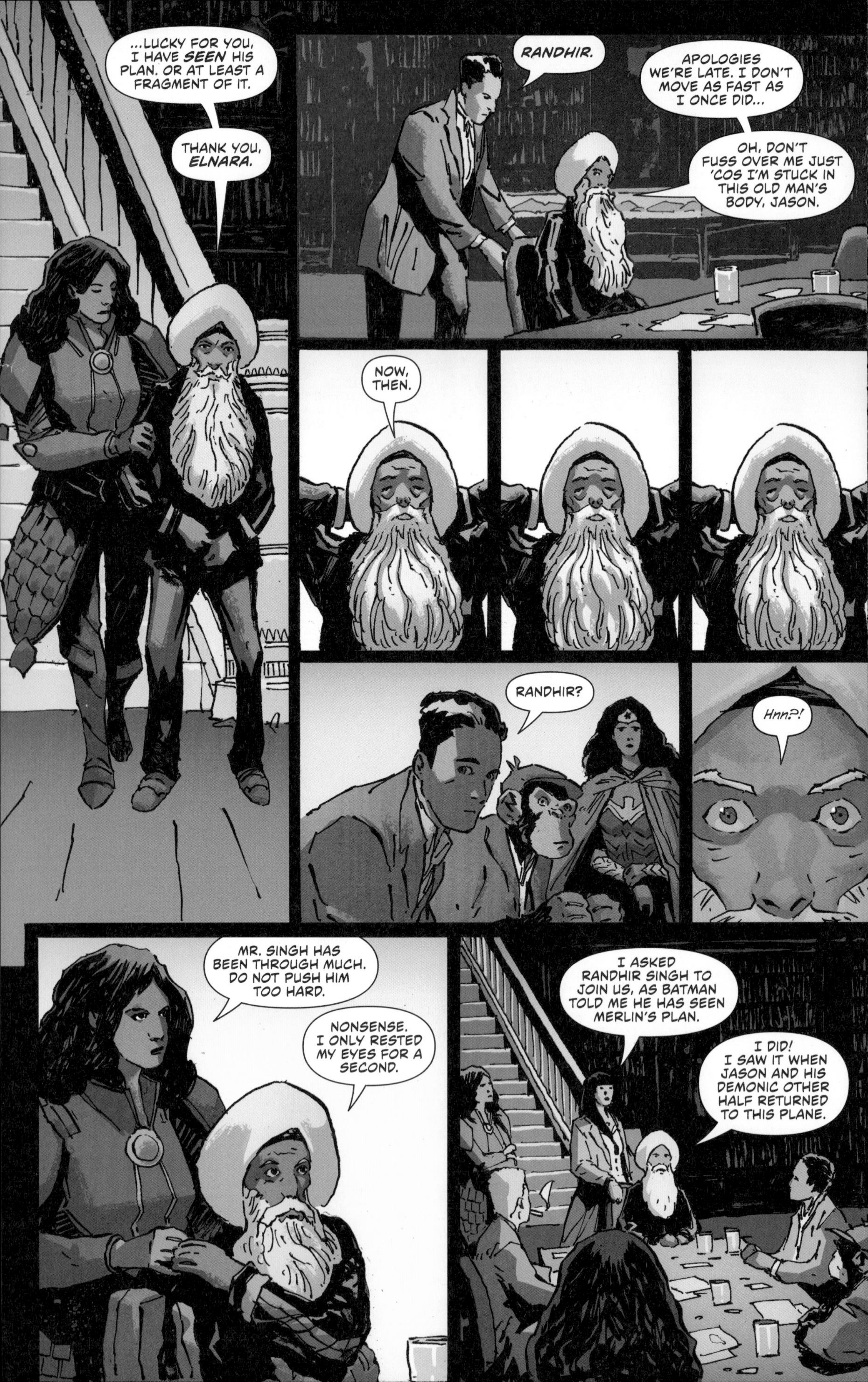

...LUCKY FOR YOU, I HAVE **SEEN** HIS PLAN. OR AT LEAST A FRAGMENT OF IT.
THANK YOU, **ELNARA.**
RANDHIR.
APOLOGIES WE'RE LATE. I DON'T MOVE AS FAST AS I ONCE DID...
OH, DON'T FUSS OVER ME JUST 'COS I'M STUCK IN THIS OLD MAN'S BODY, JASON.
NOW, THEN.
RANDHIR?
Hnn?!
MR. SINGH HAS BEEN THROUGH MUCH. DO NOT PUSH HIM TOO HARD.
NONSENSE. I ONLY RESTED MY EYES FOR A SECOND.
I ASKED RANDHIR SINGH TO JOIN US, AS BATMAN TOLD ME HE HAS SEEN MERLIN'S PLAN.
I DID! I SAW IT WHEN JASON AND HIS DEMONIC OTHER HALF RETURNED TO THIS PLANE.

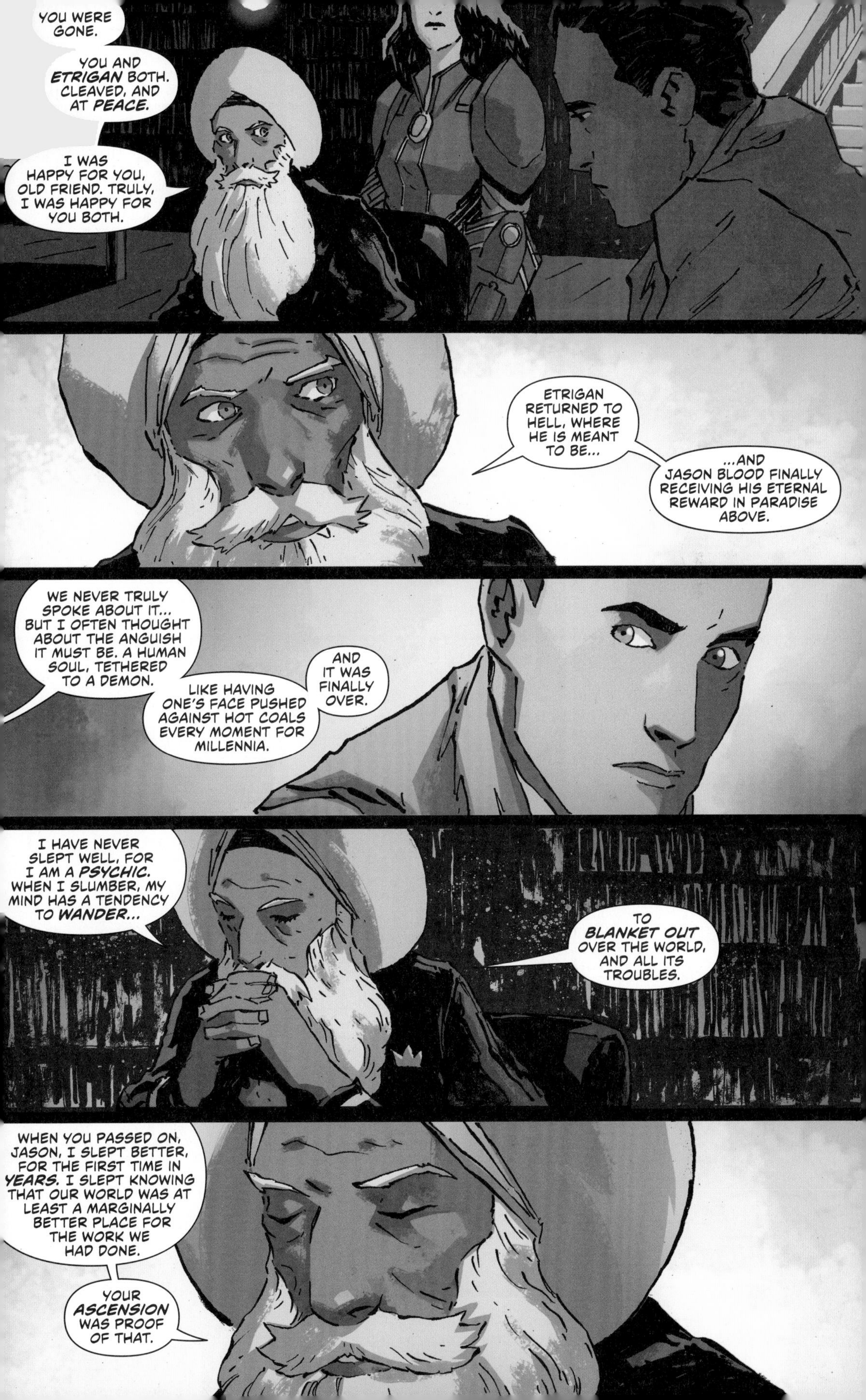
YOU WERE GONE.
YOU AND ETRIGAN BOTH. CLEAVED, AND AT PEACE.
I WAS HAPPY FOR YOU, OLD FRIEND. TRULY, I WAS HAPPY FOR YOU BOTH.
ETRIGAN RETURNED TO HELL, WHERE HE IS MEANT TO BE...
...AND JASON BLOOD FINALLY RECEIVING HIS ETERNAL REWARD IN PARADISE ABOVE.
WE NEVER TRULY SPOKE ABOUT IT... BUT I OFTEN THOUGHT ABOUT THE ANGUISH IT MUST BE. A HUMAN SOUL, TETHERED TO A DEMON.
LIKE HAVING ONE'S FACE PUSHED AGAINST HOT COALS EVERY MOMENT FOR MILLENNIA.
AND IT WAS FINALLY OVER.
I HAVE NEVER SLEPT WELL, FOR I AM A PSYCHIC. WHEN I SLUMBER, MY MIND HAS A TENDENCY TO WANDER...
TO BLANKET OUT OVER THE WORLD, AND ALL ITS TROUBLES.
WHEN YOU PASSED ON, JASON, I SLEPT BETTER, FOR THE FIRST TIME IN YEARS. I SLEPT KNOWING THAT OUR WORLD WAS AT LEAST A MARGINALLY BETTER PLACE FOR THE WORK WE HAD DONE.
YOUR ASCENSION WAS PROOF OF THAT.

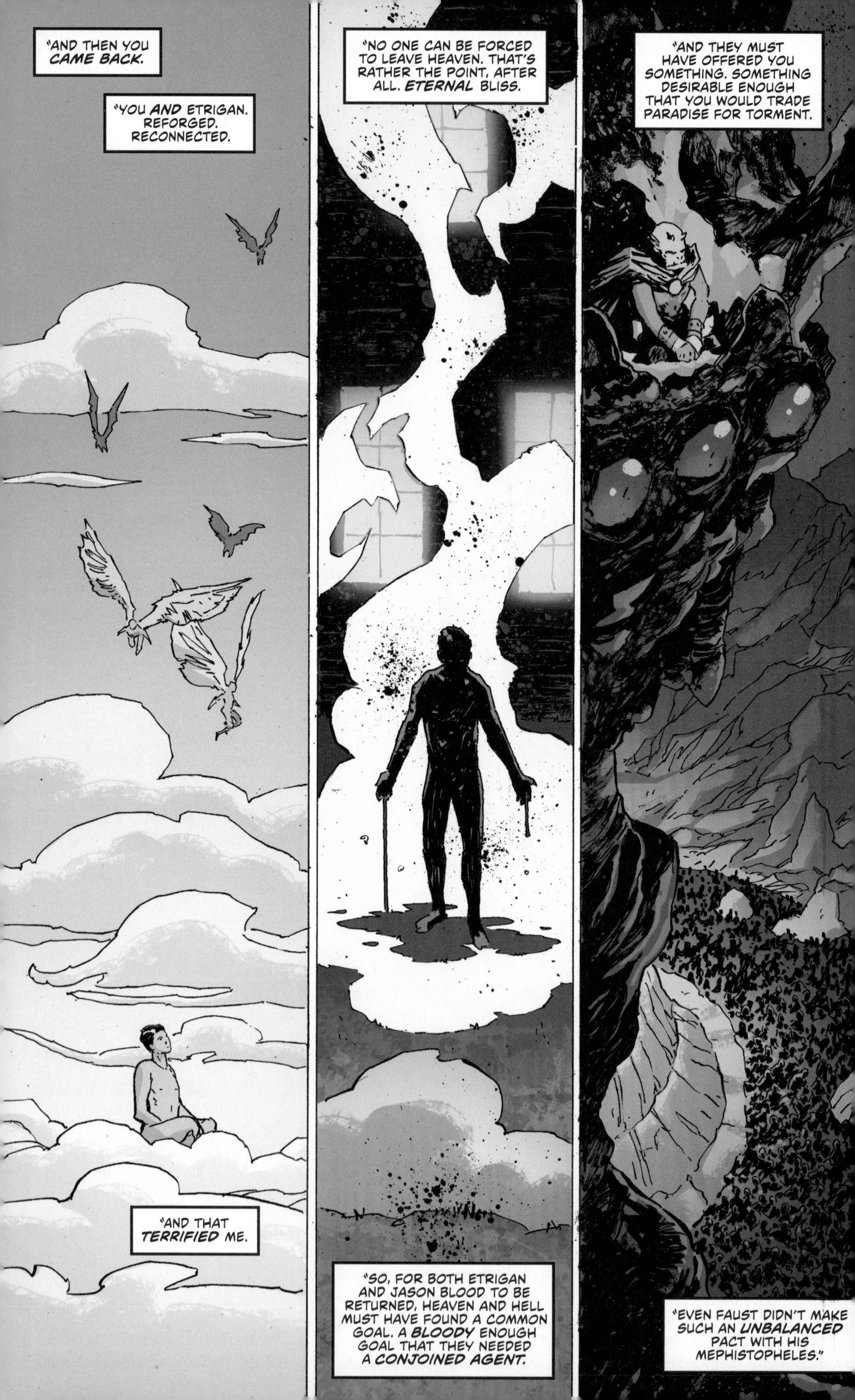
"AND THEN YOU *CAME BACK*.
"YOU *AND* ETRIGAN. REFORGED. RECONNECTED.
"AND THAT *TERRIFIED* ME.
"NO ONE CAN BE FORCED TO LEAVE HEAVEN. THAT'S RATHER THE POINT, AFTER ALL. *ETERNAL* BLISS.
"SO, FOR BOTH ETRIGAN AND JASON BLOOD TO BE RETURNED, HEAVEN AND HELL MUST HAVE FOUND A COMMON GOAL. A *BLOODY* ENOUGH GOAL THAT THEY NEEDED A *CONJOINED AGENT*.
"AND THEY MUST HAVE OFFERED YOU SOMETHING. SOMETHING DESIRABLE ENOUGH THAT YOU WOULD TRADE PARADISE FOR TORMENT.
"EVEN FAUST DIDN'T MAKE SUCH AN *UNBALANCED* PACT WITH HIS MEPHISTOPHELES."

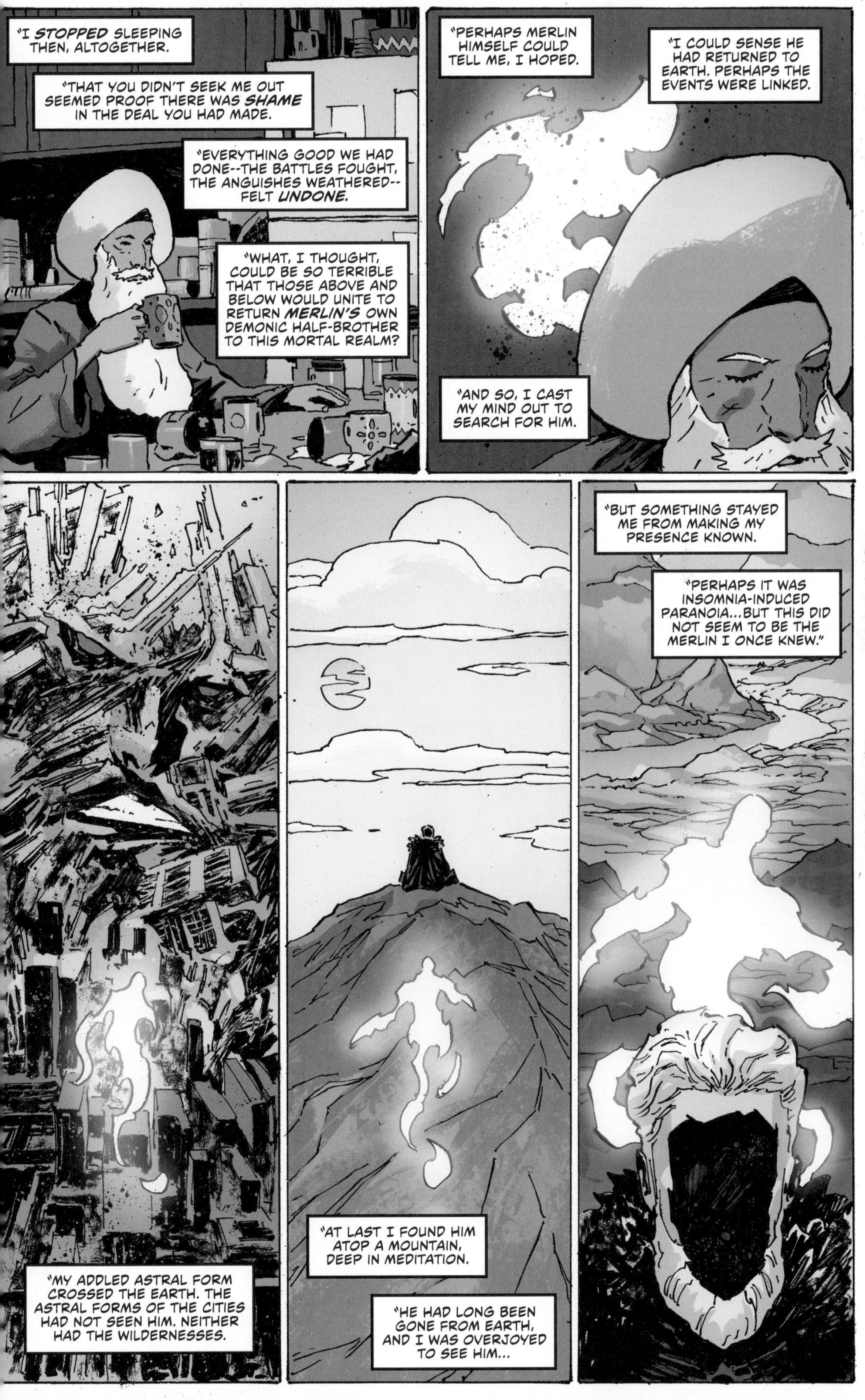
"I STOPPED SLEEPING THEN, ALTOGETHER.
"THAT YOU DIDN'T SEEK ME OUT SEEMED PROOF THERE WAS SHAME IN THE DEAL YOU HAD MADE.
"EVERYTHING GOOD WE HAD DONE--THE BATTLES FOUGHT, THE ANGUISHES WEATHERED--FELT UNDONE.
"WHAT, I THOUGHT, COULD BE SO TERRIBLE THAT THOSE ABOVE AND BELOW WOULD UNITE TO RETURN MERLIN'S OWN DEMONIC HALF-BROTHER TO THIS MORTAL REALM?
"PERHAPS MERLIN HIMSELF COULD TELL ME, I HOPED.
"I COULD SENSE HE HAD RETURNED TO EARTH. PERHAPS THE EVENTS WERE LINKED.
"AND SO, I CAST MY MIND OUT TO SEARCH FOR HIM.
"MY ADDLED ASTRAL FORM CROSSED THE EARTH. THE ASTRAL FORMS OF THE CITIES HAD NOT SEEN HIM. NEITHER HAD THE WILDERNESSES.
"AT LAST I FOUND HIM ATOP A MOUNTAIN, DEEP IN MEDITATION.
"HE HAD LONG BEEN GONE FROM EARTH, AND I WAS OVERJOYED TO SEE HIM...
"BUT SOMETHING STAYED ME FROM MAKING MY PRESENCE KNOWN.
"PERHAPS IT WAS INSOMNIA-INDUCED PARANOIA...BUT THIS DID NOT SEEM TO BE THE MERLIN I ONCE KNEW."

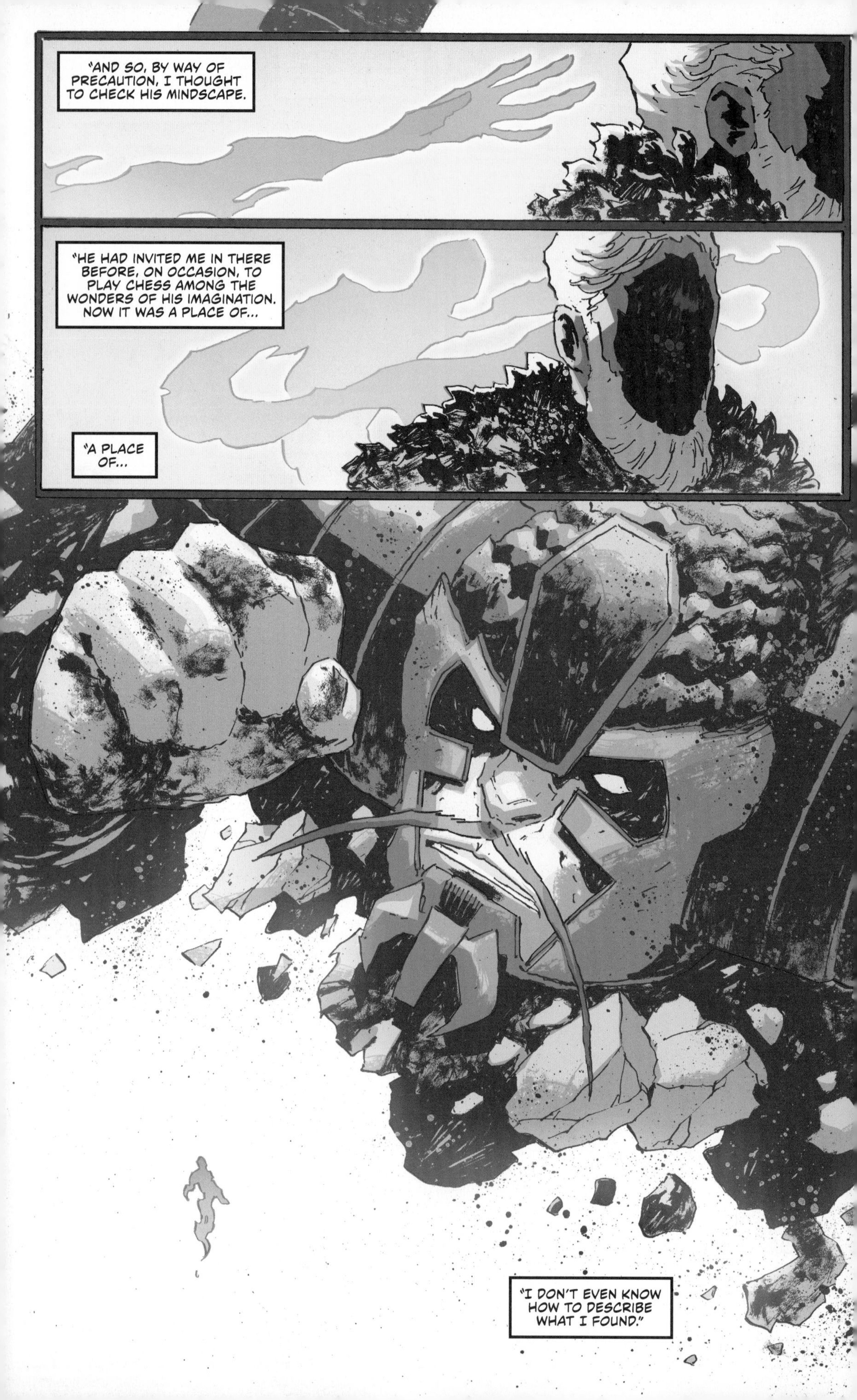
"AND SO, BY WAY OF PRECAUTION, I THOUGHT TO CHECK HIS MINDSCAPE.
"HE HAD INVITED ME IN THERE BEFORE, ON OCCASION, TO PLAY CHESS AMONG THE WONDERS OF HIS IMAGINATION. NOW IT WAS A PLACE OF...
"A PLACE OF...
"I DON'T EVEN KNOW HOW TO DESCRIBE WHAT I FOUND."

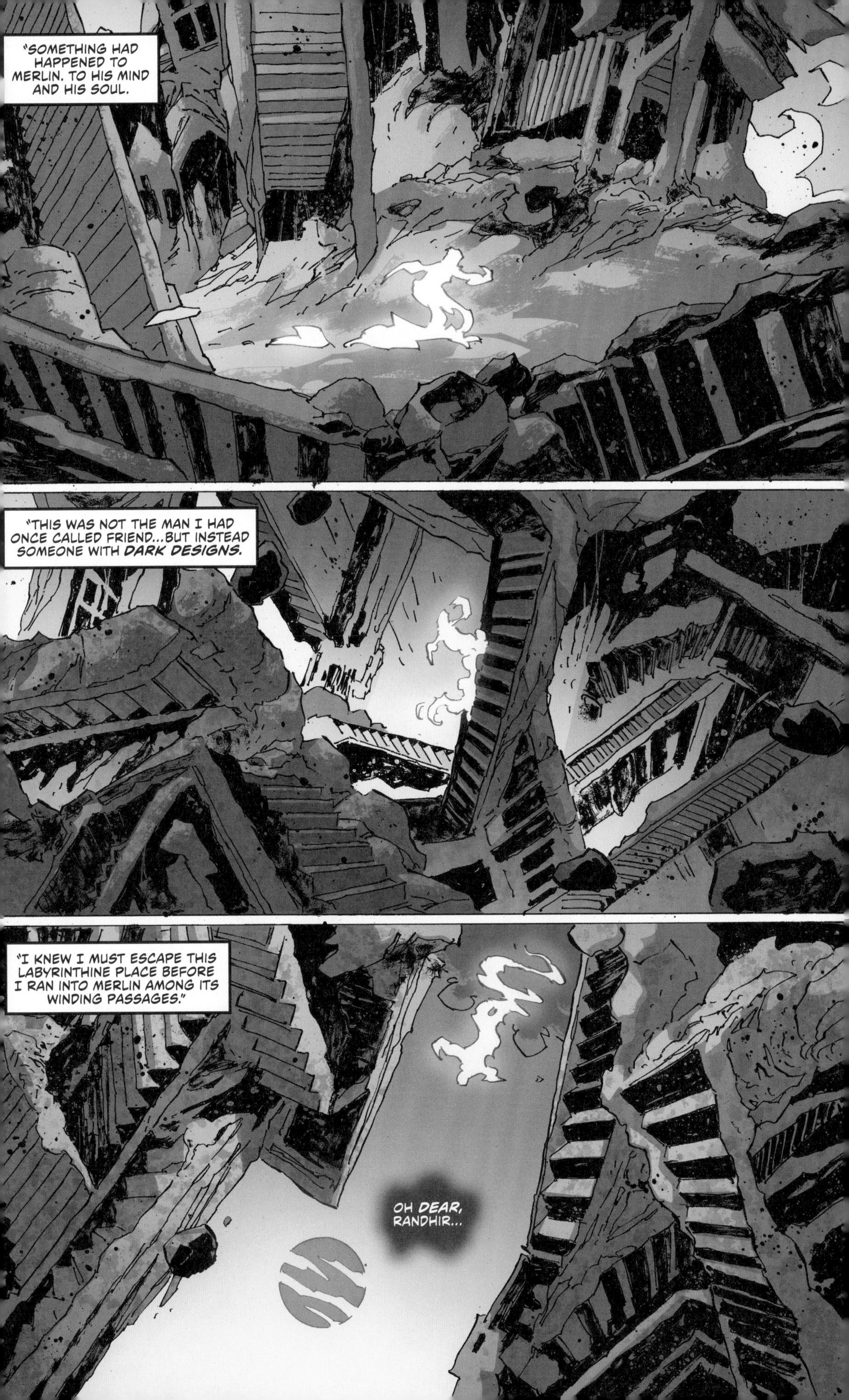
"SOMETHING HAD HAPPENED TO MERLIN. TO HIS MIND AND HIS SOUL.
"THIS WAS NOT THE MAN I HAD ONCE CALLED FRIEND...BUT INSTEAD SOMEONE WITH DARK DESIGNS.
"I KNEW I MUST ESCAPE THIS LABYRINTHINE PLACE BEFORE I RAN INTO MERLIN AMONG ITS WINDING PASSAGES."
OH DEAR, RANDHIR...

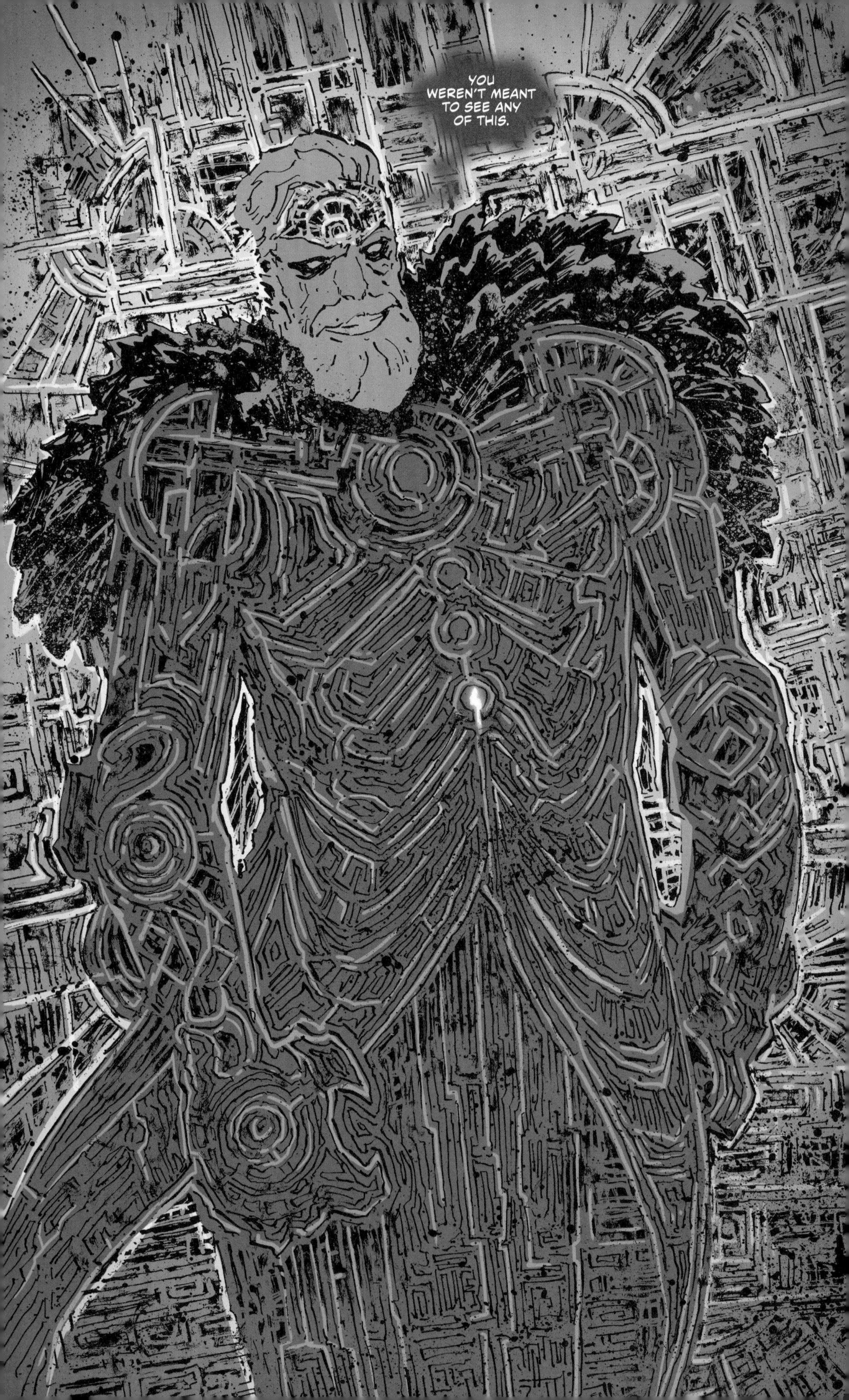
YOU WEREN'T MEANT TO SEE ANY OF THIS.

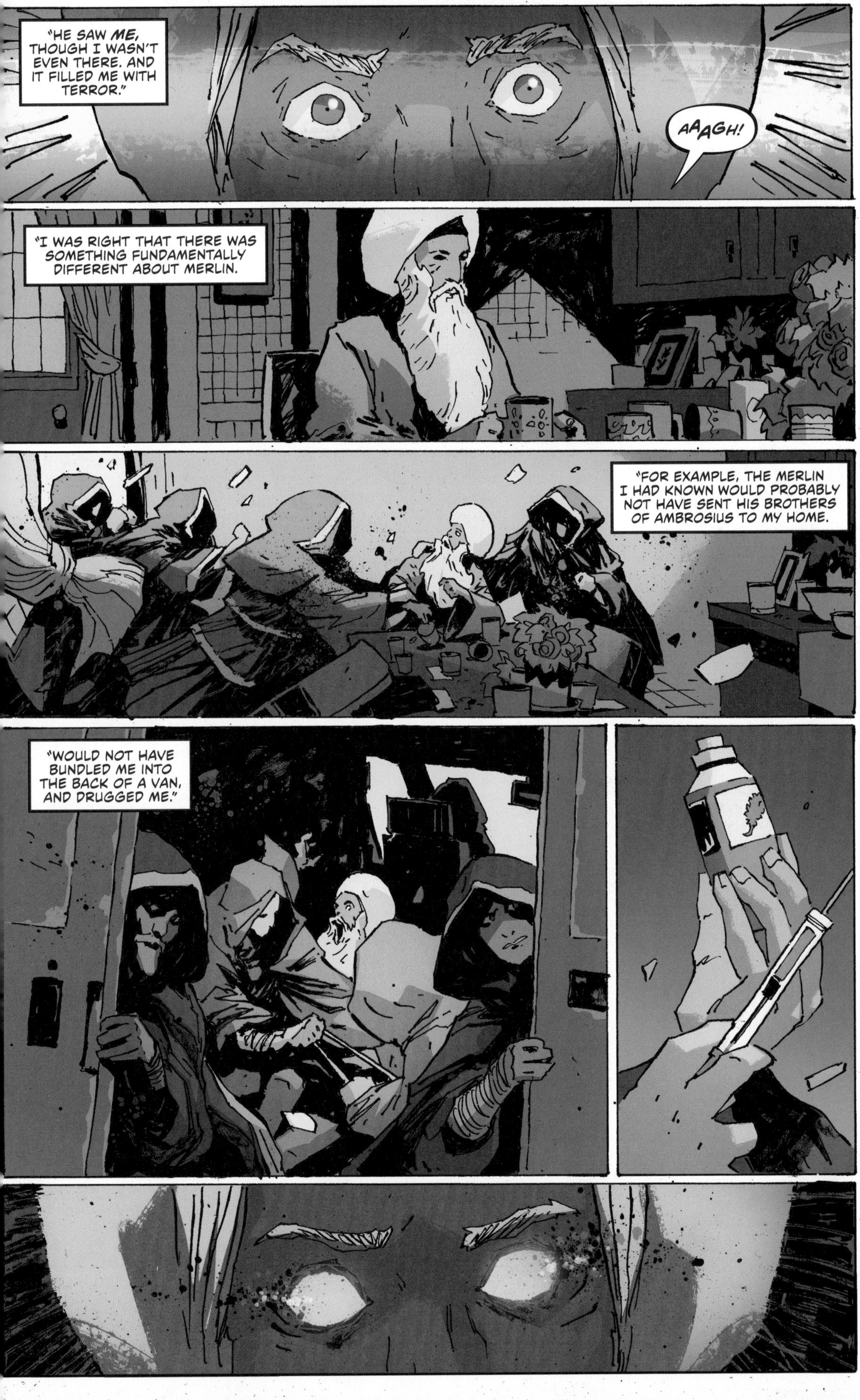
"HE SAW ME, THOUGH I WASN'T EVEN THERE. AND IT FILLED ME WITH TERROR."
AAAGH!
"I WAS RIGHT THAT THERE WAS SOMETHING FUNDAMENTALLY DIFFERENT ABOUT MERLIN.
"FOR EXAMPLE, THE MERLIN I HAD KNOWN WOULD PROBABLY NOT HAVE SENT HIS BROTHERS OF AMBROSIUS TO MY HOME.
"WOULD NOT HAVE BUNDLED ME INTO THE BACK OF A VAN, AND DRUGGED ME."

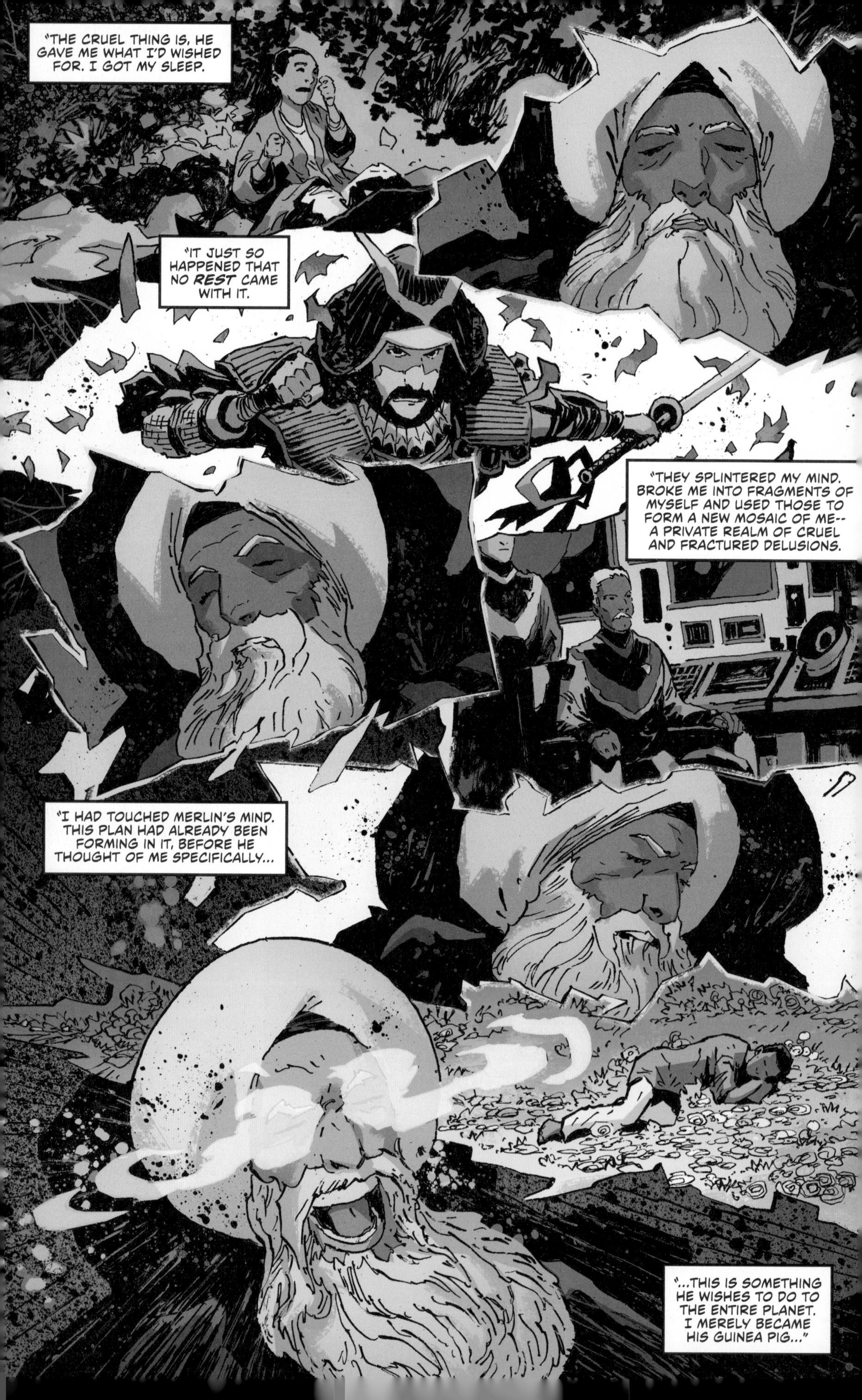
"THE CRUEL THING IS, HE GAVE ME WHAT I'D WISHED FOR. I GOT MY SLEEP.
"IT JUST SO HAPPENED THAT NO REST CAME WITH IT.
"THEY SPLINTERED MY MIND. BROKE ME INTO FRAGMENTS OF MYSELF AND USED THOSE TO FORM A NEW MOSAIC OF ME-- A PRIVATE REALM OF CRUEL AND FRACTURED DELUSIONS.
"I HAD TOUCHED MERLIN'S MIND. THIS PLAN HAD ALREADY BEEN FORMING IN IT, BEFORE HE THOUGHT OF ME SPECIFICALLY...
"...THIS IS SOMETHING HE WISHES TO DO TO THE ENTIRE PLANET. I MERELY BECAME HIS GUINEA PIG..."

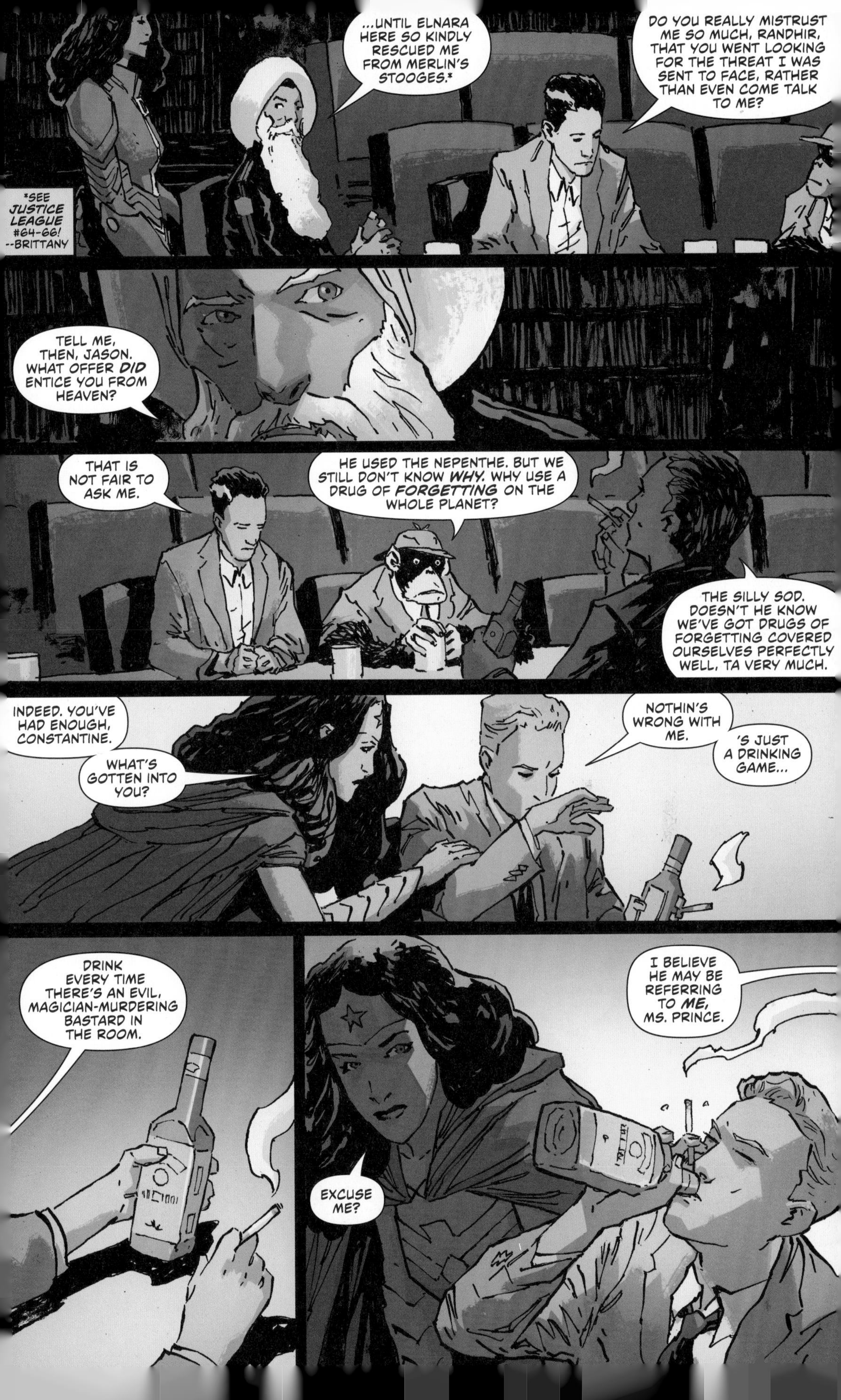
...UNTIL ELNARA HERE SO KINDLY RESCUED ME FROM MERLIN'S STOOGES.*
DO YOU REALLY MISTRUST ME SO MUCH, RANDHIR, THAT YOU WENT LOOKING FOR THE THREAT I WAS SENT TO FACE, RATHER THAN EVEN COME TALK TO ME?
*SEE JUSTICE LEAGUE #64-66! --BRITTANY
TELL ME, THEN, JASON. WHAT OFFER DID ENTICE YOU FROM HEAVEN?
THAT IS NOT FAIR TO ASK ME.
HE USED THE NEPENTHE. BUT WE STILL DON'T KNOW WHY. WHY USE A DRUG OF FORGETTING ON THE WHOLE PLANET?
THE SILLY SOD. DOESN'T HE KNOW WE'VE GOT DRUGS OF FORGETTING COVERED OURSELVES PERFECTLY WELL, TA VERY MUCH.
INDEED. YOU'VE HAD ENOUGH, CONSTANTINE.
WHAT'S GOTTEN INTO YOU?
NOTHIN'S WRONG WITH ME.
'S JUST A DRINKING GAME...
DRINK EVERY TIME THERE'S AN EVIL, MAGICIAN-MURDERING BASTARD IN THE ROOM.
I BELIEVE HE MAY BE REFERRING TO ME, MS. PRINCE.
EXCUSE ME?

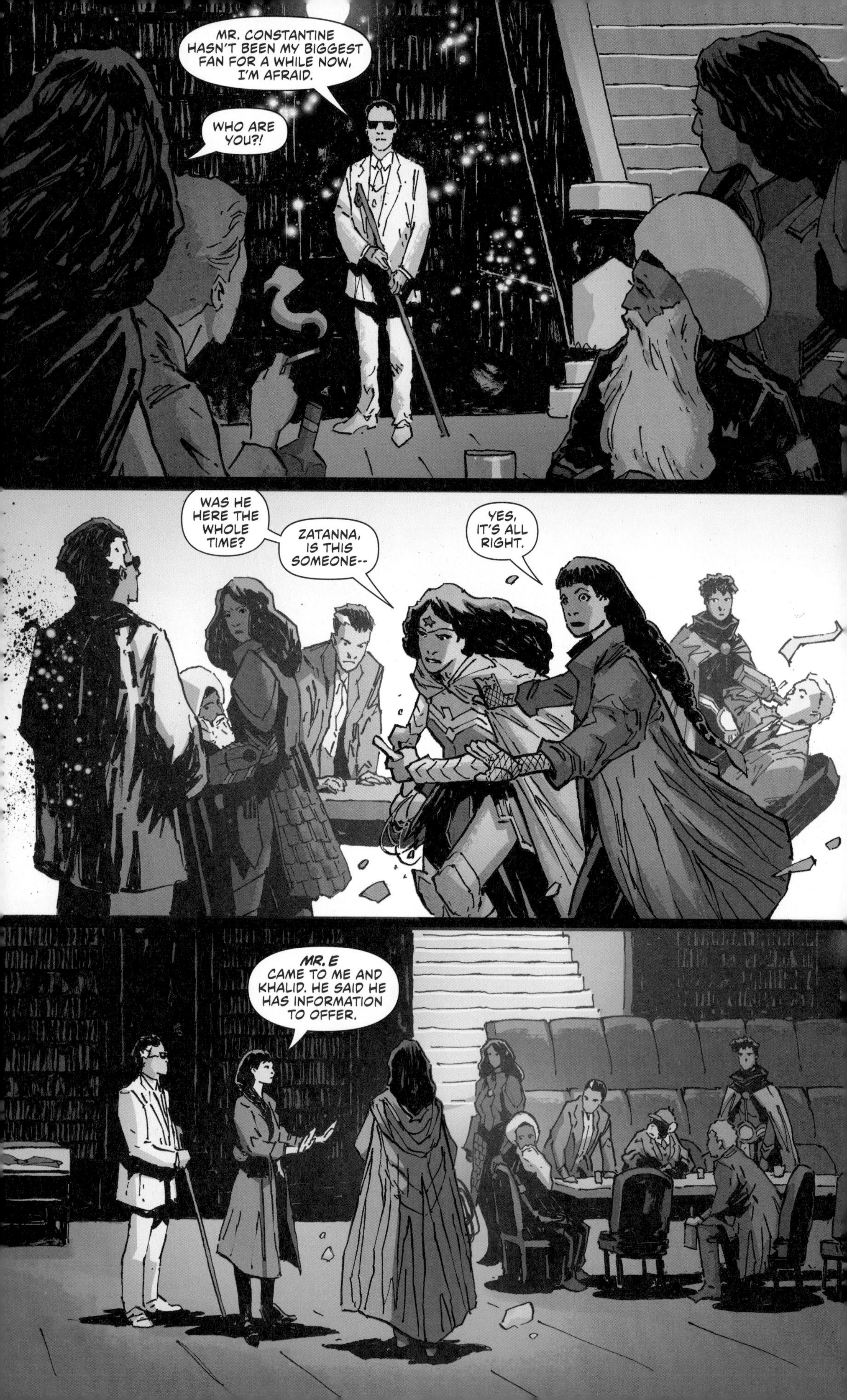

MR. CONSTANTINE HASN'T BEEN MY BIGGEST FAN FOR A WHILE NOW, I'M AFRAID.
WHO ARE YOU?!
WAS HE HERE THE WHOLE TIME?
ZATANNA, IS THIS SOMEONE--
YES, IT'S ALL RIGHT.
MR. E CAME TO ME AND KHALID. HE SAID HE HAS INFORMATION TO OFFER.

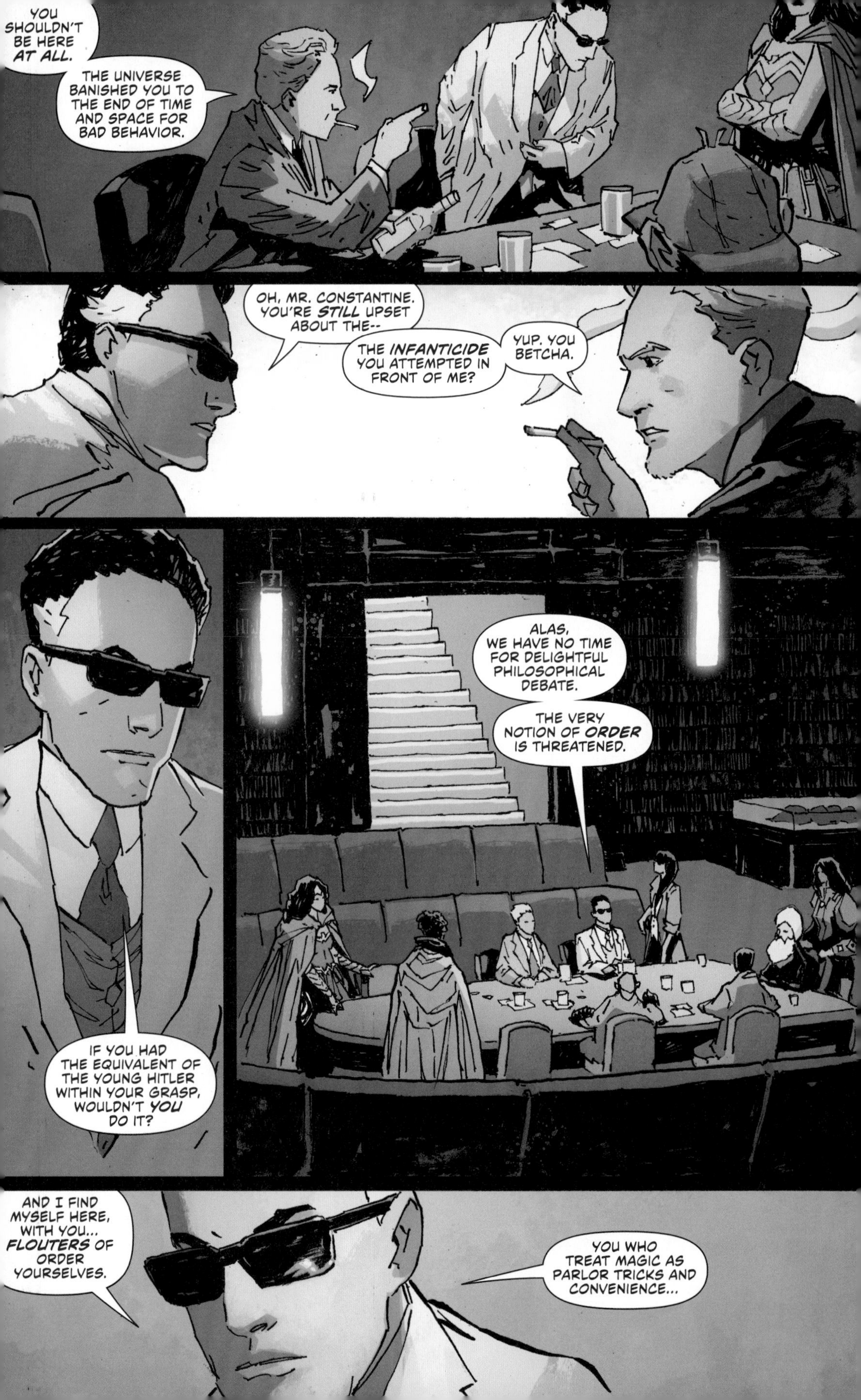
YOU SHOULDN'T BE HERE AT ALL.
THE UNIVERSE BANISHED YOU TO THE END OF TIME AND SPACE FOR BAD BEHAVIOR.
OH, MR. CONSTANTINE. YOU'RE STILL UPSET ABOUT THE--
THE INFANTICIDE YOU ATTEMPTED IN FRONT OF ME?
YUP. YOU BETCHA.
ALAS, WE HAVE NO TIME FOR DELIGHTFUL PHILOSOPHICAL DEBATE.
THE VERY NOTION OF ORDER IS THREATENED.
IF YOU HAD THE EQUIVALENT OF THE YOUNG HITLER WITHIN YOUR GRASP, WOULDN'T YOU DO IT?
AND I FIND MYSELF HERE, WITH YOU... FLOUTERS OF ORDER YOURSELVES.
YOU WHO TREAT MAGIC AS PARLOR TRICKS AND CONVENIENCE...

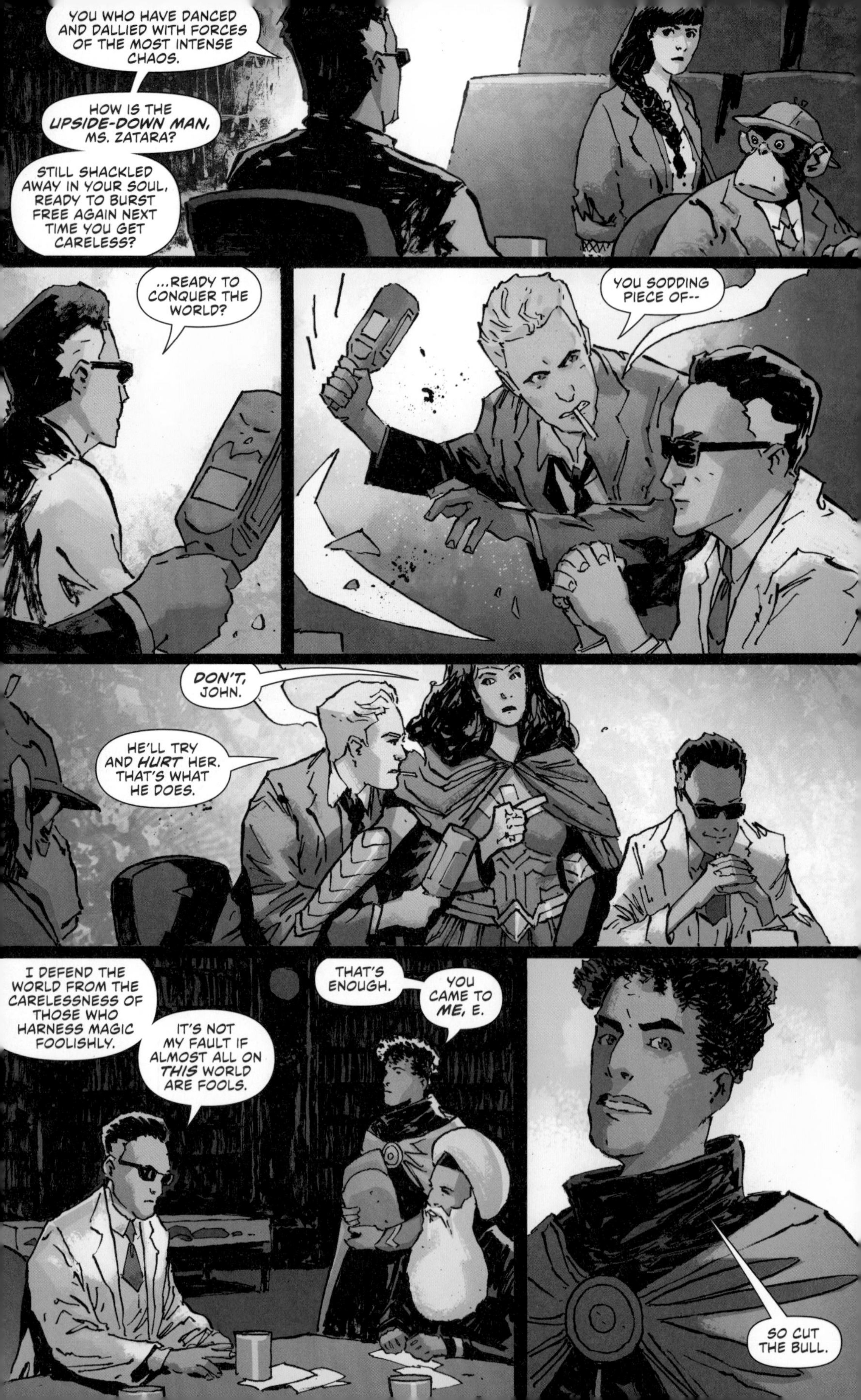
YOU WHO HAVE DANCED AND DALLIED WITH FORCES OF THE MOST INTENSE CHAOS.
HOW IS THE *UPSIDE-DOWN MAN*, MS. ZATARA?
STILL SHACKLED AWAY IN YOUR SOUL, READY TO BURST FREE AGAIN NEXT TIME YOU GET CARELESS?
...READY TO CONQUER THE WORLD?
YOU SODDING PIECE OF--
DON'T, JOHN.
HE'LL TRY AND *HURT* HER. THAT'S WHAT HE DOES.
I DEFEND THE WORLD FROM THE CARELESSNESS OF THOSE WHO HARNESS MAGIC FOOLISHLY.
IT'S NOT MY FAULT IF ALMOST ALL ON *THIS* WORLD ARE FOOLS.
THAT'S ENOUGH.
YOU CAME TO *ME*, E.
SO CUT THE BULL.

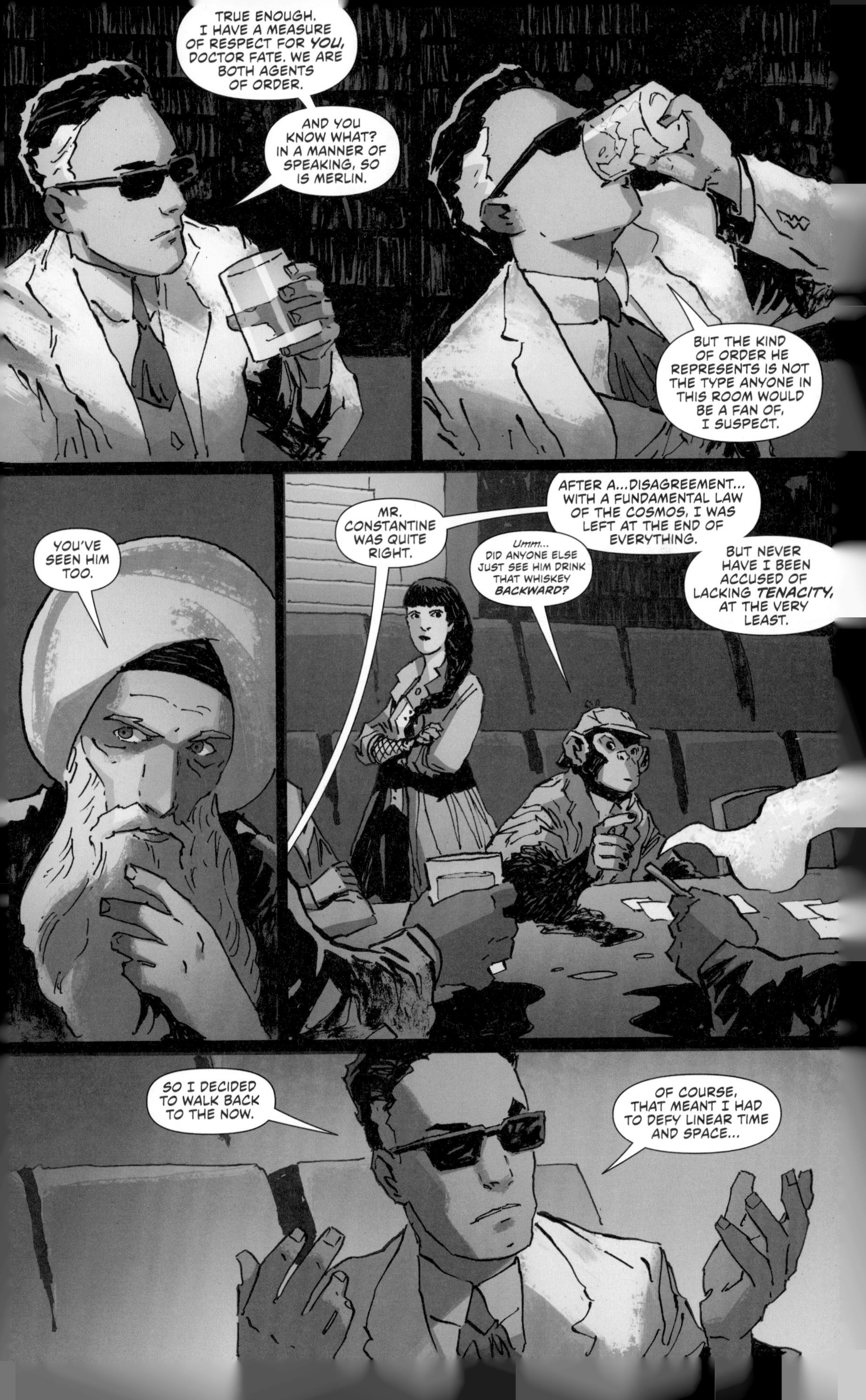
TRUE ENOUGH. I HAVE A MEASURE OF RESPECT FOR *YOU*, DOCTOR FATE. WE ARE BOTH AGENTS OF ORDER.
AND YOU KNOW WHAT? IN A MANNER OF SPEAKING, SO IS MERLIN.
BUT THE KIND OF ORDER HE REPRESENTS IS NOT THE TYPE ANYONE IN THIS ROOM WOULD BE A FAN OF, I SUSPECT.
YOU'VE SEEN HIM TOO.
MR. CONSTANTINE WAS QUITE RIGHT.
AFTER A...DISAGREEMENT... WITH A FUNDAMENTAL LAW OF THE COSMOS, I WAS LEFT AT THE END OF EVERYTHING.
Umm... DID ANYONE ELSE JUST SEE HIM DRINK THAT WHISKEY *BACKWARD?*
BUT NEVER HAVE I BEEN ACCUSED OF LACKING *TENACITY*, AT THE VERY LEAST.
SO I DECIDED TO WALK BACK TO THE NOW.
OF COURSE, THAT MEANT I HAD TO DEFY LINEAR TIME AND SPACE...

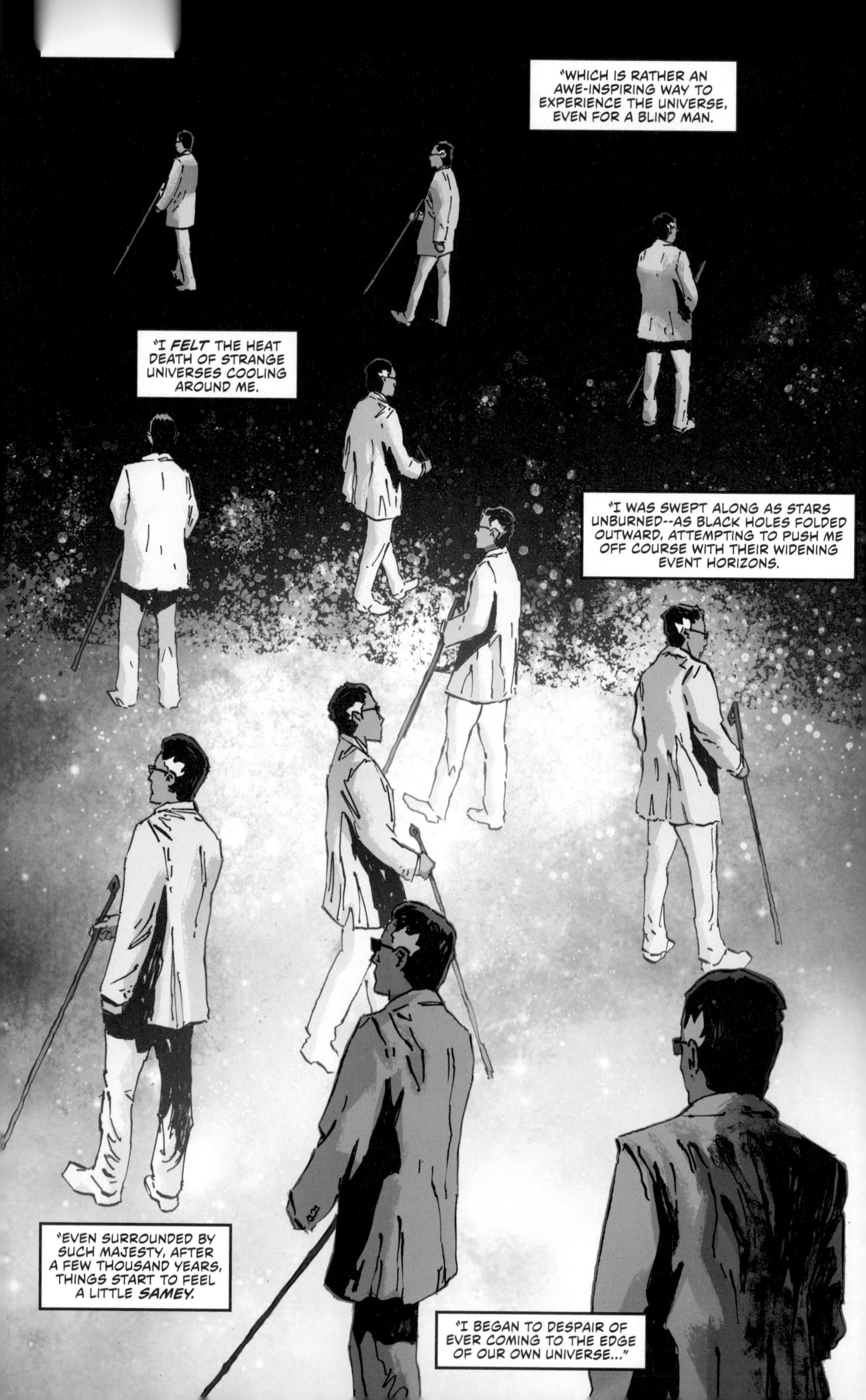
"WHICH IS RATHER AN AWE-INSPIRING WAY TO EXPERIENCE THE UNIVERSE, EVEN FOR A BLIND MAN.
"I *FELT* THE HEAT DEATH OF STRANGE UNIVERSES COOLING AROUND ME.
"I WAS SWEPT ALONG AS STARS UNBURNED--AS BLACK HOLES FOLDED OUTWARD, ATTEMPTING TO PUSH ME OFF COURSE WITH THEIR WIDENING EVENT HORIZONS.
"EVEN SURROUNDED BY SUCH MAJESTY, AFTER A FEW THOUSAND YEARS, THINGS START TO FEEL A LITTLE *SAMEY.*
"I BEGAN TO DESPAIR OF EVER COMING TO THE EDGE OF OUR OWN UNIVERSE..."

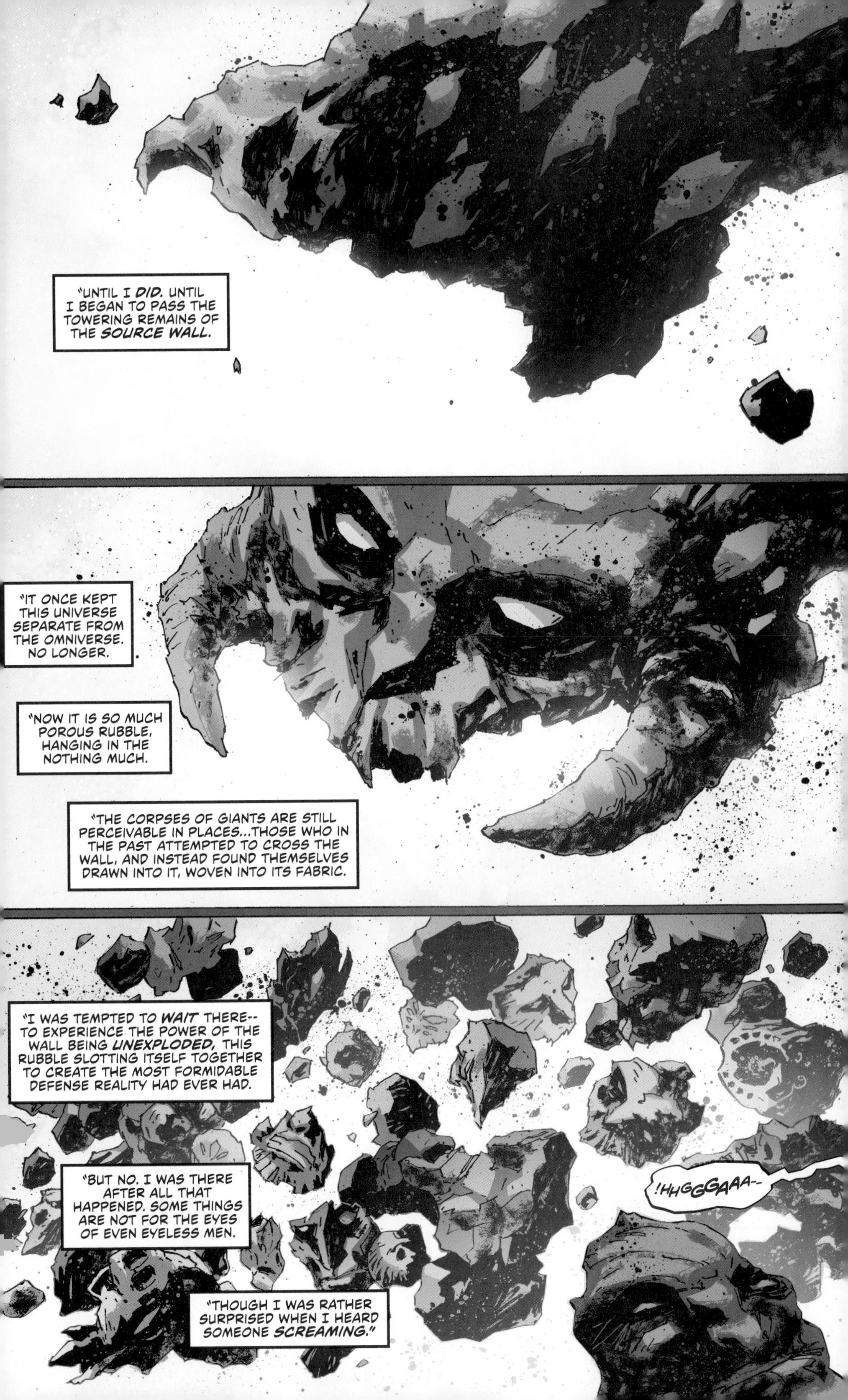
"UNTIL I DID. UNTIL I BEGAN TO PASS THE TOWERING REMAINS OF THE SOURCE WALL.
"IT ONCE KEPT THIS UNIVERSE SEPARATE FROM THE OMNIVERSE. NO LONGER.
"NOW IT IS SO MUCH POROUS RUBBLE, HANGING IN THE NOTHING MUCH.
"THE CORPSES OF GIANTS ARE STILL PERCEIVABLE IN PLACES...THOSE WHO IN THE PAST ATTEMPTED TO CROSS THE WALL, AND INSTEAD FOUND THEMSELVES DRAWN INTO IT, WOVEN INTO ITS FABRIC.
"I WAS TEMPTED TO WAIT THERE--TO EXPERIENCE THE POWER OF THE WALL BEING UNEXPLODED, THIS RUBBLE SLOTTING ITSELF TOGETHER TO CREATE THE MOST FORMIDABLE DEFENSE REALITY HAD EVER HAD.
"BUT NO. I WAS THERE AFTER ALL THAT HAPPENED. SOME THINGS ARE NOT FOR THE EYES OF EVEN EYELESS MEN.
!HHGGGAAA--
"THOUGH I WAS RATHER SURPRISED WHEN I HEARD SOMEONE SCREAMING."

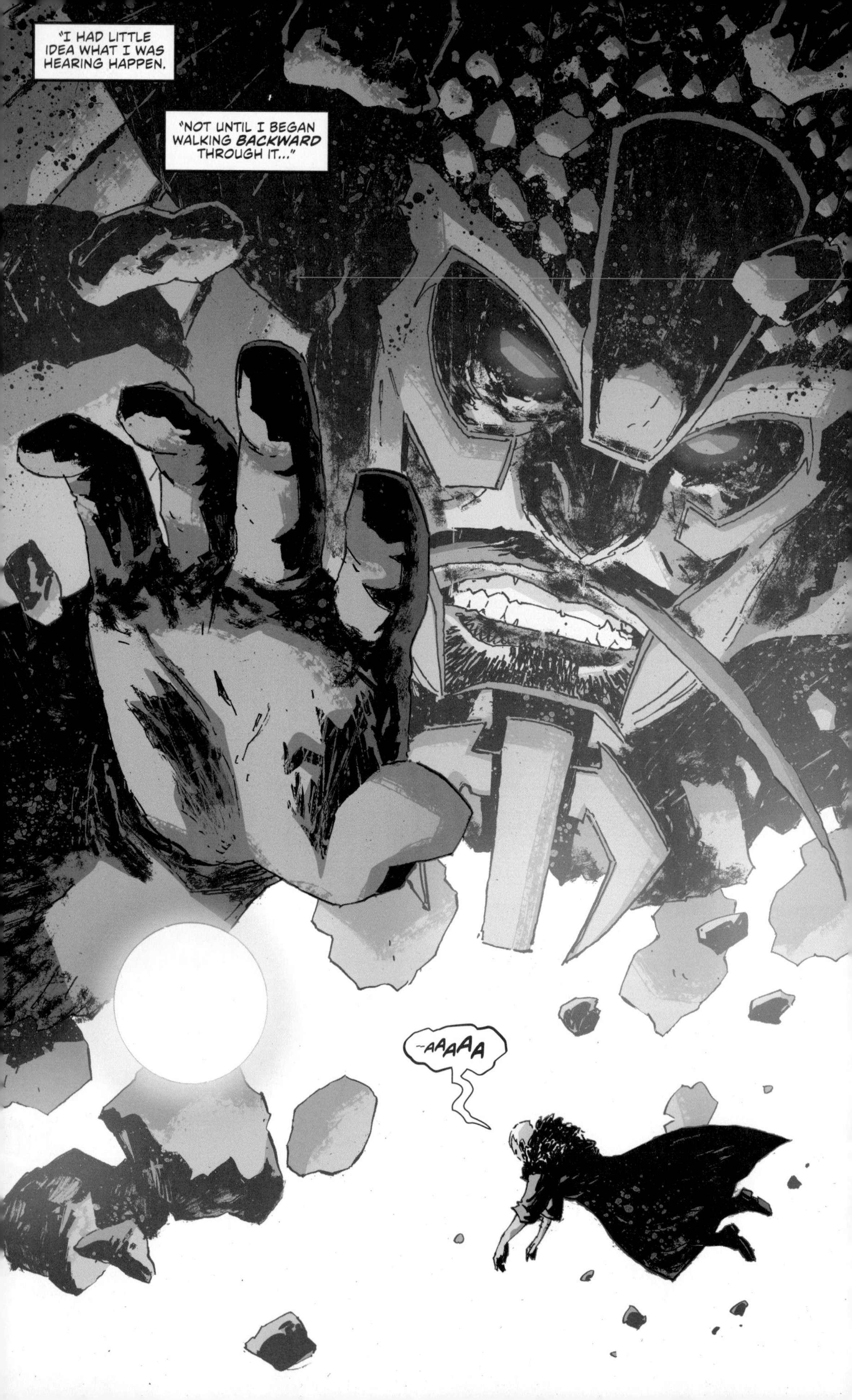
"I HAD LITTLE IDEA WHAT I WAS HEARING HAPPEN.
"NOT UNTIL I BEGAN WALKING BACKWARD THROUGH IT..."
--AAAAA

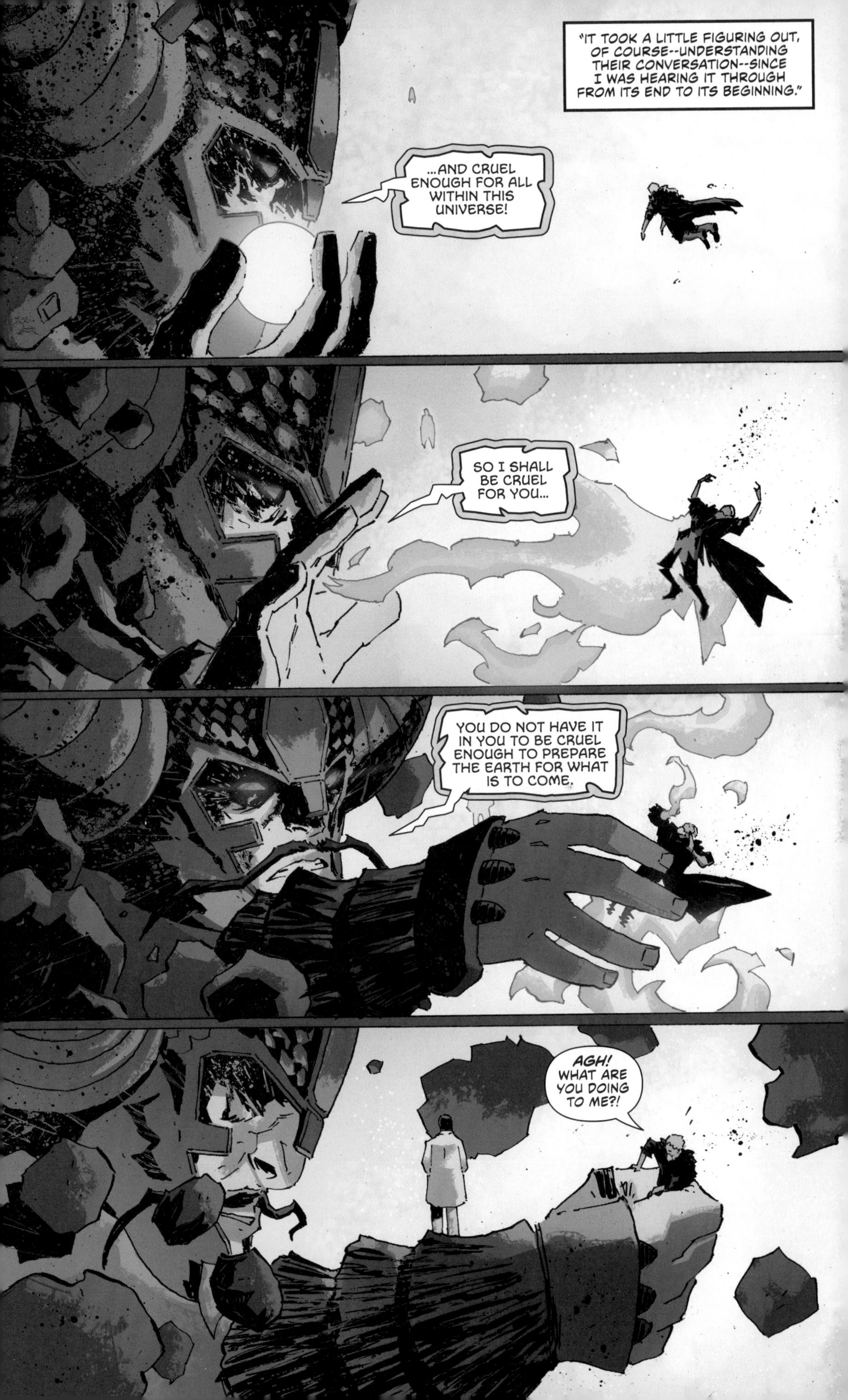
"IT TOOK A LITTLE FIGURING OUT, OF COURSE--UNDERSTANDING THEIR CONVERSATION--SINCE I WAS HEARING IT THROUGH FROM ITS END TO ITS BEGINNING."
...AND CRUEL ENOUGH FOR ALL WITHIN THIS UNIVERSE!
SO I SHALL BE CRUEL FOR YOU...
YOU DO NOT HAVE IT IN YOU TO BE CRUEL ENOUGH TO PREPARE THE EARTH FOR WHAT IS TO COME.
AGH! WHAT ARE YOU DOING TO ME?!

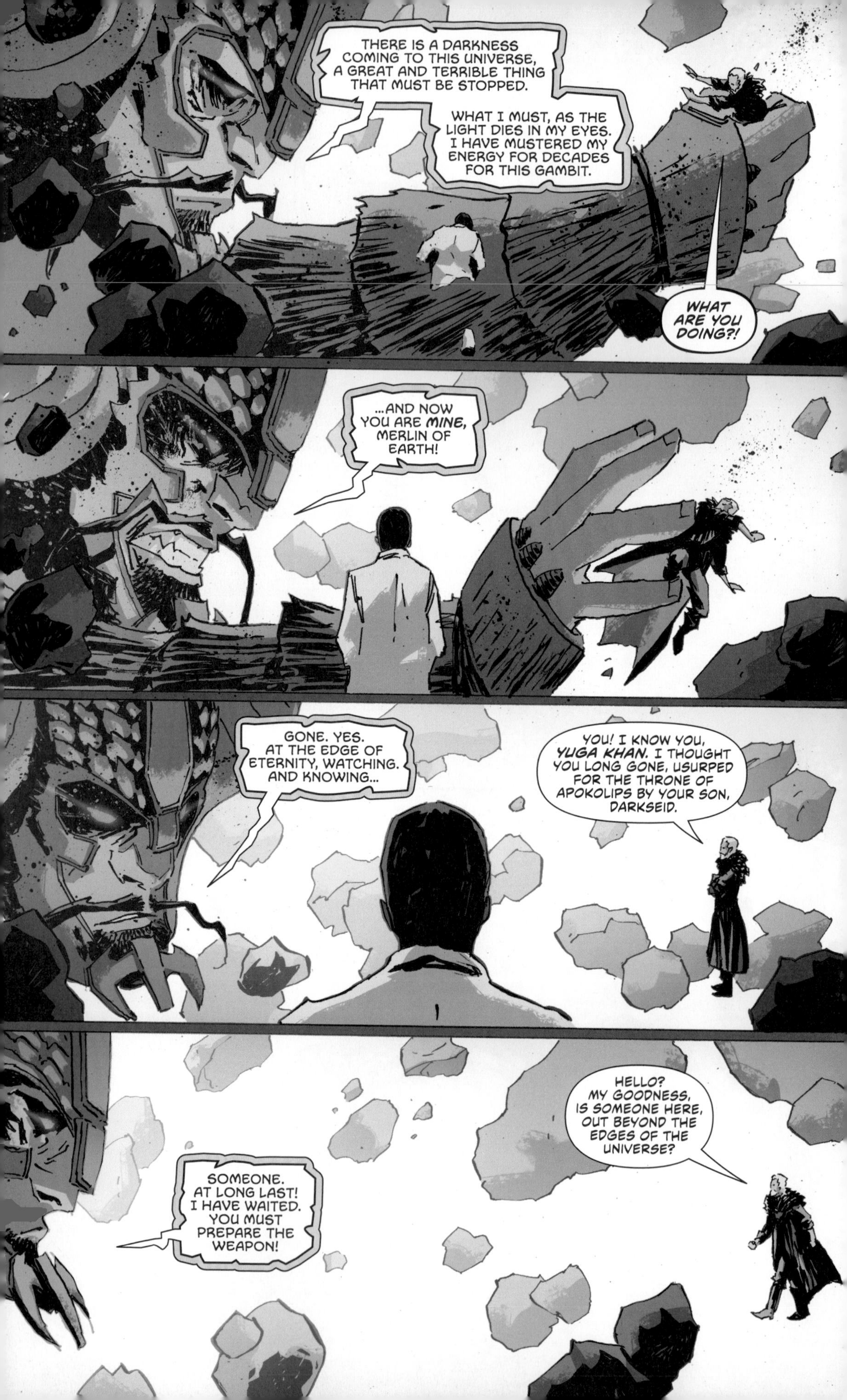
THERE IS A DARKNESS COMING TO THIS UNIVERSE, A GREAT AND TERRIBLE THING THAT MUST BE STOPPED.
WHAT I MUST, AS THE LIGHT DIES IN MY EYES. I HAVE MUSTERED MY ENERGY FOR DECADES FOR THIS GAMBIT.
WHAT ARE YOU DOING?!
...AND NOW YOU ARE MINE, MERLIN OF EARTH!
GONE. YES. AT THE EDGE OF ETERNITY, WATCHING. AND KNOWING...
YOU! I KNOW YOU, YUGA KHAN. I THOUGHT YOU LONG GONE, USURPED FOR THE THRONE OF APOKOLIPS BY YOUR SON, DARKSEID.
HELLO? MY GOODNESS, IS SOMEONE HERE, OUT BEYOND THE EDGES OF THE UNIVERSE?
SOMEONE. AT LONG LAST! I HAVE WAITED. YOU MUST PREPARE THE WEAPON!

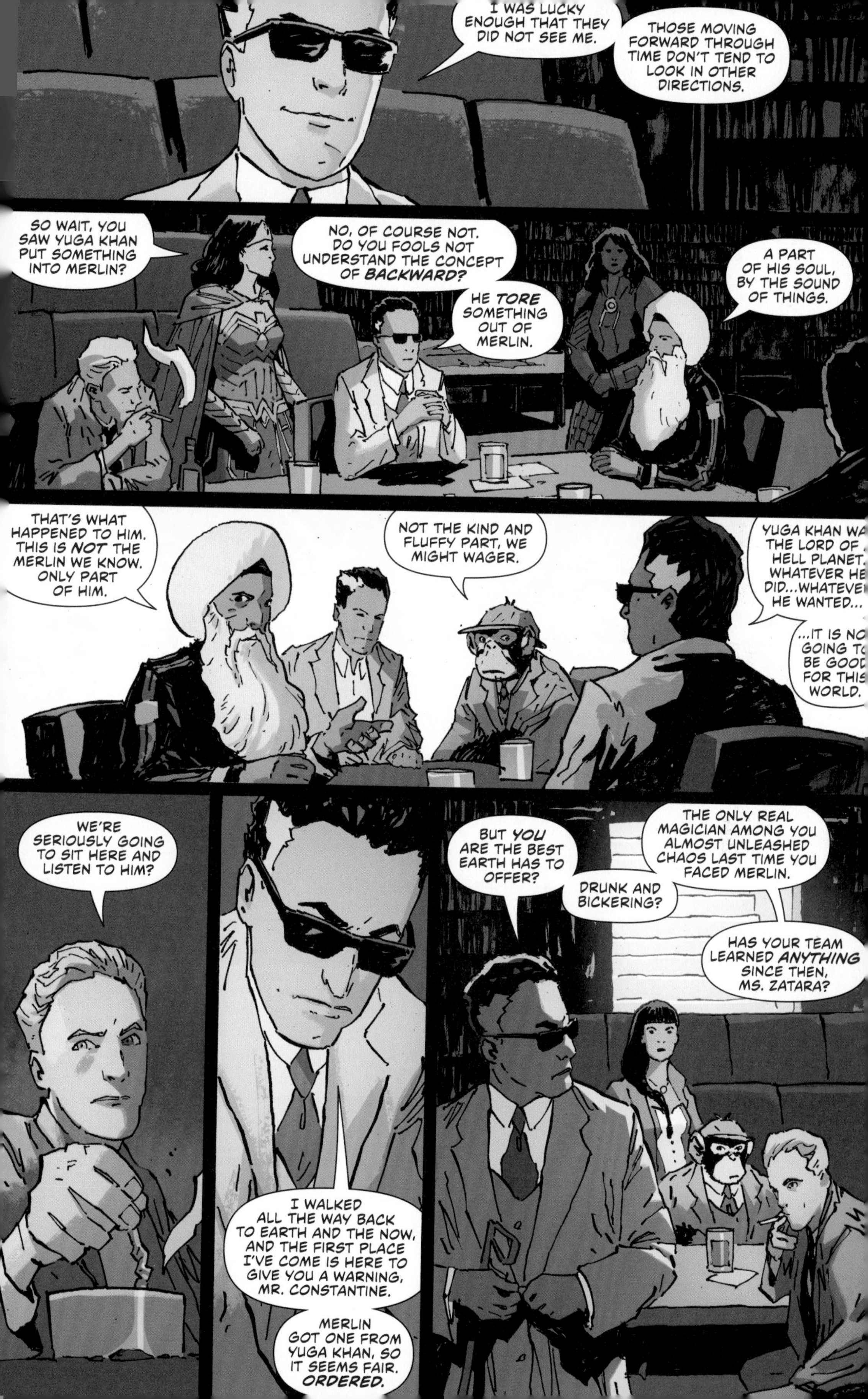
I WAS LUCKY ENOUGH THAT THEY DID NOT SEE ME.
THOSE MOVING FORWARD THROUGH TIME DON'T TEND TO LOOK IN OTHER DIRECTIONS.
SO WAIT, YOU SAW YUGA KHAN PUT SOMETHING INTO MERLIN?
NO, OF COURSE NOT. DO YOU FOOLS NOT UNDERSTAND THE CONCEPT OF BACKWARD?
HE TORE SOMETHING OUT OF MERLIN.
A PART OF HIS SOUL, BY THE SOUND OF THINGS.
THAT'S WHAT HAPPENED TO HIM. THIS IS NOT THE MERLIN WE KNOW. ONLY PART OF HIM.
NOT THE KIND AND FLUFFY PART, WE MIGHT WAGER.
YUGA KHAN WA THE LORD OF HELL PLANET. WHATEVER HE DID...WHATEVE HE WANTED...
...IT IS NO GOING TO BE GOOD FOR THIS WORLD.
WE'RE SERIOUSLY GOING TO SIT HERE AND LISTEN TO HIM?
I WALKED ALL THE WAY BACK TO EARTH AND THE NOW, AND THE FIRST PLACE I'VE COME IS HERE TO GIVE YOU A WARNING, MR. CONSTANTINE.
MERLIN GOT ONE FROM YUGA KHAN, SO IT SEEMS FAIR. ORDERED.
BUT YOU ARE THE BEST EARTH HAS TO OFFER?
DRUNK AND BICKERING?
THE ONLY REAL MAGICIAN AMONG YOU ALMOST UNLEASHED CHAOS LAST TIME YOU FACED MERLIN.
HAS YOUR TEAM LEARNED ANYTHING SINCE THEN, MS. ZATARA?

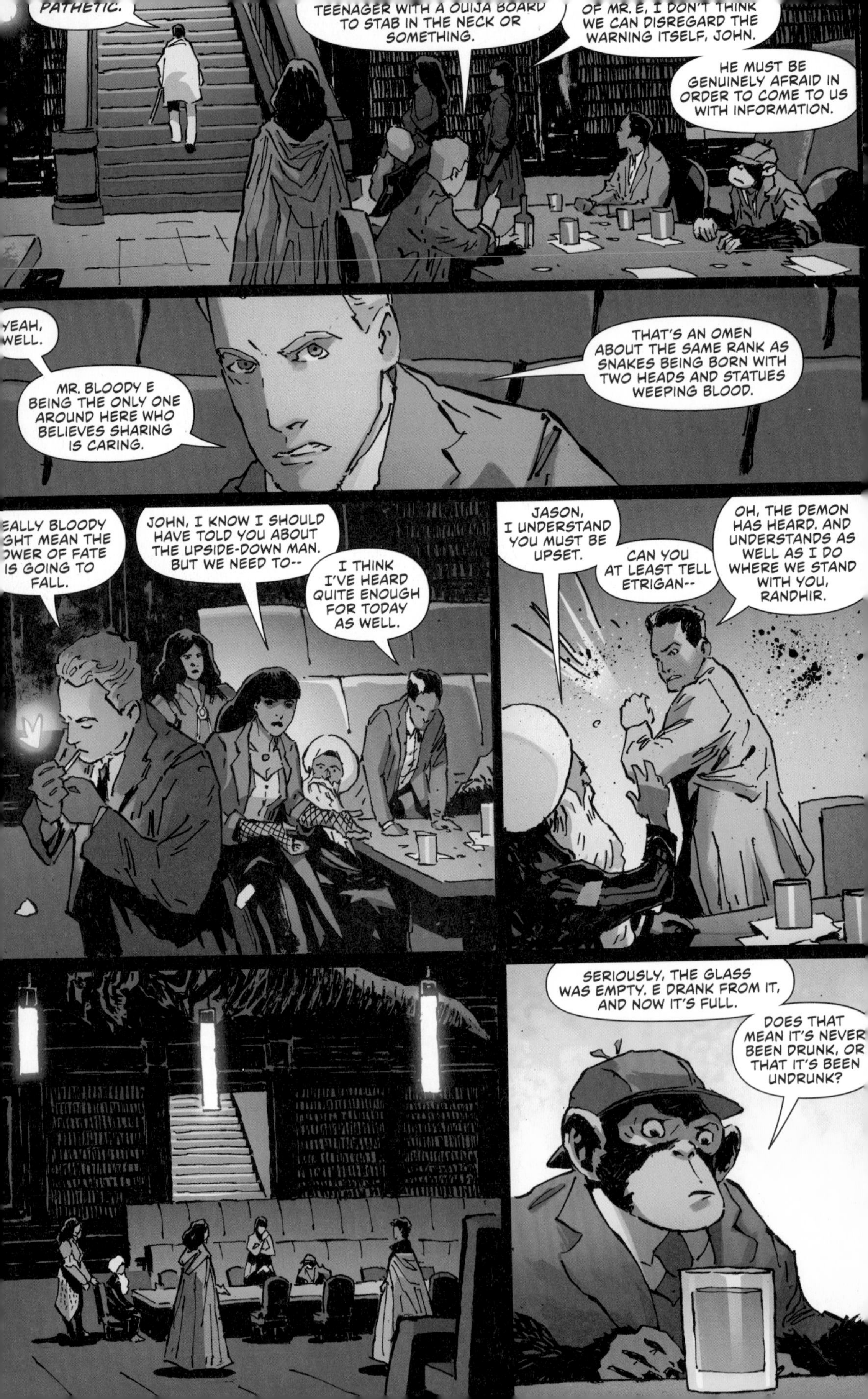
PATHETIC.
TEENAGER WITH A OUIJA BOARD TO STAB IN THE NECK OR SOMETHING.
OF MR. E, I DON'T THINK WE CAN DISREGARD THE WARNING ITSELF, JOHN.
HE MUST BE GENUINELY AFRAID IN ORDER TO COME TO US WITH INFORMATION.
YEAH, WELL.
MR. BLOODY E BEING THE ONLY ONE AROUND HERE WHO BELIEVES SHARING IS CARING.
THAT'S AN OMEN ABOUT THE SAME RANK AS SNAKES BEING BORN WITH TWO HEADS AND STATUES WEEPING BLOOD.
EALLY BLOODY GHT MEAN THE OWER OF FATE IS GOING TO FALL.
JOHN, I KNOW I SHOULD HAVE TOLD YOU ABOUT THE UPSIDE-DOWN MAN. BUT WE NEED TO--
I THINK I'VE HEARD QUITE ENOUGH FOR TODAY AS WELL.
JASON, I UNDERSTAND YOU MUST BE UPSET.
CAN YOU AT LEAST TELL ETRIGAN--
OH, THE DEMON HAS HEARD. AND UNDERSTANDS AS WELL AS I DO WHERE WE STAND WITH YOU, RANDHIR.
SERIOUSLY, THE GLASS WAS EMPTY. E DRANK FROM IT, AND NOW IT'S FULL.
DOES THAT MEAN IT'S NEVER BEEN DRUNK, OR THAT IT'S BEEN UNDRUNK?

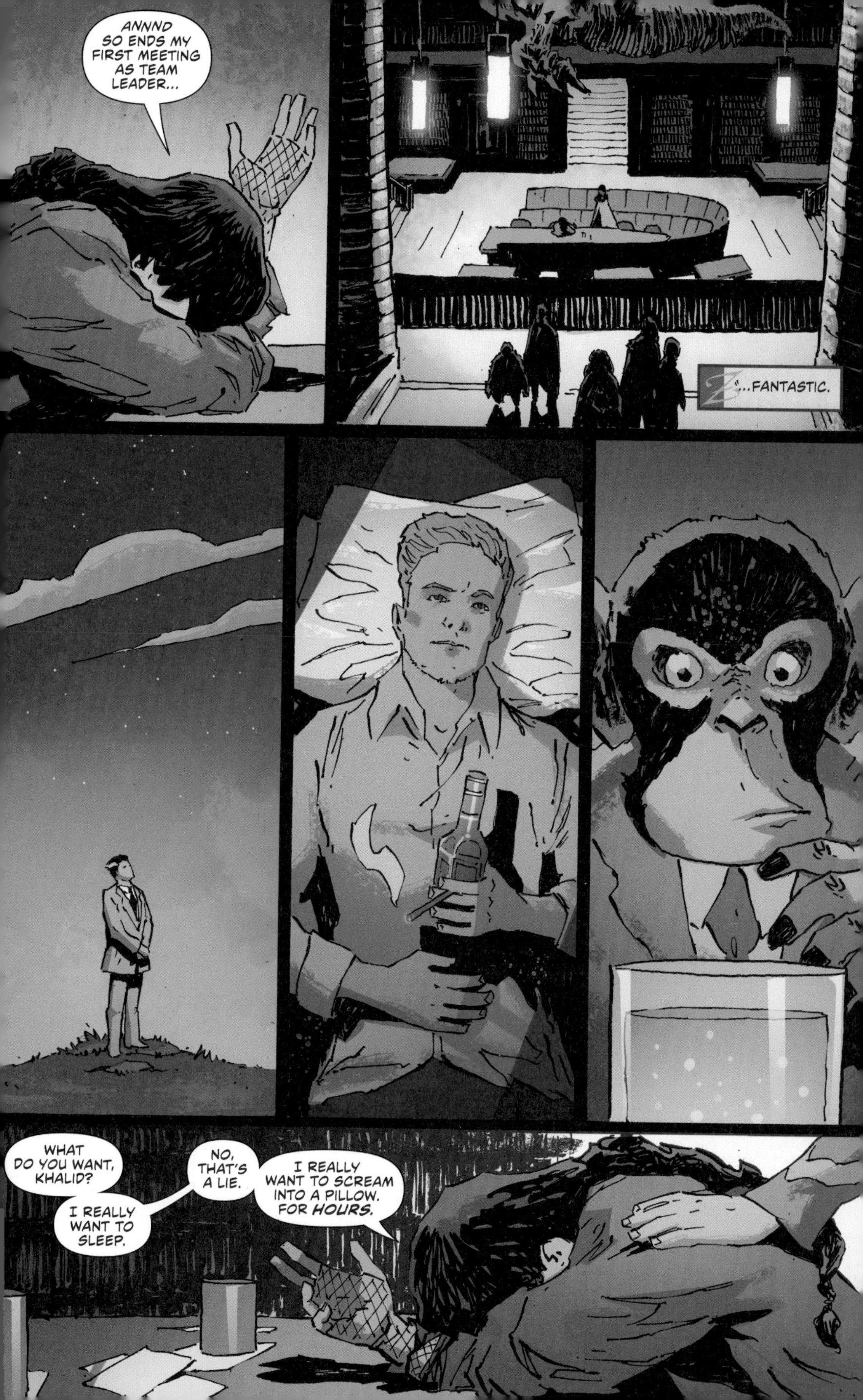
ANNND SO ENDS MY FIRST MEETING AS TEAM LEADER...
...FANTASTIC.
WHAT DO YOU WANT, KHALID?
I REALLY WANT TO SLEEP.
NO, THAT'S A LIE.
I REALLY WANT TO SCREAM INTO A PILLOW. FOR *HOURS*.

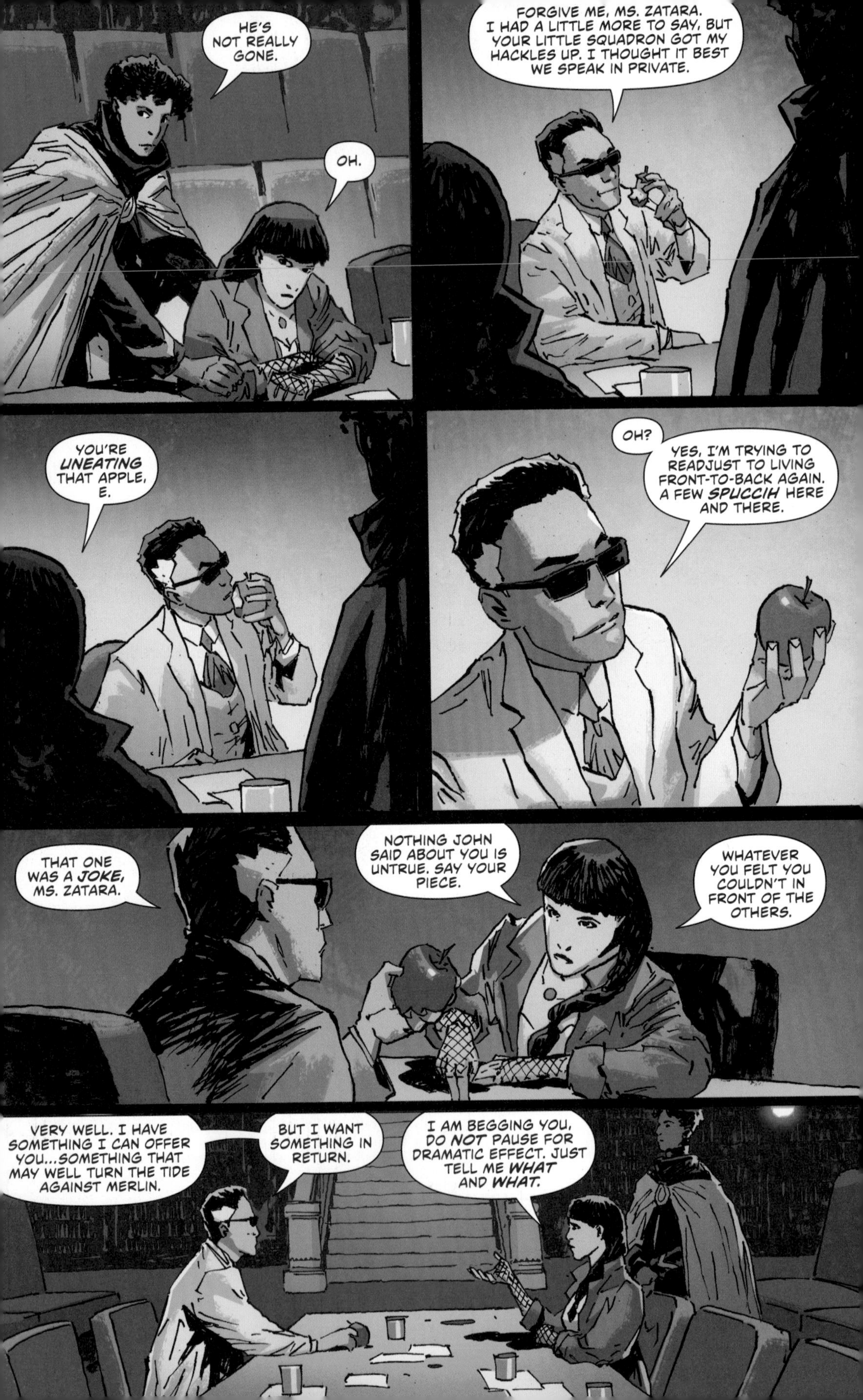
HE'S NOT REALLY GONE.
OH.
FORGIVE ME, MS. ZATARA. I HAD A LITTLE MORE TO SAY, BUT YOUR LITTLE SQUADRON GOT MY HACKLES UP. I THOUGHT IT BEST WE SPEAK IN PRIVATE.
YOU'RE UNEATING THAT APPLE, E.
OH?
YES, I'M TRYING TO READJUST TO LIVING FRONT-TO-BACK AGAIN. A FEW SPUCCIH HERE AND THERE.
THAT ONE WAS A JOKE, MS. ZATARA.
NOTHING JOHN SAID ABOUT YOU IS UNTRUE. SAY YOUR PIECE.
WHATEVER YOU FELT YOU COULDN'T IN FRONT OF THE OTHERS.
VERY WELL. I HAVE SOMETHING I CAN OFFER YOU...SOMETHING THAT MAY WELL TURN THE TIDE AGAINST MERLIN.
BUT I WANT SOMETHING IN RETURN.
I AM BEGGING YOU, DO NOT PAUSE FOR DRAMATIC EFFECT. JUST TELL ME WHAT AND WHAT.

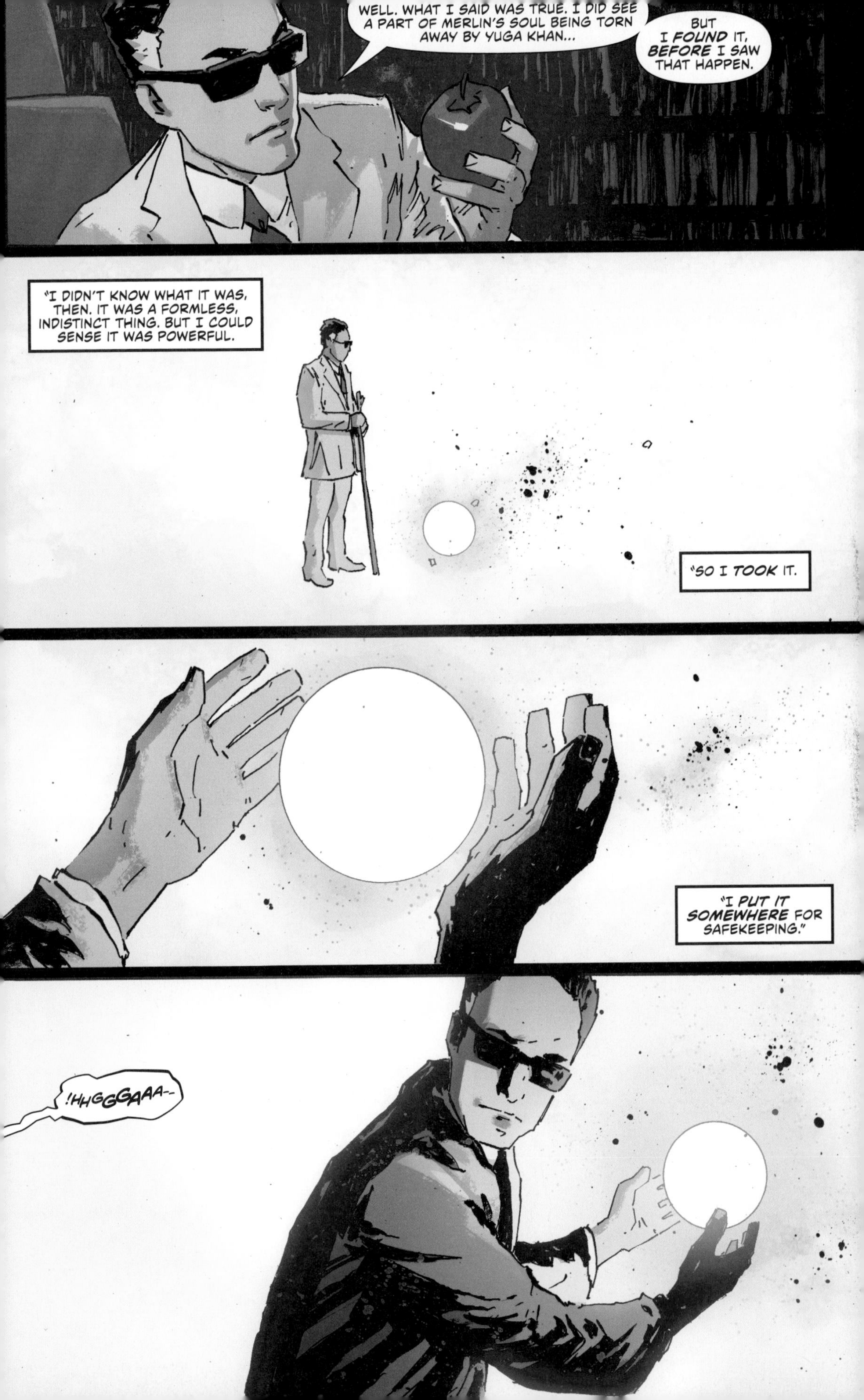
WELL. WHAT I SAID WAS TRUE. I DID SEE A PART OF MERLIN'S SOUL BEING TORN AWAY BY YUGA KHAN...
BUT I FOUND IT, BEFORE I SAW THAT HAPPEN.
"I DIDN'T KNOW WHAT IT WAS, THEN. IT WAS A FORMLESS, INDISTINCT THING. BUT I COULD SENSE IT WAS POWERFUL.
"SO I TOOK IT.
"I PUT IT SOMEWHERE FOR SAFEKEEPING."
!HHGGGAAA--

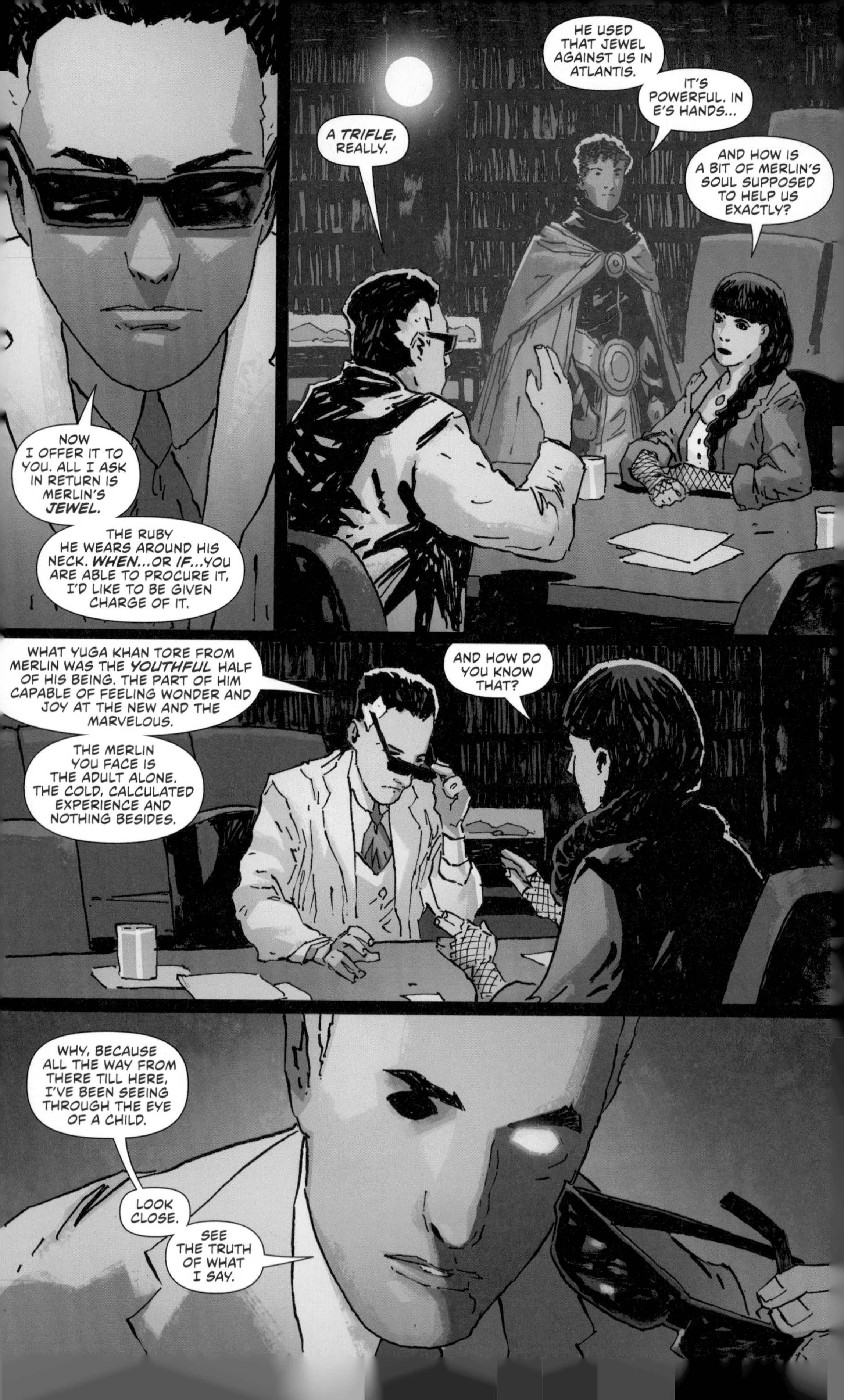
NOW I OFFER IT TO YOU. ALL I ASK IN RETURN IS MERLIN'S *JEWEL.*
THE RUBY HE WEARS AROUND HIS NECK. *WHEN...*OR *IF...*YOU ARE ABLE TO PROCURE IT, I'D LIKE TO BE GIVEN CHARGE OF IT.
A *TRIFLE,* REALLY.
HE USED THAT JEWEL AGAINST US IN ATLANTIS.
IT'S POWERFUL. IN E'S HANDS...
AND HOW IS A BIT OF MERLIN'S SOUL SUPPOSED TO HELP US EXACTLY?
WHAT YUGA KHAN TORE FROM MERLIN WAS THE *YOUTHFUL* HALF OF HIS BEING. THE PART OF HIM CAPABLE OF FEELING WONDER AND JOY AT THE NEW AND THE MARVELOUS.
THE MERLIN YOU FACE IS THE ADULT ALONE. THE COLD, CALCULATED EXPERIENCE AND NOTHING BESIDES.
AND HOW DO YOU KNOW THAT?
WHY, BECAUSE ALL THE WAY FROM THERE TILL HERE, I'VE BEEN SEEING THROUGH THE EYE OF A CHILD.
LOOK CLOSE.
SEE THE TRUTH OF WHAT I SAY.

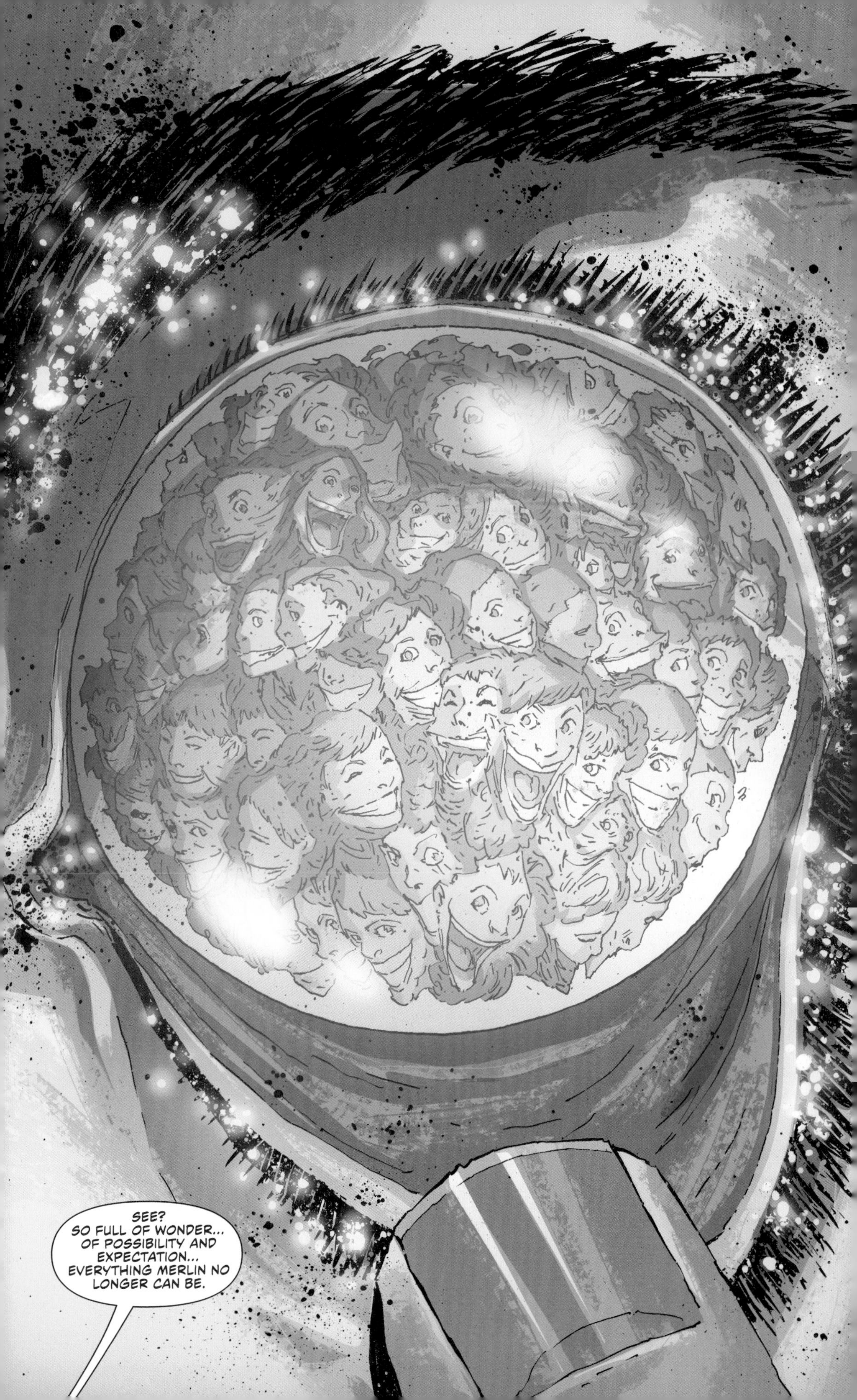
SEE? SO FULL OF WONDER... OF POSSIBILITY AND EXPECTATION... EVERYTHING MERLIN NO LONGER CAN BE.

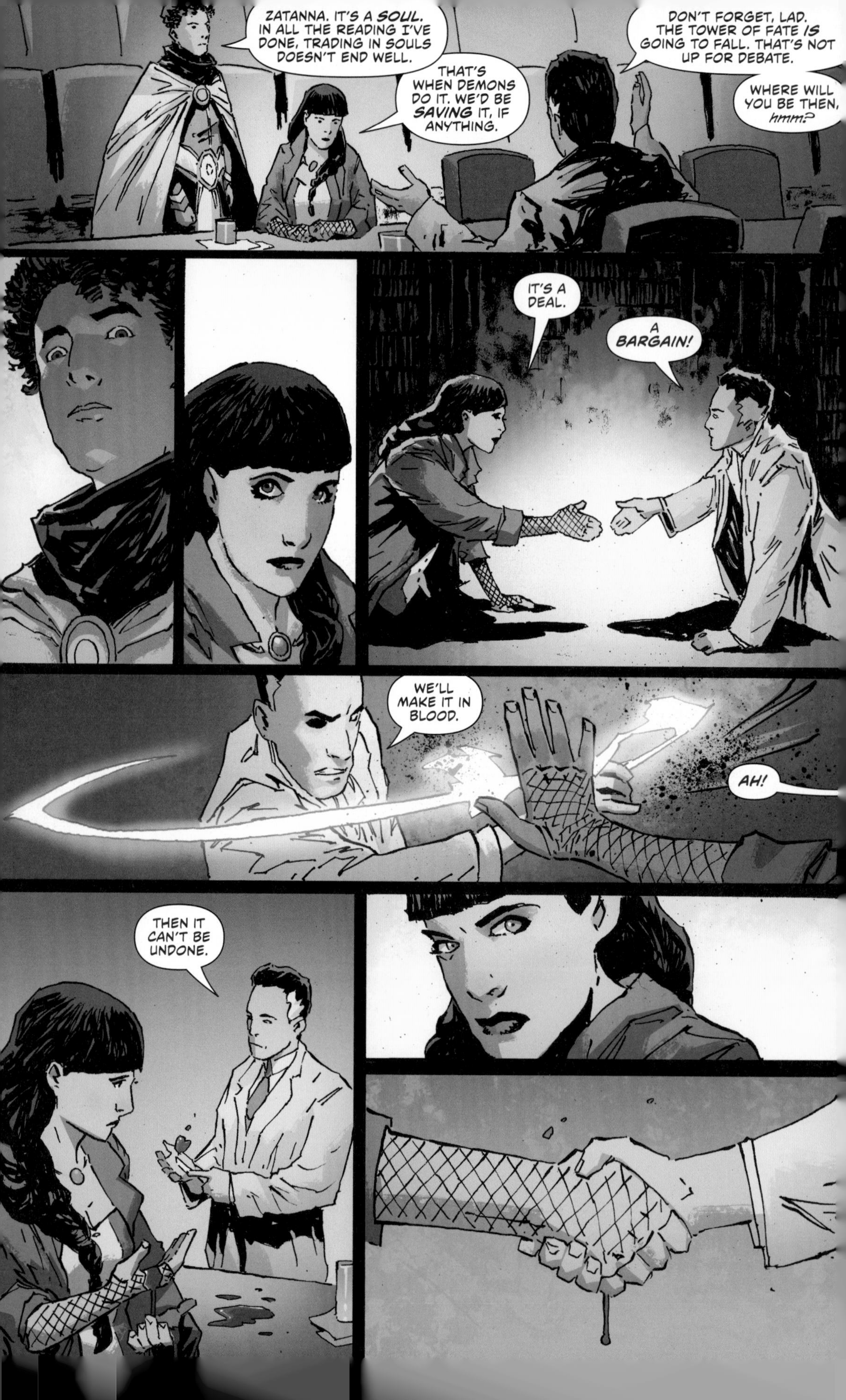
ZATANNA. IT'S A SOUL. IN ALL THE READING I'VE DONE, TRADING IN SOULS DOESN'T END WELL.
THAT'S WHEN DEMONS DO IT. WE'D BE SAVING IT, IF ANYTHING.
DON'T FORGET, LAD. THE TOWER OF FATE IS GOING TO FALL. THAT'S NOT UP FOR DEBATE.
WHERE WILL YOU BE THEN, hmm?
IT'S A DEAL.
A BARGAIN!
WE'LL MAKE IT IN BLOOD.
AH!
THEN IT CAN'T BE UNDONE.

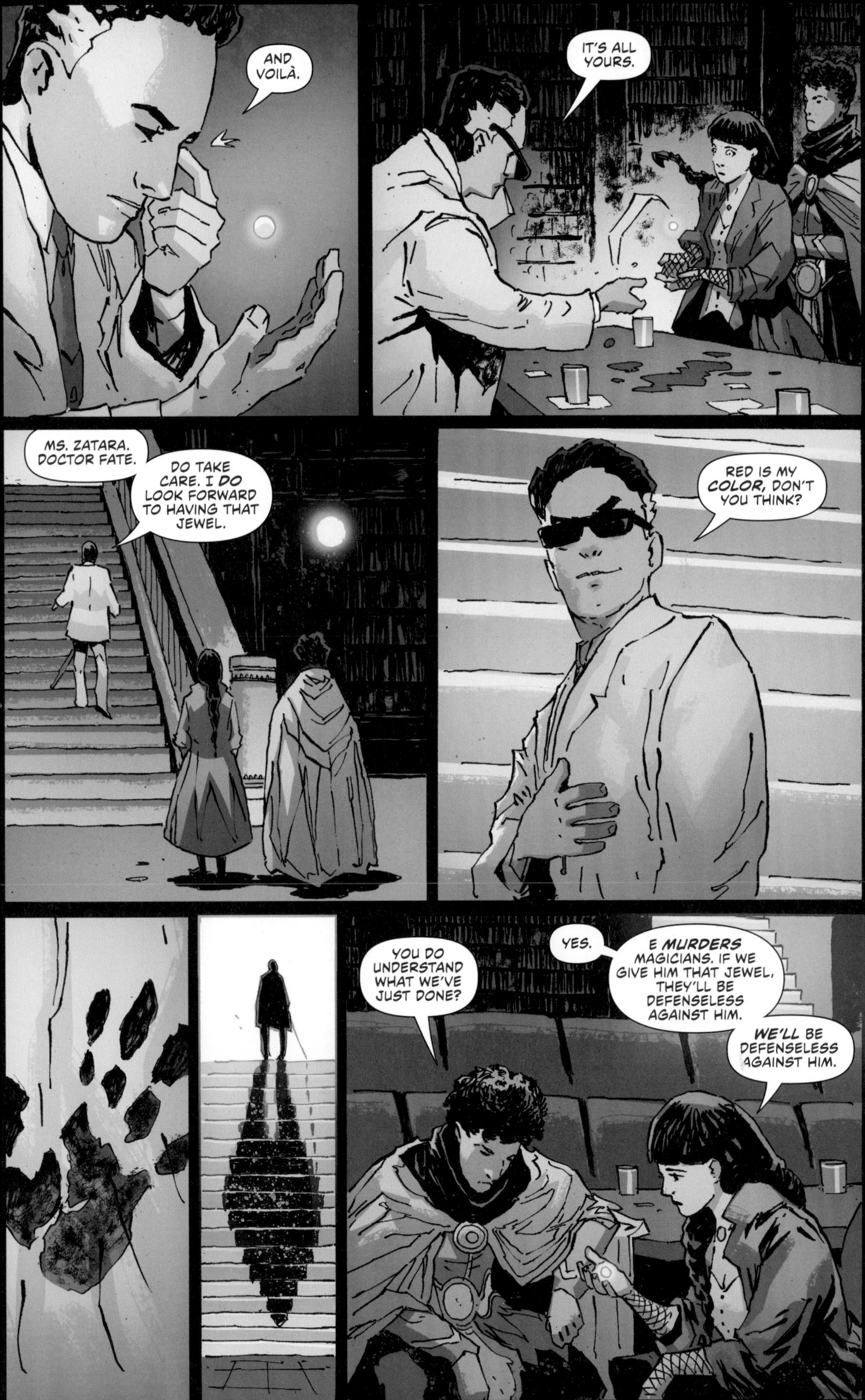
AND VOILÀ.
IT'S ALL YOURS.
MS. ZATARA. DOCTOR FATE.
DO TAKE CARE. I *DO* LOOK FORWARD TO HAVING THAT JEWEL.
RED IS MY *COLOR,* DON'T YOU THINK?
YOU DO UNDERSTAND WHAT WE'VE JUST DONE?
YES.
E *MURDERS* MAGICIANS. IF WE GIVE HIM THAT JEWEL, THEY'LL BE DEFENSELESS AGAINST HIM.
WE'LL BE DEFENSELESS AGAINST HIM.

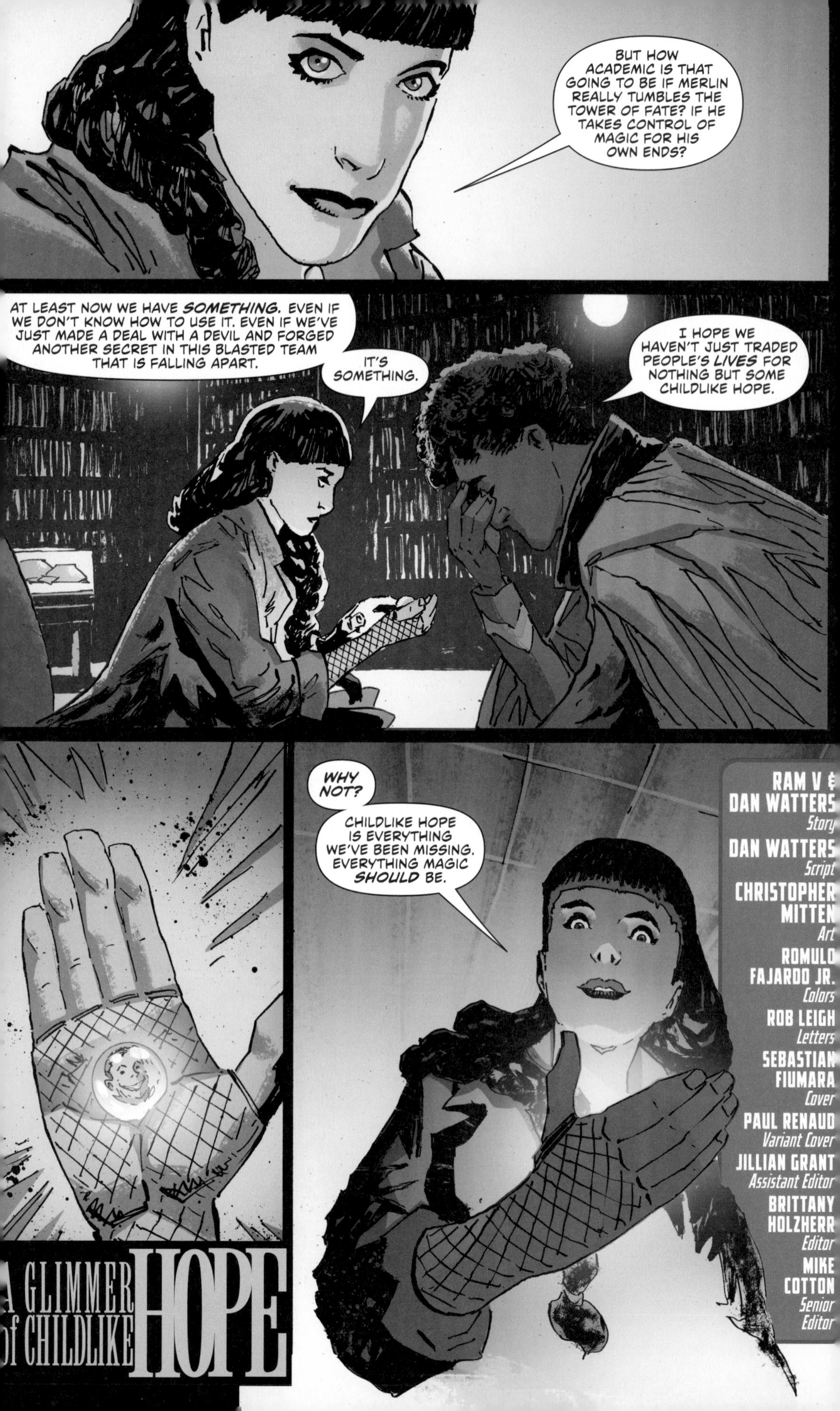
BUT HOW ACADEMIC IS THAT GOING TO BE IF MERLIN REALLY TUMBLES THE TOWER OF FATE? IF HE TAKES CONTROL OF MAGIC FOR HIS OWN ENDS?
AT LEAST NOW WE HAVE SOMETHING. EVEN IF WE DON'T KNOW HOW TO USE IT. EVEN IF WE'VE JUST MADE A DEAL WITH A DEVIL AND FORGED ANOTHER SECRET IN THIS BLASTED TEAM THAT IS FALLING APART.
IT'S SOMETHING.
I HOPE WE HAVEN'T JUST TRADED PEOPLE'S LIVES FOR NOTHING BUT SOME CHILDLIKE HOPE.
A GLIMMER of CHILDLIKE HOPE
WHY NOT?
CHILDLIKE HOPE IS EVERYTHING WE'VE BEEN MISSING. EVERYTHING MAGIC SHOULD BE.
RAM V & DAN WATTERS Story
DAN WATTERS Script
CHRISTOPHER MITTEN Art
ROMULO FAJARDO JR. Colors
ROB LEIGH Letters
SEBASTIAN FIUMARA Cover
PAUL RENAUD Variant Cover
JILLIAN GRANT Assistant Editor
BRITTANY HOLZHERR Editor
MIKE COTTON Senior Editor

Design Gallery

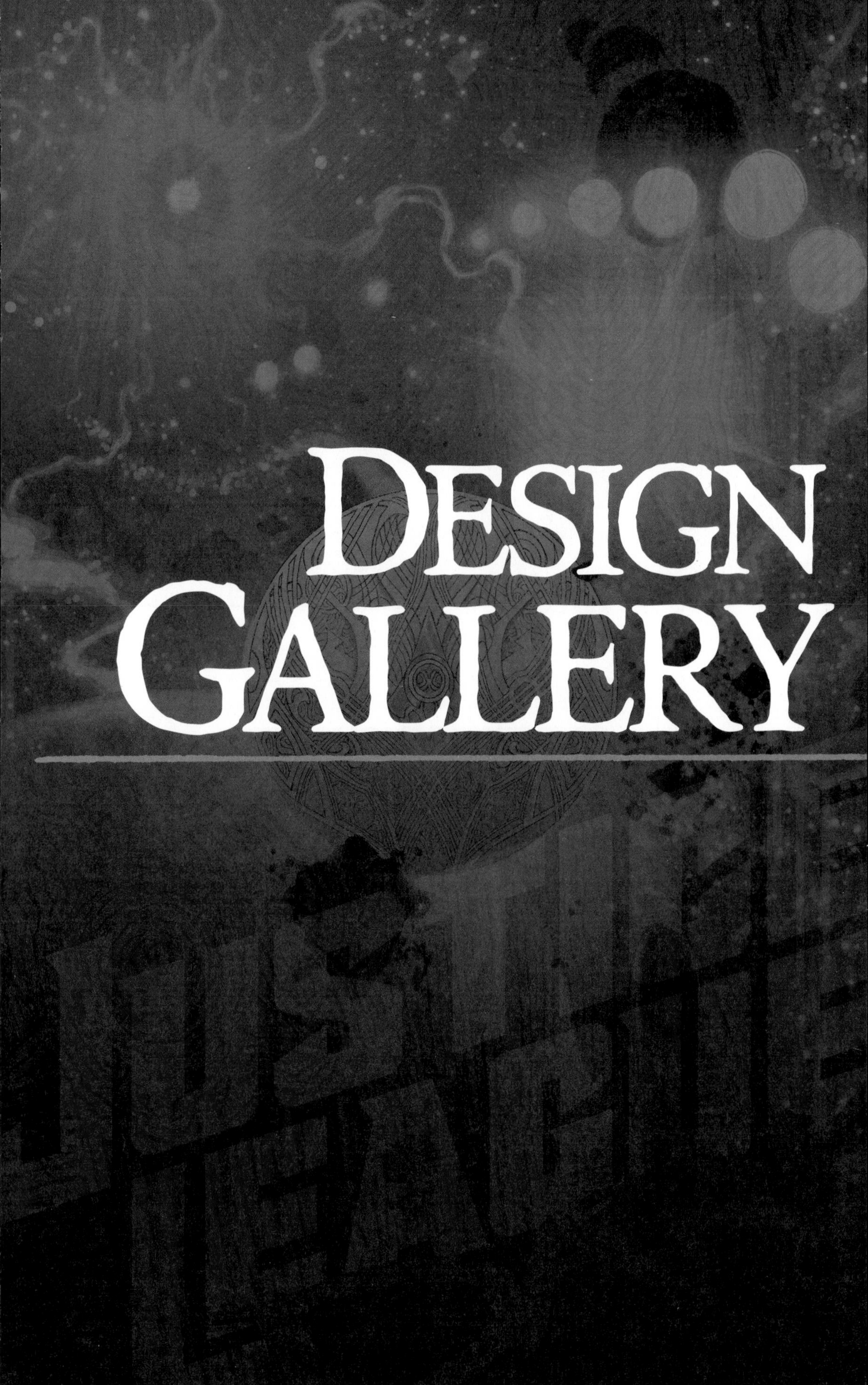

Justice League Dark 2021 Annual #1 main cover sketches by SEBASTIAN FIUMARA

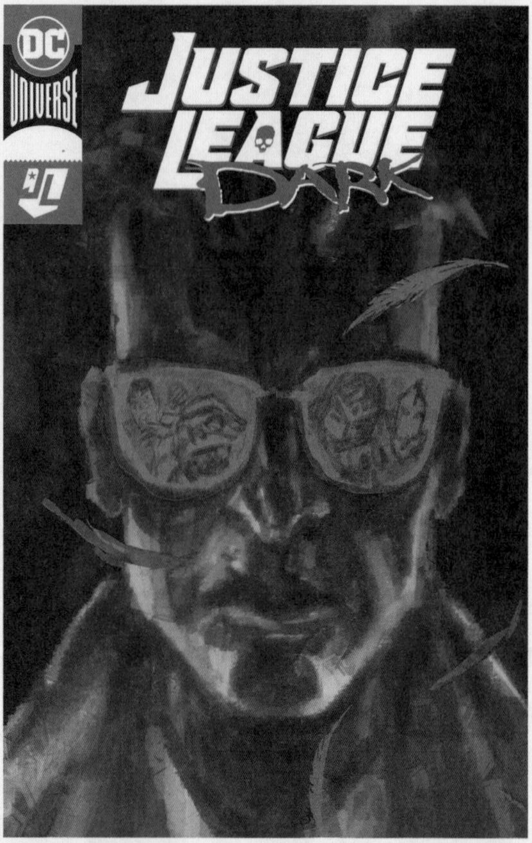
DC
UNIVERSE
JUSTICE
LEAGUE
DARK

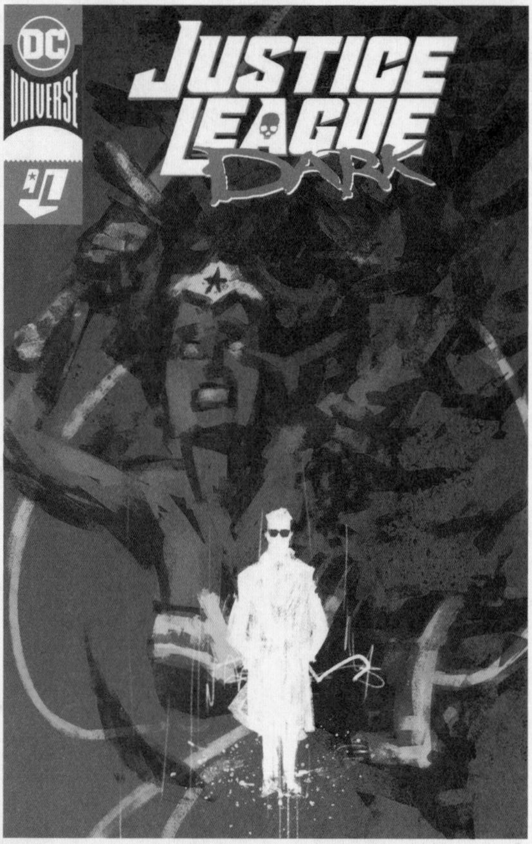
DC
UNIVERSE
JUSTICE
LEAGUE
DARK

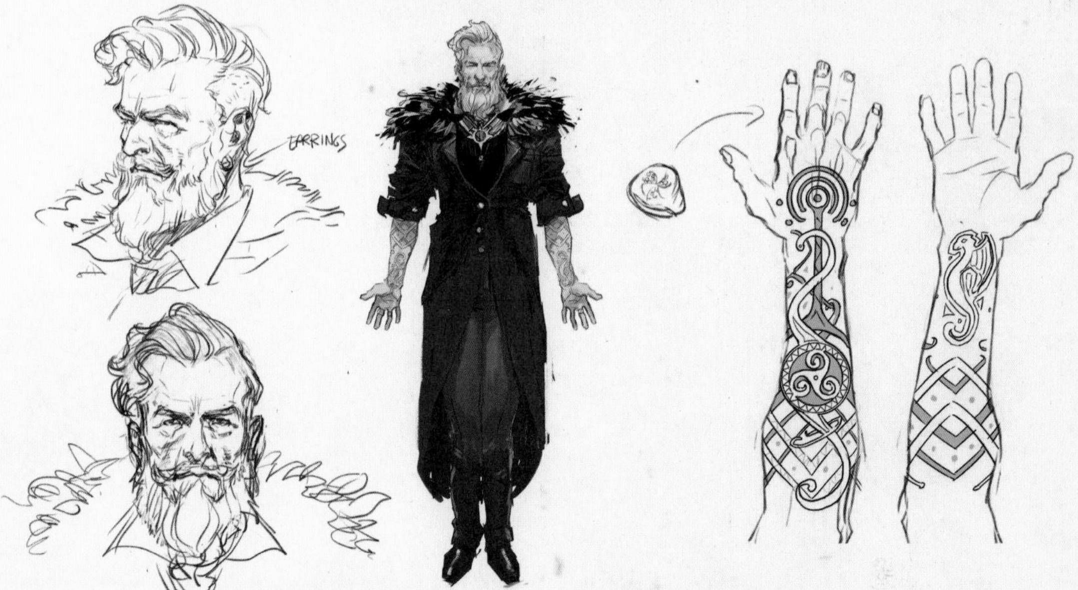
EARRINGS

MERLIN

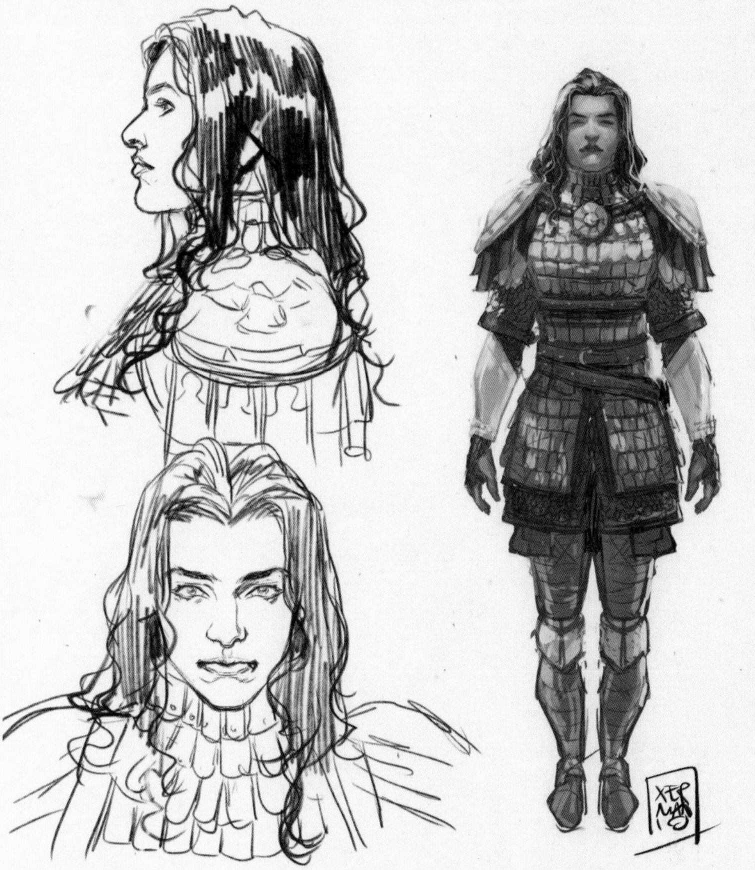

ELNARA ROSHTU

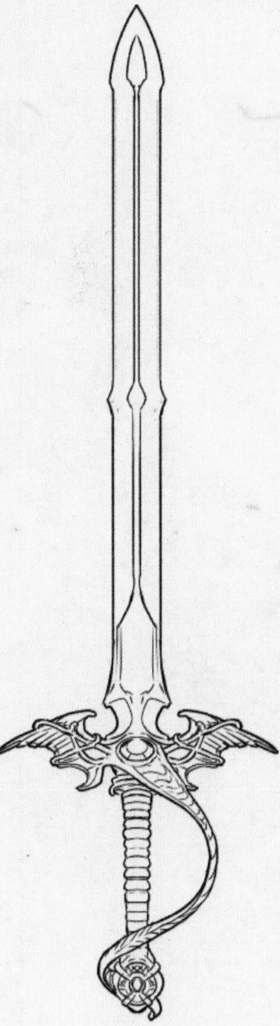

ANGEL'S SWORD

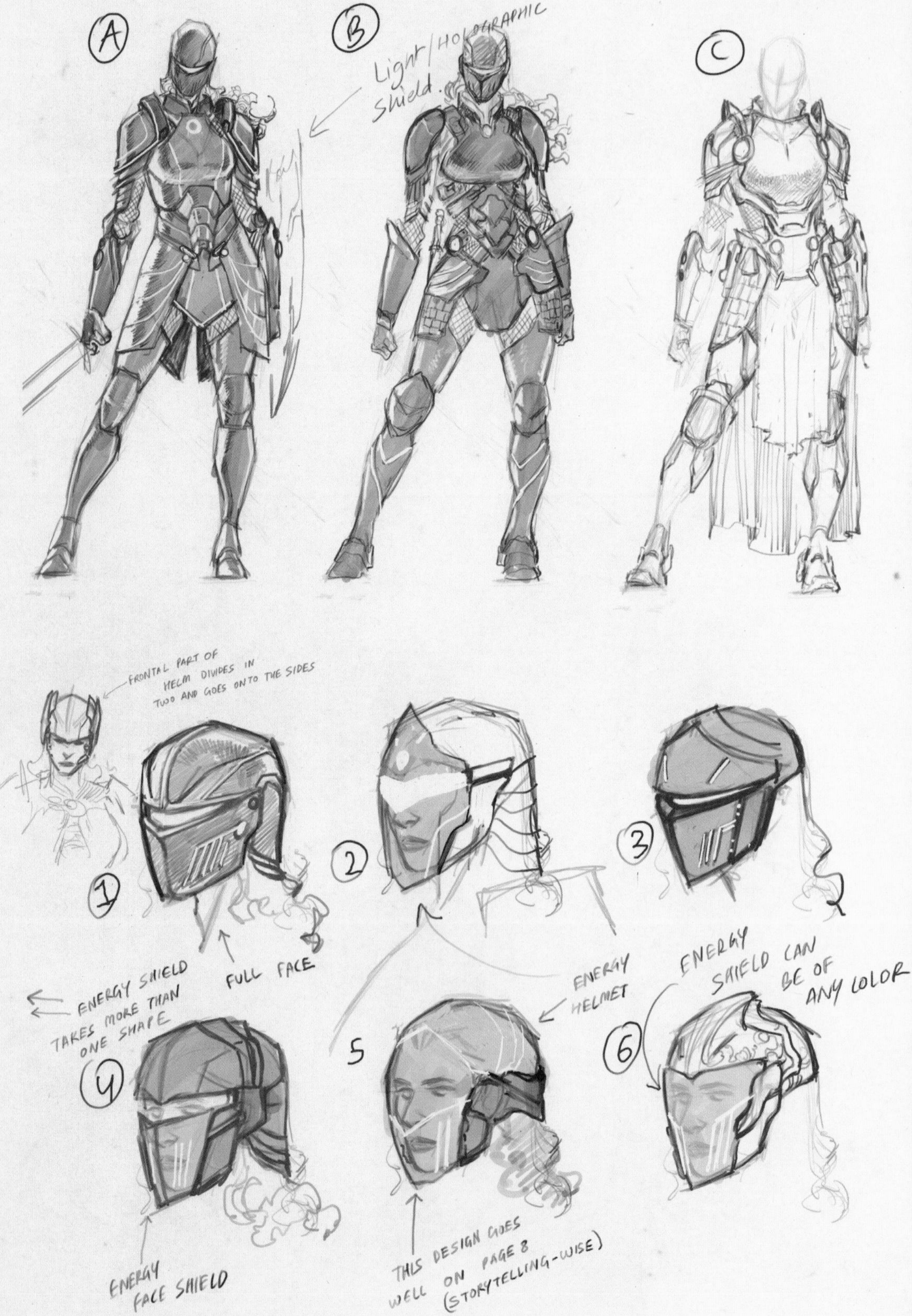

A
B
Light/HOLOGRAPHIC Shield.
C
FRONTAL PART OF HELM DIVIDES IN TWO AND GOES ONTO THE SIDES
1
2
3
FULL FACE
ENERGY SHIELD TAKES MORE THAN ONE SHAPE
ENERGY HELMET
ENERGY SHIELD CAN BE OF ANY COLOR.
4
5
6
ENERGY FACE SHIELD
THIS DESIGN GOES WELL ON PAGE 8 (STORYTELLING-WISE)

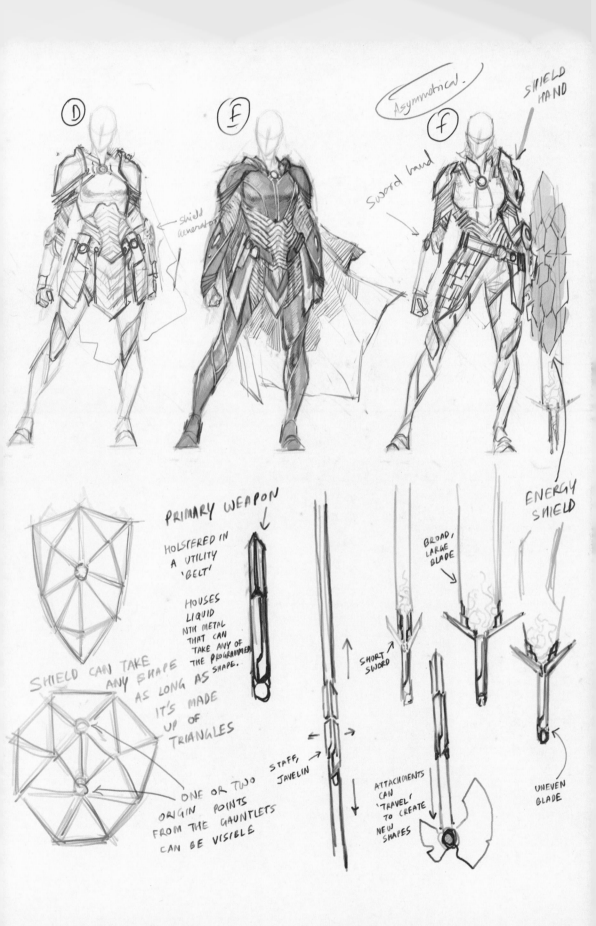

Ⓓ

Ⓕ

Asymmetrical.

Ⓕ

shield generator

Sword hand

SHIELD HAND

PRIMARY WEAPON

HOLSTERED IN A UTILITY 'BELT'

HOUSES LIQUID NTH METAL THAT CAN TAKE ANY OF THE PROGRAMMED SHAPE.

SHIELD CAN TAKE ANY SHAPE AS LONG AS IT'S MADE UP OF TRIANGLES

ONE OR TWO ORIGIN POINTS FROM THE GAUNTLETS CAN BE VISIBLE

STAFF, JAVELIN

SHORT SWORD

ATTACHMENTS CAN 'TRAVEL' TO CREATE NEW SHAPES

ENERGY SHIELD

BROAD, LARGE BLADE

UNEVEN BLADE

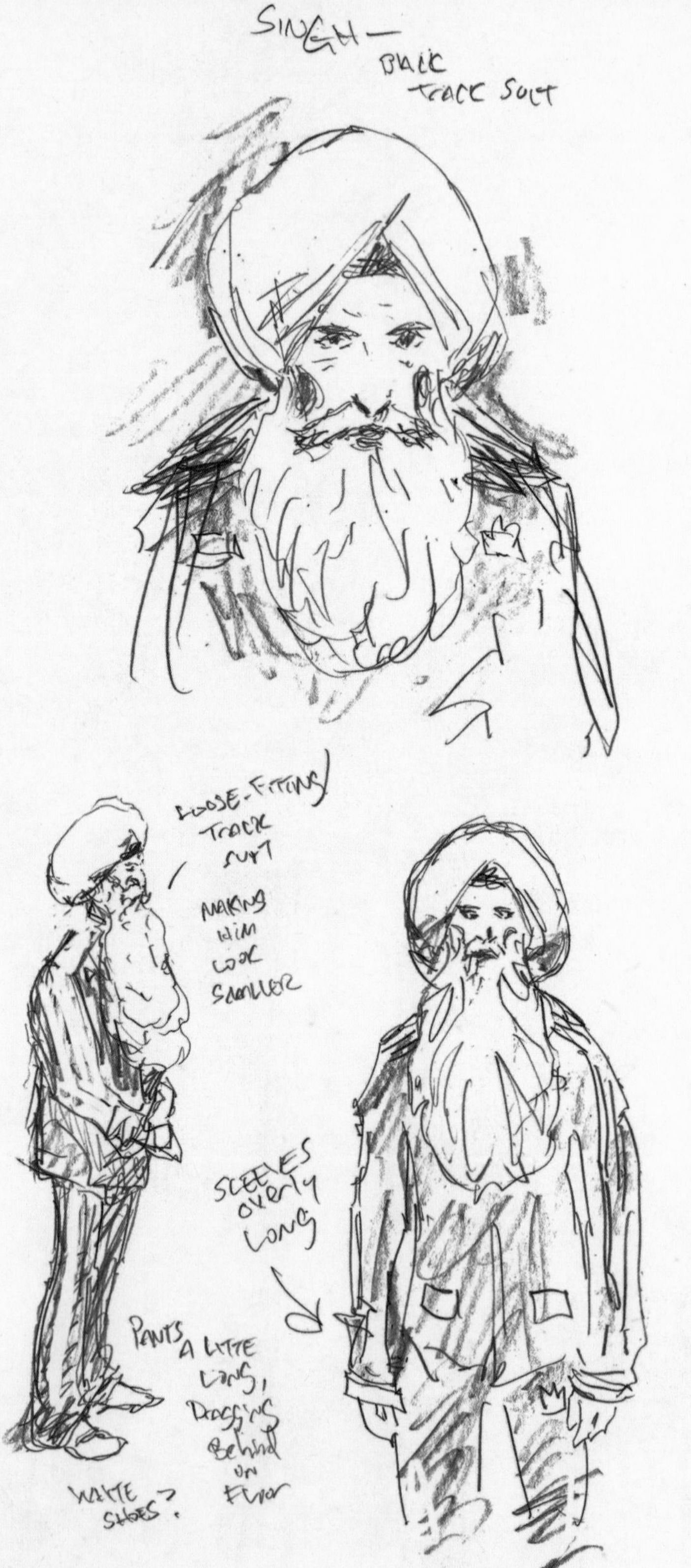
SINGH —
BLACK TRACK SUIT
LOOSE-FITTING TRACK SUIT
MAKING HIM LOOK SMALLER
SLEEVES OVERLY LONG
PANTS A LITTLE LONG, DRAGGING BEHIND ON FLOOR
WHITE SHOES?

Justice League Dark 2021 Annual #1 pgs. 1-10 layouts by CHRISTOPHER MITTEN

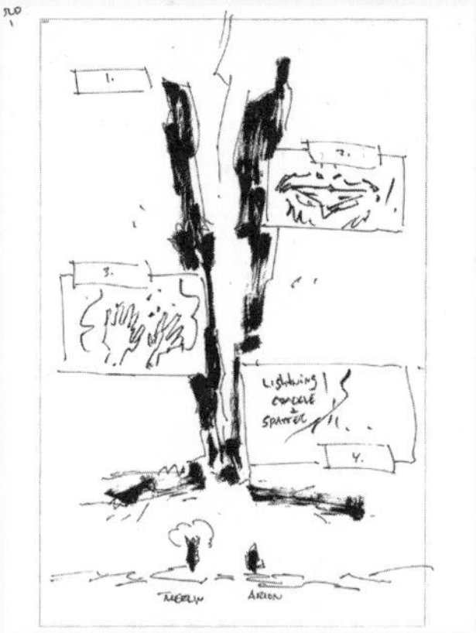
MERLIN
ARION

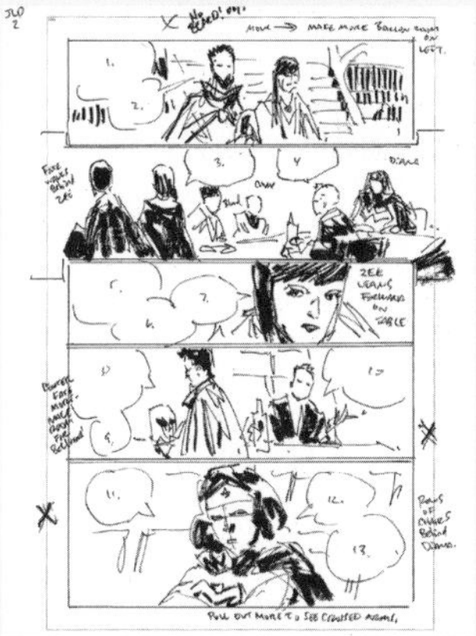

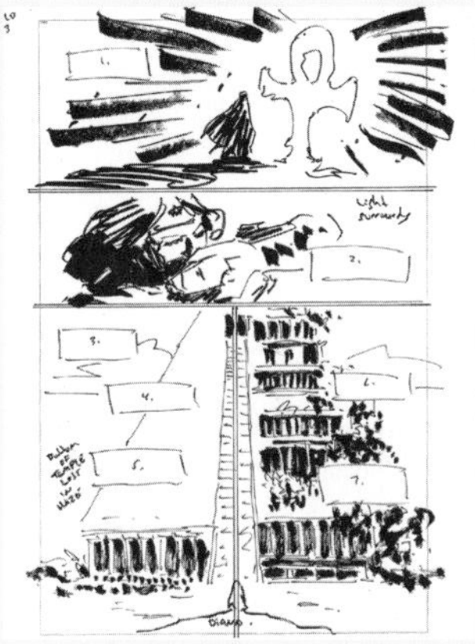

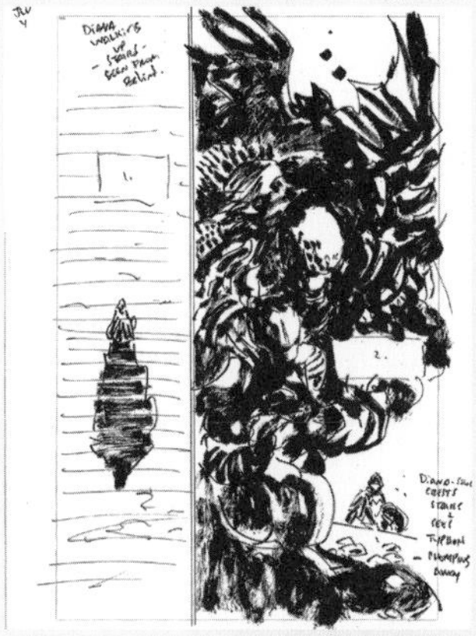

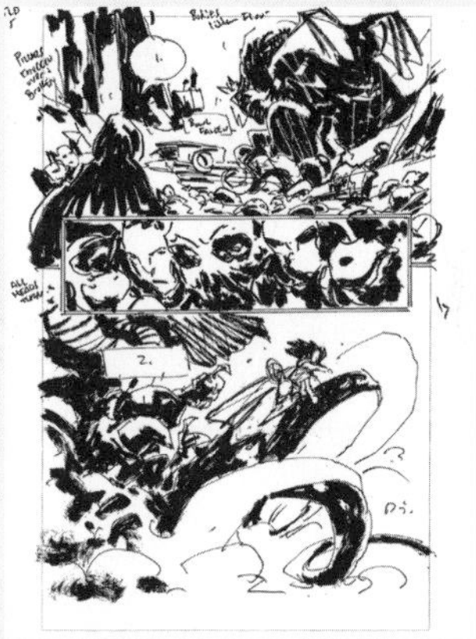

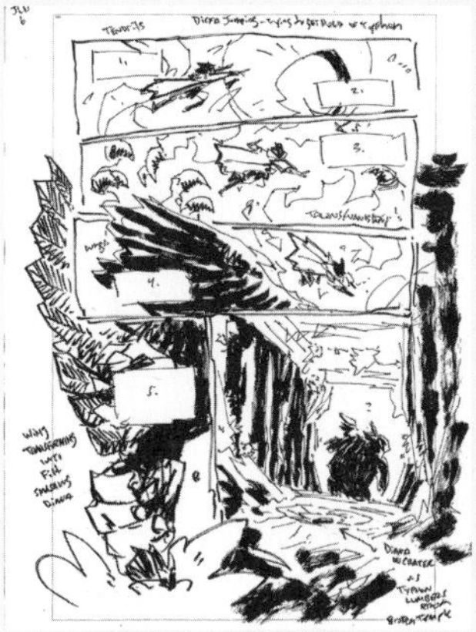

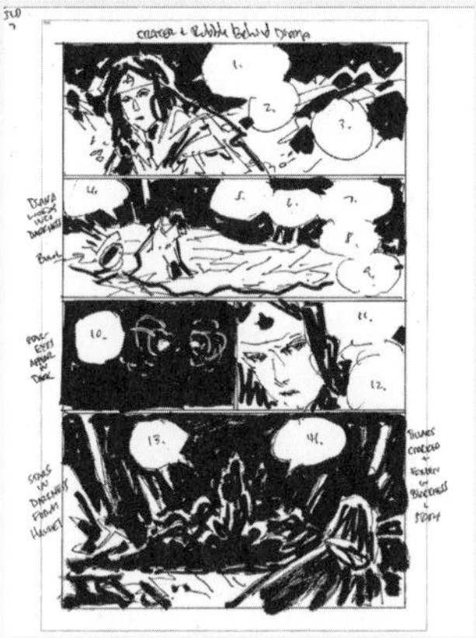

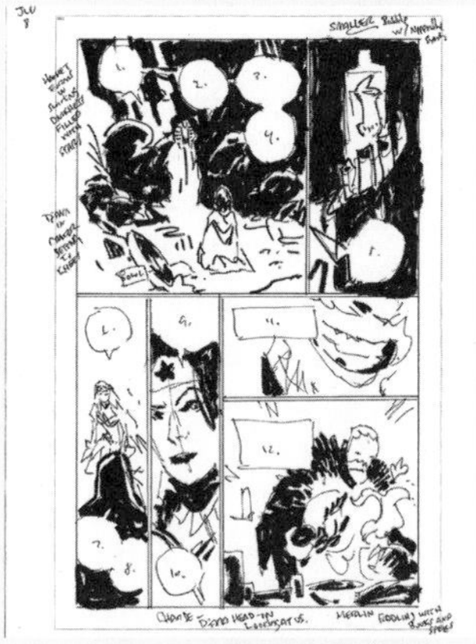

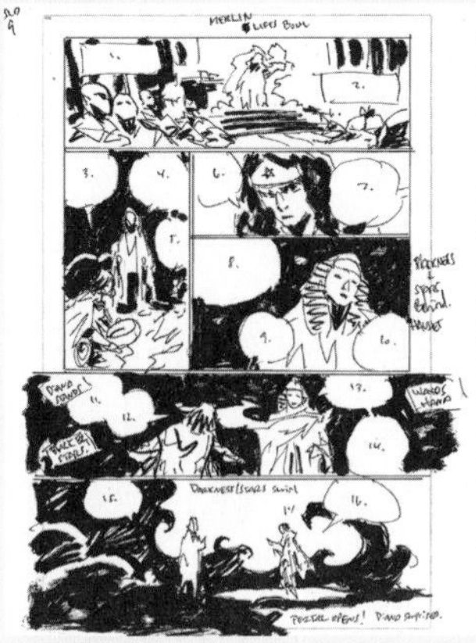

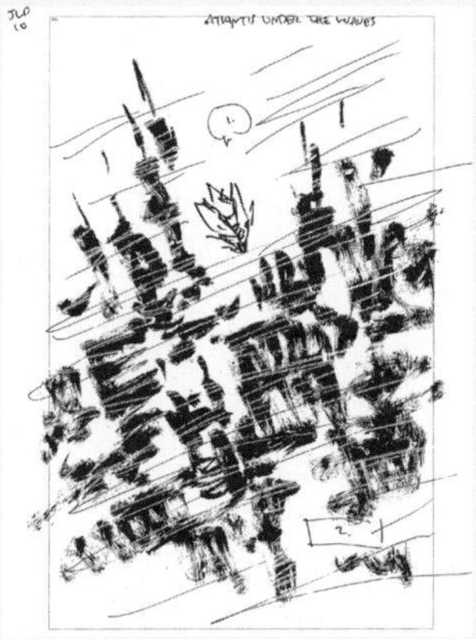
ATLANTIS UNDER THE WAVES

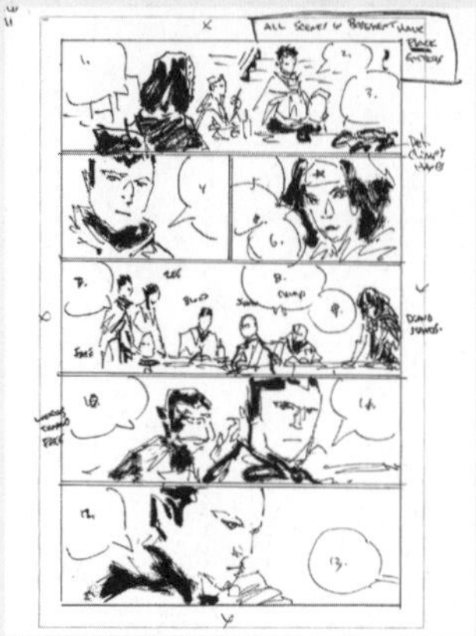

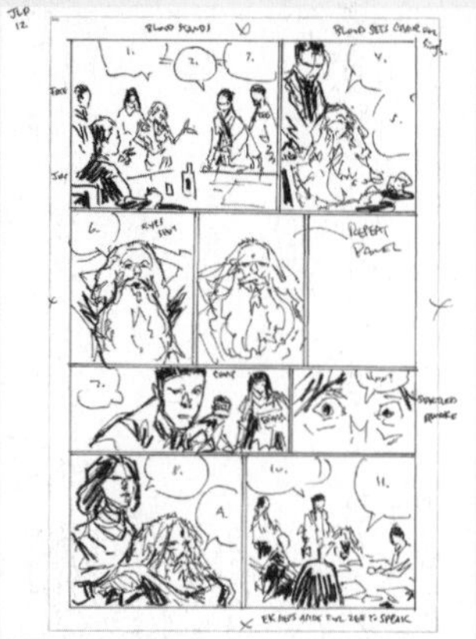

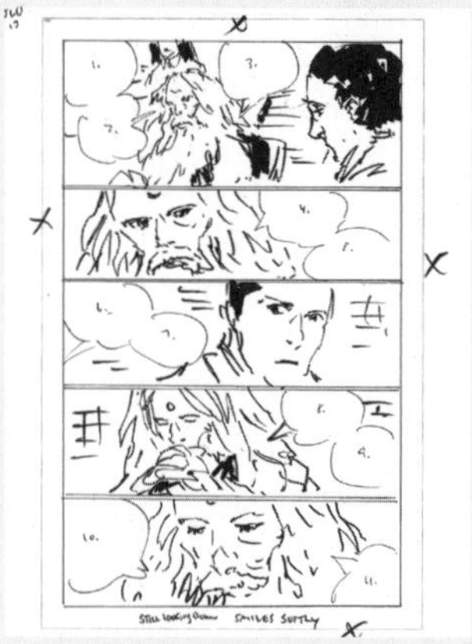
STILL LOOKING DOWN SMILES SOFTLY

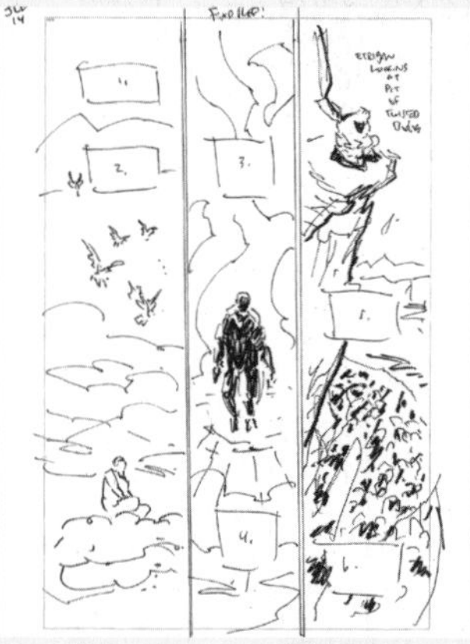

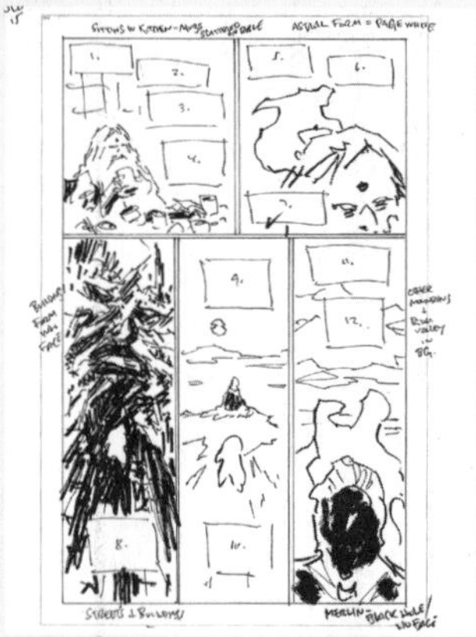

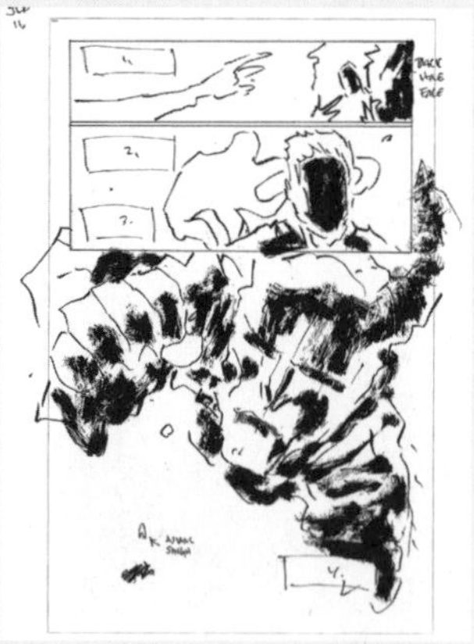

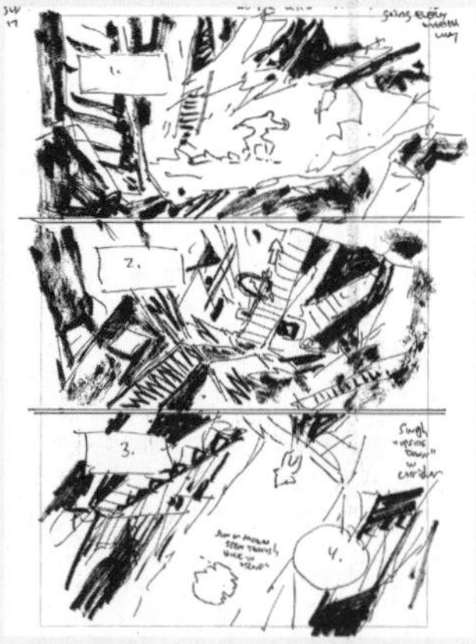

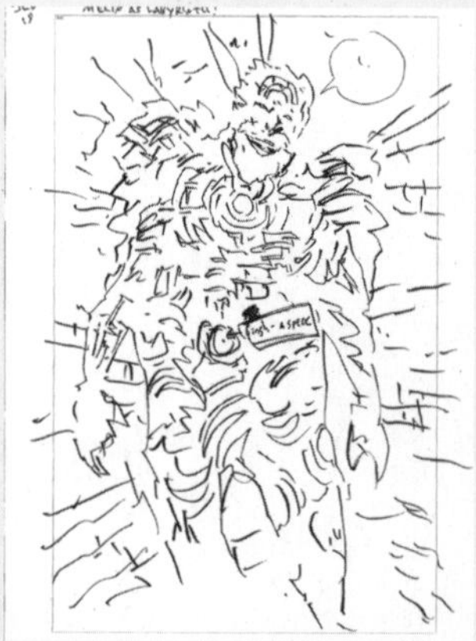

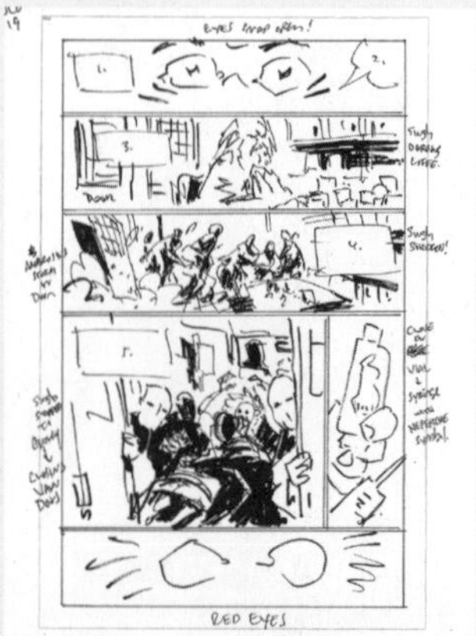
EYES SNAP OPEN!
RED EYES

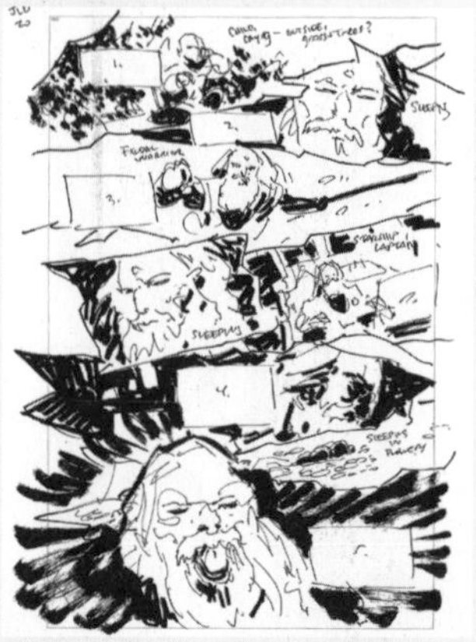